A

JOURNEY

THROUGH THE

KINGDOM OF OUDE,

IN 1849-1850;

BY DIRECTION OF THE RIGHT HON. THE EARL OF DALHOUSIE, GOVERNOR-GENERAL.

WITH PRIVATE CORRESPONDENCE RELATIVE TO THE ANNEXATION OF OUDE TO BRITISH INDIA, &c.

BY MAJOR-GENERAL SIR W. H. SLEEMAN, K.C.B.
Resident at the Court of Lucknow.

IN TWO VOLUMES.
VOL. II.

LONDON:
RICHARD BENTLEY,
Publisher in Ordinary to Her Majesty.
1858.

CONTENTS OF THE SECOND VOLUME.

CHAPTER I.

CHAPTER II.

CHAPTER III.

CHAPTER IV.

CHAPTER V.

CHAPTER VI.

DIARY

OF

A TOUR THROUGH OUDE.

CHAPTER I.

Sundeela—The large landholders of the district—Forces with the Amil—Tallookdars of the district—Ground suited for cantonments and civil offices—Places consecrated to worship—Hutteea Hurun—Neem Sarang, traditions regarding—Landholders and peasantry of Sundeela—Banger and Sandee Palee, strong against the Government authorities from their union—*Nankar* and *Seer*. Nature and character of—Jungle—Leaves of the peepul, bur, &c., used as fodder—Want of good houses and all kinds of public edifices—Infanticide—Sandee district—Security of tenure in groves—River Gurra—Hafiz Abdulla, the governor—Runjeet Sing, of Kutteearee—Thieves in the Banger district—Infanticide—How to put down the crime—Palee—Richness of the foliage, and carpeting of spring crops—Kunojee Brahmins—Success of the robber's trade in Oude—Shahabad—Timber taken down the little river Gurra to the Ganges, from the Tarae forest—Fanaticism of the Moosulman population of Shahabad; and insolence and impunity with which they oppress the Hindoos of the town.

The baronial proprietors in the Sundeela district are Murdun Sing, of Dhurawun, with a rent-roll of 38,000; Gunga Buksh, of Atwa, with one of 25,000; Chundeeka Buksh, of Birwa, with one of 25,000; and Somere Sing, of Rodamow, with one of 34,000. This is the rent-roll declared and entered in the accounts; but it is much below the real one. The Government officers are afraid to measure their lands, or to make any inquiries on the estates into their value, lest they should turn robbers and plunder the country, as they are always prepared to do. They have always a number of armed and brave retainers, ready to support them in any enterprise, and can always add to their number on emergency. There is never any want of loose characters ready to fight for the sake of plunder alone. A tallookdar, however, when opposed to his government, does not venture to attack another tallookdar or his tenants. He stands too much in need of his aid, or at least of his neutrality and forbearance.

January 18, 1850.—Halted at Sundeela. To the north of the town there is a large uncultivated plain of *oosur* land, that would answer for cantonments; but the water lies, for some time after rain, in many places. The drainage is defective, but might be made good towards a rivulet to the north and west. There is another open plain to the west of the town, between the suburbs and the small village of Ausoo Serae, where the Trigonometrical Survey has one of its towers. It is about a mile from east to west, and more from north to south, and well adapted for the location of troops and civil establishments. The climate is said to be very good. The town is large and still populous, but the best families seem to be going to decay, or leaving the place. Many educated persons from Sundeela in our civil establishments used to leave their families here; but life and property have become so very insecure, that they now always take them with them to the districts in which they are employed, or send them to others. I observed many good houses of burnt brick and cement, but they are going fast to decay, and are all surrounded by numerous mud-houses without coverings, or with coverings of the same material, which are hidden from view by low parapets. These houses have a wretched appearance.

The Amil has twelve guns with him; but the bullocks are all so much out of condition from want of food that they can scarcely walk; and the Amil was obliged to hire a few plough-bullocks from the cultivators, to draw out two guns to my camp to fire the salute. They get no grain, and there is little or no grass anywhere on the fallow and waste lands, from the want of rain during June, July, and August. The Amil told me, that he had no stores or ammunition for the guns; and that their carriages were all gone, or going, to pieces, and had received no repairs whatever for the last twelve years. I had in the evening a visit from Rajah Murdun Sing, of *Dharawun*, a stout and fat man, who bears a fair character. He is of the Tilokchundee Bys clan, who cannot intermarry with each other, as they are all of the same gote or family. It would, according to their notions, be incestuous.

January 19, 1850.—Hutteeah Hurrun, thirteen miles. The plain level as usual, and of the loose doomuteea soil, fertile in natural powers everywhere, and well tilled around the villages, which are more numerous than in any other part that we have passed over. The water is everywhere near the surface, and wells are made at little cost. A well is dug at a cost of from five to ten rupees; and in the muteear, or argillaceous soil, will last for irrigation for forty years. To line it with burnt bricks without cement will cost from one to two hundred rupees; and to add cement will cost a hundred more. Such lining is necessary in light soil, and still more so in sandy or *bhoor*. They frequently line their wells at little cost with long thick cables, made of straw and twigs, and twisted round the surface inside. The fields are everywhere irrigated from wells or pools, and near villages well manured; and the wheat and other spring crops are excellent. They have been greatly benefited by the late rains, and in no case injured. The ground all the way covered with white hoar frost, and the dews heavy in a cloudless sky. Finer weather I have never known in any quarter of the world.

This place is held sacred from a tradition, that Ram, after his expedition against Cylone, came here to bathe in a small tank near our present camp, in order to wash away the sin of having killed a *Brahmin* in the person of Rawun, the monster king of that island, who had taken away his wife, Seeta. Till he had done so, he could not venture to revisit his capital, Ajoodheea. There are many legends regarding the origin of the sanctity of this and the many other places around, which pilgrims must visit to complete the *pykurma*, or holy circuit. The most popular seems to be this. Twenty-eight thousand sages of great sanctity were deputed, with the god Indur at their head, on a mission to present an address to Brimha, as he reposed upon the mountain Kylas, praying that he would vouchsafe to point out to them the place in Hindoostan most worthy to be consecrated to religious worship. He took a discus from the top-knot on his head, and, whirling it in the air, directed it to proceed in search. After much search it rested at a place near the river Goomtee, which it deemed to be most fitted for the purification of one's faith, and which thenceforth took the name of *Neem Sarung*, a place of devotion. The twenty-eight thousand sages followed, and were accompanied by Brimha himself, attended by the Deotas, or subordinate gods. He then summoned to the place no less than *three crores and half*, or thirty millions and half of *teeruts*, or angels, who preside each over his special place of religious worship. All settled down at places within ten miles of the central point, Neem Sarung; but their departure does not seem to have impaired the sanctity of the places whence they came. The angels, or spirits, who presided over them sent out these offshoots to preside at Neemsar and the consecrated places around it, as trees send off their grafts without impairing their own powers and virtues.

Misrik, a few miles from this, and one of the places thus consecrated, is celebrated as the residence of a very holy sage, named Dudeej. In a great battle between the Deotas and the Giants, the Deotas were defeated. They went to implore the aid of the drowsy god, Brimha, upon his snowy mountain top. He told them to go to Misrik and arm themselves with the *bones* of the old sage, Dudeej. They found Dudeej alive and in excellent health; but they thought it their duty to explain to him their orders. He told them, that he should be very proud indeed to have his bones used as arms in so holy a cause; but he had unfortunately vowed to bathe at all the sacred shrines in India before he died, and must perform his vow. Grievously perplexed, the Deotas all went and submitted their case to their leader, the god Indur. Indur consulted his chaplain, Brisput, who told him, that there was really no difficulty whatever in the case—that the angels of all the holy shrines in India had been established at and around Neemsar by Brimha himself; and the Deotas had only to take water from all the sacred places over which they presided, and pour it over the old sage, to get both him and themselves out of the dilemma. They did so, and the old sage, expressing himself satisfied, gave up his life. In what mode it was taken no one can tell me. The Deotas armed themselves with his bones, attacked the Giants forthwith, and gained an easy and complete victory. The wisdom of the orders of drowsy old Brimha, in this case, is as little questioned by the Hindoos of the present day as that of the orders of drunken old Jupiter was in the case of Troy, by the ancient Greeks and Romans. Millions, "wise in their generation," have spent their lives in the reverence of both.

There is hardly any sin that the waters of these dirty little ponds are not supposed to be capable of washing away; and, over and above this, they are supposed to improve all the good, and reduce to order all the bad passions and emotions of those who bathe in them, by propitiating the aid of the deity, and those who have influence over him.

A good deal of the land, distant from villages, lies waste, though capable of good tillage; and from the all-pervading cause, the want of confidence in the Government and its officers, and of any feeling of security to life, property, and industry. Should this cause be removed, the whole surface of the country would become the beautiful garden which the parts well cultivated and peopled now are. It is all well studded with fine trees—single and in clusters and groves. The soil is good, the water near the surface, and to be obtained in any abundance at little outlay, and the peasantry are industrious, brave, and robust. Nothing is wanted but good and efficient government, which might be easily secured. I found many Kunojee Brahmins in the villages along the road, who tilled their own fields without the aid of ploughmen; and they told me, that when they had no longer the means to hire ploughmen, they were permitted to hold their own ploughs—that is, they were not excommunicated for doing so.

In passing along, with wheat-fields close by on our left, while the sun is a little above the horizon on the right, we see a *glory* round the shadows of our heads as they extend into the fields. All see these *glories* around their own heads, but cannot see them around those of their neighbours. They stretch out from the head and shoulders, with gradually-diminished splendour, to some short distance. This beautiful and interesting appearance arises from the leaves and stalks of the wheat being thickly bespangled with dew. The observer's head being in the direct rays of the sun, as they pass over him to that of his shadow in the field, he carries the glory with him. Those before and behind him see the same glory around the shadows of their own heads, but cannot see it round that of the head of any other person before or behind; because he is on one or other side of the direct rays which pass over them. It is best seen when the sky is most clear, and the dew most heavy. It is not seen over bushy crops such as the arahur, nor on the grass plains.

January 20, 1850.—Beneegunge, eight miles, over a slightly-undulating plain of light sandy soil, scantily cultivated, but well studded with fine trees of the best kind. Near villages, where the land is well watered and manured, the crops are fine and well varied. All the pools are full from the late rain, and they are numerous and sufficient to water the whole surface of the country, with a moderate fall of rain in December or January. If they are not available, the water is always very near the surface, and wells can be made for irrigation at a small cost. The many rivers and rivulets which enter Oude from the Himmalaya chain and Tarae forest, and flow gently through the country towards the Ganges, without cutting very deeply into the soil, always keep the water near the surface, and available in all quarters and in any quantity for purposes of irrigation. Never was country more favoured by nature, or more susceptible of improvement under judicious management. There is really hardly an acre of land that is not capable of good culture, or that need be left waste, except for the sites of towns and villages, and ponds for irrigation, or that would be left waste under good government. The people understand tillage well, and are industrious and robust, capable of any exertion under protection and due encouragement.

The Government has all the revenues to itself, having no public debt and paying no tribute to any one, while the country receives from the British Government alone fifty lacs, or half a million a-year; first, in the incomes of guaranteed pensioners, whose stipends are the interest of loans received by our Government at different times from the sovereigns of Oude, as a provision for their relatives and dependents in perpetuity, and as endowments for their mausoleums and mosques, and other religious and eleemosynary establishments; second, in the interest paid for Government securities held by people residing in Oude; third, in the payment of pensions to the families of men who have been killed in our service, and to invalid native officers and sipahees of our army residing there; fourth, in the savings of others who still serve in our army, while their families reside in Oude; and those of the native officers of our civil establishments, whose families remain at their homes in Oude; fifth, in the interest on a large amount of our Government securities held by people at Lucknow, who draw the interest not from the

Resident's Treasury, but from the General Treasury in Calcutta, or the Treasuries of our bordering districts, in order to conceal their wealth from the King and his officers. Over and above all this our Government has to send into Oude, to be expended there, the pay of five regiments of infantry and a company of artillery, which amounts to some six or seven lacs more. Oude has so many places of pilgrimage, that it receives more in the purchase of the food and other necessaries required by the pilgrims, during their transit and residence, than it sends out with pilgrims who visit shrines and holy places in other countries. It requires little from other countries but a few luxuries for the rich—in shawls from Kashmere and the Punjab, silks, satins, broad-cloth, muslins, guns, watches, &c. from England.

A great portion of the salt and saltpetre required is raised within Oude, and so is all the agricultural produce, except in seasons of drought; and the arms required for the troops are manufactured in Oude, with the exception of some few cannon and shells, and the muskets and bayonets for the few disciplined regiments. The royal family and some of the Mahommedan gentlemen at Lucknow send money occasionally to the shrines of Mecca, Medina, Kurbala, and Nujuf Ashruf, in Turkish Arabia; and some Hindoos send some to Benares and other places of worship, to be distributed in charity or laid out in useful works in their name. Some of the large pensions enjoyed by the relatives and dependents of former sovereigns, under the guarantee of our Government, go in perpetuity to the shrines in Turkish Arabia, in default of both *will* and *heir*. When Ghazee-od Deen succeeded his father on the musnud in 1814, contrary to his expectation and to his father's wish, he gave the minister about fifty lacs of rupees to be expended in charity at those shrines, and in canals, saraees, and other works of utility. Letters, full of expressions of gratitude and descriptions of these useful works, were often shown to him; but the minister, Aga Meer, is said to have kept the whole fifty lacs to himself, and got all these letters written by his private secretaries. Some few Hindoo and Mahommedan gentlemen, when they have lost their places and favour at the Oude Court, go and reside at Cawnpoor, and some few other places in the British territory for greater security; but generally it may be said, that in spite of all disadvantages Mahommedan gentlemen from Oude, in whatever country they may serve, like to leave their families in Oude, and to return and spend what they acquire among them. They find better society there than in our own territories, or society more to their tastes; better means for educating their sons; more splendid processions, festivals, and other inviting sights, in which they and their families can participate without cost; more consideration for rank and learning, and more attractive places for worship and religious observances. The little town of Karoree, about ten or twelve miles from Lucknow, has, I believe, more educated men, filling high and lucrative offices in our civil establishments, than any other town in India except Calcutta. They owe the greater security which they there enjoy, compared with other small towns in Oude, chiefly to the respect in which they are known to be held by the British Government and its officers, and to the influence of their friends and relatives who hold office about the Court of Lucknow.

January 21, 1849.—Sakin, ten miles north-west. The country well studded with fine trees, and pretty well cultivated, but the soil is light from a superabundance of sand; and the crops are chiefly autumn, except in the immediate vicinity of villages, and cut in December. The surface on which they stood this season appears to be waste, except where the stalks of the jowar and bajara are left standing for sale and use, as fodder for cattle. These stalks are called kurbee, and form good fodder for elephants, bullocks, &c., during the cold, hot, and rainy season. They are said to keep better when left on the ground, after the heads have been gathered, than when stacked. The sandy soil, in the vicinity of villages, produces fine spring crops of all kinds, wheat, gram, sugar-cane, arahur, tobacco, &c., being well manured by drainage from the villages, and by the dung stored and spread over it; and that more distant would produce the same, if manured and irrigated in the same way.

The head men or proprietors of some villages along the road mentioned, "that the fine state in which we saw them was owing to their being strong, and able to resist the Government authorities when disposed, as they generally were, to oppress or rack-rent them; that the landholders owed their strength to their union, for all were bound to turn out and afford aid to their neighbour on hearing the concerted signal of distress; that this league, '*offensive and defensive*,' extended all over the Baugur district, into which we entered about midway between this and our last stage; and that we should see how much better it was peopled and cultivated in consequence than the district of Mahomdee, to which we were going; that the strong only could keep anything under the Oude Government; and as they could not be strong without union, all landholders were solemnly pledged to aid each other, *to the death*, when oppressed or attacked by the local officers." They asked Captain Weston, who was some miles behind me, what was the Resident's object in this tour, whether the Honourable Company's Government was to be introduced into Oude? He told them that the object was solely to see the state of the country and condition of the people, with a view to suggest to the King's Government any measures that might seem calculated to improve both; and asked them whether they wished to come under the British rule? They told him, "that they should like much to have the British rule introduced, if it could be done without worrying them with its complicated laws and formal and distant courts of justice, of which they had heard terrible accounts."

The Nazim of the Tundeeawun or Baugur district met me on his border, and told me, "that he was too weak to enforce the King's orders, or to collect his revenues; that he had with him one efficient company of Captain Bunbury's corps, with one gun in good repair, and provided with draft-bullocks, in good condition; and that this was the only force he could rely upon; while the landholders were strong, and so leagued together for mutual defence, that, at the sound of a matchlock, or any other concerted signal, all the men of a dozen large villages would, in an hour, concentrate upon and defeat the largest force the King's officers could assemble; that they did so almost every year, and often frequently within the same year; that he had nominally eight guns on duty with him, but the carriage of one had already gone to pieces; and those of the rest had been so long without repair that they would go to pieces with very little firing; that the draft-bullocks had not had any grain for many years, and were hardly able to walk; and he was in consequence obliged to hire plough-bullocks, to draw the gun required to salute the Resident; but he had only ten days ago received an order to give them grain himself, charge for it in his accounts, and hold himself responsible for their condition; that they had been so starved, that he was obliged to restrict them to a few ounces a-day at first, or they would have all died from over-eating." This order has arisen from my earnest intercession in favour of the artillery draft-bullocks; but so many are interested in the abuse, that the order will not be long enforced. Though the grain will, as heretofore, be paid for from the Treasury, it will, I hear, be given to the bullocks only while I am out on this tour.

In the evening some cultivators came to complain that they had been robbed of all their bhoosa (chaff) by a sipahee from my camp. I found, on inquiry, that the sipahee belonged to Captain Hearsey's five companies of Frontier Police; that these companies had sixteen four-bullock hackeries attached to them for the carriage of their tents and luggage; and that these hackeries had gone to the village, and taken all that the complainants had laid up for their own cattle for the season; that such hackeries formerly received twenty-seven rupees eight annas a-month each, and their owners were expected to purchase their own fodder; but that this allowance had for some years been cut down to fourteen rupees a-month, and they were told *to help themselves to fodder wherever they could find it;* that all the hackeries hired by the King and his local officers, for the use of troops, establishments, &c. had been reduced at the same rate, from twenty-seven eight annas a-month to fourteen, and their owners received the same order. All villages near the roads along which the troops and establishments move are plündered of their bhoosa, and all those within ten miles of the place, where they may be detained for a week or fortnight, are plundered in the same way.

The Telinga corps and Frontier Police are alone provided with tents and hackeries by Government. The Nujeeb corps are provided with neither. The Oude Government formerly allowed for each four-bullock hackery thirty rupees a-month, from which *two rupees and half* were deducted for the perquisites of office. The owners of the hackeries were expected to purchase bhoosa and other fodder for their bullocks at the market price; but they took what they requred without payment, in *collusion with* the officers under whom they were employed, or in *spite* of them; and the Oude Government in 1845 cut the allowance down to seventeen rupees and half, out of which *three rupees and half* are cut for perquisites, leaving fourteen rupees for the hackeries: and their owners and drivers have the free privilege of helping themselves to bhoosa and other fodder wherever they can find them. Some fifty or sixty of these hackeries were formerly allowed for each Telinga corps with guns, now only twenty-two are allowed; and when they move they must, like Nujeeb corps, seize what more they require. They are allowed to charge nothing for their extra carriage, and therefore pay nothing.

January 22, 1849.—Tundeeawun, eight miles west. The country level, and something between doomuteen and muteear, very good, and in parts well cultivated, particularly in the vicinity of villages; but a large portion of the surface is covered with jungle, useful only to robbers and refractory landholders, who abound in the purgunnah of Bangur. In this respect it is reputed one of the worst districts in Oude. Within the last few years the King's troops have been frequently beaten and driven out with loss, even when commanded by an European officer. The landholders and armed peasantry of the different villages unite their *quotas of auxiliaries*, and concentrate upon them on a concerted signal, when they are in pursuit of robbers and rebels. Almost every able-bodied man of every village in Bangur is trained to the use of arms of one kind or another, and none of the King's troops, save those who are disciplined and commanded by European officers, will venture to move against a landholder of this district; and when the local authorities cannot obtain the aid of such troops, they are obliged to conciliate the most powerful and unscrupulous by reductions in the assessment of the lands or additions to their *nankar*.

To illustrate the spirit and system of union among the chief landholders of the Bangur district, I may here mention a few facts within my own knowledge, and of recent date. Bhugwunt Singh, who held the estate of Etwa Peepureea, had been for some time in rebellion against his sovereign; and he had committed many murders and robberies, and lifted many herds of cattle within our bordering district of Shajehanpoor; and he had given shelter, on his own estate, to a good many atrocious criminals, from that and others of our bordering district. He had, too, aided and screened many gangs of Budhuks, or dacoits by hereditary profession. The Resident, Colonel Low, in 1841, directed every possible effort to be made for the arrest of this formidable offender, and Captain Hollings, the second in command of the 2nd battalion of Oude local infantry, sent intelligencers to trace him.

They ascertained that he had, with a few followers, taken up a position two hundred yards to the north of the village of Ahroree, in a jungle of palas-trees and brushwood in the Bangur district, about twenty-eight miles to the south-west of Seetapoor, where that battalion was cantoned, and about fourteen miles west from Neemkar. Captain Hollings made his arrangements to surprise this party; and on the evening of the 3rd of July 1841, he marched from Neemkar at the head of three companies of that battalion, and a little before midnight he came within three-quarters of a mile of the rebel's post. After halting his party for a short time, to enable the officers and sipahees to throw off all superfluous clothing and utensils, Captain Hollings moved on to the attack. When the advanced guard reached the outskirts of the robber's position about midnight, they were first challenged and then fired upon by the sentries. The subadar in command of this advance guard fell dead, and a non-commissioned officer and a sipahee severely wounded.

The whole party now fired in upon the gang and rushed on. One of the robbers was shot, and the rest all escaped out on the opposite side of the jungle. The sipahees believing, since the surprise had been complete, that the robbers must have left all their wealth behind them, dispersed, as soon as the firing ceased and the robbers disappeared, to get every man as much as he could. While thus engaged they were surrounded by the Gohar, (or body of auxiliaries which these landholders send to each other's aid on the concerted signal,) and fired in upon from the front, and both right and left flanks. Taken by surprise, they collected together in disorder, while the assailants from the front and sides continued to pour in their fire upon them; and they were obliged to retire in haste and confusion, closely followed by the auxiliaries, who gained confidence, and pressed closer as their number increased by the quotas they received from the villages the detachment had to pass in their retreat.

All efforts on the part of Captain Hollings to preserve order in the ranks were vain. His men returned the fire of their pursuers, but without aim or effect. At the head of the auxiliaries were Punchum Sing, of Ahroree, and Mirza Akbar Beg, of Deureea; and they were fast closing in upon the party, and might have destroyed it, when Girwur Sing, tomandar, came up with a detachment of the Special Police of the Thuggee and Dacoitee Department. At this time the three companies were altogether disorganized and disheartened, as the firing and pursuit had lasted from midnight to daybreak; but on seeing the Special Police come up and join with spirit in the defence, they rallied, and the assailants, thinking the reinforcement more formidable than it really was, lost confidence and held back. Captain Hollings mounted the fresh horse of the tomandar, and led his detachment without further loss or molestation back to Neemkar. His loss had been one subadar, one havildar, and three sipahees killed; one subadar, two havildars, one naik, and fourteen sipahees wounded and missing. Captain Hollings' groom was shot dead, and one of his palankeen-bearers was wounded. His horse, palankeen, desk, clothes, and all the superfluous clothing and utensils, which the sipahees had thrown off preparatory to the attack fell into the hands of the assailants. Attempts were made to take up and carry off the killed and wounded; but the detachment was so sorely pressed that they were obliged to leave both on the ground. The loss would have been much greater than it was, but for the darkness of the night, which prevented the assailants from taking good aim; and the detachment would, in all probability, have been cut to pieces, but for the timely arrival of the Special Police under Girwur Sing.

Such attacks are usually made upon robber bands about the first dawn of day; and this attack at midnight was a great error. Had they not been assailed by the auxiliaries, they could not, in the darkness, have secured one of the gang. It was known, that at the first shot from either the assailing or defending party in that district, all the villages around concentrate their quotas upon the spot, to fight to the death against the King's troops, whatever might be their object; and the detachment ought to have been prepared for such concentration when the firing began, and returned as quickly as possible from the place when they saw that by staying they could not succeed in the object.

Four months after, in November, Punchum Sing, of Ahroree, himself cut off the head of the robber, Bhugwunt Sing, with his own hand, and sent it to the governor, Furreed-od Deen, with an apology for having *by mistake* attacked Captain Hollings' detachment. The governor sent the head to the King, with a report stating that he had, at the peril of his life, and after immense toil, hunted down and destroyed this formidable rebel; and his Majesty, as a reward for his valuable services, conferred upon Furreed-od Deen a title and a first-rate dress of honour. Soon after, in the same month of July 1841, his Majesty the King of Oude's second regiment of infantry, under the command of a very gallant officer, Captain W. D. Bunbury, was encamped near the village of Belagraon, when information was brought that certain convicts, who had escaped from the gaol at Bareilly, had taken refuge in the village of Parakurown, about fifty miles to the north-west of his camp. Captain Bunbury immediately detached three companies, with two six-pounders, under his brother, Lieutenant A. C. Bunbury, to arrest them. After halting for a short time at Gopamow, to allow his men to take breath, Lieutenant Bunbury pushed on, and reached the place a little before the dawn of day. He demanded the surrender of the outlaws from the chief of the village, named Ajrael Sing, a notoriously bad character, who insolently refused to give them up. A fight commenced, in which one of the convicts, and some others, were killed; but at last Lieutenant Bunbury succeeded in securing Arjael Sing himself, with some few of his followers, and the outlaws.

Hearing the firing of the field-pieces, the surrounding villages concentrated their quotas of auxiliaries upon the place, and attacked Lieutenant Bunbury's detachment on all sides. He had taken possession of the village; but finding it untenable against so large and increasing a body of assailants, he commenced his retreat. He had scarcely reached the outskirts when he found himself surrounded by overwhelming numbers of these auxiliaries, through whom he was obliged to fight his way for a distance of fourteen miles to Pahanee. The armed peasantry of every village, on the right and left of the road as they passed, turned out and joined the pursuers in their attempt to rescue his prisoners. Lieutenant Bunbury's conduct of this retreat was most gallant and judicious; and his men behaved admirably. When the assailants appeared likely to overwhelm him, he abandoned one of his two guns, and hastened on, leaving three men lying under them apparently wounded, and unable to move. On this they pressed on, sword in hand, to despatch the wounded men, and seize the guns. When the assailants were within thirty or forty yards of the gun, they started up, and poured in upon the dense crowd a discharge of grape with deadly effect. A party then doubled back from the main body of the detachment, protected the artillery men in limbering up the gun, and escorting it to the main body, which again resumed its march. This experiment was repeated several times with success as they passed other villages, from which further auxiliaries poured out, till they approached Pahanee, where they found support. In this retreat Lieutenant Bunbury lost sixty men out of his three companies, or about one-third of his number; but he retained all his prisoners. Ajrael Sing soon after died of the wounds he had received in defending the convicts in his village; and the rest of the prisoners were all sent to the Oude Durbar. Lieutenant Bunbury is now in the Honourable Company's Service, and in the 34th Regiment of Bengal Native Infantry.

On the 23rd of January 1849, Captain Hearsey, of the Oude Frontier Police, sent his subadar-major, Ramzan Khan, with a party of one hundred and fifty men of that police, to arrest a notorious robber, Mendae Sing, and other outlaws, from the Shajehanpoor district, who had found an asylum in the village of Sahurwa, in the Mahomdee district, whence they carried on their depredations upon our villages across the border. The party reached Sahurwa the next morning a little before sunrise. The subadar-major having posted his men so as to prevent the escape of the outlaws, demanded their surrender from the village authorities. They were answered by a volley of matchlock-balls; and finding the village too strong to be taken by his small detachment without guns, he withdrew to a more sheltered position to the westward, and detached a havildar with fifty men to take possession of a large gateway to the south of the village. During this movement the villagers continued to fire upon them; and the quotas of auxiliaries from the surrounding villages, roused by the firing, came rushing on from all quarters. Seeing no chance of being able either to take the village or to maintain his position against such numbers, the subadar-major drew off his detachment, and proceeded for support to Pahanee, a distance of twelve miles. He reached that place pursued by the auxiliaries, and with the loss of one havildar and one sipahee killed, and three sipahees very severely wounded. There are numerous instances of this sort in which the King's troops have been attacked and beaten back, and their prisoners rescued by the landholders of Bangur, and the adjoining districts of Mahomdee and Sandee Palee. They are never punished for doing so, as the King is too weak, and the aid of the British troops, for the purpose, has seldom been given.

It would be of advantage to remove the Regiment of Oude Local Infantry from Seetapoor to Tundeeawun, where its presence and services are much more required. The climate is as good, and all that native soldiers require for food and clothing are cheaper. The drainage is good; and to the east of the town there is one of the finest plains for a cantonment that I have ever seen. There are but few wells, but new ones can be made at a trifling cost; and the Oude Government would willingly incur the outlay required for these and for all the public buildings required for the new cantonments, to secure the advantage of such a change. The cost of the public buildings would be only 12,000 rupees; and the same sum would have to be given in compensation for private buildings — total 24,000. The refractory landholders would soon be reduced to order, and prevented from any longer making their villages dens of robbers as they now do; and the jungles around would all soon disappear. These jungles are not thick, or unhealthy, consisting of the small dhak or palas tree, with little or no underwood; and the surface they now occupy would soon be covered with fine spring crops, and studded with happy village communities, were people encouraged by an assurance of protection to settle upon it, and apply their capital and labour to its cultivation. The soil is everywhere of the finest quality, the drainage is good, and there are no jheels. A few ponds yield the water required for the irrigation of the spring crops, during their progress to maturity, from November to March: they are said all to become dry in the hot season. It is, I think, capable of being made the finest part of this fine country of Oude.

It was in contemplation to make the road from Lucknow to Shajehanpoor and Bareilly pass through this place, Tundeeawun, by which some thirty miles of distance would be saved, and a good many small rivers and water-courses avoided. Why this design was given up I know not; but I believe the only objection was the greater insecurity of this line from the bad character of the great landholders of the Bangur and Sandee Palee districts; and the greater number of thieves and robbers who, in consequence, reside in them. There has been but little outlay in works of any kind in the whole line through Seetapore; and when measures have been taken to render this line more secure, a good road will, I hope, be made through Tundeeawun. It was once a populous place, but has been falling off for many years, as the disorders in the district have increased. The Nazim resides here. The last Nazim, Hoseyn Allee, who was removed to Khyrabad, at the end of last year, is said to have given an increase of *nankar* to the refractory landholders of this district during that year, to the extent of forty thousand rupees a-year, to induce them to pay the Government demand, and desist from plunder. By this means he secured a good reputation at Court, and the charge of a more profitable and less troublesome district; and left the difficult task of resuming this lavish increase of the *nankar* to his successor, Seonath, the son of Dilla Ram, who held the contract of the district for some twenty years up to the time of his death, which took place last year. Seonath is a highly respectable and amiable man; but he is very delicate in health, and, in consequence, deficient in the vigour and energy required to manage so turbulent a district. He has, however, a deputy in Kidder Nath, a relative, who has all the ability, vigour, and energy required, if well supported and encouraged by the Oude Durbar. He was deputy under Dilla Ram for many years, and the same under Hoseyn Allee last year. He is a man of great intelligence and experience; and one of the best officers of the Oude Government that I have yet seen.

There are two kinds of recognised perquisites which landholders enjoy in Oude and in most other parts of India—the *nankar* and the *seer* land. The *nankar* is a portion of the recognised rent-roll acknowledged by the ruler to be due to the landholder for the risk, cost, and trouble of management, and for his perquisite as hereditary proprietor of the soil when the management is confided to another. It may be ten, twenty, or one hundred per cent. upon the rent-roll of the estate, which is recognised in the public accounts, as the holder happens to be an object of fear or of favour, or otherwise; and the real rent-roll may be more or less than that which is recognised in the public accounts. The actual rent which the landholder receives may increase with improvements, and he may conceal the improvement from the local authorities, or bribe them to conceal it from Government; or it may diminish from lands falling out of tillage, or becoming impoverished by over-cropping, or from a diminution of demand for land produce; and the landholder may be unable to satisfy the local authorities of the fact, or to prevail upon them to represent the circumstance to Government. The amount of the *nankar* once recognised remains the same till a new rate is recognised by Government; but when the Government becomes weak, the local authorities assume the right to recognise new rents, to suit their own interest, and pretend that they do so to promote that of their sovereign.

I may instance the Amil of this district last year. He was weak, while the landholders were strong. They refused to pay, on the plea of bad seasons. He could send no money to the Treasury, and was in danger of losing his place. The man who had to pay a revenue of ten thousand could not be induced to pay five: he enjoyed an acknowledged *nankar* of two thousand upon a recognised rent-roll of twelve thousand; and, to induce him to pay, he gives him an increase to this *nankar* of one thousand, making the *nankar* three thousand, and reducing the revenue to nine thousand. Being determined to render the increase to his *nankar* permanent, whether the Government consents or not, the landholder agrees to pay the ten thousand for the present year. The collector sends the whole or a part of the one thousand as gratuities to influential men at Court, and enters it in the public accounts as irrecoverable balance. The present Amil, finding that the increase to the *nankar* has not been acknowledged by Government, demands the full ten thousand rupees for the present year. The landholder refuses to pay anything, takes to the jungles, and declares that he will resist till his permanent right to the increase be acknowledged.

The Amil has taken the contract at the rate of last year, as the Government had sanctioned no increase to the *nankar*, and he pleads in vain for a remission in the rate, which he pledged himself to pay, or an increase of means to enforce payment among so turbulent and refractory a body of landholders. As I have before mentioned, the Oude Government has this season issued an order to all revenue collectors to refuse to recognise any increase to the *nankar* that has been made since the year A.D. 1814, or Fusilee 1222, when Saadut Allee died, as none has since that year received the sanction of Government, though the *nankar* has been more than doubled within that period in the manner above described by local authorities. The increase to the *nankar*, and the alienation in rent-free tenure of lands liable to assessment in 1814 by local authorities and influential persons at Court, are supposed to amount in all Oude to forty lacs of rupees a-year. None of them have been formally recognised by the Court, but a great part of them has been tacitly acquiesced in by the minister and Dewan for the time being. They cannot enforce the order for reverting to the *nankar* of 1814, and if they attempt to do so the whole country will be in disorder. Indeed, the minister knows his own weakness too well to think seriously of ever making such an attempt. The *seer* lands are those which the landholders and their families till themselves, or by means of their servants or hired cultivators. Generally they are not entered at all in the rent-rolls; and when they are entered, it is at less rates than are paid for the other lands. The difference between the no rent, or less rates, and the full rates is part of their perquisites. These lands are generally shared out among the members of the family as hereditary possessions.

January 23, 1850.—Behta, ten miles, over a plain of fine muteear soil. The greater part of the surface is, however, covered by a low palas jungle. The jungle remains, because no one will venture to lay out his capital in rooting up the trees and shrubs, and bringing the land under culture where the fruits of his industry, and his own life and those of his family, would be so very insecure, and because the powerful landholders around require the jungles to run to when in arms against the Government officers, as they commonly are. The land under this jungle is as rich in natural powers as that in tillage; and nothing can be finer than the crops in the cultivated parts, particularly in those immediately around villages. There are numerous large trees in the jungles; but the fine peepul and banyan trees are torn to pieces for the use of the elephants and camels of the establishments of the local officers, and for the cows, bullocks, and buffaloes of the peasantry. The cows and buffaloes are said to give greater quantities of milk when fed on the leaves of these trees than when fed on anything else available in the dry season; but the milk is said to be of inferior quality. All the cultivated and peopled parts are beautifully studded with single trees and groves.

No respectable dwelling-house is anywhere to be seen, and the most substantial landholders live in wretched mud-hovels with invisible covers. I asked the people why, and was told that they were always too insecure to lay out anything in improving their dwelling-houses; and, besides, did not like to have such local ties, where they were so liable to be driven away by the Government officers or by the landholders in arms against them, and their reckless followers. The local officers of Government, of the highest grade, occupy houses of the same wretched description, for none of them can be sure of occupying them a year, or of ever returning to them again when once removed from their present offices; and they know that neither their successors nor any one else will ever purchase or pay rent for them. No mosques, mausoleums, temples, seraees, colleges, courts of justice, or prisons to be seen in any of the towns or villages. There are a few Hindoo shrines at the half-dozen places which popular legends have rendered places of pilgrimage, and a few small tanks and bridges made in olden times by public officers, when they were more secure in their tenure of office than they are now. All the fine buildings raised by former rulers and their officers at the old capital of Fyzabad are going fast to ruin. The old city of Ajoodhea is a ruin, with the exception of a few buildings along the bank of the river raised by wealthy Hindoos in honour of Ram, who once lived and reigned there, and is believed by all Hindoos to have been an incarnation of Vishnoo.

I have often mentioned that the artillery draft-bullocks receive no grain, and are everywhere so poor that they can hardly walk, much less draw heavy guns and tumbrils. The reason is this, the most influential men at Court obtain the charge of feeding the cattle in all the different establishments, and charge for a certain quantity of grain or other food at the market price for each animal. They contract for the supply of the cattle with some grain-merchant of the city, who undertakes to distribute it through his own agents. The contractor for the supply of the artillery draft-bullocks sends an agent with those in attendance upon every collector of the land revenue, and he gives them as little as possible. The contractor, afraid of making an enemy of the influential man at Court, who could if he chose deprive him of his contract or place, never presumes to interfere, and the agent gives the poor bullocks no grain at all. The collector, or officer in charge of the district, is, however, obliged every month to pay the agent of the contractor the full market price of the grain supposed to be consumed—that is, one seer and half a-day by every bullock. The same, or some other influential person at Court, obtains and transfers in the same way the contract for the feeding of the elephants, horses, camels, bullocks, and other animals kept at Lucknow for use or amusement, and none of them are in much better condition than the draft-bullocks of the artillery in the remote districts—all are starved, or nearly starved, and objects of pity. Those who are responsible for their being fed are too strong in Court favour to apprehend any punishment for not feeding them at all.

In my ride this morning I asked the people of the villages through and near which we passed whether infanticide prevailed: they told me that it prevailed amongst almost all the Rajpoot families of any rank in Oude; that very poor families of those classes retained their daughters, because they could get something for them from the families of lower grade, into which they married them; but that those who were too well off in the world to condescend to take money for their daughters from lower grades, and were obliged to incur heavy costs in marrying them into families of the same or higher grade, seldom allowed their infant daughters to live.

"It is strange," I observed, "that men, who have to

undergo such heavy penance for killing a cow, even by accident, should have to undergo none for the murder of their own children, nor to incur any odium among the circle of society in which they live—not even among Brahmins and the ministers of their religion."

"They do incur odium, and undergo penance," said Rajah Bukhtawur Sing; "do they not?" said he to some Brahmins standing near. They smiled, but hesitated to reply. "They know they do," said the Rajah, "but are afraid to tell the truth, for they and their families live in villages belonging to these proud Rajpoot landholders, and would be liable to be turned out of house and home were they to tell what they know." One of the Brahmins then said, "All this is true, sir; but after the murder of every infant the family considers itself to be an object of displeasure to the deity, and after the twelfth day they send for the family priest (Prohut), and, by suitable gratuities, obtain absolution. This is necessary, whether the family be rich or poor; but when the absolution is given, nothing more is thought or said about the matter. The Gour and other Rajpoots who can afford to unite their daughters in marriage to the sons of Chouhans, Byses, and other families of higher grade, though they cannot obtain theirs in return for their sons, commit less murders of this kind than others; but all the Rajpoot clans commit more or less of them. Habit has reconciled them to it; but it appears very shocking to us Brahmins and all other classes. They commonly bury the infants alive as soon as possible after their birth. We, sir, are helpless, living as as we do among such turbulent and pitiless landholders, and cannot presume to admonish or remonstrate: our lives would not be safe for a moment were we to say anything, or seem to notice such crimes."

I do not think that any landholder of this class, in the Bangur district, would feel much compunction for the commission of any crime that did not involve their expulsion from caste, or degradation in rank. Great crimes do not involve these penalties: they incur them only by small peccadillos, or offences deemed venal among other societies. The Government of Oude, as it is at present constituted, will never be able to put down effectually the great crimes which now stain almost every acre of land in its dominions. It is painful to pass over a country abounding so much in what the evil propensities of our nature incite men to do, when not duly restrained; and so little in what the good prompt us to perform and create, when duly protected and encouraged, under good government.

January 24, 1850.—Sandee, fourteen miles, over a plain of light domuteea soil, which becomes very sandy for the last four or five miles. The crops are scanty upon the more sandy parts, except in the vicinity of villages; but there is a little jungle, and no undue portion of fallow for so light a soil. About five miles from our last ground, we came through the large and populous village of Bawun; about three miles further, through another of nearly the same size, Sungeechamow; and about three miles further on, through one still larger, Admapoor, which is three miles from Sandee. Sandee and Nawabgunge join each other, and are on the bank of the Gurra river, a small stream whose waters are said to be very wholesome. We passed the boundary of the Bangur district, just before we entered the village of Sungeechamow, which lies in that of Sandee.

There is a Hindoo shrine on the right of the road between Sandee and Admapoor, which is said to be considered very sacred, and called Burmawust. It is a mere grove, with a few priests, on the bank of a large lake, which extends close up to Sandee on the south. The river Gurra flows under the town to the north. The place is said to be healthy, but could hardly be so, were this lake to the west or east, instead of the south, whence the wind seldom blows. This lake must give out more or less of malaria, that would be taken over the village, for the greater portion of the year, by the prevailing easterly and westerly winds. I do not think the place so eligible for a cantonment at Tundeeawun, in point either of salubrity, position, or soil.

January 25, 1850.—Halted at Sandee. The lake on the south side, mentioned yesterday, abounds in fish, and is covered with wild fowl; but the fish we got from it yesterday was not good of its kind. I observed very fine groves of mango-trees close to Sandee, planted by merchants and shopkeepers of the place. The oldest are still held by the descendants of those by whom they were first planted more than a century ago; and no tax whatever is imposed upon the trees of any kind, or upon the lands on which they stand. Many young groves are growing up around, to replace the old ones as they decay; and the greatest possible security is felt in the tenure by which they are held by the planter, or his descendants, though they hold no written lease, or deed of gift; and have neither written law nor court of justice to secure it to them. Groves and solitary mango, semul, tamarind, mhowa and other trees, whose leaves and branches are not required for the food of elephants and camels, are more secure in Oude than in our own territories; and the country is, in consequence, much better provided with them. While they give beauty to the landscape, they alleviate the effects of droughts to the poorer classes from the fruit they supply; and droughts are less frequently and less severely felt in a country so intersected by fine streams, flowing from the Tarae forest, or down from the perpetual snows of neighbouring hills, and keeping the water always near the surface. These trees tend also to render the air healthy, by giving out oxygen in large quantities during the day, and absorbing carbonic acid gas. The river Gurra enters the Ganges about twelve miles below Sandee. Boats take timber on this stream from the Phillibeet district to Cawnpoor. It passes near the town of Shajehanpoor; and the village of Palee, twenty miles north-west from Sandee, where we shall have to recross it.

January 26, 1850.—Busora, twelve miles north-west from Sandee, over a plain of light sandy soil, or bhoor, with some intervals of oosur. The tillage extends over as much of the surface as it ought in so light a soil; and the district of Sandee Palee generally is said to be well cultivated. It has been under the charge of Hafiz Abdoollah, a very honest and worthy man, for seven years up to his death, which took place in November last. He is said never to have broken faith with a landholder; but he was too weak in means to keep the bad portion under control; and too much occupied in reading or repeating the *Koran*, which he knew all by heart, as his name imports. His son Ameer Gholam Allee, a lad of only thirteen years of age, has been appointed his successor. He promises to be like his father in honesty and love of the holy book.*

About half way we passed the village of Bhanapoor,

* He has been since removed, and was in prison as a defaulter, July 1851.

held by zumeendars of the *Dhaukurree* Rajpoot clan, who told me, that they gave their daughters in marriage to the Rykwars, but more to the Sombunsie Rajpoots, who abound in the district, and hold the greater part of the lands; that these Sombunsies have absorbed almost all the lands of the other classes by degrees, and are now seizing upon theirs; that the Sombunsies give their daughters in marriage only to the Rathore and Chouhan Rajpoots, few of whom are to be found on the Oude side of the Ganges; and, in consequence, that they take such as they preserve to our districts on the other side of that river, but murder the greater part rather than condescend to marry them to men of the other Rajpoot clans whom they deem to be of inferior grade, or go to the expense of uniting them in marriage to clans of higher or equal grade in Oude. Some Sombunsies, who came out to pay their respects from the next village we passed, told us, that they did not give their daughters even to the Tilokchundee Bys Rajpoots; but in this they did not tell the truth.

At the next village, the largest in the parish, Barone, the chief landholder, Kewul Sing, came out and presented his offering of a fine fighting-ram. He was armed with his bow, and "quiver full of arrows;" but told me, that he thought a good gun, with pouch and flask, much better, and he carried the bow and quiver merely because they were lighter. He was surrounded by almost all the people of the town, and told me, that the family held in copartnership fifty-two small villages, immediately around *Barone*—that this village had been attacked and burnt down by Captain Bunbury and his regiment the year before last, without any other cause that they could understand save that he had recommended him not to encamp in the grove close by. The fact was, that none of the family would pay the Government demand, or obey the old Amil, Hafiz Abdoollah; and it was necessary to make an example. On being asked whether his family and clan, the Sombunsies, preserved or destroyed their daughters, he told me, in the midst of his village community, that he would not deceive me; that they, one and all, destroyed their infant daughters; but that one was, occasionally, allowed to live *(ek-adh)*; that the family was under a taint for twelve days after the murder of an infant, when the family priest (Prohut) was invited and fed in due form; that he then declared the absolution complete, and the taint removed.

The family priest was present, and I asked him what he got on such occasions? He said, that to remove the taint, or grant absolution after the murder of a daughter, he got little or no money; he merely partook of the food prepared for him in due form; but that, on the birth of a son, he got ten rupees from the parents. All the assembled villagers bore testimony to the truth of what the patriarch and the priest told me. They said, that no one would enter a house in which an infant daughter had been destroyed, or eat or drink with any member of the family till the Prohut had granted the absolution, which he did after the expiration of twelve days, as a matter of course, depending as he did upon the good-will of the landholders, who were all of the same clan, Sombunsies. Few other Brahmins will condescend to eat, drink, or associate with these family and village priests, who take the sins of such murderers upon their own heads.

The old patriarch rode on with me upon his pony, five miles to my tents, as if I should not think the worse of him for having murdered his own daughters, and permitted others to murder theirs. I told him, that I could hold no converse with men who were guilty of such crimes; and that the vengeance of God would crush them all, sooner or latter. For his only excuse he told me, that it was a practice, derived from a long line of ancestors, wiser and better than they were; and that it prevailed in almost every Rajpoot family in the country; that they had, in consequence, become reconciled to it, and knew not how to do without it. Family pride is the cause of this terrible evil!

The estate of Kuteearee, on the left-hand side of the road towards the Ramgunga and Ganges, is held by Runjeet Sing, of the Kuteear Rajpoot clan. His estate yields to him about one hundred and twenty thousand rupees a-year, while he is assessed at only sixteen thousand. While Hakeem Mehndee was in banishment at Futtehgurh, about fifteen years ago, he became intimate with Runjeet Sing, of Kuteearee; and when he afterwards became minister, in 1837, he is said to have obtained for him the King's seal and signature to a perpetual lease at this rate, from which is deducted a *nankar* of four thousand, leaving an actual demand of only twelve thousand. Were such grants, in perpetuity, respected in Oude, the ministers and their minions would soon sell the whole of his Majesty's dominions, and leave him a beggar. He has not yet been made to pay a higher rate; not, however, out of regard for the King's pledge, but solely out of that for Runjeet's fort of Dhunmutpoor, on the bank of the Ganges, his armed bands, and his seven pieces of cannon. He has been diligently employing all his surplus rents in improving his defensive means; and, besides his fort and guns, is said to have a large body of armed and disciplined men. He has seized upon a great many villages around, belonging to weaker proprietors: and is every year adding to his estate in this way. In this the old Amil, Hafiz Abdoollah, acquiesced, solely because he had not the means nor the energy to prevent it. He got his estate excluded from the jurisdiction of the local authorities, and placed in the Huzoor Tuhseel.

Like others of his class, who reside on the border, he has a village in the British territory to reside in, unmolested, when charged by the Oude authorities with heavy crimes and balances. He had been attacked and and driven across the Ganges, in 1837, for contumacy and rebellion; deprived of his estate, and obliged to reside at Futtehgurh, where he first became acquainted with Hakeem Mehndee. The Oude Government has often remonstrated against the protection which this contumacious and atrocious landholder receives from our subjects and authorities.* Crimes in this district are not quite so numerous as in Bangur; but they are of no less atrocious a character. The thieves and robbers of Bangur, when taken and taxed with being so, say, "of course we are robbers—if we were not, how should we have been permitted to reside in Bangur?" All are obliged to fight and plunder with the landholders, or to rob for them on distant roads, and in distant villages.

My camp has been robbed several times within the time I have been out, and the property has been traced to villages in the Sundeela and Bangur districts. In the Sundeela district it can be recovered when traced with a

* See the Resident's letter to Government North-Western Provinces, 3rd August, 1837. The King's letter to the Resident, 7th April, 1837. The same to the same, 19th May, 1837. Depositions and urzies. Runjeet Sing was attacked by the King's troops and driven across the Ganges again in June 1851, and died during the contest, which is being continued by his son. 1851.—W. H. S.

small force, and the thieves taken; but in the Bangur district it would require a large military force well commanded, and a large train of artillery to recover the one or seize the other.

A respectable landholder of this place, a Sombunsie, tells me, that the custom of destroying their female infants has prevailed from the time of the first founder of their race; that a rich man has to give food to many Brahmins, to get rid of the stain, on the twelfth or thirteenth day, but that a poor man can get rid of it by presenting a little food in due form to the village priest; that they cannot give their daughters in marriage to any Rajpoot families, save the Rhathores and Chouhans; that the family of their clan who gave a daughter to any other class of Rajpoots, would be excluded from caste immediately and for ever; that those who have property have to give all they have with their daughters to the Chouhans and Rhathores, and reduce themselves to nothing; and can take nothing from them in return, as it is a great stain to take "*kuneea dan*," or virgin price, from any one; that a Sombunsie may, however, when reduced to great poverty, take the "*kuneea dan*" from the Chouhans and Rhathores for a virgin daughter without being excommunicated from the clan, but even he could not give a daughter to any other clan of Rajpoots without being excluded for ever from caste; that it was a misfortune no doubt, but it was one that had descended among them from the remotest antiquity, and could not be got rid of; that mothers wept and screamed a good deal when their first female infants were torn from them, but after two or three times giving birth to female infants, they become quiet and reconciled to the usage, and said, "do as you like;" that some poor parents of their clan did certainly give their daughters for large sums to wealthy people of lower clans, but lost their caste for ever by so doing; that it was the dread of sinking, in substance from the loss of property, and in grade from the loss of caste, that alone led to the murder of female infants; that the dread prevailed more or less in every Rajpoot clan, and led to the same thing; but most in the clan that restricted the giving of daughters in marriage to the smallest number of clans.

The infant is destroyed in the room where it is born, and there buried. The floor is then plastered over with cow-dung, and on the thirteenth day the village or family priest must cook and eat his food in that room. He is provided with wood, ghee, barley, rice, and tillee (sesamum). He boils the rice, barley, and sesamum in a brass vessel, throws the ghee over them when they are dressed, and eats the whole. This is considered as a *hom*, or burnt-offering, and by eating it in that place the priest is supposed to take the whole *hutteea* or sin upon himself, and to cleanse the family from it. I am told that they put the milk of the mudar shrub "asclepias gigantea," into the mouth of the infant to destroy it, and cover the mouth with the fæces that first pass from the infant's bowels. It soon dies; and after the expiation the parents again occupy the room, and there receive the visits of their family and friends, and gossip as usual!

Rajah Bukhtawar Sing tells me, that he has heard the whole process frequently described in this way by the midwives who have attended the birth. These midwives are however generally sent out of the room with the mother when the infant is found to be a girl. In any law for the effectual prevention of this crime, it would be necessary to prescribe a severe punishment for the priest, as an accessary after the fact. The only objection to this is, I think, that it might deprive the Court of the advantage of an important witness when required at the trial of the parents, but when necessary he might be admitted as King's evidence. All the people here that I talk to on the subject, say that the crime has been put down in the greater part of the British territories, and that judicious measures honestly and firmly carried out would put it down in Oude, and do away with the scruples which one clan of Rajpoots have to give their daughters in marriage to another. Unable to murder their daughters, they would be glad to dispose of them in marriage to all clans of Rajpoots. It might be put down in Oude, as it was put down by Mr. Willoughby, of Bombay, in the districts under his charge, by making the abolition one of the conditions on which all persons of the Rajpoot clans hold their lands, and strictly enforcing the observance of that condition. The Government of Oude as now constituted could do nothing whatever towards putting it down in this or any other way.

January 27, 1850.—Palee, eight miles north-west. The road half way from Sandee to Busora, and half way from Busora to Palee, passes over a very light, sandy soil—bhoor. I have already stated that kutcha wells, or wells without burnt brick and cement, will not last in this sandy soil, while it stands more in need of irrigation. The road for the last half way of this morning's stage passes over a good doomuteea soil. The whole country is however well cultivated, and well studded with fine trees; and the approach to Palee is at this season very picturesque. The groves of mango and other fine trees amidst which the town stands, on the right bank of the Gurra river, appear very beautiful as one approaches, particularly now that the surrounding country is covered by so fine a carpet of rich spring crops. The sun's rays, falling upon such rich masses of foliage, produce an infinite variety of form, colour, and tint, on which the eye delights to repose. We intended to have our camp on the other side of the river, but no good ground could be found for it, without injury to the crops, within three miles from Palee, and we must cross it on our way to Shahabad to-morrow.

This small river flows along a little to the right of our march this morning. About half way we passed a very pretty village, held and cultivated by families of Kunojee Brahmins, who *condescend* to hold and drive their own ploughs. Other families of this class pride themselves upon never condescending to drive their own ploughs, and consider themselves in consequence a shade higher in caste. Other Brahmin families have different shades or degrees of caste, like the Kunojeeas; but I am not aware that any family of any other class of Brahmins condescend to hold their own ploughs. I told them, that "God seemed to favour their exertions, and bless them with prosperity, for I had not seen a neater village or village community." They seemed to be all well pleased with my compliment. At Palee resides Bulbhuder Sing, a notorious robber, who was lately seized and sent as a felon to Lucknow. After six months' confinement he bribed himself out, got possession of the estate which he now holds, and to which he had no right whatever, and had it excluded from the jurisdiction of the local authorities, and transferred to the "Hozoor Tuhseel." He has been ever since diligently employed in converting it into a den of robbers, and in the usual way seizing upon other people's lands, stock, and property of all kinds.

Hundreds in Oude are doing the same thing in the same way. Scores of those who suffer from the depredations of this class of offenders, complain to me every day; but I can neither afford them redress, nor hold out any hope of it from any of the Oude authorities. It is a proverb, "that those who are sentenced to six years' imprisonment in Oude, are released in six months, and those who are sentenced to six months, are released in six years." Great numbers are released every year at Lucknow for *thanksgivings*, or *propitiation*. If the King or any member of his family becomes sick, prisoners are released, that they may recover; and when they recover, others are released as a grateful, and, at the same time, profitable acknowledgment, since the Government relieves itself from the cost of keeping them; and its servants appropriate the money paid for their ransom. Those who are in for long periods are, for the most part, great offenders, who are the most able and most willing to pay high for their release; those who are in for short ones are commonly the small ones, who are the least able and least disposed to give anything. The great offenders again are those who are most disposed, and most able, to revenge themselves on such persons as have aided the Government in their arrest or conviction; and they do all they can to murder and rob them and their families and relatives, as soon as they are set at large, in order to deter others from doing the same. This would be a great evil in any country, but is terrible in Oude, where no police is maintained for the protection of life and property. The cases of atrocious murders and robberies which come before me every day, and are acknowledged by the local authorities, and neighbours of the sufferers, to have taken place, are frightful. Such sufferings, for which no redress is to be found, would soon desolate any part of India less favoured by nature.

In the valley of the Nerbudda, for instance, such sufferings would render a district desolate for ages. The people, driven off from an estate, go and settle in another better governed. The grass grows rankly from the richness of the soil, and the humidity of the air, and becomes filled with deer and other animals, that are food for beasts of prey. Tigers, leopards, wolves, wild dogs, &c. follow, to feed upon them; and they render residence and industry unsafe. Malaria follows, and destroys what persons the tigers leave. I have seen extensive tracts of the richest soil and most picturesque scenery, along the banks of the Nerbudda, which had been rendered desolate for ages by the misrule of only a few years. It is the same in the Tarae forest, which separates Oude from Nepaul. But in the rest of Oude, from the Ganges to this belt of forest, no such effects follow misrule, however great and prolonged. Here no grass grows too rankly, few deer fill it, few tigers, leopards, wolves, or wild dogs come in pursuit of them, and no malaria is feared. If a landholder takes to rebellion and plunder, he is followed by all his retainers and clansmen; and their families, and the cultivators of other classes, feeling no longer secure, go and till lands on other estates, till they are invited back. The cowherds and shepherds, who live by the produce of their cattle and sheep, remain and thrive by the abundance of pasture lands, from which the rich spring and harvest crops have disappeared. These cattle and sheep graze over them, and enrich the soil by restoring to it a portion of those elements of fertility, of which a long succession of harvests had robbed it. Over and above what they leave on the grounds, over which they graze, large stores of manure are collected for future use by the herdsmen, who now exclusively occupy the villages. The landholder and his followers, in the meantime, subsist and enrich themselves by the indiscriminate plunder of the surrounding country; and are at last invited back by a weak and wearied Government, to reoccupy the lands, improved by this salutary fallow, at a lower rate of rent, or no rent at all for some years, and a remission of all balances for past years, on account of *paemalee*, or treading down of crops, during the disorder that has prevailed.

The cultivators return to occupy their old lands, so enriched, at reduced rates of rent; and, in two or three years, these lands become again carpeted with a beautiful variety of spring and autumn crops. The crops, in our districts, on the opposite side of the river Ganges, bear no comparison with those on the Oude side. The lands are all overcropped and under-stocked with cattle and sheep from the want of pasture lands. There is little manure, the water is too far below the surface to admit of sufficient irrigation, without greater outlay than the farmers and cultivators can afford; the rotation of crops is insufficient, and no salutary fallow comes to the relief of the soil, from the labour of men living and working under the efficient protection of a strong and able Government. The difference in the crops is manifest to the beholder, and shown in the rate of rents paid for the lands where the price of land produce is the same in both; the same river conveying the produce of both to and from the same markets.

A Murhutta army, under the Peshwa, Ballajee, invaded the districts, about the source of the Nerbudda river, about one hundred and seven years ago, A.D. 1742. They ravaged these districts, as they did all others which they invaded; but they, like the greater part of the Oude

Tarae, remain waste; while the others, like the rest of Oude, soon recovered and become prosperous from the circumstances above stated. The soil of some of the districts, about the source of the Nerbudda, then ravaged, is among the finest in the world; but the long grass and rich foliage, by which it is covered, are occupied, like the pampos of South America, almost exclusively by wild cattle, buffaloes, deer, and tigers. The district of Mundula, which intervenes between them and the rich and highly-cultivated district of Jubbulpoor, in the valley of that river, was populous and well cultivated when we took possession of it in the year 1817; but it has become almost as waste under our rule by a more gradual but not less desolating process. Not considering the diminishing markets for land produce, our assessments of the land revenue were too high, and the managing officers never thought the necessity of reduction established, till the villages were partially or wholly deserted. The farmers and cultivators all emigrated, by degrees, into the neighbouring districts of Nagpoor and Rewa, where they had more consideration and lighter assessments, and the markets for land produce were improving. The lands of Mundula became waste, and covered with rank grass filled with deer; tigers followed to feed upon them, and carried off all the poor peasantry, who remained and attempted to cultivate small patches; malaria followed and completed the work.

Like the *tharoos* of the Oude forest, the Gonds born in this malaria are the only people who can live in it; and the ravages of tigers and endemial disease prevent their numbers from increasing. Those who once emigrate never come back, and population and tillage have been decreasing ever since we took possession, or for thirty-three years. The same process has been going on in other parts of the Nerbudda valley with the same results. In Oude, from the causes above described, lands of the same denomination and kind often yield double the rate of rent that they yield in our own conterminous districts, or districts on the opposite side of the Ganges, and other rivers that separate our territories from those of Oude. Under a tolerable Government, Oude would soon become one of the most beautiful countries in India; but the lands would fall off, in fertility, as ours do from over-cropping, no doubt.

January 28, 1850.—Shahabad, ten miles. We crossed, close under Palee, the little river Gurra, which continued for some miles to flow along, in its winding course, close by on our left. It is here some five or six miles to the south-west of the town. The soil we have come over is chiefly muteear, or the doomuteea, tightened by a mixture of clay, or argillaceous earth. Rich crops of rice are grown on this muteea, which retains its moisture so much better than the looser doomutea soil.

Half-way we came through a neat village, the lands of which are subdivided between the members of a large family of Kunojee Brahmins, who came out to see us pass, and pay their respects. The cultivation was so fine that I *hoped* they were of the class who condescended to hold their own ploughs. I asked them; and they, with seeming pride, told me that they did not—that they employed servants to hold their ploughs for them. When I told them that this was their *misfortune*, they seemed much amused, but were all well-behaved and respectful, though they must have thought my notion very odd.

The little Gurra flows from the Oude Tarae forest by the town of Phillibheet, where boats are built, to be taken down to Cawnpoor, on the Ganges, for sale. About four hundred, great and small, are supposed to be taken down the Gurra every year, in the season of the rains. They take down the timber of the Tarae forest, rice, and other things; and all are sold, with their cargoes, at Cawnpoor, or other places on the Ganges. The timbers are floated along on both sides of the boats. Palee is a good place for a cantonment, or seat of public civil establishments, and Shahabad is no less so. The approach to both, from the south-east, is equally beautiful, from the rich crops which cover the ground up to the houses, and the fine groves and majestic single trees which surround them.

Shahabad is a very ancient and large town, occupied chiefly by Pathan Mussulmans, who are a very turbulent and fanatical set of fellows. Subsookh Rae, a Hindoo, and the most respectable merchant in the district, resided here, and for some time consented to officiate, as the deputy of poor old Hafiz Abdoollah, for the management of the town, where his influence was great. He had lent a good deal of money to the heads of some of the Pathan families of the town, but finding few of them disposed to repay, he was last year obliged to refuse further loans. They determined to take advantage of the coming mohurrum festival to revenge the *affront* as men commonly do who live among such a fanatical community. The tazeeas are commonly taken up, and carried in procession, ten days after the new moon is first seen, at any place where they are made; but in Oude all go by the day in which the moon is seen from the capital of Lucknow. As soon as she is seen at Lucknow, the King issues an order throughout his dominions for the tazeeas to be taken in procession ten days after. The moon was this year, in November, first seen on the 30th of the month at

Lucknow; but at Shahabad, where the sky is generally clearer, she had been seen on the 29th. The men to whom Subsookh Rae had refused further loans determined to take advantage of this incident to wreak their vengeance; and when the deputy promulgated the King's order for the tazeeas to be taken in procession ten days after the 30th, they instigated all the Mahommedans of the town to insist upon taking them out ten days after the 29th, and persuaded them that the order had been fabricated, or altered, by the malice of their Hindoo deputy, *to insult their religious feelings.* They were taken out accordingly, and having to pass the house of Subsookh Rae, when their excitement, or spirit of religious fervour, had reached the highest pitch, they there put them down, broke open the doors, entered in a crowd, and plundered it of all the property they could find, amounting to above seventy thousand rupees. Subsookh Rae was obliged to get out, with his family, at a back door, and run for his life. He went to Shajehanpoor, in our territory, and put himself under the protection of the magistrate. Not content with all this, they built a small miniature mosque at the door with some loose bricks, so that no one could go either out or in without the risk of knocking it down, or so injuring this *mock mosque* as to rouse, or enable the evil-minded to rouse, the whole Mahommedan population against the offender. Poor Subsookh Rae has been utterly ruined, and ever since seeking in vain for redress. The Government is neither disposed nor able to afford it, and the poor boy who has now succeeded his *learned* father in the contract is helpless. The little mock mosque, of uncemented bricks, still stands as a monument of the insolence of the Mahommedan population, and the weakness and apathy of the Oude Government.

CHAPTER II.

Infanticide—Nekomee Rajpoots—Fallows in Oude created by disorders—Their cause and effect—Tillage goes on in the midst of sanguinary conflicts—Runjeet Sing, of Kutteearee—Mahomdee district—White Ants—Traditional decrease in the fertility of the Oude soil—Risks to which cultivators are exposed—Obligations which these risks impose upon them—Infanticide—The Amil of Mahomdee's narrow escape—An infant disinterred and preserved by the father after having been buried alive—Insecurity of life and property—Beauty of the surface of the country, and richness of its foliage—Mahomdee district—State and recent history of—Relative fertility of British and Oude soil—Native notions of our laws and their administration—Of the value of evidence in our Courts—Infanticide—Boys only saved—Girls destroyed in Oude—The priests who give absolution for the crime abhorred by the people of all other classes—Lands in our districts becoming more and more exhausted from over-cropping—Probable consequences to the Government and people of India—Political and social error of considering land private property—Hakeem Mehndee and subsequent managers of Mahomdee—Frauds on the King in charges for the keep of animals—Kunojee Brahmins—Unsuccessful attempt to appropriate the lands of weaker neighbours—Gokurnath, on the border of the Tarae—The sakhoo or saul trees of the forest.

LALTA SING, of the Nikomee Rajpoot tribe, whom I had lately an opportunity of assisting, for his good services in arresting outlays from our territories, has just been to pay his respects. Our next encamping ground is to be on his estate of Kurheya and Para. He tells me that very few families of his tribe now destroy their female infants; that tradition ascribes the origin of this evil to the practice of the Mahommedan emperors of Delhi of demanding daughters in marriage from the Rajpoot princes of the country; that some of them were too proud to comply with the demand, and too weak to resist it in any other way than that of putting all their female infants to death. This is not impossible. He says that he believes the *Dhankuries*, whom I have described above to be really the only tribe of Rajpoots among whom no family destroys its infant daughters in Oude; that all tribes of Rajpoots get money with the daughters they take from tribes a shade lower in caste, to whom they cannot give theirs in return; and pay money with the daughters they give in marriage to tribes a shade higher, who will not give their daughters to them in return. The native collector of Shahabad, a gentlemanly Mahommedan, came out two miles to pay his respects on my approach, and we met on a large space of land, lying waste, while all around was covered with rich crops. I asked, "Pray why is this land left waste?" "It is, sir, altogether unproductive." "Why is this? It seems to me to be just as good as the rest around, which produces such fine crops." "It is called *khubtee*—slimy, and is said to be altogether barren." "I assure you, sir," said Rajah Bukhtawar Sing, "that it is good land, and capable of yielding good crops, under good tillage, or it would not produce the fine grass you see upon it. You must not ask men like this about the kinds and qualities of soils, for they really know nothing whatever about them: they are *city gentlemen's sons*, who get into high places, and pass their lives in them without learning anything but how to screw money out of such as we are, who are born upon the soil, and depend upon its produce all our lives for subsistence. Ask him, sir, whether either he or any of his ancestors ever knew anything of the difference between one soil and another."

The collector acknowledged the truth of what the old man said, and told me that he really knew nothing about the matter, and had merely repeated what the people told him. This is true with regard to the greater part of the local revenue officers employed in Oude. "One of these city gentlemen, sir," said Bukhtawar Sing, "when sent out as a revenue collector, in Saadut Allee's time, was asked by his assistants what they were to do with a crop of sugar-cane which had been attached for balances, and was becoming too ripe, replied, '*Cut it down, to be sure, and have it stacked!*' He did not know that sugar-cane must, as soon as cut, be taken to the mill, or it spoils." "I have heard of another," said the old Rusaldar Nubbee Buksh, "who, after he entered upon his charge, asked the people about him to show him the tree on which grew the fine *istamālee** rice which they used at Lucknow." "There is no question, sir," said Bukhtawar Sing, "that is too absurd for these cockney gentlemen to ask when they enter upon such revenue charges as these. They are the aristocracy of towns and cities, who are learned enough in books and court ceremonies and intrigues, but utterly ignorant of country life, rural economy, and agricultural industry."

For a cantonment or civil station, the ground to the north of Shahabad, on the left-hand side of the road leading to Mahomdee, seems the best. It is a level plain, of a stiff soil formed of clay and sand, and not very productive.

The country, from Sandee and Shahabad to the rivers Ganges and Ramgunga, is one rich sheet of spring culti-

* The *istamālee* rice is rice of fine quality, which has been kept for some years before used. To be good, rice must be kept for some years before used, and that only which has been so kept is called *istamalee* or *useable*.

vation; and the estate of Kuteearee, above described, is among the richest portions of this sheet. The portions on which the richest crops now stand became waste during the disorders which followed the expulsion of Runjeet Sing, in the usual way, in 1837, and derived the usual benefit from the salutary fallow. A stranger passing through such a sheet of rich cultivation, without communing with the people, would little suspect the fearful crimes that are every year committed upon it, from the weakness and apathy of the Government, and the bad faith and bad character of its officers and chief landholders. The land is tilled in spite of all obstacles, because all depend upon its produce for subsistence; but there is no indication of the beneficial interference of the Government for the protection of life, property, and character, and for the encouragement of industry and the display of its fruits. The land is ploughed, and the seed sown, often by stealth at night, in the immediate vicinity of a sanguinary contest between the Government officers and the landholders. It is only when the latter are defeated, and take to the jungles, or the Honourable Company's districts, and commence their indiscriminate plunder, that the cultivator ceases from his labours, and the lands are left waste.

Runjeet Sing two or three years ago seized upon the village of Mulatoo, in his vicinity, to which he had no claim whatever, and he has forcibly retained it. It had long paid Government ten thousand a-year, but he has consented to pay only one thousand. Lands yielding above nine thousand he has cut off from its rent-roll, and added to those of his hereditary villages on the borders. Last year he seized upon the village of Nudua, with a rent-roll of fourteen hundred rupees, and he holds it with a party of soldiers and two guns. The Amil lately sent out a person with a small force to demand the Government dues; but they were driven back, as he pretends that he got it in mortgage from Dumber Sing, who had taken a short lease of that and other khalsa villages, and absconded as a defaulter; and that he has purchased the lands from the cultivating proprietors, and is, therefore, bound to pay no revenue whatever for them to the King. All defaulters and offenders who take refuge on his estate he instigates to plunder, and provides with gangs, on condition of getting the greater part of the booty. He thinks that he is sure of shelter in the British territory, should he be driven from Oude; he feels also sure of aid from other large landholders of the same class in the neighbourhood.

January 30, 1850.—Kurheya Para, twelve miles, over a plain of excellent muteear soil, a good deal of which is covered with jungle. Para is a short distance from Kurheya, and our camp is midway between the two villages. The boundary of the Sandee Palee and Mahomdee districts we crossed about four miles from our present encampment. This district of Mahomdee was taken in contract by Hakeem Mehndee, at three lacs and eleven thousand rupees a-year, in 1804 A. D., and in a few years he brought it into full tillage, and made it yield above seven lacs. It has been falling off ever since it was taken from him, and now yields only between three and four lacs. The jungle is studded with large peepul-trees, which are all shorn of their small branches and leaves. The landholders and cultivators told me that they were taken off by the cowherds who grazed their buffaloes, bullocks, and cows in these jungles; that they formed their chief and, in the cold season, their best food, as the leaves of the peepul-tree were supposed to give warmth to the stomach, and to increase the quantity of the milk; that the cowherds were required to pay nothing for the privilege of grazing their cattle in these jungles, by the person to whom the lands belonged, because they enriched the soil with their manure, and all held small portions of land under tillage, for which they paid rent; that they had the free use of the peepul-trees in the jungles, but were not permitted to touch those on the cultivated lands and in villages.

White ants are so numerous in the argillaceous muteear soil, in which their food abounds, that it is really dangerous to travel on an elephant, or *swiftly* on horseback, over a new road cut or enlarged through any portion of it that has remained long untilled. The two fore legs of my elephant went down yesterday morning into a deep pit made by them, but concealed by the new road, which has been made over it for the occasion of my visit near Shahabad, and it was with some difficulty that he extricated them. We have had several accidents of the same kind since we came out. In cutting a new road they cut through large ant-hills, and leave no trace of the edifices or the gulf below them, which the little insects have made in gathering their food and raising their lofty habitation. They are not found in the bhoor or oosur soils, and in comparatively small numbers in the doomuteea or lighter soil, but they abound in the muteear soil in proportion to its richness. Cultivation, where the crops are irrigated, destroys them, and the only danger is in passing over new roads cut through jungle, or lands that have remained long untilled, or along the sides of old pathways, from which these land-marks have been removed in hastily widening them for wheeled carriages.

A Brahmin cultivator, whose cart we had been obliged to press into our own service for this stage, came along with me almost all the way. He said, "The spring crops of this season, sir, are no doubt very fine; but in days of yore, before the curse of *Bhurt Jee* (the brother of Ram) came upon the landholders and cultivators of Oude, they were much finer; when he set out from his capital of Ajoodheea for the conquest of Cylone, he left the administration to his brother, Bhurt Jee, who made a liberal settlement of the land tax. He put a ghurra or pitcher, with a round bottom, turned upside down, into every half acre (beegha) of the cultivated land, and required the landholder or cultivator to leave upon it, as much of the grain produced as the rounded bottom would retain, which could not be one ten-thousandth part of the produce; he lived economically, and collected at this rate during the many years that his brother was absent. But when his brother returned and approached the boundary of his dominions, he met hosts of landholders and cultivators clamouring against the *rapacity and oppression* of his brother's administration. The humanity of Ram's disposition was shocked, sir, at all this, and he became angry with his brother before he heard what he had to say. When Bhurt had satisfied his brother that he had not taken from them the thousandth part of what he had a right to take, and Ram had, indeed, taken from them himself, he *sighed* at the wickedness and ingratitude of the agricultural classes of Oude; and the baneful effects of this sad *sigh* has been upon us ever since, sir, in spite of all we can do to avert them. In order to have the blessing of God upon our labours, it is necessary for us to fulfil strictly all the responsibilities under which we hold and till the land; first, to pay punctually the just demands of Government; second, all the wages of the labour employed; third, all the charities to the poor; fourth, all the offerings to our respective tutelary gods; fifth, a special offering to Mahabeer, alias Hunooman. These payments and offerings, sir, must all be made before the cultivator can safely take the surplus produce to his store-room for sale and consumption."

Old Bukhtawar Sing, who was riding by my side, said, "A conscientious farmer or cultivator, sir, when he finds that his field yields a great deal more than the usual returns, that is when it yields twenty instead of the usual return of ten, gives the whole in charity, lest evil overtake him from his unusual good luck and inordinate exultatation."

I asked the Brahmin cultivator why all these offerings were required to be made by cultivators in particular? He replied, "There is, sir, no species of tillage in which the lives of numerous *insects* are not sacrificed, and it is to atone for these numerous murders, and the ingratitude to Bhurt, that cultivators, in particular, are required to make so many offerings;" and, he added, "much sin, sir, is no doubt brought upon the land by the murder of so many female infants. I believe, sir, that all the tribes of Rajpoots murder them; and I do not think than one in ten is suffered to live. If the family or village priest did not consent to eat with the parents after the murder, no such murders could take place, sir; for none, even of their nearest relatives, will ever eat with them till the Brahmin has done so."

The bearers of the tonjohn in which I sat, said, "We do not believe, sir, that one girl in twenty among the Rajpoots is preserved. Davey Buksh, the Gonda Rajah, is, we believe, the only one of the Biseyn Rajpoot tribe who preserves his daughters;* his father did the same, and his sister, who was married to the Bhudoreea Rajah of Mynpooree, came to see him lately on the occasion of a pilgrimage to Ajoodheea, on the death of her husband; of the six Kulhuns families of Chehdwara, two only preserve their daughters—Surnam Sing of Arta, and Jeskurn of Kumeear; but whether their sons or successors in the estates will do the same is uncertain." These bearers are residents of that district.

I may here remark, that oak-trees in the hills of the Himmelah chain are disfigured in the same manner, and for the same purpose, as the peepul and banyan trees are here; their small branches and leaves are torn off to supply fodder for bullocks and other animals. The ilex of the hills has not, however, in its nakedness the majesty of the peepul and banyan of the plains, though neither of them can be said to be "when unadorn'd, adorn'd the most."

January 31, 1850.—Puchgowa, north-east, twelve miles over a plain of doomuteea soil, a good deal of which is out of tillage at present. On the road we came through several neat villages, the best of which was occupied exclusively by the families of the Kunojeea Brahmin proprietors, and the few persons of inferior caste who ploughed their lands for them, as they are a shade too high in caste to admit of their holding their own ploughs. They are, however, very worthy people, and seemed very much pleased at being put so much at their ease in a talk with the great man about their own domestic and rural economy. They told me, that they did not permit Rajpoots to reside in or have anything to do with their village.

* There are a great many families of the Biseyn Rajpoots who never destroy their infant daughters.

"Why?" I asked.—"Because, sir, if they once get a footing among us, they are, sooner or later, sure to turn us all out." "How?"—"They get lands by little and little at lease, soon refuse to pay rent, declare the lands to be their own, collect bad characters for plunder, join the Rajpoots of their own clan in all the villages around in their enterprises, take to the jungles on the first occasion of a dispute, attack, plunder, and burn the village, murder us and our families, and soon get the estate for themselves, on their own terms from the local authorities, who are wearied out by the loss of revenue arising from their depredations; our safety, sir, depends upon our keeping entirely aloof from them."

Under a government so weak, the only men who prosper seem to be these landholders of the military classes who are strong in their union, clan feeling, courage, and ferocity. The villages here are numerous though not large, and by far the greater part are occupied by Rajpoots of the Nikomee tribe.

The Amil of the Mahomdee district, Krishun Sahae, had come out so far as Para to meet me, and have my camp supplied. He had earned a good reputation as a native collector of long standing in the Shajehanpore district, under Mr. Buller; but being ambitious to rise more rapidly than he could hope to do, under our settled government, he came to Lucknow with a letter of introduction from Mr. Buller to the Resident, Colonel Richmond, paid his court to the Durbur, got appointed Amil of the Mahomdee district, under the *amanee* system, paid his nazuranas on his investiture, in October last, and entered upon his charge. A few days ago it pleased the minister to appoint to his place Aboo Toorab Khan, the nephew and son-in-law of Moonowur-ood Dowla; and orders were sent out immediately, by a camel-messenger, to the commandants of the corps on duty with Krishun Sahae, to seize and send him, his family, and all his relations and dependents, with all his property to be found upon them, to Lucknow. The wakeel, whom he kept at Court for such occasions, heard of the order for the supercession and arrest, and forthwith sent off a note to his master by the fastest foot-messenger he could get. The camel-messenger found that the Amil had left Mahomdee, and gone out two stages to Para, to meet the Resident. He waited to deliver his message to the commandants and subordinate civil officers of the district, and see that they secured all the relatives, dependents, and property of the Amil that could be found. The foot-messenger, more wise, went on, and delivered his letter to Krishun Sahae, at Para, on the evening of Tuesday the 29th. He ordered his elephant very quietly, and mounting, told the driver to take him to a village on the road to Shajehanpoor.

On reaching the village about midnight, the driver asked him whither he was going—"I am flying from my enemies," said Krishun Sahae; "and we must make all haste, or we shall be overtaken before we reach the boundary." "But," said the driver, "my house and family are at Lucknow, and the one will be pulled to the ground and the other put into gaol if I fly with you." Krishun Sahae drew out a pistol and threatened to shoot him if he did not drive on as told. They were near a field of sugar-cane, and the driver hedged away towards it, without the Amil's perceiving his intention. When they got near the field the elephant dashed in among the cane to have a feast; and the driver in his *seeming* effort to bring him out, fell off and disappeared under the high cane. The Amil did all he could to get out his elephant, but the animal felt that he was no longer in danger of severe treatment from above, and had a very comfortable meal before him in the fine ripe cane, and would not move. The poor Amil was obliged to descend, and make all possible haste on foot across the border, attended by one servant who had accompanied him in his flight. The driver ran to the village and got the people to join him in the pursuit of his master, saying that he was making off with a good deal of the King's money. With an elephant load of the King's money in prospect, they made all the haste they could; but the poor Amil got safely over the border into British territory. They found the elephant dining very comfortably on the sugar-cane. After abusing the driver and all his female relations for deluding them with the hope of a rich booty, they permitted him to take the empty elephant to the new Amil at Mahomdee. News of all this reached my camp last night.

I omitted to mention that, at Busora on the 27th, a Rajpoot landholder of the Sombunsie tribe, came to my camp with a petition regarding a mortgage, and mentioned that he had a daughter, now two years of age; that when she was born he was out in his fields, and the females of the family put her into an earthen pot, buried her in the floor of the apartment, where the mother lay, and lit a fire over the grave; that he made all haste home as soon as he heard of the birth of a daughter, removed the fire and earth from the pot, and took out his child. She was still living, but two of her fingers which had not been sufficiently covered were a good deal burnt. He had all possible care taken of her, and she still lives; and both he and his wife are very fond of her. Finding that his tale interested me, he went home for the child; but his village was far off, and he has not been able to overtake me. He had given no orders to have her preserved, as his wife was confined sooner than he expected; but the family took it for granted that she was to be destroyed, and in running home to preserve her he acted on the impulse of the moment. The practice of destroying female infants is so general among this tribe, that a family commonly destroys the daughter as soon as born, when the father is from home, and has given no special orders about it, taking it to be his wish as a matter of course.

Several respectable landholders of the Chouhan, Nikomee, and other tribe of Rajpoots, were talking to me yesterday evening, and as they were connected by marriage with Rajpoot families of the same and higher clans in the British territories, I asked them whether some plan could not be devised to suppress the evil in Oude, as it had been suppressed there; for the disorders which prevailed seemed to me to be only a visitation from above for such an all-pervading sin. They told me that there would be little difficulty in putting down this system under an honest and strong Government that would secure rights, enforce duties, and protect life and property, as in the British territories. Atrocious and cruel as this crime is in Oude, it is hardly more so than that which not long ago prevailed in France and other nations of Europe, of burying their daughters alive in nunneries in order to gratify the same family pride.

It is painful to me to walk out of my tent of an evening, for I have every day large crowds seeking redress for grievous wrongs, for which I see no hope of redress: men and women, who have had their dearest relatives murdered, their houses burnt down, their whole property taken away, their lands seized upon, their crops destroyed by ruffians residing in the same or neighbouring villages, and actually in the camp of the Amil, without the slightest fear of being punished or made to surrender any portion of what they have taken. The Government authorities are too weak, even to enforce the payment of the Government demand, and have not the means to seize or punish offenders of any kind, if they have the inclination. In some districts they not only acquiesce in the depredations of these gangs of robbers, but act in collusion with their leaders, in order to get their aid in punishing defaulters or pretended defaulters, among the landholders. They murder the landholders, and as many as possible of their families, and as a reward for their services the local authorities make over their lands to them at reduced rates.

The Nazim of Sandee Palee told me on taking leave, that he had only two wings of Nujeeb Regiments with him, one of which was fit for some service, and in consequence, spread over the district on detached duties. The other was with him, but out of the five hundred, for which he had to issue monthly pay, he should not be able to get ten men to follow him on any emergency. They are obliged to court and conciliate the strong and reckless who prey upon the weak and industrious; and in consequence become despised and detested by the people. I feel like one moving among a people afflicted with incurable diseases, who crowd around him in hope, and are sent away in despair. I try to make the local authorities exert themselves in behalf of the sufferers; but am told that they have already done their utmost in vain; that if they seize robbers and murderers and send them to Lucknow, they are sure to purchase their enlargement and return to wreak their vengeance on them and on all who have aided them in their arrest and conviction; that if they attempt to seize one of the larger landholders, who refuses to pay the Government demand, seizes upon the lands of his weaker neighbours, and murders and robs them indiscriminately, he removes across the Ganges, into one of the Honourable Company's districts, and thence sends his myrmidons to plunder and lay waste the whole country, till he is invited back by a weak and helpless Government upon his own terms; that formerly British troops were employed in support of the local authorities against offenders of this class; but that of late years all such aid and support have been withdrawn from the Oude Government, while the offenders find all they require from the subjects and police authorities of the bordering British districts.

The country we passed over to-day, between Para and Puchgowa, is a plain, beautifully studded with groves and fine solitary trees, in great perfection. The bandha or mistletoe, upon the mhowa and mango trees, is in full blossom, and adds much to their beauty; the soil is good, and the surface everywhere capable of tillage, with little labour or outlay; for the jungle where it prevails the most is of grass, and the small palas-trees (butea-frondosa) which may be easily uprooted. The whole surface of Oude is, indeed, like a gentleman's park of the most beautiful description, as far as the surface of the ground and the foliage go. Five years of good Government would make it one of the most beautiful parterres in nature. To plant a large grove, as it ought to be, a Hindoo thinks it necessary to have the following trees:—

The banyan, or burgut; peepul, ficus religiosa; mango; tamarind; jamun, eugenia jambolana; bele, cratoeva marmelos; pakur, ficus venosa; mhowa, bassia latifolia; oula, phyllanthus emblica; goolur, figus glomerata; kytha, feronia elephantum; kuthal, or jack; moulsaree, mimusops elengi; kuchnar, bauhinea variegata; neem, melia azadirachta; bere, fizyphus jujuba; horse-radish, sahjuna; sheeshum, dalbergia sisa; toon, adrela toona; and chundun, or sandal.

Where he can get or afford to plant only a small space, he must confine himself to the more sacred and generally useful of these trees; and they are the handsomest in appearance. Nothing can be more beautiful than one of those groves surrounded by fields teeming with rich spring crops, as they are at present; and studded here and there with fine single banyan, peepul, tamarind, mhowa, and cotton trees, which, in such positions, attain their highest perfection, as if anxious to display their greatest beauties, where they can be seen to the most advantage. Each tree has there free space for its roots, which have the advantage of the water supplied to the fields around in irrigation, and a free current of air, whose moisture is condensed upon its leaves and stems by their cooler temperature, while its carbonic acid and ammonia are absorbed and appropriated to their exclusive use. Its branches, unincommoded by the proximity of other trees, spread out freely, and attain their utmost size and beauty.

I may here mention what are the spring crops which now in a luxuriance not known for many years, from fine falls of rain in due season, embellish the surface over which we are passing:—

Spring Crops.—Wheat; barley; gram; arahur, of two

kinds (pulse); musoor (pulse); alsee (linseed); surson (a species of fine mustard); moong (pulse); peas, of three kinds; mustard; sugar-cane, of six kinds; koosum (safflower); opium; and palma christi.

February 1, 1850.—Mahomdee, eleven miles, over a level plain of muteear soil of the best quality, well supplied with groves and single trees of the finest kind; but a good deal of the land is out of tillage, and covered with the rank grass, called garur, the roots of which form the fragrant khus, for tatties, in the hot winds; and dhak (butea frondosa) jungle. Several villages, through and near which we passed, belong to Brahmin zumeendars, who were driven away last year by the rapacity of the contractor, Mahomed Hoseyn, a senseless oppressor, who was this year superseded by a very good officer and worthy man, who was driven out with disgrace, as described yesterday, while engaged in inviting back the absconded cultivators to these deserted villages, and providing them with the means of bringing their lands again into tillage. Hoseyn Allee had seized and sold all their plough-bullocks, and other agricultnral stock, between the autumn and spring harvests, together with all the spring crops, as they became ripe, to make good the increased rate of revenue demanded; and they were all turned out beggars, to seek subsistence among their relatives and friends, in our bordering district of Shajehanpoor. The rank grass and jungle are full of neelgae and deer of all kinds; and the cowherds, who remain to graze their cattle on the wide plains, left waste, find it very difficult to preserve their small fields of corn from their trespass. They are said to come in herds of hundreds around these fields during the night, and to be frequently followed by tigers, several of which were killed last year, by Captain Hearsey, of the Frontier Police. Waste lands, more distant from the great Tarae forest, are free from tigers.

I had a long talk with the Brahmin communities of two of these villages, who had been lately invited back from the Shajehanpoor district, by Krishun Sahae, and resettled on their lands. They are a mild, sensible, and most respectable body, whom a sensible ruler would do all in his power to protect and encourage; but these are the class of landholders and cultivators whom the reckless governors of districts, under the Oude Government, most grievously oppress. They told me—"that nothing could be better than the administration of the Shajehanpoor district by the present collector and magistrate, Mr. Buller, whom all classes loved and respected; that the whole surface of the country was under tillage, and the poorest had as much protection as the highest in the land; that the whole district was, indeed, a garden." "But the returns, are they equal to those from your lands in Oude?"—"Nothing like it, sir; they are not half as good; nor can the cultivator afford to pay half the rate that we pay when left to till our lands in peace." "And why is this?"—"Because, sir, ours is sometimes left waste to recover its powers, as you now see all the land around you, while theirs has no rest." "But do they not alternate their crops, to relieve the soil?"—"Yes, sir, but this is not enough: ours receive manure from the herds of cattle and deer that graze upon it while fallow; and we have greater stores of manure than they have, to throw over it when we return and resume our labours. We alternate our crops, at the same time, as much as they do; and plough and cross-plough our lands more." "And where would you rather live—there, protected as the people are from all violence, or here, exposed as you are to all manner of outrage and extortion."—"We would rather live here, sir, if we could; and we were glad to come back." "And why? There the landholders and cultivators are sure that no man will be permitted to exact a higher rate of rent or revenue than that which they voluntarily bind themselves to pay during the period of a long lease; while here you are never sure that the terms of your lease will be respected for a single season."—"That is all true, sir, but we cannot understand the '*aen* and *kanoon*' (the rules and regulations), nor should we ever do so; for we found that our relations, who had been settled there for many generations, were just as ignorant of them as ourselves. Your Courts of justice (adawluts) are the things we most dread, sir; and we are glad to escape from them as soon as we can, in spite of all the evils we are exposed to on our return to the place of our birth. It is not the fault of the European gentlemen who preside over them, for they are anxious to do, and have justice done, to all; but, in spite of all their efforts, the wrong-doer often escapes, and the sufferer is as often punished."

"The truth, sir, is seldom told in these Courts. There they think of nothing but the number of witnesses, as if all were alike; here, sir, we look to the quality. When a man suffers wrong, the wrong-doer is summoned before the elders, or most respectable men of his village or clan; and if he denies the charge and refuses redress, he is told to bathe, put his hand upon the peepul-tree, and declare aloud his innocence. If he refuses, he is commanded to restore what he has taken, or make suitable reparation for the injury he has done; and if he refuses to do this, he is punished by the odium of all, and his life becomes miserable. A man dares not, sir, put his hand upon that sacred tree and deny the truth—the gods sit in it and know all things; and the offender dreads their vengeance. In your adawluts, sir, men do not tell the truth so often as they do among their own tribes, or village communities —they perjure themselves in all manner of ways, without shame or dread; and there are so many men about these Courts, who understand the 'rules and regulations,' and are so much interested in making truth appear to be falsehood, and falsehood truth, that no man feels sure that right will prevail in them in any case. The guilty think they have just as good a chance of escape as the innocent. Our relations and friends told us, that all this confusion of right and wrong, which bewildered them, arose from the multiplicity of the 'rules and regulations,' which threw all the power into the hands of bad men, and left the European gentlemen helpless!"

"But you know that the crime of murdering female infants, which pervades the whole territory of Oude, and brings the curse of God upon it, has been suppressed in the British territory, in spite of these '*aens* and *kanoons*?'" —"True, sir, it has been put down in your bordering districts; but the Rajpoot families who reside in them manage to escape your vigilance, and keep up the evil practice. They intermarry with Rajpoot families in Oude, and the female infants, born of the daughters they give in marriage to Oude families, are destroyed in Oude without fear or concealment; while the daughters they receive in marriage, from Oude families, are sent over the border into Oude, when near their confinement, on the pretence of visiting their relations. If they give birth to boys, they bring them back with them into your districts; but if they give birth to girls, they are destroyed in the same manner, and no questions are ever asked about them." "Do you ever eat or drink with Rajpoot parents who destroy their female infants?"—"Never, sir! we are Brahmins, but we can take water in a brass vessel from the hands of a Rajpoot, and we do so when his family is unstained with this crime; but nothing would ever tempt us to drink water from the hands of one who permitted his daughters to be murdered." "Do you ever eat with the village or family priest who has given absolution to parents who have permitted their daughters to be murdered, by eating in the room where the murder has been perpetrated?"—"Never, sir; we abhor him as a participator in the crime; and nothing would ever induce one of us to eat or associate with him: he takes all the sin upon his own head by doing so, and is considered by us as an outcast from the tribe, and accursed! It is they who keep up this fearful usage. Tigers and wolves cherish their offspring, and are better than these Rajpoots, who out of family or clan pride, destroy theirs. As soon as their wives give birth to sons, they fire off guns, give largely in charity, make offerings to shrines, and rejoice in all manner of ways; but when they give birth to poor girls, they bury them alive without pity, and a dead silence prevails in the house; it is no wonder, sir, that you say that the curse of God is upon the land in which such sins prevail!"

The quality of testimony, no doubt, like that of every other commodity, deteriorates under a system, which renders the good of no more value *in exchange* than the bad. The formality of our Courts here, as everywhere else, tends to impair, more or less, the quality of what they receive. The simplicity of Courts, composed of little village communities and elders, tends, on the contrary, to improve the quality of the testimony they get; and in India, it is found to be best in the isolated hamlets of hills and forests, where men may be made to do almost anything rather than *tell a lie.* A Marhatta pandit, in the valley of the Nerbudda, once told me, that it was almost impossible to teach a wild Gond of the hills and jungles the *occasional* value of a lie! It is the same with the Tharoos and Booksas, who are, almost exclusively the cultivators of the Oude Tarae forest, and with the peasantry of the Himmalaya chain of mountains, before they have come much in contact with people of the plains, and become subject to the jurisdiction of our Courts. These Courts are, everywhere, our *weak point* in the estimation of our subjects; and they should be, everywhere, simplified to meet the wants and wishes of so simple a people.

That the lands, under the settled Government of the Honourable East India Company, are becoming more and more deteriorated by overcropping is certain; and an Indian statesman will naturally inquire, what will be the probable consequence to the people and the Government? To the people, the consequence must be, a rise in the price of land produce, proportioned to the increased cost of producing and bringing to market what is required for consumption. The price in the market must always be sufficient to cover the cost of producing, and bringing what is required from the poorest and most distant lands to which that market is at any time obliged to have recourse for supply; and as these lands deteriorate in their powers of fertility, recourse must be had to lands more distant, or more cost must be incurred in manure, irrigation, &c., to make these, already had recourse to, to produce the same quantity, or both. The price in the market must rise to meet the increased outlay required, or that outlay will not be made; and the market cannot be supplied.

As men have to pay more for the land produce they require, they will have less to lay out in other things; and as they cannot do without the land produce, they must be satisfied with less of other things, till their incomes increase to meet the necessity for increased outlay. People will get this increase in proportion as their labour, services, talents, or acquirements are more or less indispensable to the society; and the price of other things will diminish, as the cost of producing and bringing them to market diminishes, with improvements in manufactures, and in the facilities of transport. No very serious injury to the people of our territories is, therefore, to be apprehended from the inevitable deterioration in the natural powers of the soil, under our settled Government, which gives so much security to life, property, and character, and so much encouragement to industry.

The consequence to the Government will be less serious than might at first appear. Under a system of limited settlements of the land-revenue, such as prevail over all our dominions, except in Bengal, the Government is in reality the landlord; and our land-revenue is in reality land-rent.* We alienate a portion of that rent for limited

* I believe our Government committed a great *political* and *social* error, when it declared all the land to be the property of the lessees: and all questions regarding it to be cognizable by Judicial Courts. It would have been better for the people, as well as the Government, had all such questions been left to the Fiscal and Revenue Courts. There is the same regular series of these Courts, from the Tuhseeldar to the Revenue Sudder Board, as of the Judicial Courts, from the Moonsiff to the Judicial Sudder Board; and they are all composed of the same class of persons, with the same character and motives to honest exertion. Why force men to run the gauntlet through both series? It tends to make the Government to be considered as a rapacious tax-gatherer, instead of a liberal landlord, which it really is; and to foster the growth of a host of native pettifogging attorneys, to devour, like white ants, the substance of the landholders of all classes and grades.

periods in favour of those with whom we make such settlements, and take all the rest ourselves. On an average, perhaps, our Government takes one-sixth of the gross produce of the land; and the persons, with whom the settlements are made, take another sixth. The net rent, which the Government and they divide equally between them, may be taken, on an average, at one-third of the gross produce of the land. The cultivator would, I believe, always be glad to take and cultivate land, on an average, on condition of giving one-third of the gross produce, or the value of one-third, to be divided between the Government and its lessee; and the lessee will always consider himself fortunate if he gets one-half of this third, to cover the risk and cost of management.

Where the soil of a particular village in a district deteriorates, an immediate reduction in the assessment must be given, or the lands will be deserted. If the Government does not consent to such a reduction, the lessee must sustain the whole burthen, for he cannot shift it off upon the cultivators, without driving them from the lands. The lessee may sustain the whole burthen for one or two years; but if the officers of Government attempt to make him sustain it longer, they drive him after his cultivators, and the land is left waste. I have seen numerous estates of villages and some districts made waste by such attempts in India. I have seen land in such estates, which, when unexhausted, yielded, on an average, twelve returns of the seed, without either manure or irrigation, and paid a rent of twenty shillings an acre, become so exhausted by overcropping in a few years as to yield only three or four returns, and unable to pay four shillings an acre—indeed, unable to pay any rent at all. The cultivator, by degrees, ceases to sow the more exhausting and profitable crops, and is at last obliged to have recourse to manure, or desert his land altogether; but no manure will enable him to get the same quantity of produce as he got before, while what he gets sells at the same rate in the market. He can, therefore, no longer pay the same rate of rent to Government and its lessee. He has got a less quantity of produce, and it has cost him much more to raise it, while it continues to sell at the same price in the market.

But when the lands of a whole country, or a large extent of country, deteriorate in the same manner, and all cultivators are obliged to do the same thing, the price of land produce must rise in the markets, so as to pay the additional costs of supply. All but the poorest and most distant to which these markets must have recourse for supply, at any particular time, will pay rent, and pay it at a rate proportioned to their greater fertility or nearer proximity to the markets. Such markets must pay for land produce a price sufficient to cover the costs of producing and bringing it from the poorest and most distant lands, to which they are obliged at any particular time to have recourse for supply. All land produce of the same quality must, at the same time and place, sell in the market at the same price; and all that is over and above the cost of producing and bringing it to market will go to the proprietors of the land, that is, to the Government and its lessees. The poorest and most distant land, to which any market may have recourse at any particular time, may pay no rent, because the price is no more than sufficient to pay the cost of producing and bringing their supply to that market; but all that is less poor and distant will pay rent, because the price which their produce brings in that market will be more than sufficient to pay the cost of producing and bringing their supply to that market.

The increase in the price of land produce which must take place, as the lands become generally exhausted by overcropping, will, probably, prevent any great falling off in the money rate of rents and revenues, from the land in our Indian possessions; and with the improvements in manufactures, and in the facilities of transport, which must tend to reduce the price of other articles, that money will purchase more of them in the market; and the establishments which have to be maintained out of these rents and revenues may not become more costly. Government and its lessees may have the same incomes in money, and the greater price they and their establishments are obliged to pay for land produce may be compensated by the lesser price they will have to pay for other things.

As facilities for irrigation are extended and improved in wells and canals, new elements of fertility will be supplied to the surface, in the soluble salts contained in their waters. The well-waters will bring these salts from great depths, and the canal-waters will collect them as they flow along, or percolate through, the earth; and as they rise, by capillary attraction, they will convey them to the surface, where they are required for tillage. The atmosphere, in water, ammonia, and carbonic-acid gas will continue to supply plants with the oxygen, hydrogen, nitrogen, and carbon which they require from it; and judicious selection and supply of manure will provide the soil with those elements in which it happens to be deficient. Peace, security, instruction, and a due encouragement to industry, will, it may be hoped, secure to the people all that they require from our Government, and to our Government all that it can fairly require from the people.

The soil of Mahomdee is as fine as that of any part of Oude that I have seen; and the soil of Oude, generally, is equal to the best that I have seen in any part of India. It is all of the kinds above described—muteear (argillaceous), doomuteea (light), bhoor (sandy), and oosur (barren), as far as I have seen. In some parts, the muteear is more productive than in others; and the same may be said of all the other denominations of soil. In the poorer parts of the muteear, the stiff clay, devoid of decayed vegetable and animal matter, seems to superabound, as the sand does in the lightest or poorer portions of the soil, called doomuteea, which runs into bhoor. The oosur, or soil rendered unproductive by a superabundance of substances not suitable to the growth of plants, seems to be common to both kinds. In all soils, except the oosur, fine trees grow, and good crops are produced under good tillage; but in the muteear, the outlay to produce them is the least. It is an error to suppose that a soil, even of pure sand, must be absolutely barren. Quartz-sand commonly contains some of the inorganic substances necessary to plants—silica, lime, potash, alumina, oxide of iron, magnesia, &c.—and they are rendered soluble, and fit for the use of plants by atmospheric air and water, impregnated with carbonic-acid gas, as all water is more or less. The only thing required from the hand of man, besides water, to render them cultivable, is vegetable or animal substances, to supply them, as they decay or decompose, with organic acids.

The late Hakeem Mehndee, took the contract of the Mahomdee district, as already stated, in the year A.D. 1804, when it was in its present bad state, at 3,11,000 rupees a-year; and he held it till the year 1819, or for sixteen years. He had been employed in the Azimgurh district, under Boo Allee Hakeem, the contractor; and during the negotiations for the transfer of that district, with the other territories to the British Government, which took place in 1801; he lost his place, and returned to Lucknow, where he paid his court to the then Dewan, or Chancellor of the Exchequer, who offered him the contract of the Mahomdee district, at three lacs and eleven thousand rupees a-year, on condition of his depositing in the Treasury a security bond for thirty-two thousand rupees. There had been a liaison between him and a beautiful dancing-girl, named Peeajoo, who had saved a good deal of money. She advanced the money, and Hakeem Mehndee deposited the bond, and got the contract. The greater part of the district was then, as now, a waste; and did not yield more than enough to cover the Government demand, gratuities to courtiers, and cost of management. The Hakeem remained to support his influence at Court, while his brother, Hadee Allee Khan, resided at Mahomdee, and managed the district. The Hakeem and his fair friend were married, and lived happily together till her death, which took place before that of her husband, while she was on a pilgrimage to Mecca. While she lived, he married no other woman; but on her death he took to himself another, who survived him; but he had no child by either. His vast property was left to Monowur-od Dowlah, the only son of his brother, Hadee Allee Khan, and to his widow and dependents. The district improved rapidly under the care of the two brothers; and, in a few years, yielded them about seven lacs of rupees a-year. The Government demand increased with the rent-roll to the extent of four lacs of rupees a-year. This left a large income for Hakeem Mehndee and his family, who had made the district a garden, and gained the universal respect and affection of the people.

In the year 1807, Hakeem Mehndee added, to the contract of Mahomdee, that of the adjoining district of Khyrabad, at five lacs of rupees a-year, making his contract nine lacs. In 1816, he added the contract for the Bahraetch district, at seven lacs and seventy-five thousand; but he resigned this in 1819, after having held it for two years, with no great credit to himself. In 1819, he lost the contract for Mahomdee and Khyrabad, from the jealousy of the prime minister, Aga Meer. In April 1818, the Governor-General the Marquess of Hastings passed through his district of Khyrabad, on his way to the Tarae forest, on a sporting excursion, after the Marhatta war. Hakeem Mendee attended him during this excursion, and the Governor-General was so much pleased with his attentions, courteous manners, and sporting propensities, and treated him with so much consideration and kindness, that the minister took the alarm, and determined to get rid of so formidable a rival. He in consequence made the most of the charge preferred against him, of the murder of Amur Sing; and demanded an increase of five lacs of rupees a-year, or fourteen lacs of rupees a-year, instead of nine. This Hakeem Mehndee would not consent to give; and Shekh Imam Buksh was, in 1819, sent to supersede him, as a temporary arrangement.

In 1820, Poorun Dhun, and Govurdhun Dass, merchants of Lucknow, took the contract of the two districts at twelve lacs of rupees a-year, or an increase of three lacs; and from that time, under a system of rack-renting, these districts have been falling off. Mahomdee is now in a worse state than Khyrabad, because it has had the bad luck to get a worse set of contractors. Hakeem

Mehndee retired with his family, first to Shajehanpoor, and then to Futtehgurh, on the Ganges, and resided there, with his family, till June 1830, when he was invited back by Nusseer-do Deen Hyder, to assume the office of prime minister. He held the office till August 1832, when he was removed by the intrigues of the Kumboos, Taj-od Deen Hoseyn, and Sobhan Allee Khan, who persuaded the King that he was trying to get him removed from the throne, by reporting to the British Government the murder of some females, which had, it is said, actually taken place in the palace. Hakeem Mehndee was invited from his retirement by Mahomed Allee Shah, and again appointed minister in 1837; but he died three months after, on the 24th of December, 1837.

During the thirty years which have elapsed since Hakeem Mehndee lost the contract of Mahomdee, there have been no less than seventeen governors, fifteen of whom have been contractors; and the district has gradually declined from what it was, when he left it, to what it was when he took it—that is from a rent-roll of seven lacs of rupees a-year, under which all the people were happy and prosperous, to one of three, under which all the people are wretched. The manager, Krishun Sahae, who has been treated as already described, would, in a few years, have made it what it was when the Hakeem left it, had he been made to feel secure in his tenure of office, and properly encouraged and supported. He had, in the three months he had charge, invited back from our bordering districts hundreds of the best classes of landholders and cultivators, who had been driven off by the rapacity of his predecessor, re-established them in their villages, and set them to work in good spirit, to restore the lands which had lain waste from the time they deserted them; and induced hundreds to convert to sugar-cane cultivation the lands which they had destined for humbler crops, in the assurance of the security which they were to enjoy under his rule. The one class tells me, they must suspend all labours upon the waste lands till they can learn the character of his successor; and the other, that they must content themselves with the humbler crops till they can see whether the richer and more costly ones will be safe from his grasp, or that of the agents, whom he may employ to manage the district for him. No man is safe for a moment under such a Government, either in his person, his character, his office, or his possession; and with such a feeling of insecurity among all classes, it is impossible for a country to prosper.*

I may here mention one among the numerous causes of the decline of the district. The contract for it was held for a year and half, in A.D. 1847-48, by Ahmed Allee. Feeling insecure in his tenure of office, he wanted to make as much as possible out of things as they were, and resumed Guhooa, a small rent-free village, yielding four hundred rupees a-year, held by Bahadur Sing, the tallookdar of Peepareea, who resides at Pursur. He had recourse to the usual mode of indiscriminate murder and plunder, to reduce Ahmed Allee to terms. At the same time, he resumed the small village of Kombee, yielding three hundred rupees a-year, held rent-free by Bhoder Sing, tallookdar of Magdapoor, who resided in Koombee; and, in consequence, he united his band of marauders to that of Bahadur Sing; and together they plundered and

* Krishun Sahae has been restored, but does not feel secure in his tenure of office.

burnt to the ground some dozen villages, and laid waste the purgunnah of Peepareea, which had yielded to Government twenty-five thousand rupees a-year, and contained the sites of one hundred and eight villages, of which, however, only twenty-five were occupied.

During the greater part of the time that these depredations were going on, the two rebels resided in our bordering district of Shajehanpoor, whence they directed the whole. Urgent remonstrances were addressed to the magistrate of that district, but he required *judicial* proof of their participation in the crimes, that were committed by their followers, upon the innocent and unoffending peasantry; and no proof that the contractor could furnish being deemed sufficient, he was obliged to consent to restore the rent-free villages. The lands they made waste, still remain so, and pay no revenue to Government.

Saadut Allee Khan (who died in 1814), when sovereign of Oude, was fond of this place, and used to reside here for many months every year. He made a garden, about a mile to the east of the town, upon a fine open plain of good soil, and planted an avenue of fine trees all the way. The trees are now in perfection, but the garden has been neglected; and the bungalow in the centre, in which he resided, is an entire ruin. He kept a large establishment of men and cattle, for which sixty thousand rupees a-year were regularly charged in the accounts of the manager of the district, through his reign and those of Ghazee-od Deen, Nuseer-od Deen Hyder, Mahomed Allee Shah, and Amjud Allee Shah, and the first year of the reign of his present Majesty, Wajid Allee Shah; though, with the exception of two bullocks and two gardeners, the cattle had all disappeared, and the servants been all discharged some thirty years before.

In October last, when six guns were required from the great park of artillery at Lucknow, to be sent out on detached duty with the Gungoor Regiment, an inspection of the draft-bullocks took place, and it was found, that the Court favourite who had charge of the park had made away with no less than one thousand seven hundred and thirty of them, and only twenty could be found to take the guns. He had been charging for the food of these one thousand seven hundred and thirty for a long series of years. On mentioning this fact to a late minister, he told me of two facts within his own knowledge, illustrative of these sort of charges. This same Court favourite, in the reign of Nuseer-od Deen Hyder, in 1835, received charge of sixteen bullocks, of surpassing beauty, which had been presented to the King, and he was allowed to draw, from the Treasury, a rupee a-day, for the food of each bullock.

In the reign of Mahomed Allee Shah, his prudent successor, a muster of all the bullocks was called for, and Ghalib Jung, to whom the muster was intrusted, to spite the favourite, called for these sixteen bullocks. The favourite had disposed of them, though he continued to draw the allowance; and, to supply their place, he sent to the bazaar and seized sixteen of the bullocks which had that day brought corn to market. They were presented to Ghalib Jung for muster. He pretended to be very angry, declared that it was disgraceful to keep such poor creatures on the King's establishment, and still more so to charge a rupee a-day for the food of each, and ordered them to be sold forthwith by auction. Soon after they had been sold, the poor men to whom they belonged came up to claim them, but could never get either the bullocks or their price, nor could the favourite ever be persuaded to refund any portion of the money he had drawn for the sixteen he had sold.*

In the early part of the reign of Ghazee-od Deen Hyder, a fine dog from the Himmalaya Hills was presented to him, and made over to the charge of one of the favourites, who drew a rupee a-day for his food. Soon after his Majesty became ill and very irritable, and one day complained much of this dog's barking. He was told that the only way to silence a dog of this description was to give him a seer of conserve of roses to eat every day, and a bottle of rose-water to drink. His Majesty ordered them to be given forthwith, and his repose was never after disturbed by the dog's barking. A rupee a-day continued to be drawn for these things for the dog for the rest of the long reign of Ghazee-od Deen Hyder, and through that of his successor, Nuseer-od Deen, which lasted for ten years, and ended in 1837, though the animal had died soon after the order for these things was given, or in 1816, and he believed it continued to be drawn up to the present day.

The cantonment at Mahomdee stands between this garden of Saadut Allee's and the town, and this is the best site for any civil or military establishments that may be required at Mahomdee. The Nazims usually reside in the fort in the town.

February 2, 1850.—Halted at Mahomdee. The spring crops around the town are very fine, and the place is considered to be very healthy. There is, however, some peculiarity in the soil, opposed to the growth of the poppy. The cultivators tell me that they have often tried it; that it is stunted in growth, whatever care be taken of it, and yields but little juice, and that of bad quality,

* The favourite, in both these cases, was Anjum-od Dowlah.

though it attains perfection in the Shahabad and other districts around. The doomuteea soil is here esteemed better than the muteear, though it requires more labour in the tillage. It is said that *mote* and *mash*, two pulses, do not thrive in the muteear soil so well as in the doomuteea.

February 3, 1850.—Poknapoor, eight miles. We crossed the Goomtee about midway, over a bridge of boats that had been prepared for us. The boats came up the river thus far for timber, and were detained for the occasion. The stream is here narrow, and said to flow from a basin (the phoola talao) in the Tarae forest, some fifty miles to the north, at Madhoo Tanda. There is some tillage on the verge of the stream on the other side; but from the river to our tents, four miles, there is none. The country is level and well studded with groves and fine single trees, bur, peepul, mhowa, mango, &c., but covered with rank grass.

Near the river is a belt of the sakhoo and other forest-trees, with underwood, in which tigers lodge and prey upon the deer, which cover the grass plain, and frequently upon the bullocks, which are grazed upon it in great numbers. Several bullocks have been killed and eaten by them within the last few days; and an old fakeer, who has for some months taken up his lodging on this side the river under a peepul-tree, in a straw hut just big enough to hold him, told us that he frequently saw them come down to drink in the stream near his lodging. We saw a great many deer in passing, but no tigers. The soil near the river is sandy, and the ground uneven, but still cultivable; and on this side of the sandy belt it is all level and of the best kind of doomuteea. Our tents are in a fine grove of mango-trees, in the midst of a waste, but level and extensive, plain of this soil, not a rood of which is unfit for the plough or incapable of yielding crops of the finest quality. It is capable of being made, in two or three years, a beautiful garden.

The single trees, which are scattered all over it, have been shorn of their leaves and small branches by the cow-herds for their cattle, but they would all soon clothe themselves again under protection. The groves are sufficiently numerous to furnish sites for the villages and hamlets required. All the large sakhoo-trees have been cut down and taken away on the ground we have come over, which is too near the river for them to be permitted to attain full size. Not an acre or a foot of the land is oosur, or unfit for tillage. Poknapoor is in the estate of Etowa, which forms part of the pergunnah of Peepareea, to which Bahadur Sing, the person above described, lays claim. He holds a few villages round his residence at Pursur; but the pergunnah is under the management of a Government officer, under the Amil of Mahomdee. The Rajah, Syud Ashruf Allee Khan, of Mahomdee, claims a kind of suzerainty over all the district, and over this pergunnah of Peepareea among the rest. From all the villages tilled and peopled he is permitted to levy an income for himself at the rate of two rupees a-village. This the people pay with some reluctance, though they recognise his right.

The zumeendars of Poknapoor are Kunojee Brahmins, who tell me that they can do almost everything in husbandry save holding their own ploughs: they can drive their own harrows and carts, reap, their own crops, and winnow and tread out their own corn; but if they once condescend to *hold their own ploughs* they sink in grade, and have to pay twice as much as they now pay for wives for their sons from the same families, and take half of what they now take for their daughters from the same families, into which they now marry them. They have, they say, been settled in these pergunnahs, north-east of the Goomtee River. for fifty-two generations as farmers and cultivators; and their relatives, who still remain at Aslamabad, a village one koss south-east of Mahomdee, which was the first abode of the tribe in Oude, have been settled there for no less than eighty-four generations. They form village communities, dividing the lands among the several members, and paying over and above the Government demand a liberal allowance to the head of the village and of the family settled in it, to maintain his respectability and to cover the risk and cost of management, either in kind, in money, or in an extra share of the land.

The lands of Poknapoor are all divided into two equal shares, one held by *Dewan* and the other by *Ramnath*, who were both among the people with whom I conversed. Teekaram, who has a share in Dewan's half, mentioned that about thirteen years ago the Amil, Khwaja Mahmood, wanted to increase the rate of the Government demand on the village from the four hundred, which they had long paid, to four hundred and fifty; that they refused to pay, and Hindoo Sing, the Rajpoot tallookdar of Rehreea, one koss east of Poknapoor, offered to take the lease at four hundred and fifty, and got it. They refused to pay, and he, at the head of his gang of armed followers, attacked, plundered, and burnt down the village, and killed his, Teekaram's, brother Girdharee, with his two sons, and inflicted three severe cuts of a sabre on the right arm of his wife, who is now a widow among them. Hindoo Sing's object was to make this village a permanent addition to his estate; but, to his surprise, the Durbar took serious notice of the outrage, and he fled into the Shajehanpoor district, where he was seized by the magistrate, Mr. Buller, and made over to the Oude authorities for trial. He purchased his escape from them in the usual way; but soon after offered to surrender to the collector, Aboo Torab Khan, on condition of pardon for all past offences.

The collector begged the Brahmins to consent to pardon him for the murders, on condition of getting from Hindoo Sing some fifty beeghas of land, out of his share in Rehreea. They said they would not consent to take five times the quantity of the land among such a turbulent set; but should be glad to get a smaller quantity, rent-free, in their own village, for the widow of Girdharee. The collector gave them twenty-five beeghas, or ten acres, in Poknapoor; and this land Teekaram still holds, and out of the produce supports the poor widow. A razenamah, or pardon, was given by the family, and Hindoo Sing has ever since lived in peace upon his estate. The lease of the village was restored to the Brahmin family, at the reduced rate of two hundred and fifty, but soon after raised to four hundred, and again reduced to two hundred and fifty, after the devastation of Bahadur Sing and Bhoder Sing.

These industrious and unoffending Brahmins say that since these Rajpoot landholders came among them, many generations ago, there has never been any peace in the district, except during the time that Hakeem Mehndee held the contract, when the whole plain that now lies waste became a beautiful *chummun* (parterre); that since his removal, as before his appointment, all has been confusion; that the Rajpoot landholders are always quarrelling either among themselves or with the local Government authorities; and, whatever be the nature or the cause of quarrel, they always plunder and murder, indiscriminately, the unoffending communities of the villages around, in order to reduce these authorities to their terms; that when these Rajpoot landholders leave them in peace, the contractors seize the opportunity to increase the Government demand, and bring among them the King's troops, who plunder them just as much as the rebel landholders, though they do not often murder them in the same reckless manner. They told me that the hundreds of their relatives who had gone off during the disorders and taken lands, or found employment in our bordering districts, would be glad to return to their own lands, groves, and trees, in Oude, if they saw the slightest chance of protection, and the country would soon become again the beautiful parterre which Hakeem Mehndee left it thirty years ago, instead of the wilderness in which they were now so wretched; that they ventured to cultivate small patches here and there, not far from each other, but were obliged to raise small platforms, upon high poles, in every field, and sit upon them all night, calling out to each other, in a loud voice, to keep up their spirits, and frighten off the deer which swarmed upon the grass plain, and would destroy the whole of the crops in one night, if left unprotected; that they were obliged to collect large piles of wood around each platform, and keep them burning all night, to prevent the tigers from carrying off the men who sat upon them; that their lives were wretched amidst this continual dread of man and beast, but the soil and climate were good, and the trees and groves planted by their forefathers were still standing and dear to them; and they hoped, now that the Resident had come among them, to receive, at no distant day, the protection they required. This alone is required to render this the most beautiful portion of Oude, and Oude the most beautiful portion of India.

February 4, 1850.—Gokurnath, thirteen miles, north-east, over a level plain of the same fine muteear soil, here and there running into doomuteea and bhoor, but in no case into oosur. The first two miles over the grass plain, and the next four through a belt of forest trees, with rank grass and underwood, abounding in game of all kinds, and infested by tigers. Bullocks are often taken by them, but men seldom. The sal (*alias* sakhoo) trees are here stunted, gnarled, and ugly, while in the Tarae forest they are straight, lofty, and beautiful. The reason is, that beyond the forest their leaves are stripped off and sold for *plates*. They are carried to distant towns, and stored up for long periods, to form breakfast and dinner plates, and the people in the country use hardly anything else. Plates are formed of them by sewing them together, when required; and they become as pliable as leather, even after being kept for a year or more, by having a little water sprinkled over them. They are long, wide, and tough, and well suited to the purpose. All kinds of food are put upon them, and served up to the family and guests. The cattle do not eat them, as they do leaves of the peepul, bur, neem, &c. The sakhoo, when not preserved, is cut down, when young, for beams, rafters, &c., required in building. In the Tarae forest, the proprietors of the lands on which they stand preserve them till they attain maturity, for sale to the people of the plains; and they are taken down the Ghagra and other rivers that flow through the forest to the Ganges, and vast numbers are sold in the Calcutta market. The fine tall sakhoos in the Tarae forest are called "sayer;" the knotted, stunted, and crooked shakoos, beyond the forest, are called "khohurs."

There are but few teak (or sagwun) trees in this part of

the Tarae forest. The country is everywhere studded with the same fine groves and single trees, and requires only tillage to become a garden. From the belt of jungle to our camp at Gokurnath, seven miles, the road runs over an open grass plain, with here and there a field of corn. The sites of villages are numerous, but few of them are occupied at present. All are said to have been in a flourishing state, and filled by a happy peasantry, when Hakeem Mehndee lost the government. Since that time these villages and hamlets have diminished by degrees, in proportion as the rapacity of the contractors and the turbulence of the Rajpoot landholders have increased.

The first village we passed through, after emerging from the belt of jungle, was Pureylee, which is held and occupied by a large family of cultivating proprietors of the Koormee caste. Up to the year 1847, it had for many years been in a good condition, and paid a revenue of two thousand rupees a-year to Government. In that year Ahmud Allee, the collector, demanded a thousand more. They could not pay this, and he sold all their bullocks and other stock to make up the demand; the lands became waste as usual; and Lonee Sing, of Mitholee, offered the next contractor one thousand rupees a-year for the lease, and got it. The village has now been permanently absorbed in his estate, in the usual way; and, as the Koormees are a peaceful body, they have quietly acquiesced in the arrangement, and get all the aid they require from their new landlord. Before this time they had held their lands, as proprietors, directly under Government. From allodial* proprietors they are become feudal tenants under a powerful Rajpoot chief.

* By allodial, I mean, lands held in proprietary right, immediately under the crown, but liable to the land-tax.

CHAPTER III.

Lonee Sing, of the Ahbun Rajpoot tribe—Dispute between Rajah Bukhtawar Sing and a servant of one of his relatives—Cultivation along the border of the Tarae forest—Subdivision of land among the Ahbun families—Rapacity of the King's troops, and establishments of all kinds—Climate near the Tarae—Goitres—Not one-tenth of the cultivable lands cultivated, nor one-tenth of the villages peopled—Criterion of good tillage—Ratoon crops—Manure available—Khyrabad district better peopled and cultivated than that of Mahomdee, but the soil over-cropped—Blight—Rajah Ajeet Sing and his estate of Khymara—Ousted by collusion and bribery—Anrod Sing of Oel, and Lonee Sing—State of Oude forty years ago compared with its present state—The Nazim of the Khyrabad district—Trespasses of his followers—Oel Dhukooa—*Khalsa* lands absorbed by the Rajpoot barons—Salarpoor—Sheobuksh Sing, of Kuteysura—*Bhulmunsee*, or property tax—Beautiful groves of Lahurpoor—Residence of the Nazim—Wretched state of the force with the Nazim—Gratuities paid by officers in charge of districts, whether in contract or trust—Rajah Argun Sing's estate of Dhorehra—Hereditary gang robbers of the Oude Tarae suppressed—Mutiny of two of the King's Regiments at Bhitolee—Their rapacity and oppression—Singers and fiddlers who govern the King—Why the Amils take all their troops with them when they move—Seetapoor, the cantonment of one of the two Regiments of Oude Local Infantry—Sipahees not equal to those in Magness's, Barlow's, and Banbury's, or in our Native Regiments of the Line—Why—The Prince Momtaz-od Dowlah—Evil effects of shooting monkeys—Doolaree, alias Mulika Zumanee—Her history, and that of her son and daughter.

LONEE SING, who visited me yesterday afternoon with a respectable train, has, in this and other ways less creditable, increased his estate of *Mitholee* from a rent-roll of forty to one of one hundred and fifty thousand rupees a-year, out of which he pays fifty thousand to Government, and he is considered one of its best subjects. He is, as above stated, of the Ahbun Rajpoot clan, and a shrewd and energetic man. The estate was divided into six shares. It had formed one under Rajah Davey Sing, whose only brother, Bhujun Sing, lived united with him, and took what he chose to give him for his own subsistence and that of his family. Davey Sing died without issue, leaving the whole estate to his brother, Bhujun Sing, who had two sons, Dul Sing and Maun Sing, among whom he divided the estate.* Dul Sing had six sons, but Maun Sing had none. He, however, adopted Bhowanee Sing, to whom he left his portion of the estate. Dul Sing's share became subdivided among his six sons; but Khunjun Sing, the son of his eldest son, when he became head of the family, got together a large force, with some guns, and made use of it in the usual way by seizing upon the lands of his weaker neighbours. He attacked his nephew, Bhowanee Sing, and took all his lands; and got, on one pretence or another, the greater part of those of his other relatives.

He died without issue, leaving his possessions and military force to Lonee Sing, his brother, who continued to pursue the same course. In 1847 he, with one thousand armed men and five guns, attacked his cousin, Monnoo Sing, of Mohlee, the head of the family of the fourth son of Dul Sing, killed four and wounded two persons; and, in collusion with the local governor, seized upon all his estate. Redress was sought for in vain; and as I was passing near, Monnoo Sing and his brother Chotee Sing came to me at Mahomdee to complain. Monnoo Sing remained behind sick at Mahomdee; but Chotee Sing followed me on. He rode on horseback behind my elephant, and I made

* *Mitholee* contains the sites of one thousand four hundred and eighty-six villages, only one-third of which are now occupied.

him give me the history of his family as I went along, and told him to prepare for me a genealogical table, and an account of the mode in which Lonee Sing had usurped the different estates of the other members of the family. This he gave to me on the road between Poknapoor and Gokurnath by one of his belted attendants, who, after handing it up to me on the elephant, ran along under the nose of Rajah Bukhtawur Sing's fine chestnut horse without saying a word.

I asked the Rajah whether he knew Lonee Sing? "Yes," said he; "everybody knows him: he is one of the ablest, best, and most substantial men in Oude; and he keeps his estate in excellent order, and is respected by all people."—"Except his own relations," said the belted attendant; "these he robs of all they have, and nobody interposes to protect them, because he has become wealthy, and they have become poor!" "My good fellow," said the Rajah, "he has only taken what they knew not how to hold, and with the sanction of the King's servants."—"Yes," replied the man, "he has got the sanction of the King's servants, no doubt, and any one who can pay for it may get that now-a-days to rob others of the King's subjects. Has not Lonee Sing robbed all his cousins of their estates, and added them to his own, and thereby got the means of bribing the King's servants to let him do what he likes?" "What," said the Rajah, with some asperity, "should you, a mere soldier, know about State affairs? Do you suppose that all the members of any family can be equal? Must there not be a head to all families to keep the rest in order? Nothing goes on well in families or governments where all are equal, and there is no head to guide; and the head must have the means to guide the rest."—"True," said the belted attendant, "all can't be equal in the rule of States; but in questions of private right, between individuals and subjects, the case is different; and the ruler should give to every one his due, and prevent the strong from robbing the weak. I have five fingers in my hand: they serve me, and I treat them all alike. I do not let one destroy or molest the other." "I tell you," said the Rajah, with increasing asperity, "that there must be heads of families as well as heads of States, or all would be confusion; and Lonee Sing is right in all that he has done. Don't you see what a state his district is in, now that he has taken the management of the whole upon himself? I dare say all the waste that we see around us has arisen from the want of such heads of families."—"You know," said the man, "that this waste has been caused by the oppression of the King's officers, and their disorderly and useless troops, and the strong striving to deprive the weak of their rights."

"You know nothing about these matters," said the Rajah, still more angrily. "The wise and strong are everywhere striving to subdue the weak and ignorant, in order that they may manage what they hold better than they can. Don't you see how the British Government are going on, taking country after country year after year, in order to manage them better than they were managed under others? and don't you see how these countries thrive under their strong and just Government? Do you think that God would permit them to go on as they do unless he thought that it was for the good of the people who come under their rule?" Turning to me, the Rajah continued: "When I was one day riding over the country with Colonel Low, the then Resident, as I now ride with you, sir, he said, with a sigh, 'In this country of Oude what darkness prevails! No one seems to respect the right of another; and every one appears to be grasping at the possessions of his neighbour, without any fear of God or the King'—'True, sir,' said I; 'but do you not see that it is the necessary order of things, and must be ordained by Providence? Is not your Government going on taking country after country, and benefiting all it takes? And will not Providence prosper their undertakings as long as they do so? The moment they come to a stand, all will be confusion. Sovereigns cannot stand still, sir; the moment *their bellies are full* (their ambition ceases), they and the countries they govern retrograde. No sovereign in India, sir, that has any regard for himself or his country, can with safety sit down and say that *his belly is full* (that he has no further ambition of conquest): he must go on to the last.'"*

The poor belted attendant of Chotee Sing was confounded with the logic and eloquence of the old Rajah, and said nothing more; and Chotee Sing himself kept quietly behind on his horse, with his ears well wrapped up in warm cloth, as the morning was very cold, and he was not well. He looked very grave, and evidently thought the Rajah had outlived his understanding. But the fact is that the Rajah has, by his influence at Court, taken all the lands held by his two elder nephews, Rughbur Sing and Ramadeen, and made them over to their youngest brother, Maun Sing, whom he has adopted, made his heir, and the head of the family. He has, in

* The Rajah's reasoning was drawn from the practice in Oude, of seizing upon the possessions of weaker neighbours, by means of gangs of robbers. The man who does this, becomes the slave of his gangs, as the imperial robber, who seizes upon smaller states by means of his victorious armies, becomes their slave, and, ultimately, their victim. The history of India is nothing more than the biography of such men, and the Rajah has read no other.

consequence, for the present a strong fellow-feeling with Lonee Sing; and, in all this oration at least, "his wishes were father to his thoughts."

The sharpest retort that I remember ever having had myself was given to me by a sturdy and honest old landholder of the middle class, whom I had known for a quarter of a century on the bank of the Nerbudda, in 1843. During the insurrection in the Saugor and Nerbudda territories, which commenced in 1842, I was sent down by the Governor-General Lord Ellenborough to ascertain if possible the causes which had led to it. I conversed freely with the landholders, and people of all classes in the valley, who had been plundered by the landed aristocracy of the jungles on the borders, and had one afternoon some fifty in my tent seated on the carpet. After a good deal of talk about the depredations of the jungle barons upon the people of the cultivated plains, and remonstrance at the want of support on their part to the Government officers, I said to Umrao Sing, one of the most sturdy and honest among them, "Why did you withhold from the local officers the information which you must have had of the movements and positions of the rebels and their followers, who were laying the country waste? In no part of India have the farmers and cultivators been more favoured in light assessments and protection to life and property; but there are some men who never can be satisfied; give them what you will, they will always be craving after more."—"True, sir," said Umrao Sing, looking me steadily in the face, and with the greatest possible gravity, "there are some people who never can be satisfied, give them what you will. Give them the whole of Hindoostan, and they will go off to Kabul to take more!"

There was a pause, during which all looked very grave, for they thought that the old man had exceeded the bounds of the privilege he had long enjoyed of expressing his thoughts freely to European gentlemen; and Umrao Sing continued: "The fact is, sir, that after you had, by good government, made us all happy and prosperous, and proud to display the wealth we had acquired on our persons, and in our houses and villages, you withdrew all your troops from among us, and left us a prey to the wild barons of the hills and jungles on our borders, whose families had risen to wealth, distinction, and large landed possessions under former misrule and disorder, and who are always longing for the return of such disorders, that they may have some chance of recovering the consequence and influence which they have lost under a settled and strong Government: they saw that your troops had been taken off for distant conquests, and heard of nothing but defeats and disasters, and readily persuaded themselves that your rule was at an end; for what could men, born and bred in the jungles, know of your resources to retrieve such disasters?

"After the Mahratta war, in 1817, you prohibited the people of your newly-acquired districts from carrying arms, not dreaming that the only persons who would obey or regard your order were the peaceful landholders and peasantry of the plains, who were satisfied with your Government, and anxious for its duration, but exposed to the envy and hatred of the Gond and Lodhee chiefs, who occupied the hills and jungles on their borders.

"When they came down upon us, you had no means left to protect us; and having no longer any arms or any experience of the use of them, after a quarter of a century of peace, we were unable to defend our villages, our houses, or our families; if we attempted to defend them, we and our families were killed; if we did not, we were robbed and threatened with death, if we gave you information to their prejudice. We saw that they could carry their threats into execution, for your local officers had not the means to protect us from their vengeance, and we suffered in silence; but you must not infer from this that we were tired of your rule, or pleased with their depredations; all here can testify that we longed for the return of your strength and their downfal. It is true, however," added he, "that the new European officers placed over us did not treat us with the same courtesy and consideration as the old ones, or seem to entertain the same kindly feeling towards us; and our communion with them was less free and cordial."

All approved of my old friend's speech, and declared that he had given expression to the thoughts and feelings of all present, and of all the people of the plains, who lived happily under our rule, and prayed earnestly for its duration. The portion of the estate of Mitholee, held by Lonee Sing, now contains the sites of six hundred and four villages, about one-half of which are occupied; four hundred and eighty-four of these lie in the Mahomdee district, and one hundred and twenty in that of Khyrabad. The number and names of the villages are still kept up in the accounts.

February 5, 1850.—Kurrunpoor Mirtaha, ten miles over a plain of fine muteear soil, scantily cultivated, but bearing excellent spring crops where it is so. Not far from our last camp at Gokurnath, we entered a belt of jungle three miles wide, consisting chiefly of stunted, knotty, and crooked sakhoo trees, with underwood and rank chopper grass. This belt of jungle is the same we passed through, as above described, between Poknapoor and Gokurnath. It runs from the great forest to the north, a long way down south-east, into the Khyrabad district. From this belt to our present ground, six miles, the road passes over a fine plain, nine-tenths of which is covered with this grass, but studded with mango-groves and fine single trees. The forest runs along to the north of our road—which lay east—from one to three miles distant, and looked very like a continued mango-grove. The level plain of rich soil extends up through the forest to the foot of the hills, and is all the way capable of the finest cultivation. Here and there the soil runs into light doomuteea; and in some few parts even into bhoor, in proportion as the sand abounds; but generally the soil is the fine muteear, and very fertile. The whole plain is said to have been in cultivation thirty years ago, when Hakeem Mehndee held the contract; but the tillage has been falling off ever since, under the bad or oppressive management of successive contractors.

The estate through which we have been passing is called Bharwara, and contains the sites of nine hundred and eighty-nine villages, about one-tenth of which are now occupied. The landholders are all of the Ahbun Rajpoot tribe; but a great part of them have become Musulmans. They live together, however, though of different creeds, in tolerable harmony; and eat together on occasions of ceremony, though not from the same dishes. No member of the tribe ever forfeited his inheritance by changing his creed. Nor did any one of them, I believe, ever change his creed, except to retain his inheritance, liberty, or life, threatened by despotic and unscrupulous rulers. They dine on the same floor, but there is a line marked off to separate those of the party who are Hindoos from those who are Musulmans. The Musulmans have Mahommedan names, and the Hindoos Hindoo names; but both still go by the common patronymic name of Ahbuns. The Musulmans marry into Musulman families, and the Hindoos into Hindoo families of the highest castes, Chouhans, Rathores, Rykwars, Janwars, &c. Of course all the children are of the same religion and caste as their parents. They tell me that the conversion of their ancestors was effected by force, under a prince or chief called "Kala Pahar." This must have been Mahommed Firmally, *alias* Kala Pahar—to whom his uncle Bheilole, King of Delhi, left the district of Bahraetch as a separate inheritance a short time before his death, which took place A. D. 1488. This conversion seems to have had the effect of doing away with the murder of female infants in the Ahbun families who are still Hindoos; for they could not get the Musulman portion of the tribe to associate with them if they continued it.

The estate of Bharwara is divided into four parts, Hydrabad, Hurunpoor, Aleegunge, and Sekunderabad. Each division is subdivided into parts, each held by a separate branch of the family; and the subdivision of these parts is still going on, as the heads of the several branches of the family die, and leave more than one son. The present head of the Ahbun family is Mahommed Hussan Khan, a Musulman, who resides in his fort in the village of Julalpoor, near the road over which we passed. The small fort is concealed within, and protected by a nice bamboo-fence that grows round it. He holds twelve villages rent free, as *nankar*, and pays revenue for all the rest that compose his share of the great estate. The heads of families who hold the other shares enjoy in the same manner one or more villages rent free, as *nankar*. These are all well cultivated, and contain a great many cultivators of the best classes, such as Koormees, Lodhies, and Kachies.

We passed through one of them, Kamole, and I had a good deal of talk with the people, who were engaged in pressing out the juice of sugar-cane. They told me that the juice was excellent, and that the syrup made from it was carried to the district of Shajehanpoor, in the British territory, to be made into sugar. Mahommed Hussan Khan came up, as I was talking with the people, and joined in the conversation. All seemed to be delighted with the opportunity of entering so freely into conversation with a British Resident who understood farming, and seemed to take so much interest in their pursuits. I congratulated the people on being able to keep so many of their houses well covered with grass-choppers; but they told me, "that it was with infinite difficulty they could keep them, or anything else they had, from the grasp of the local authorities and the troops and camp-followers who attended them, and desolated the country like a flock of locusts; that they are not only plundered but taxed by them—first, the sipahees take their choppers, beams, and rafters off their houses—then the people in charge of artillery bullocks and other cattle take all their stores of bhoosa, straw, &c., and threaten to turn the cattle loose on their fields, if not paid a gratuity—the people who have to collect fuel for the camp (bildars) take all their stores of wood, and doors and windows also, if not paid for their redemption—then the people in charge of elephants and camels threaten to denude of their leaves and small branches all the peepul, burgut, and other trees most sacred and dear to them, near their homes, unless paid for their forbearance; and—though last, not least—men, women, and children are seized, not only to carry the plunder and other burthens gratis for sipahees and servants of all kinds and grades, and camp-followers, but to be robbed of their clothes, and made to pay ransoms to get back, while all the plough-bullocks are put in requisition to draw the guns which the King's bullocks are unable to draw themselves. In short, that the approach of King's servants is dreaded as one of the greatest calamities that can befal them."

I should here mention, that all the Telinga regiments, fourteen in number, are allowed tents and hackeries to carry them. The way in which the bullocks of such carts are provided with fodder has been already mentioned; but no tents or conveyance of any kind are allowed for the Nujeeb corps, thirty-two in number. Whenever they move (and they are almost always moving), they seize whatever conveyance and shelter they require from the people of the country around. Each battalion, even in its ordinary incomplete state, requires four hundred or five hundred porters, besides carts, bullocks, horses, ponies, &c. Men, women, and children, of all classes, are seized, and made to carry the baggage, arms, accoutrements, and *cages of pet birds*, belonging to the officers and sipahees of these corps. They are stripped of their clothes, confined, and starved from the time they are seized; and as it is difficult to catch people to relieve them along the road, they are commonly taken on two or three stages. If they run away, they forfeit all their clothes which remain in the hands of the sipahees; and a great many die along the road of fatigue, hunger, and exposure to the sun. Numerous cruel instances of this have been urged by me on the notice of the King, but without any good effect.

The line of march of one of these corps is like the road to the temple of Juggurnaut! When the corps is about to move, detachments are sent out to seize conveyance of all kinds; and for one cart required and taken, fifty are seized, and released for a donation in proportion to their value, the respectability of the proprietors, and the necessity for their employment at home at the time. The sums thus extorted by detachments they share with their officers, or they would never be again sent on such lucrative service.

It appears that in this part of Oude the people have not for many years suffered so much from the depredations of the refractory landholders as in other parts; and that the desolate state of the district arises chiefly from the other three great evils that afflict Oude—the rack-renting of the contractors; the divisions they create and foster among landholders; and the depredations of the troops and camp-followers who attend them. But the estate has become much subdivided, and the shareholders from this cause, and the oppression of the contractors, have become poor and weak; and the neighbouring landholders of the Janwar and other Rajpoot tribes have taken advantage of their weakness to seize upon a great many of their best villages. Out of Kurumpoor, within the last nine years, Anorud Sing, of Oel, a Janwar Rajpoot, in collusion with local authorities, has taken twelve; and Umrao Sing, of Mahewa, of the same tribe, has taken eighteen, making twenty villages from the Kurumpoor division. These landholders reside in the Khyrabad district, which adjoins that of Mahomdee, near our present camp.

The people everywhere praise the climate—they appear robust and energetic, and no sickness prevails, though many of the villages are very near the forest. The land on which the forest stands contains, in the ruins of well-built towns and fortresses, unquestionable signs of having once been well cultivated and thickly peopled: and it would soon become so again under good government. There is nothing in the soil to produce sickness; and, I believe, the same soil prevails up through the forest to the hills. Sickness would, no doubt, prevail for some years, till the underwood and all the putrid leaves should be removed. The water that stagnates over them, and percolates through the soil into the wells, from which the people drink, and the exhalations which arise from them and taint the air, confined by the dense mass of forest-trees, underwood, and high grass, are, I believe, the chief cause of the diseases which prevail in this belt of jungle.

It is however remarkable, that there are two unhealthy seasons in the year in this forest—one at the latter end of the rains in August, September, and October, and the other before the rains begin to fall in the latter part of April, the whole of May, and part of June. The diseases in the latter are, I believe, more commonly fatal than they are in the former; and are considered by the people to arise solely from the poisonous quality of the water, which is often found in wells to be covered with a thin crust of petrolium. Diseases of the same character prevail at the same two seasons in the jungles, above the sources of the Nerbudda and Sohun rivers, and are ascribed by the people to the same causes—those which take place after the rains, to bad air; and those which take place immediately before the rains, after the cold and dry seasons, to bad water. The same petrolium, or liquid bitumen, is found floating on the spring waters in the hot season, when the most fatal diseases break out in the jungles, about the sources of the Nerbudda and Sohun, as in the Oude Tarae; and, in both places, the natives appear to me to be right in attributing them to the water; but whether the poisonous quality of the water be imparted to it by bitumen from below, or by the putrid leaves of the forest trees from above, is uncertain; the people drink from the bituminous spring waters at this season, as well as from stagnant pools in the beds of small rivers, which have ceased to flow during part of the cold, and the whole of the hot, season. These pools become filled with the leaves of the forest trees which hang over them.

The bitumen, in all the jungles to which I refer, arises, I believe, from the *coal measures*, pressed down by the overlying masses of sandstone strata, common to both the Himmalaya chain of mountains over the Tarae forest, and the Vendeya and Sathpoor ranges of hills at the sources of the Nerbudda and Sohun rivers. It is, however, possible that the water of these stagnant pools, tainted by the putrid leaves, may impart its poison through the medium of the air in exhalations; and I have known European officers, who were never conscious of having drunk either of the waters above described, take the fever (owl) in the month of May in the Tarae, and in a few hours become raving mad. These tainted waters may possibly act in both ways—directly, and through the medium of the air.

While on the subject of the causes or sources of disease, I may mention two which do not appear to me to have been sufficiently considered and provided against in India. First, when a new cantonment is formed and occupied in haste, during or after a campaign, terraces are formed of the new earth dug up on the spot to elevate the dwellings of officers and soldiers from the ground, which may possibly become flooded in the rains; and over the piles of fresh earth officers commonly form wooden floors for their rooms to secure them from the damp, new earth. Between this earth and the wooden floor a small space of a foot or two is commonly left. The new earth, thus thrown up from places that may not have been dug or ploughed for ages, absorbs rapidly the oxygen from the air above, and gives out carbonic acid, nitrogen and hydrogen gases, which render the air above unfit for men to breathe. This noxious air accumulates in the space below the wooden floor, and, passing through the crevices, is breathed by the officers and soldiers as they sleep.

Between the two campaigns against Nepal in 1814 and 1815, the brigade in which my regiment served formed such a cantonment at Nathpoor, on the right bank of the river Coosee. The land which these cantonments occupied had been covered with a fine sward on which cattle grazed for ages, and was exceedingly rich in decayed vegetable and animal matter. The place had been long remarked for its salubrity by the indigo-planters and merchants of all kinds who resided there; and on the ground which my regiment occupied there was a fine pucka-house, which the officer commanding the brigade and some of his staff occupied. In the rains the whole plain, being very flat, was often covered with water, and thousands of cattle grazed upon it during the cold and hot seasons. The officers all built small bungalows for themselves on the plan above described; and the medical officers all thought that they had, in doing so, taken all possible precautions. The men were provided with huts, as much as possible on the same plan. These dwellings were all ready before the rains set in, and officers and soldiers were in the finest state of health and spirits.

In the middle and latter part of the rains, officers and men began to suffer from a violent fever, which soon rendered the European officers and soldiers delirious, and prostrated the native officers and sipahees; so that three hundred of my own regiment, consisting of about seven hundred, were obliged to be sent to their homes on sick leave. The greater number of those who remained continued to suffer, and a great many died. Of about ten European officers present with my regiment, seven had the fever, and five died of it, almost all in a state of delirium. I was myself one of the two who survived, and I was for many days delirious.

Of the medical officers of the brigade, the only one, I believe, who escaped the fever was Adam Napier, who, with his wife and children, occupied apartments in the brigadier's large pucka-house. Not a person who resided in that house was attacked by the fever. There was another pucka-house a little way from the cantonments, close to the bank of the river, occupied by an indigo-planter, a Mr. Ross. No one in that house suffered. The fever was confined to those who occupied the houses and huts which I have described. All the brigade suffered much, but my regiment, then the first battalion of the 12th Regiment, and now the 12th Regiment, suffered most; and it was stationed on the soil which had remained longest unturned and untilled on what had been considered a park round the pucka-house, in which the brigadier resided. I believe that I am right in attributing this sickness exclusively to the circumstances which I have mentioned; and I am afraid that, during the thirty-five years that have since elapsed, similar circumstances have continued to produce similar results. I am myself persuaded, that had the sward remained unbroken, and the houses and huts been raised upon it, over wooden platforms placed upon it, to secure officers and men from the damp ground, there would have been little or no sickness in that brigade.

The second of the two causes or sources of disease, to which I refer, is the insufficient room which is allowed for the accommodation of our European troops in India. Within the room assigned for the non-commissioned officers and soldiers, they soon exhaust the atmosphere around of its oxygen or vital air, while they expire or exhale carbonic acid, nitrogen and hydrogen gases, which render it altogether unfit to sustain animal life; and death or disease must soon overtake those who inhale or inspire it.

I may illustrate this by a fact within my own observation. In 1817, a flank battalion of six hundred European soldiers was formed at Allahabad, where I then was with my regiment to escort the Governor-General the Marquess of Hastings. With these six hundred soldiers there were thirty-two European officers. The soldiers and non-commissioned officers were put into the barracks in the fort, where they had not sufficient room. The commissioned officers resided in bungalows in the cantonments, or in tents on the open plain. The men were effectually prevented from exposing themselves to the sun, and from indulging in any kind of intemperance, and every possible care was taken of them. The commissioned officers lived as they liked, denied themselves no indulgence, and were driving about all day, and every day, in sun and rain, to visit each other and their friends. A fever, similar to that above described, broke out among the soldiers and non-commissioned officers in the fort, and great numbers died. Of the six hundred, only sixteen escaped the fever. When too late, they were removed from the fort into tents on the plain. From that day the deaths diminished, and he sick began to recover. Of the thirty-two commissioned officers only one, I think, was ever sick at all, and his sickness was of a kind altogether different; and, it is impossible to resist the conclusion, that the non-commissioned officers and soldiers got their disease from want of sufficient room, and, consequently, of sufficient pure air to breathe. Subsequent experience has, I believe, tended to confirm the conclusion; and, I may safely say, that more European soldiers have died from a disregard of it, than from all the wars that we have had within the thirty-three years that have since elapsed. The cause is still in operation, and continues to produce the same fatal results, and will continue to do so till we change the system of accommodating our European troops in India.

The buildings in which they are lodged should all have thatched or tiled roofs, through which the hot and impure air, which has been already breathed, may pass, and be replaced within by the pure air of the atmosphere around, instead of roofs of pucka-masonry which confine this air to be breathed over again by the people within; and double or quadruple the space now allowed to each man should be given. At the cost now incurred in providing them with this insufficient room, under roofs of pucka-masonry, they could be provided with four times the space, under roofs of thatch and tiles, which would be so much more safe and suitable.

The state of the Bharwara district may be illustrated by that of one of its four divisions or mahals, Alleegunge.

In the last year of Hakeem Mehudee's rule (1818), this division was assessed at one hundred and thirty-eight thousand rupees, with the full consent of the people, who were all thriving and happy. The assessment was, indeed, made by the heads of the principal Ahbun families of the district, with Mahommed Hussan Khan as chief assessor. One hundred and thirty-two thousand were collected, and six thousand were remitted in consequence of a partial failure of the crops. Last year, by force and violence, the landholders of this division were made to agree to an assessment upon the lands in tillage of ten thousand and five hundred rupees, of which not six thousand can be collected. The other three divisions are in the same state. Not one-tenth of the land is in tillage, nor are one-tenth of the villages peopled. The soil is really the finest that I have seen in India; and I have seen no part of India in which so small a portion of the surface is unfit for tillage. The moisture rises to the surface just as it is required; and a tolerable crop is got by a poor man who cannot afford to keep a plough, and merely burns down the grass and digs the surface with his spade, or pickaxe, before he sows the seed. Generally, however, the tillage, in the portion cultivated, is very good. The surface is ploughed and cross-ploughed from six to twenty, or even thirty, times in the season; and the harrow and roller are often applied till every clod is pulverized to dust.

The test of first-rate preparation for the seed is that a ghurra, or earthen pitcher, full of water, let fall upon the field from a man's head, shall not break. The clods in the muteear soil are so pulverised only in the fields that are to be irrigated, or to the surface of which moisture rises from below as the weather becomes warm. The people say that it does so rise when required in land even a good way from the forest, and that the clods are, in consequence, not necessary to retain it. This is the only part of India in which I have known the people take ratoon, or second crops of sugar-cane from the same roots; and the farmers and cultivators tell me that the second crop is almost as good as the first. The fields in tillage are well supplied with manure, which is very abundant where so large a portion of the surface is waste, and affords such fine pasture. They are also well watered, for the water is near the surface, and in the tight muteear soil a kutcha well, or well without masonry, will stand good for twenty seasons. To make pucka-wells, or wells lined with burnt bricks and cement, would be costly. Each well of this kind costs about one hundred rupees. The kutcha-wells, which are lined with nothing, or with thick ropes of twigs and straw, cost only from five to ten rupees. The people tell me that oppression and poverty have made them less fastidious than they were formerly; that formerly it was considered disgraceful to plough with buffaloes, or to use them in carts, but they are now in common use for both purposes; that vast numbers of the Kunojee Brahmins and others, who could not formerly drive their own ploughs, drive them now; and that all will in time condescend to do so, as the penalties of higher payments with and for daughters in marriage cease to be exacted from men whose necessities have become so pressing.

March 6, 1850.—Halted at Kurunpoor, where the gentlemen of my camp shot some floricans, hares, partridges, and a porcupine along the bank of the small river Ole, which flows along from north-west to south-east within three miles of Kurunpoor.

March 7, 1850.—Teekur, twelve miles. The road,

for three miles, lay through grass jungle to the border of the Khyrabad district, whence the plain is covered with cultivation, well studded with trees, clusters of bamboos, and well peopled with villages, all indicating better management. A great many fields are reduced to the fine dust above described to receive the sugar-cane, which is planted in February. The soil is muteear, but has in many parts become impaired by over-cropping. The people told me that the crops were not so rich as they ought to be, from the want of manure, which is much felt here, where there is so little pasture for cattle. The wheat has almost everywhere received an orange tint from the geerwa, or blight, which covers the leaves, but, happily, has not as yet settled upon the stalks to feed on the sap. This blight, the cultivators say, arises from the late and heavy rain they have had, and the easterly wind that prevailed for a few days. The geerwa is a red fungus, which, when it adheres to the stems, thrusts its roots through the pores of the epidermis and robs the grain of the sap as it ascends. When easterly winds and sultry weather prevail, the pores of the epidermis appear to be more opened and exposed to the inroads of these fungi than at other times. If the wind continue westerly for a fortnight more, little injury may be sustained; but should easterly winds and sultry weather prevail, the greater part may be lost. "We cultivators and landholders," said Bukhtawur Sing, "are always in dread of something, and can never feel quite easy: if little rain falls, we complain of the want of more; if a good deal comes down, we are in dread of this blight, and never dare to congratulate ourselves on the prospect of good returns." To the justice and wisdom of this observation all assented.*

* Westerly winds and cold weather prevailed, and the blight did

The landholders of this purgunnah are chiefly Janwar Rajpoots. Kymara, a fine village, through which we passed, about five miles from Kurunpoor, is the residence of the present head of this family, Rajah Ajeet Sing. He has a small fort close by, in which he is now preparing to defend himself against the King's forces. The poor old man came out with all his village community to meet and talk with me, in the hope that I might interpose to protect him. He is weak in mind and body, has no son, and, having lately lost his only brother and declared heir to the estate, his cousins and more distant relations are scrambling for the inheritance. The usual means of violence, collusion, and intrigue have been had recourse to. The estate is in the Huzoor Tuhseel, and not under the jurisdiction of the contractor of Khyrabad. The old man seemed care-worn and very wretched, and told me that the contractor, whom I should meet at Teekur, had only yesterday received orders from Court to use all his means to oust him from possession, and make over the estate to his cousin, Jodha Sing, who had lately left him in consequence of a dispute, after having, since the death of his brother, aided him in the management of the estate; that he had always paid his revenues to the King punctually, and last year he owed a balance of only one hundred and sixty rupees, when *Anrod Sing*, his distant relative, wanted him to declare his younger brother, Dirj Bijee Sing, his heir to the estate, in lieu of Jodha Sing.

This he refused to do, and Anrod Sing came, with a force of two thousand armed men, supported by a detach-

---

little apparent injury to the crops; but the wheat crops, generally, over Oude and the adjoining districts, was shrivelled and deficient in substance. It had "run to stalk" from the excess of rain.

ment from Captain Barlow's regiment, and laid siege to his fort, on the pretence that he was required to give security for the more punctual payment of the revenue. To defend himself, he was obliged to call in the aid of his clan and neighbours, and expend all that he had or could borrow, and, at last, constrained to accept Anrod Sing's security, for no merchants would lend money to a poor man in a state of siege. Anrod Sing had now gone off to Lucknow, and bribed the person in charge of the Huzoor Tuhseel, Gholam Ruza Khan, one of the most corrupt men in the corrupt Court of Lucknow, to get an order issued by the Minister to have him turned out, and the estate made over to Jhoda Sing, from whom he would soon get it on pretence of accumulated balances, and make it over, in perpetuity, to his brother, Dirj Bijee Sing. In this attempt, the old man said, a good many lives must be lost and crops destroyed, for his friends would not let him fall without a struggle.*

As soon as we left the poor old man, Bukhtawur Sing said, "This, sir, is the way in which Government officers manage to control and subdue these sturdy Rajpoot landholders. While they remain united, as in the Bangur district, they can do nothing with them, and let them keep their estates on their own terms; but the moment a quarrel takes place between them they take advantage of

* The old man has been attacked and turned out with the loss of some lives, in spite of the Resident's remonstrance, and the estate has been made over to Jodha Sing, on the security for the payment of the revenue of Anrod Sing. Jodha Sing is, naturally, of weak intellect; and Anrod Sing will soon have him turned out as an incompetent defaulter, and get the estate for himself, or for his younger brother. Luckily *Anrod Sing* and *Lonee Sing*, of Mitholee, are at daggers-drawn about some villages, which Anrod Sing has seized, and to which Lonee Sing thinks he has a better right. Their dread of each other will be useful to the Government and the people.

it: they adopt the cause of the strongest, and support him in his aggressions upon the other members of his family or clan till all become weak by division and disorder, and submit. Forty or fifty years ago, sir, when I used to move about the country on circuit with Saadut Allee Khan, the then sovereign, as I now move with you, there were many Rajpoot landholders in Oude stronger than any that defy the Government now; but they dared not then hold their heads so high as they do now. The local officers employed by him were men of ability, experience, and character, totally unlike those now employed. Each had a wing of one of the Honourable Company's regiments and some good guns with him, and was ready and able to enforce his master's orders and the payment of his just demands; but, since his death, the local officers have been falling off in character and strength, while the Rajpoot landholders have risen in pride and power. The aid of the British troops has, by degrees, been altogether withdrawn, and the landholders of this class despise the Oude Government, and many of them resist its troops whenever they attempt to enforce the payment of even its most moderate demands. The revenues of the State fall off as the armed bands of these landholders increase, and families who, in his time, kept up only fifty armed men, have now five hundred, or even a thousand or two thousand, and spend what they owe to Government in maintaining them. To pay such bands they withhold the just demands of the State, rob their weaker neighbours of their possessions, and plunder travellers on the highway, and men of substance, wherever they can find them.

"When Saadut Allee made over one-half of his dominions to the British Government in 1801, he was bound to reduce his military force and rely altogether upon the support of your Government. He did so; but the force he retained, though small, was good; and while that support was afforded things went on well—he was a wise man, and made the most of the means he had. Since that time, sir, the Oude force has been increased four-fold, as your aid has been withdrawn; but the whole is not equal to the fourth part which served under Saadut Allee. You see how insignificant it everywhere is, and how much it is despised even by the third-class Rajpoot landholders. You see, also, how they everywhere prey upon the people, and are dreaded and detested by them: the only estates free from their inroads are those under the 'Huzoor Tuhseel,' into which the Amils and their disorderly hosts dare not enter. If the landholders could be made to feel that they would not be permitted to seize other men's possessions, nor other men to seize theirs, as long as they obeyed the Government and paid its just dues, they would disband these armed followers, and the King might soon reduce his. He will never make them worth anything; there are too many worthless, but influential persons about the Court, interested in keeping up all kinds of abuses, to permit this. These abuses are the chief source of their incomes: they rob the officers and sipahees, and even the draft-bullocks; and you everywhere see how the poor animals are starved by them."

Within a mile of the camp I met the Nazim, Hoseyn Allee Khan, who told me that Rajah Goorbuksh Sing, of Ramnuggur Dhumeree, had fulfilled all the engagements entered into before me at Byramghat, on the Ghagra, on the 6th of December, and was no longer opposed to the Government; and that the only large landholder in his district who remained so at present was Seobuksh Sing, of Kateysura, a strong fort, mounted with seven guns, near the road over which I am to pass the day after to-morrow, between Oel and Lahurpoor. As he came up on his little elephant along the road, I saw half-a-dozen of his men, mounted on camels, trotting along through a fine field of wheat, now in ear, with as much unconcern as if they had been upon a fine sward to which they could do no harm. I saw one of my people in advance make a sign to them, on which they made for the road as fast as they could. I asked the Nazim how he could permit such trespass. He told me, "That he did not see them, and unless his eye was always upon them he could not prevent their doing mischief, for they were the King's servants, who never seemed happy unless they were trespassing upon some of his Majesty's subjects." Nothing, certainly, seems to delight them so much as the trespasses of all kinds which they do commit upon them.

March 8, 1850.—Oel, five miles, over a plain of the same fine muteear soil, beautifully cultivated and studded with trees, intermixed with numerous clusters of the graceful bamboo. A great-grandson of the monster Nadir Shah, of Persia, Ruza Kolee Khan, who commands a battalion in the King of Oude's service, rode by me, and I asked him whether he ever saw such a cultivated country in Persia. "Never," said he: "Persia is a hilly country, and there is no tillage like this in any part of it. I left Persia, with my father, twenty-two years ago, when I was twenty-two years of age, and I have still a very distinct recollection of what it was then. There is no country in the world, sir," said the Nazim, "like Hindoostan, when it enjoys the blessings of a good government. The purgunnah of Kheree, in which we now are, is all held by the heads of three families of Janwar Rajpoots: Rajah Ajub Sing, of Kymara; Anrod Sing, of Oel; and Umrao Sing, of Mahewa. There are only sixty-six villages of Khalsa, or Crown lands left, yielding twenty-one thousand rupees a-year. The rest have been all absorbed by the heads of these Rajpoot families.

	Villages.		Jumma.		
Kymara	82	. . .	13,486	0	0
Oel.	170	. . .	54,790	0	0
Mahewa	70	. . .	20,835	0	0
	322		89,111	0	0
Khalsa	66	. . .	21,881	0	0
	388	. . .	1,10,992	0	0

"These heads of families have each a fort, surrounded by a strong fence of bamboos, and mounted with good guns; and the King cannot get so large a revenue from them as he did thirty years ago, in the time of Hakeem Mehndee, though their lands are as well tilled now as they were then, and yield more rent to their holders. They spend it all in keeping up large armed bands to resist the Government; but they certainly take care of their cultivators and tenants of all kinds, and no man dares molest them.

"But," said Bukhtawur Sing, "this beautiful scene would all be changed were they encouraged or permitted to contend with each other for the possession of the lands. I yesterday saw a great number of the merchants of Kymara following the Resident's camp; and, on asking them why, they told me that the order from Court obtained by Gholam Ruza for you (the Nazim) to assist the Oel chief, Anrod Sing, in despoiling Rajah Ajub Sing of his estate, had driven out all who had no fields of corn or other local ties to detain them, and had anything to lose by remaining. The chief and his retainers were repairing their fort, and preparing to fight for their possessions to the last; and if you take your disorderly force against them according to orders, the crops now in the ground will be all destroyed, and the numerous fields now prepared to receive sugar-cane and the autumn seed will be left waste: they will make reprisals upon Oel; others of their clan will join in the strife; and this district will be what that of Bharwara, which we have just left, now is. The merchants are in the right, sir, to make off: no property in such a scene is ever safe. There is no property, sir, like that in the Honourable Company's paper: it is the only property that we can enjoy in peace. You feel no anxiety about it. It doubles itself in fifteen or sixteen years; and you go on from generation to generation enjoying your five per cent., and neither fearing nor annoying anybody."

The two villages of Oel and Dhukwa adjoin each other, and form a large town; but the dwelling-houses have a wretched appearance, consisting of naked mud walls, with but a few more grass-choppers than are usually found upon them in Oude towns. There is a good-looking temple, dedicated to Mahadeo, in the centre of the town, and the houses are close upon the ditch of the fort, which has its bamboo-fence inside its ditch and outer mud walls. I have written to the Durbar to recommend that the order for the attack upon Rajah Ajub Sing be countermanded, and more pacific measures adopted for the settlement of the claims of the Exchequer and Anród Sing upon poor old Ajub Sing.

The Kanoongoes of this place tell me that the dispute has arisen from a desire, on the part of the old man's wife, to set aside the just claim of Jodha Sing, the old man's nephew, to the inheritance, in favour of a lad whom she has adopted and brought up, by name Teeka Sing, in whose name the estate is now managed by a servant; that Jodha Sing is the rightful heir, and managed the estate well for his uncle, after the death of his brother, till lately, when his aunt persuaded his uncle to break with him, which he did with reluctance; that Jodha Sing now lives in retirement at his village of Barkerwa; that Anrod Sing's design upon the inheritance for his younger brother, Dirj Bijee Sing, is unjust; and that he is, in consequence, obliged to prosecute it on the pretence of recovering money due, and supporting the claim of Jodha Sing, and in collusion with the officers of Government; that Gholam Ruza, who has charge of the Huzoor Tuhseel, is ready to adopt the cause of any one who will pay him; and that Anrod Sing is now at Lucknow paying his court to him, and getting these iniquitous orders issued.

Oel was transferred to the Huzoor Tuhseel in 1834, Kymara in 1836, and Mahewa in 1839. These Rajpoot landholders do not often seize upon the lands of a relative at once, but get them by degrees by fraud and collusion with Government officers, so that they may share the odium with them. They instigate these officers to demand more than the lands can pay; offer the enhanced rate, and get the lands at once; or get a mortgage, run up the account, and foreclose by their aid. They no sooner get the estate than they reduce the Government demand, by collusion or violence, to less than what the former proprietor had paid.

March 9, 1850.—Lahurpoor, twelve miles, over a plain of doomuteea soil, well studded with groves and single trees, but not so fully cultivated the last half way as the first. For the first half way the road lies through the estate of Anrod Sing, of Oel; but for the last it runs through that of Seobuksh Sing, a Gour Rajpoot, who has a fort near the town of Kuteysura, five miles from Lahurpoor, and seven from Oel. It is of mud, and has a ditch all round, and a bamboo-fence inside the outer walls. It is of great extent, but not formidable against well-provided troops. The greater part of the houses in the town are in ruins, and Seobuksh has the reputation of being a reckless and improvident landholder. He is said not only to take from his tenants higher rates of rent than he ought, but to extort from them very often *a property tax*, highly and capriciously rated. This is what the people call the *bhalmansae*, of which they have a very great abhorrence. "You are a *bhala manus*" (a gentleman, or man of substance), he says to his tenant, "and must have property worth at least a thousand rupees. I want money sadly, and must have one-fifth: give me two hundred rupees." This is what the people call "*bhalmansae*," or rating a man according to his substance; and to say that a landlord or governor does this, is to say that he is a reckless oppressor, who has no regard to obligations or to consequences.

There are manifest signs of the present landholder, Seobuksh Sing, being of this character; but others, not less manifest, of his grandfather having been a better man, in the fine groves which surround Lahurpoor, and the villages between this place and Kuteysura, all of which are included in his estate. These groves were, for the most part, planted during the life of his grandfather by men of substance, who were left free to dispose of their property as they thought best.

All the native gentlemen who rode with me remarked

on the beauty of the approach to Lahurpoor, in which a rich carpet of spring crops covers the surface up to the groves, and extends along under the trees which have been recently planted. There are many young groves about the place, planted by men who have acquired property by trade, and by the savings out of the salaries and perquisites of office at Lahurpoor, which is the residence of the Nazim, or local governor, during several months in the year; and the landlord, Seobuksh, cannot venture to exact his *property-tax* from them. The air and water are much praised, and the general good health of the troops, civil establishments, and residents of all classes, show that the climate must be good. The position, too, is well chosen with reference to the districts, and the character of the people under the control of the governor of the Khyrabad district.

The estate of Seobuksh is very extensive. The soil is all good and the plain level, so that every part of it is capable of tillage. Rutun Sing, the father of Seobuksh, is said to have been a greater rack-renter, rebel, and robber than his son is, and together they have injured the estate a good deal, and reduced it from a rent-roll of one hundred thousand to one of forty. Its rent-roll is now estimated in the public accounts at 54,640, out of which is deducted a *nankar* of 17,587, leaving a Government demand of only 37,053. This he can't pay; and he has shut himself up sullenly in his mud fort, where the Nazim dares not attack him. He is levying contributions from the surrounding villages, but has not yet plundered or burnt down any. He was lately in prison for two years; but released on the security of Rajah Lonee Sing, of Mitholee, whose wife is his wife's sister. He, however, says that he was pledged to produce him when required, not before the *present Nazim*, but his *predecessor;* and that he is no longer bound by this pledge. This reasoning would, of course, have no weight with the Government authorities, nor would it be had recourse to were Lonee Sing less strong. Each has a strong fort and a band of steady men. The Nazim has not the means to attack Seobuksh, and dares not attack Lonee Sing, as his estate of Pyla is in the "Huzoor Tuhseel," and under the protection of Court favourites, who are well paid by him.

Lonee Sing's estate of Mitholee is in the Mahomdee district, and under the jurisdiction of the Amil; and it is only the portion, consisting of one hundred and four recently-acquired villages, which he holds in the Pyla estate, in the Khyrabad district, that has been made over to the Huzoor Tuhseel.* He offered an increased rate for these villages to the then Amil, Bhowood Dowlah, in the year A.D. 1840. It was accepted, and he attacked, plundered, and murdered a good many of the old proprietors, and established such a dread among them, that he now manages them with little difficulty. Basdeo held fourteen of these villages under mortgage, and sixteen more under lease. He had his brother, maternal uncle, and a servant killed by Lonee Sing, and is now reduced to beggary. Lonee Sing took the lease in March, 1840, and commenced this attack in May.

The Nazim had with him, of infantry, 1. Futteh Aesh Nujeebs. 2. Wuzeree, ditto. 3. Zuffur, Mobaruk Telinga. 4. Futteh Jung ditto; Ruza Kolee Khan. 5. Captain Barlow's ditto. Eleven guns. But, being unable to get any duty from the three regiments first named, he offered to dispense with the two first, on condition that

* Anrod Sing holds twenty-eight villages in the Pyla estate, acquired in the same way as those held by Lonee Sing.

the command of the third should be placed at his disposal for his son or nephew.

This request was complied with; and, on paying a fee of five thousand rupees, he got the dress of investiture, and offered it to Lieutenant Orr, a very gallant officer, the second in command of Captain Barlow's corps, as the only way to render the corps so efficient as he required it to be. The Durbar took away the two regiments; but, as soon as they heard that Lieutenant Orr was to command the third, they appointed Fidda Hoseyn, brother of the ruffian Mahommed Hoseyn, who had held the district of Mahomdee, and done so much mischief to it. Fidda Hoseyn, of course, paid a high sum for the command to be exacted from his subordinates, or the people of the district in which it might be employed; and the regiment has remained worse than useless. Of the eleven guns, five are useless on the ground, and without bullocks. The bullocks for the other six are present, but too weak to draw anything. They had had no grain for many years; but within the last month they have had one-half seer each per day out of the one seer and half paid for by Government. There is no ammunition, stores, or anything else for the guns, and the best of the carriages are liable to fall to pieces with the first discharge. They are not allowed to repair them, but must send them in to get them changed for others when useless. The Durbar knows that if they allow the local officers to charge for the repair of guns, heavy charges will be made, and no gun ever repaired; and the local officers know that if they send in a gun to be repaired at Lucknow, they will get in exchange one *painted* to look well, but so flimsily done up that it will go to pieces the first or second time it is fired.

Captain Barlow's corps is a good one, and the men are finer than any that I have seen in our own infantry regiments, though they get only five rupees a-month each, while ours get seven. They prefer this rate under European officers in the Oude service, to the seven rupees a-month which sipahees get in ours, though they have no pension establishment or extra allowance while marching. They feel sure that their European commandants will secure them their pay sooner or later; they escape many of the harassing duties to which our sipahees are liable; they have leave to visit their homes one month in twelve; they never have to march out of Oude to distant stations, situated in bad climates; they get fuel and fodder, and often food, for nothing; their baggage is always carried for them at the public cost. But to secure them their pay, arms, accoutrements, clothing, &c., the commandant must be always about the Court himself, or have an *ambassador* of some influence there at great cost. Captain Barlow is almost all his time at Court, as much from choice as expediency, drawing all his allowances and emoluments of all kinds, while his second in command performs his regimental duties for him. The other officers like this, because they know that the corps could not possibly be kept in the state it is without it. Captain Barlow has lately obtained three thousand rupees for the repair of his six gun-carriages, tumbrils, &c., that is, five hundred for each. They had not been repaired for ten years; hardly any of the others have been repaired for the last twenty or thirty years.

The Nazim of this district of Khyrabad has taken the farm of it for one year at nine lacs of rupees, that is one lac and a half less than the rate at which it was taken by his predecessor last year. He tells me, that he was obliged to enter into engagements to pay in gratuities fifty thousand to the minister, of which he has as yet paid only five thousand; twenty-five thousand to the Dewan, Balkishun, and seven thousand to Gholam Ruza, who has charge of the Huzoor Tuhseel—that he was obliged to engage to pay four hundred rupees a-month, in salaries, to men named by the Dewan, who do no duty, and never show their faces to him; and similar sums to the creatures of the minister and others—that he was obliged to pay gratuities to a vast number of understrappers at Court—that he was not made aware of the amount of these gratuities, &c., till he had received his dress of investiture, and had merely promised to pay what his predecessor had paid—that when about to set out, the memorandum of what his predecessor had paid was put into his hand, and it was then too late to remonstrate or draw back. There may be some exaggeration in the rate of the gratuities demanded; but that he has to pay them to the persons named I have no doubt whatever, because all men in charge of districts have to pay them to those persons, whether they hold the districts in contract or in trust.

The Zuffer Mobaruk regiment, with its commandant, Fidda Hoseyn, is now across the Ghagra in charge of Dhorehra, an estate in the forest belonging to Rajah Arjun Sing, who has absconded in consequence of having been ruined by the rapacity of a native collector last year; and they are diligently employed in plundering all the people who remain. The estate paid 2,75,000 a-year till these outrages began; and it cannot now pay fifty thousand. Arjun Sing and Seobuksh Sing, of Kuteysura, are the only refractory landholders in the Khyrabad district at present.

March 10, 1850.—Halted at Lahurpoor. There is good ground for large civil and military establishments to the south of the town, about a mile out, on the left of the road leading to Khyrabad. It is a fine open plain of light soil. New pucka-wells would be required; and some low ground, near the south and north, would also require to be drained, as water lies in it during the rains. There is excellent ground nearer the town on the same side, but the mango-groves are thick and numerous, and would impede the circulation of air. The owners would, moreover, be soon robbed of them were a cantonment, or civil station, established among or very near to them. The town and site of any cantonment, or civil station, should be taken from the Kuteysura estate, and due compensation made to the holder, Seobuksh. The town is a poor one; and the people are keeping their houses uncovered, and removing their property under the apprehension that Seobuksh will attack and plunder the place. All the merchants and respectable landholders, over the districts bordering on the Tarae forest, through which we have passed, declare, that all the colonies of Budukh dacoits, who had, for many generations, up to 1842, been located in this forest, have entirely disappeared. Not a family of them can now be found anywhere in Oude. Six or eight hundred of their brave and active men used to sally forth every year, and carry their depredations into Bengal, Behar, and all the districts of the north-west provinces. Their suppression has been a great benefit conferred upon the people of India by the British Government.

March 11, 1850.—Kusreyla, ten miles, over a plain of excellent muteear soil scantily cultivated, but studded with fine trees, single and in groves. Kusreyla is among the three hundred villages which have been lately taken in mortgage from the proprietors, and in lease from Government, by Monowur-od Dowlah, the nephew and heir of the late Hakeem Mehndee. He is inviting and locating in these villages many cultivators of the best classes; and they will all soon be in a fine state of tillage. No soil can be finer, and no acre of it is incapable of bearing fine crops. The old proprietors and lessees, to whom he had lent money on mortgage, have persuaded him to foreclose, that they may come under so substantial and kind a landholder. They prefer holding the sub-lease under such a man, to holding the lease directly under Government, subject to the jurisdiction of the Nazim. Monowur-od Dowlah pays forty thousand rupees a-year for the whole to Government, and has had the whole transferred to the Huzoor Tuhseel.

The Nazim of Khyrabad rode by my side during this morning's march, and at my request he described the mutiny which took place in two of the regiments that attended him in the siege of Bhitolee, just before I crossed the Ghagra at Byramghat. These were the Futteh Aesh, and the Wuzeeree. Their commandants are Allee Hoseyn, a creature of one of the singers, Kootab Allee; and Mahommed Akhbur, a creature of the minister's. They were earnestly urged by the minister and Nazim to join their regiments for the short time they would be on this important service, but in vain; nothing could induce them to quit the Court. All the corps mentioned above, as attending the Nazim, were present, and the siege had begun when, on the 17th of November, some shopkeepers in camp, having been robbed during the night by some thieves, shut up their shops, and prepared to leave the camp in a body. The siege could not go on if the traders all left the place; and he sent a messenger to call the principal men that he might talk to them. They refused to move, and the messenger, finding that they were ready to set out, seized one of them by the waist-band, and when he resisted, struck him on the head with a stick, and said he would make him go to his master. The man called out to some sipahees of the Wuzeeree regiment, who were near, to rescue him. They did so: the messenger struggled to hold his grasp, but was dragged off and beaten. He returned the blows; the sipahees drew their swords: he seized one of the swords and ran off towards his master's tent, waiving it over his head, to defend himself, followed by some of the sipahees. The others ran back to the grove in which their regiment and the Futteh Aesh were bivouaced; both regiments seized their arms and ran towards the Nazim's tents; and when they got within two hundred yards, commenced firing upon them.

The Nazim had with him only a few of his own armed servants. They seized their arms, and begged permission to return the fire, but were restrained till the regiment came near, and two tomandars, or officers, who stood by the Nazim, were shot down, one dead, and the other disabled. His men could be restrained no longer, and they shot down two of the foremost of the assailants. The Nazim then sent off to Lieutenant Orr, who was exercising his corps with blank cartridge on the parade; and, supposing that one of these regiments was doing the same thing near the Nazim's tents, he paid no attention to them. He and his brother, the Adjutant, ran forward, and entreated the two regiments to cease firing; and the Nazim sent out Syud Seoraj-od Deen (the commandant of the Bhurmar regiment, stationed in the adjoining district of Ramnugger Dhumeree, who had just come to him on a visit), with the Koran in his hand, to do the same. The remonstrances of both were in vain. They continued to fire upon the Nazim, and Lieutenant Orr went off to bring up his regiment, which stood ready to move on the parade. Alarmed at this, the two regiments ran off to their grove, and the firing ceased.

During all this time, the other two regiments, the Zuffer Mobaruk and Futteh Jung, stood looking on as indifferent spectators; and afterwards took great credit to themselves for not joining in this attempt to blow up the viceroy, who was obliged, the next day, to go to their camp and apologize humbly for his men having presumed to return their fire, which he declared that they had done without his orders! On his doing this, they consented to forego their claim to have the unhappy messenger sent to their camp to be *executed;* and to remain with him during the siege. As to taking any part in the siege and assault on the fort, that was altogether out of their line. Ruza Kolee Khan, the commandant of the Futteh Jung, was at Lucknow during this mutiny, but he joined a few days after. Lieutenant Orr gave me the same narrative of the affair at the dinner-table last night; and said, that he and his brother had a very narrow escape—that his regiment would have destroyed all the mutineers had they been present; and he left them on the parade lest he might not be able to restrain them in such a scene. Even this mutiny of the two regiments could not tempt their commandants to leave Court, where they are still enjoying the favour of their patrons, the minister and the singers, and a large share of the pay and perquisites of their officers and sipahees, though the regiments have been sent off to the two disturbed districts of Sundela and Salone.

They dare not face the most contemptible enemy, but they spare not the weak and inoffensive of any class, age, or sex. A respectable landholder, in presenting a petition, complaining of the outrages committed upon his village and peasantry, said a few days ago—" The oppression of these revenue collectors, and their disorderly troops, is ntolerable, sir—they plunder all who cannot resist them, but cannot lift their arms, or draw their breath freely in the presence of armed robbers and rebels—it is a proverb, sir, that *insects* prey upon soft *wood*; and these men prey only upon the peaceful and industrious, who are unable to defend themselves." The Nazim tells me, that the lamentations of the poor people, plundered and maltreated, were incessant and distressing during the whole time these two orps were with him; and that he could exercise no control whatever over them, protected as they were, in all their iniquities, by the Court favour their two commandants enjoyed at Lucknow.*

I asked Bukhtawur Sing, before the Nazim overtook us this morning, why it was, that these governors always took so many troops with them when they moved from place to place, merely to settle accounts and inspect the crops. " Some of them," said he, " take all the troops they can muster, to show that they are great men; but, for the most part, they are afraid to move without them. They, and the greater part of the landholders, consider each other as natural and irreconcilable enemies; and a good many of those, who hold the largest estates, are at all times in open resistance against the Government. They have their Vakeels with the contractors when they

* Kootab Allee was one of the singers who were soon after banished from Oude in disgrace. But all the influence they exercised over the King has been concentrated in the hands of the two singers who remained, Mosahib Allee and Anees-od Dowla. All are despicable *domes*; but the two, who now govern the King, are much worse characters than any of those who were banished.

are not so, and spies when they are. They know all his movements, and would waylay and carry him off if not surrounded with a strong body of soldiers, for he is always moving over the country, with every part of which they are well acquainted. Besides, under the present system of allowing them to forage or plunder for themselves, it is ruinous to any place to leave them in it for even a few days—no man, within several miles, would preserve shelter for his family, or food for his cattle, during the hot and rainy months—he is obliged to take them about with him to distribute, as equally as he can, the terrible burthen of maintaining them. Now that the sugar-cane is ripe, not one cane would be preserved in any field within five miles of any place where the Nazim kept his troops for ten days."

March 12, 1850.—Seetapoor, nine miles over a plain of muteear soil, the greater part of which is light, and yields but scanty crops without manure, which is very scarce. Immediately about the station and villages, where manure is available, the crops are good. The wind continues westerly, the sky is clear, and the blight does not seem to increase.

The 2nd Regiment of Oude Local Infantry is stationed at Seetapoor, but it has no guns or cavalry of any kind. Formerly there was a corps of the Honourable Company's Native Infantry here, with two guns and a detail of artillery. The sipahees of this corps, and of the 1st Oude Local Infantry, at Sultanpoor, are somewhat inferior in appearance to those of our own native infantry regiments, and still more so to the Oude corps under Captains Barlow, Magness, and Bunbury. They receive five rupees eight annas a-month pay, and batta, or extra allowance, when marching; and the same pay as our own sipahees of the line (seven rupees a-month) when serving with them. But the commandants cannot get recruits equal to those that enlist in our regiments of the line, or those that enlist in the corps of the officers above named. They have not the rest and the licence of the one, while they have the same drill and discipline, without the same rate of pay as the other. They have now the privilege of petitioning through the Resident like our sipahees of the line, and that of the pension establishment, while Barlow's, Bunbury's, and Magness's corps have neither. They have none but internal duties—they are hardly ever sent out to aid the King's local authorities, and do not escort treasure even for their own pay. It is sent to them by drafts from Lucknow on the local collectors of the district in which they are cantoned; and the money required for the Resident's Treasury—a great portion of which passes through the Seetapoor cantonments—is escorted by our infantry regiments of the line, stationed at Lucknow, merely because a General Order exists that no irregular corps shall be employed on such duties while any regular corps near has a relief of guards present. The corps of regular infantry at Shajehanpoor escorts the treasure six marches to Seetapoor, where it is relieved by a detachment from one of the regular corps at Lucknow, six marches distant.

The native officers and sipahees of these two corps have leave of absence to visit their families just as often and for just as long periods as those of the corps under the three above-named officers—that is, for one month out of twelve. The native officers and sipahees of these three corps are not, however, so much drilled or restrained as those of the two Oude local corps, in which no man dares to help himself occasionally to the roofs of houses and the produce of fields or gardens; nor to take presents from local authorities, as they are hardly ever sent out to assist them. The native officers and sipahees of the very best of the King of Oude's corps do all this more or less; and they become, in consequence, more attached to their officers and the service. Moreover, the commandants of the two corps of Oude local infantry never become *mediators* between large landholders and local governors as those of the King of Oude's corps so often do; nor are any landed estates ever assigned to them for the liquidation of their arrears of pay, and confided to their management. So highly do the native officers of these three Oude *Komukee* corps appreciate all the privileges and perquisites they enjoy, when out on duty under district officers, that they consider short periods of guard duty in the city, where they have none of them, as serious punishments.

The drainage about Seetapoor is into the small river Surain, which flows along on the west boundary, and is excellent; and the lands in and about the station are at all times dry. The soil, too, is good; and the place, on the whole, is well adapted for the cantonment of a much larger force.

March 13, 1850.—Khyrabad, east nine miles, over a plain of doomuteea soil with much oosur. A little outlay and labour seem, however, to make this oosur produce good crops. On entering the town on the west side, we passed over a good stone bridge over this little stream, the Surain; and to the east of the town is another over the still smaller stream of the Gond. Khyrabad is not so well drained as Seetapoor, nor would it be so well adapted for a large cantonment. It is considered to be less healthy. There is an avenue of good trees all the way from Seetapoor to Khyrabad, a distance of six miles, planted by Hakeem Mehndee. Our camp being to the eastern extremity of the town, renders the distance nine miles.

Yesterday at Seetapoor I had a visit from Monowur-od Dowla, late prime minister, and Moomtaz-od Dowla, grandson to the late King, Mahommed Allee Shah, on their way out to the Tarae forest to join Kindoo Rao, the brother of the Byza Bae, of Gwalior, in pursuit of tigers. This morning on the road, old Bukhtawur Sing, after a sigh, said: "I presented a nazur to the prince, Moomtaz-od Dowla, sir; he is the grandson of a King, and the victim of the folly and crime of shooting a monkey! His father, Asgur Allee Khan, was the eldest son of Mahommed Allee Shah, and elder brother of Amjud Allee Shah, the father of the present King. He was fond of his gun, and one day a monkey, of the red and short-tailed kind, came and sat upon one of his out-offices. He sent for his gun, and shot it dead with a ball. The very next day, sir, he had a severe attack of fever, which carried him off in three days. During this time he frequently called out in terror, 'Save me from that monkey! save me from that monkey!' —pointing to the part of the room in which he *saw him*. The monkey killed Asgur Allee Khan, sir; and no man ever escapes death or misery who wilfully kills one. Moomtaz-od Dowla might, sir, have been now King of Oude had his father not shot that monkey."

"But I thought," said I, "it was the *hanoomaun*, or long-tailed monkey, that was held sacred by the Hindoos?" —"Sir," said Bukhtawur Sing, "both are alike sacred.*

* That Asgur Allee Khan, the eldest son of the King, Mahommed Allee Shah, did shoot the monkey, got a fever a few days after, and died of it, are facts well known at Lucknow. That he often mentioned the monkey during his delirium, is generally believed; and that his death was the consequence of his shooting that animal is the opinion

Nuseer-od Deen Hyder, the predecessor of Mahommed Allee Shah, went one day shooting in the dilkhoosha park. Several of the long-tailed monkeys came and sat upon a mango-tree near him. He could not resist the temptation, and shot several of them, one after another, with ball. He returned to the palace; but had not been home more than three hours, when he and his favourite wife, the Kooduseea Begum,* had a fierce quarrel, in which both became *insane;* she was so enraged that she took poison forthwith, and, in her agony, actually spit up her liver, which had been torn to pieces by the force of the poison! The King could not stand the horrible sight, and ran off and hid himself in the race-stand, near which you fell and broke your thigh-bone in April last; there he remained shut up till she died. He had had warning, sir, for a few months after his accession to the throne: I attended him and his minister, Aga Meer, on a visit to the garden, called padshah baag, on the opposite side of the river: he had a gun with him, and, seeing a monkey on a tree, he ordered the prime minister to try his hand at it. I told Aga Meer that evil would certainly befall him or his house if he shot the animal, and begged his Majesty not to assist upon the minister's doing it. Both laughed at what they thought my folly; the minister shot the monkey; and in a few days he was out of office and in a prison. One way or other, sir, a man who wilfully destroys a monkey is sure to be punished."

---

of all the Hindoo, and a great part of the Musulman, population. His death, while his father lived, deprived his son, Moomtaz-od Dowla, of the throne.

* The Kooduseea Begum had been introduced into the palace as waiting-woman to Mulika Zumanee, whom she soon superseded in the King's affections, which she retained till her death. She was married to the King on the 17th December, 1831, and died on the 21st of August, 1834.

At Khyrabad there is a handsome set of buildings, consisting of a mausoleum over his father, a mosque, an *imambara*, and a *kudum rusool*, or shrine with the print of the prophet's foot, erected by Mucka Durzee, a tailor in the service of the King, who made a large fortune out of his master's favours, and who still lives, and provides for their repair and suitable endowment. These buildings are, like all others of the same kind, infested by a host of professional religious mendicants of both sexes and all ages, who make the air resound with their clamours for alms. Not only are such buildings so infested, but all the towns around them. I could not help observing to the native gentlemen who attended me, "that when men planted groves and avenues, and built reservoirs, bridges, caravansaries, and wells, they did not give rise to any such sources of annoyance to travellers; that they enjoyed the water, shade, and accommodation, without cost or vexation, and went on their way blessing the donor." "That," said an old Rusaldar, "is certainly taking a new and just view of the case; but still it is a surprising thing to see a man in this humble sphere of life raising and maintaining so splendid a pile of buildings."*

The town of Khyrabad has still a good many inhabitants; but the number is fast decreasing. It was the residence of the families of a good many public officers in our service and that of Oude; and the local authorities of the district used to reside here. They do so no longer; and the families of public officers have almost all gone to reside at other places. Life and property have become exceedingly insecure, and attacks by gang-robbers so

* Mucka the tailor, to whom these buildings belong, is the person mentioned in the account of the death of the King, Nuseer-od Deen Hyder, and the confinement of Ghalib Jung.

frequent that no man thinks his house and family safe for a single night. Government officers are entirely occupied in the collection of revenue, and they disregard altogether the sufferings and risks to which the people of towns are exposed. The ground around the place is low, and the climate is inferior to that of Seetapoor. Salt and saltpetre are made from the soil immediately round the town.

I have mentioned that Moomtaz-od Dowla might now have been King of Oude had his father not died before his father. The Mohammedan law excludes for ever the children of any person who dies before the person to whom he or she is the next heir from all right in the inheritance. Under the operation of this law, the sons of the eldest son of the reigning King are excluded from the succession if he dies before his father, and the crown devolves on the second son, or on the brother of the King, if he leaves no other son. The sons of all the sons who die, while their father lives, are *mahjoob-ol-irs*, that is, excluded from inheritance. In the same manner, if the next brother of the King dies before him, his sons are excluded from the succession, which devolves on the third brother, and so on through all the brothers. For instance, on the death, without any recognised issue, of Nuseer-od Deen Hyder, son of Ghazee-od Deen, he was succeeded on the throne by Mahommed Allee Shah, the third brother of Ghazee-od Deen, though four sons of the second brother, Shums-od Dowla, still lived. On the death of Mahommed Allee Shah, he was succeeded by his second son, Amjud Allee Shah, though Moomtaz-od Dowla, the son of his eldest son, Asgur Allee Khan, still lived. Shums-od Dowla died before his elder brother, Ghazee-od Deen; and Asgur Allee Khan before his father, Mahommed Allee Shah: and the sons of both became, in consequence, *mahjoob-ol-irs*, excluded from succession. The same rule guides the succession among the Delhi sovereigns. This exclusion extends to all kinds of property, as well as to sovereignty.

Moomtaz-od Dowla is married to Zeenut-on Nissa, the daughter of Mulika Zumanee, one of the consorts of Nuseer-od Deen Hyder, late King of Oude; and he has, I fear, more cause to regret his union with her than his exclusion from the throne. Zeenut-on Nissa enjoys a pension of ten thousand rupees a-month, in her own right, under the guarantee of the British Government. I may here, as an episode not devoid of interest, give a brief account of her mother, who, for some years, during the reign of Nuseer-od Deen Hyder, presided over the palace at Lucknow. Before I do so I may mention that the King, Nuseer-od Deen Hyder, had been married to a grand-daughter of the Emperor of Delhi, a very beautiful young woman, of exemplary character, who still survives, and retains the respect of the royal family and people of Lucknow. Finding the Court too profligate for her, she retired into private life soon after the marriage, and has remained there ever since upon a small stipend from the King.

Mulika Zumanee, queen of the age, was a daughter of a Hindoo of the Koormee caste, who borrowed from his neighbour, Futteh Morad, the sum of sixty rupees, to purchase cloth. He soon after died, leaving a widow, and a daughter named Dolaree, then five years of age. They were both seized and confined for the debt by Futteh Morad; but, on the mother's consenting to leave her daughter in bondage for the debt, she was released. Futteh Morad's sister, Kuramut-on Nissa, adopted

Dolaree, who was a prepossessing child, and brought her up as her daughter; but finding, as she grew up, that she was too intimate with Roostum, the son by a former husband of her brother's second wife, she insisted on their being married, and they were so. Futteh Morad soon after died, and his first wife turned the second, with her first son, Roostum, and his wife, Dolaree, and the two sons which she had borne to Futteh Morad—Futteh Allee Khan and Warus Allee Khan—out of her house. They went to Futteh Morad's aunt, Bebee Mulatee, a *learned* woman, who resided as governess in the house of Nawab Mohubbet Khan, at Roostumnugger, near Lucknow, and taught his daughters to read the Koran. Finding Dolaree to be not the most faithful of wives to Roostum, she would not admit them into the Nawab's house, but she assisted them with food and raiment; and Roostum entered the service—as a groom—of a trooper in the King's cavalry, called Abas Kolee Beg. Dolaree had given birth to a boy, who was named Mahommed Allee; and she now gave birth to a daughter; but she had cohabited with a blacksmith and an elephant-driver in the neighbourhood, and it became a much "vexed question" whether the son and daughter resembled most Roostum, the blacksmith, or the elephant-driver; all, however, were agreed upon the point of Dolaree's backslidings. Mahommed Allee, *alias* Kywan Ja, was three years of age, and the daughter, *Zeenut-on Nissa*, one year and half, when some belted attendants from the palace came to Roostumnugger in search of a wet-nurse for the young prince, Moona Jan, who had been born the night before; and Bebee Mulatee, whose reputation for learning had reached the royal family, sent off Dolaree as one of the candidates for employment. Her appearance pleased the queen, the Padshah Begum, the quality of her milk was pronounced by the royal physicians to be first rate, and she was chosen as wet-nurse for the new-born prince.

Moona Jan's father (then heir-apparent to the throne of Oude) no sooner saw Dolaree than, to the astonishment of the Queen and her Court, he fell desperately in love with her, though she seemed very plain and very vulgar to all other eyes; and he could neither repose himself, nor permit anybody else in the palace to repose, till he obtained the King's and Queen's consent to his making her his wife, which he did in 1826. She soon acquired an entire ascendancy over his weak mind, and, anxious to surround herself in her exalted station by people on whom she could entirely rely, she invited the learned Bebee Mulatee and her daughter, Jumeel-on Nissa, and her son, Kasim Beg, to the palace, and placed them in high and confidential posts. She invited at the same time Futteh Allee and Warus Allee, the sons of Futteh Morad by his second wife; and persuaded the King that they were all people of high lineage, who had been reduced, by unmerited misfortunes, to accept employments so humble. All were raised to the rank of Nawabs, and placed in situations of high trust and emoluments. Kuramut-on Nissa, too, the sister of Futteh Morad, was invited; but when Dolaree's husband—the humble Roostum—ventured to approach the Court, he was seized and imprisoned in a fort in the Bangur district till the death of Nuseer-od Deen, when he was released. He came to Lucknow, but died soon after.

Soon after the death of Ghazee-od Deen had placed the heir-apparent, her husband, on the throne, 20th of October, 1827, she fortified herself still further by high alliances: and her son, Mahommed Allee, was affianced to the daughter of Rokun-od Dowla, brother of the late King; and her daughter, Zeenut-on Nissa, to Moomtaz-od Dowla, the prince of whom I am writing. These two marriages were celebrated at a cost of about thirty lacs of rupees; Dolaree was declared the first consort of the King, under the title of "Mulika Zamanee," *queen of the age*, and received an estate in land yielding six lacs of rupees a-year for pin-money. Not satisfied with this, she prevailed upon the King to declare her son, Mahommed Allee, *alias* Kywan Ja, to be his *own and eldest son*, and heir-apparent to the throne; and to demand his recognition as such from the British Government, through its representative, the Resident. His Majesty, with great solemnity, assured the Resident, on many occasions during November and December, 1827, *that Kywan Ja was his eldest son;* and told him that had he not been so, his uncle would never have consented to bestow his daughter upon him in marriage, nor should he himself have consented to expend twenty lacs of rupees in the ceremonies. The Resident told him that the universal impression at Lucknow was, that the boy was three years of age when his mother was first introduced to his Majesty. But this had no effect; and, to remove all further doubts and discussions on the subject, he wrote a letter himself to the Governor-General, earnestly protesting that Kywan Ja was his *eldest son and heir-apparent to the throne;* and as such he was sent from Lucknow to Cawnpoor to meet and escort over Lord Combermere in December, 1827.

On the birth of Moonna Jan, the then King, Ghazee-od Deen Hyder, declared to the Resident that the boy was not his grandson, and that his son, Nuseer-od Deen, pretended that he was his son merely to please his imperious mother, the Padshah Begum, and to annoy his father, with whom they were both on bad terms. Ghazee-od Deen had, however, before his death declared that he believed Moonna Jan to be his grandson.* In February, 1832, the King, Nuseer-od Deen Hyder, first through the minister, and then in person, assured the Resident that neither of the boys was his son, and requested that he would report the same to his Government, and assure the Governor-General "that both reports, as to these boys being sons of his, were false, and arose from the same cause, *bribery* and *ambition*; that Mulika Zumanee had paid many lacs of rupees to influential people about him to persuade him to call her son his, and declare him heir-apparent to the throne; and that Fazl Allee and Sookcheyn had done the same to induce others to persuade him to acknowledge Moonna Jan to be his son. But, said his Majesty, I know positively that he is not my son, and my father knew the same."

The wary minister then, to clench the matter, remarked that his Majesty had mentioned to him that he had ceased to cohabit with Moonna Jan's mother for twenty-four months before the boy was born; and the King assured the Resident that this was quite true. Hakeem Mehndee was as anxious as Aga Meer had been to keep the King estranged from his imperious mother, and the only sure way was to make him persist in repudiating the boy or postponing his claim to the succession.

* I believe that Ghazee-od Deen's first repudiation of Moonna Jan arose entirely from a desire to revenge himself upon his termagant wife, whose furious temper left him no peace. She was, from his birth, very fond of the boy; and to question his legitimacy was to wound her in her tenderest point. This was the "*raw*" which her husband established, and which his son and successor afterwards worked upon.

Mulika Zumanee's influence over the king had, however, been eclipsed, first, by Miss Walters, Mokuddera Ouleea, whose history has already been given; secondly, by the beautiful Taj Mahal; and, thirdly, by the Kuduseea Begum. She entered the palace as a waiting-woman to Mulika Zumanee, and, on the 17th of December, 1831, the King married her; and from that day till her death, on the 21st of August, 1834, she reigned supreme in the palace and in the King's affections.

On the King's paying a visit of ceremony to Mulika Zumanee one evening, he asked for water, and it was brought to him in a gold cup, on a silver tray, by the Kuduseea Begum, then one of the women in waiting. Her face was partially unveiled; and the King, after drinking, threw the last few drops from the cup over her veil in play. In return, she threw the few drops that had been spilled on the salver upon the King's robe, or vest. He pretended to be angry, and asked her, with a frown, how she could dare to besprinkle her sovereign; she replied—"When children play together there is no distinction between the prince and the peasant. The King was charmed with her half-veiled beauty and spirit, and he paid a second visit the next day, and again asked for water. He did the same as the first day, and she returned the compliment in the same way. He came a third time and asked for water, but Mulika Zumanee had become alarmed, and it was presented by another and less dangerous person. A few days after, however, the Queen was constrained to allow her fair attendant to attend the King, and receive from him formal proposals of marriage, which she accepted.

She was handsome and generous; but there was no discrimination in her bounty, and she is said to have received from the King nearly two millions of money out of the reserved treasury for pin-money alone. Of this she saved forty-four lacs of rupees. The King never touched this money, and it formed, in a separate apartment, the greater part of the seventy lacs found in his reserved treasury on his death, out of the ten krores or ten millions sterling, which he found there when he ascended the throne in 1827.

She is said to have been the only one of his wives who ever had any real affection for the King. She was haughty and imperious in her temper; and the only female, who had any influence over her, was a Mogulanee, who taught her to read and write. She assisted her mistress very diligently in spending her pin-money, and made the fortunes of sundry of her relations. Altercations between the Kuduseea Begum and the King were not uncommon; but, on the 21st of August, 1834, the King became unusually excited, and told her that he had raised her from bondage to the throne, and could as easily cast her back into the same vile condition. Her proud spirit could not brook this, and she instantly swallowed arsenic. The King relented, and every remedy was tried, but in vain. The King watched over her agonies till she was about to expire, when he fled in a frantic state and took refuge in the apartments of the race-stand, about three miles from the palace, till the funeral ceremonies were over. It is said, that in her anxiety to give birth to an heir to the throne, she got the husband, from whom she had been divorced, smuggled into her apartments in the palace in a female dress more than once; and that this was reported to the King, and became the real cause of the dispute.

The Mogulanee attendant, who had accumulated

twenty lacs of rupees, was seized and commanded to disgorge. She offered five lacs to Court favourites on condition that they saw her safely over the river Ganges into British territory. The most grave of them were commissioned to wait upon his Majesty, and entreat him most earnestly to banish her forthwith from his territories, as she was known, in the first place, to be one of the most *potent sorceresses* in India; and, in the next, to have been exceedingly attached to her late mistress: that they had strong grounds to believe that it was her intention to send his Majesty's spirit after hers, that they might be united in the next world as they had been in this. The King got angry, and said, that he had no dread of sorceresses, and would make the old lady disgorge her twenty lacs. That very night, however, in his sleep, he saw the Kuduseea Begum enter his room, approach his bed, look upon him with a countenance still more kind and bright than in life, and then return slowly with her face still towards him, and beckoning him with her hand to follow! As soon as he awoke he became greatly agitated and alarmed, and ordered the old sorceress to be sent forthwith across the Ganges to Cawnpoor. She paid her five lacs, and took off about fifteen; but what became of her afterwards I have not heard.

One of the first cases that I had to decide, after taking charge of my office, was that of a claim to five Government notes of twenty thousand rupees each, left by Sultan Mahal, one of the late King, Amjud Allee Shah's, widows. The claimants were the reigning King, and the mother, brother, and sister of the deceased widow. She was the daughter of a greengrocer; and, in February 1846, at the age of sixteen, she went to the palace with vegetables. The King saw and fell in love with her; and she forthwith became one of his wives, under the name of "*Sultan Mahal.*" In November, 1846, the King invested eighteen lacs and thirty thousand rupees in Government notes as a provision for his wives and other female relations. The notes were to be made out in their names respectively; and the interest was to be paid to them and their heirs. Of this sum, Sultan Mahal was to have one hundred thousand; and, on the 21st of November, she drew the interest, in anticipation, up to the 30th of December of that year. The five notes for twenty thousand each, in her name, were received in the Resident's Treasury on the 20th of April, 1847. On the 28th of August, she sent an application for the Notes to the Resident, but died the next day. The King, her husband, had died on the 13th February, 1847.

Nine days after, on the 6th of September, the new King, Wajid Allee Shah, sent an application to have these five notes transferred to one of his own wives; urging, that, as his father and the Sultan Mahal had both died, he alone ought to be considered as the heir. It was decided, that the mother, sister, and brother were the rightful heirs to the Sultan Mahal; and the amount was distributed among them according to Mahommedan law. The question was, however, submitted to Government at his Majesty's request; and the decision of the Resident was upheld on the ground that the notes were in the lady's name, and she had actually drawn interest on them; and, as she died intestate, they became the property of her heirs.

By a deed of engagement with the British Government, dated the 1st of March, 1829, the King contributed to the five per cent. loan the sum of sixty-two lacs and forty thousand rupees, the interest of which, at five per cent., our Government pledged itself to pay, in perpetuity, to four females of the King's family. To Mulika Zumanee, ten thousand a-month; to her daughter, Zeenut-on Nissa, four thousand; to Mokuddera Ouleea (Miss Walters), six thousand; and to Taj Mahal, six thousand: total, twenty-six thousand rupees a-month. On the death of Mulika Zumanee, which took place on the 22nd December, 1843, her daughter succeeded to her pension of six thousand a-month.

The other portion of her pension—four thousand rupees a-month—went to her grandson, Wuzeer Mirza, the son of Kywan Ja, who had died on the 16th of May, 1838, before his mother.* Of this four thousand a-month, one thousand are given to Zeenut-on Nissa for the boy's subsistence and education, and three thousand a-month are invested in Government securities, to be paid to him when he comes of age. But, besides the six thousand rupees a-month which she inherits from her mother, Zeenut-on Nissa enjoys the pension of four thousand rupees a-month, which was assigned to her by the King in the same deed; so that she now draws eleven thousand rupees a-month, independent of her husband's income.† By this deed the stipends are to descend to the heirs of the pensioners, if they have any; and if they have none, they can bequeath their pensions to whom they please. Should they have no heirs, and leave no will, the stipends are to go to the moojtahids and moojawurs, or presiding priests of the shrine of kurbala, in Turkish Arabia, for distribution among the needy pilgrims.

* Wuzeer Mirza is not the son of Rokun-od Dowla's daughter. Kywan Ja's marriage with that lady was never consummated.

† She takes after her mother, and makes her worthy husband very miserable. She is ill-tempered, haughty, and profligate.

An European lady, who visited the zunana of the King, Nuseer-od Deen Hyder, on the anniversary of his coronation, on the 18th of October, 1828, writes thus to a female friend:—"But the present King's wives were superbly dressed, and looked like creatures of the Arabian Tales. Indeed, one (Taj Mahal) was so beautiful, that I could think of nothing but Lalla Rookh in her bridal attire. I never saw any one so lovely, either black or white. Her features were perfect, and such eyes and eye-lashes I never beheld before. She is the favourite Queen at present, and has only been married a month or two, her age, about fourteen; and such a little creature, with the smallest hands and feet, and the most timid, modest look imaginable. You would have been charmed with her, she was so graceful and fawn-like. Her dress was of gold and scarlet brocade, and her hair was literally strewed with pearls, which hung down upon her neck in long single strings, terminating in large pearls, which mixed with and hung as low as her hair, which was curled on each side her head in long ringlets, like Charles the Second's beauties. On her forehead she wore a small gold circlet, from which depended and hung, half way down, large pearls interspersed with emeralds. Above this was a paradise plume, from which strings of pearls were carried over the head, as we turn our hair. Her earrings were immense gold rings, with pearls and emeralds suspended all round in large strings, the pearls increasing in size. She had a nose-ring also with large round pearls and emeralds; and her necklaces, &c., were too numerous to be described. She wore long sleeves, open at the elbow; and her dress was a full petticoat with a tight body attached, and open only at the throat. She had several persons to bear her train when she walked; and her women stood behind her couch to arrange her head-dress, when, in moving, her pearls got entangled in the immense robe of scarlet and gold she had thrown around her. This beautiful creature is the envy of all the other wives, and the favourite at present of both the King and his mother, both of whom have given her titles — See *Mrs. Park's Wandering*, vol. i., page 87. Taj Mahal still lives and enjoys a pension of six thousand rupees a-month, under the guarantee of the British Government. She became very profligate after the King's death; and after she had given birth to one child, it was deemed necessary to place a guard over her to prevent her dishonouring the memory of the King, her husband, any further by giving birth to more.

Of Miss Walters, alias Mokuddera Ouleea, the same lady writes:—"The other newly-made Queen is nearly European, but not a whit fairer than Taj Mahal. She is, in my opinion, plain; but she is considered by the native ladies very handsome; and she was the King's favourite before he saw Taj Mahal. She was more splendidly dressed than even Taj Mahal. Her head-dress was a coronet of diamonds, with a fine crescent and plume of the same. She is the daughter of a European merchant, and is accomplished for an inhabitant of a zunana, as she writes and speaks Persian fluently, as well as Hindoostanee; and it is said that she is teaching the King English, though when we spoke to her in English, she said she had forgotten it, and could not reply. She was, I fancy, afraid of the Queen Dowager, as she evidently understood us; and when asked if she liked being in the zunana, she shook her head and looked quite melancholy. Jealousy of the new favourite, however, appeared to be the cause of her discontent, as, though they sat on the same couch, they never addressed each other."

Of Mulika Zumanee, the same lady says:—"The mother of the King's children, Mulika Zumanee, did not visit us at the Queen Dowager's; but we went to see her at her own palace. She is, after all, the person of the most political consequence, being the mother of the heir-apparent; and she has great power over her royal husband, whose ears she boxes occasionally."

CHAPTER IV.

Nuseer-od Deen Hyder's death—His repudiation of his son, Moonna Jan, leads to the succession of his uncle, Nuseer-od Dowlah—Contest for the succession between these two persons—The Resident supports the uncle; and the Padshah Begum supports the son—The ministers supposed to have poisoned the king—Made to disgorge their ill-gotten wealth by his successor—Obligations of the treaty of 1801, by which Oude was divided into two equal shares—One transferred to the British Government, one reserved by Oude—Estimated value of each at the time of treaty—Present value of each—The sovereign often warned that unless he governs as he ought, the British Government cannot support him, but must interpose and take the administration upon itself—All such warnings have been utterly disregarded—No security to life or property in any part of Oude—Fifty years of experience have proved that we cannot make the Government of Oude fulfil its duties to its people—The alternative left appears to be to take the management upon ourselves, and give the surplus revenue to the sovereign and royal family of Oude—Probable effects of such a change on the feelings and interests of the people of Oude.

When in February, 1832, the King, Nuseer-od Deen Hyder, assured the Resident that Moonna Jan was not his son, Lord William Bentinck was Governor-General of India. A more thoroughly honest man never, I believe, presided over the government of any country. The question of right to succession was long maturely and most anxiously considered, after these repeated and formal repudiations on the part of the King, Nuseer-od Deen Hyder; and Government would willingly have deferred a final decision on so important a question longer, but it was deemed unsafe any longer from the debauched habits of the King, the chance of his sudden death, and the risk of a tumult in such a city, to leave the representative of the paramount power unprepared to proclaim its will in favour of the rightful heir, the moment that a demise took place. Under these considerations, instructions were sent to the Resident, on the 15th of December, 1832, in case of the King's death without a son, or pregnant consort, to declare the eldest surviving brother of the late King, Ghazee-od Deen Hyder, heir to the throne, and have him placed upon it. According to the law already noticed (which applies as well to sovereignty as to property) the sons of Shums-od Dowlah, the second son of Saadut Allee Khan, who had died shortly before his eldest and reigning brother, Ghazee-od Deen, were excluded from all claims to the succession, and the right devolved upon the third son of Saadut Allee, Nuseer-od Dowlah. Ghazee-od Deen had only one son, the reigning sovereign, Nuseer-od Deen Hyder.

This prince had impaired his constitution by drinking and other vicious indulgences, in which he had been encouraged in early life by his designing or inconsiderate adoptive mother, the Padshah Begum; but for some time before his death, he used frequently to declare to his most intimate companions that he felt sure he should die of poison, and that at no distant period. He for some time before his death had a small well in the palace, over which he kept his own lock and key; and he kept the same over the jar, in which he drew the water from it for his own drinking. The keys were suspended by a gold chain around his neck. The persons who gave him his drink, except when taking it out of English sealed bottles, were two sisters, Dhuneea and Dulwee. The latter and youngest is now the wife of Wasee Allee Khan. The eldest, Dhuneea, still resides at Lucknow. The general impression at Lucknow and over all Oude was, that the British Government would take upon itself the management of the country on the death, without issue, of Nuseer-od Deen Hyder; and the King himself latterly seemed rather pleased than otherwise at the thought that he should be the last of the Oude kings. He had repudiated his own son, and was unwilling that any other member of the family should fill his place. The minister and the other public officers and Court favourites, who had made large fortunes, wished it, as it was understood by some, that by such a measure they would be secured from all scrutiny into their accounts, and enabled to keep securely all that they had accumulated.

About half-past eleven, on the night of the 7th July, 1837, the Durbar Wakeel, Gholam Yaheea,* came to the Resident and reported that the King had been taken suddenly ill, and appeared to be either dead or in a dying state, from the symptoms described to him by his Majesty's attendants. The Resident, Colonel Low, ordered his two Assistants, Captains Paton and Shakespear, the Head Moonshee and Head Clerk, to be in attendance, and wrote to request the Brigadier, commanding the troops in Oude, to hold one thousand men in readiness to march to the Residency at a moment's notice. The Residency is situated in the city near the Furra Buksh Palace, in which the King resided. The Resident intended that five companies of this force should be sent in advance of the main body and guns, for the purpose of placing sentries over the palace gates, treasuries, and other places containing valuables within the walls. But

* Gholam Yaheea Khan was the maternal uncle of Shurf-od Dowlah, who was, afterwards, some time minister under Mahommed Allee Shah.

this intention was not unfortunately made known to the Brigadier. Captain Magness, who commanded a corps of infantry with six guns, and a squadron of horse, had been ordered by the minister at half-past eight o'clock, to proceed with them to a place near the southern entrance of the palace, and there to wait for further instructions, and he did so. This was three hours before the minister made any report to the Resident of the King's illness, and Captain Magness was told by the people in attendance that the King was either dead or dying.

Having given these orders, the Resident proceeded to the palace, attended by Captain Paton, the first Assistant, and Dr. Stevenson, the Residency Surgeon. They found the King lying dead upon his bed, but his body was still warm, and Dr. Stevenson opened a vein in one arm. Blood flowed freely from it, but no other sign of life could be discovered. His features were placid and betrayed no sign of his having suffered any pain; and the servants in attendance declared that the only sign of suffering they had heard or seen was a slight shriek, to which the King gave utterance before he expired; that after that shriek he neither moved, spoke, nor showed any sign whatever of life. His Majesty had been unwell for three weeks, but no one had any apprehension of danger from his symptoms. He had called for some sherbet a short time before his death, and it was given to him by Dhuneea, the eldest of the two sisters.

The Resident took with him a guard of sipahees from his escort, and Captain Paton distributed them as double sentries at the inner doors of the palace, and outside the chief buildings and store-rooms, with orders to allow no one but the ministers and treasurers to pass. Captain Magness had placed one sentry before at each of these places, and he now added a second, making a party of four sipahees at each post. Captain Paton at the same time, in conjunction with the officers of the Court, placed seals on all the jewels and other valuables belonging to the King and his establishments; and as the night was very dark, placed torch-bearers at all places where they appeared to be required.

Having made these arrangements the Resident returned with Dr. Stevenson to the Residency, leaving Captain Paton at the palace; and wrote to the Brigadier to request that he would send off the five companies in advance to the palace direct, and bring down all his disposable troops, including artillery, to the city. The distance from the palace to the cantonments, round by the old stone bridge, was about four miles and half. The iron bridge, which shortens the distance by a mile and half, had not then been thrown over the Goomtee river, which flows between them. The Resident then had drawn up, for the consent of the new king, a Persian paper, declaring that he was prepared to sign any new treaty for the better government of the country that the British Government might think proper to propose to him.

It was now one o'clock in the morning of the 8th of July, and Captain Shakespear, attended by the Meer Moonshee, Iltufat Hoseyn, and the Durbar Wakeel, proceeded to the house of the new sovereign, Nuseer-od Dowlah, who then resided where the present King now resides, a distance of about a mile from the Residency. The visit was altogether unexpected; and, as the new sovereign had been for some time ill, some delay took place in arranging for the reception of the mission. After explaining the object of his visit, Captain Shakespear presented the paper, which the King perused with great attention, and then signed without hesitation. Captain Shakespear returned with it to the Resident, who repaired again to the palace, and sent Captain Paton, the first Assistant, to the Residency, to proceed thence with Captain Shakespear and the Durbar Wakeel, to the house of the new sovereign, and escort him to the palace, where he would be in readiness to receive him. He arrived about three o'clock in the morning, and being infirm from age, and exceedingly reduced from recent illness, he was, after a short conversation with the Resident, left in a small adjoining room, to repose for a few hours preparatory to his being placed on the throne and crowned in due form. His eldest surviving son, afterwards Amjud Allee Shah, his sons, the present King, Wajid Allee Shah, and Mirza Jawad Khan, the King's foster brother, Hummeed-od Dowlah, and his confidential servant, Rufeek-od Dowla, were left in the room with him; and the Resident and his Assistants sat in the verandah facing the river Goomtee, which flows under the walls, conversing on the ceremonies to be observed at the approaching coronation, and the persons to be invited to assist at it, when they were suddenly interrupted by the intelligence that the Padshah Begum, the adoptive mother of the late King, with a large armed force, and the young pretender, Moonna Jan, were coming on to seize upon the throne, and might soon be expected at the principal entrance to the palace to the north-west.

When the Resident was about to proceed to the palace, the first time about midnight, he was assured by the minister, Roshun-od Dowla, that every possible precaution had been taken by him to prevent the Padshah Begum from attempting any such enterprise, or from leaving her residence with the young pretender; that he had placed strong bodies of troops in every street or road by which she could come. But, to make more sure, and prevent her leaving her residence at the Almas gardens, five miles from the palace, the Resident sent off one of his chobdars, Khoda Buksh, with two troopers and a verbal message, enjoining her to remain quietly at her palace. These men found her with her equipage in the midst of a large mass of armed followers, ready to set out for the palace. They delivered their message from the Resident, but were sent back with her Wakeel, Mirza Allee, to request that she might be permitted to look upon the dead body of the late King, since she had not been permitted to see him for so long a period before his death. But they reached the Resident with this message, only ten minutes before the Begum's troops were thundering for admittance at the gate. The Resident gave the chobdar a note for the officer in command of the five companies, supposed to be in advance on their way down from cantonments; but before he could get with this note five hundred yards from the palace, he met the Begum and her disorderly band filling the road and pressing on as fast as they could. Unable to proceed, he returned to the palace with all haste, and gave the Resident the first notice of their near approach. Captain Magness had placed two of his six guns at each of the three entrances to the south and west, but was now ordered to collect all, and proceed to the north-western entrance, towards which the Begum was advancing. Before he could get to that entrance she had passed in, and he returned to the south-western entrance for further orders.

On passing the mausoleum of Asuf-od Dowlah, where the Kotwal or head police officer of the city resided, she summoned him, with all his available police, to attend his sovereign to the throne of his ancestors. He promised obedience, but, with all his police, stood aloof, thinking that her side might not be the safe one to take in such an emergency. A little further on she passed Hussun Bagh, the residence of the chief consort of the late King and niece of the emperor of Delhi, and summoned and brought her on, to give some countenance to her audacious enterprise. The Resident admonished the minister for his negligence and falsehood in the assurance he had given him; and directed Rajah Bukhtawur Sing, with his squadron of one hundred and fifty horse, and Mozuffer-od Dowlah, the father of Ajum-od Dowlah, and Khadim Hoseyn, the son-in-law of Sobhan Allee Khan, the deputy-minister, with all the armed men they could muster, to arrest the progress of the pretender; but nothing whatever was done, and the excited mass came on, and augmented as it came in noise and numbers. All whom the Resident sent to check them, out of fear or favour, avoided collision, and sought safety either in their homes or among the pretender's bands.

Captain Paton, as soon as he heard the pretender's men approach, rushed to the gate to the north-west, towards which the throng was approaching rapidly. He had only four belted attendants with him, and the gate was guarded only by a small party of useless sipahees, under the control of three or four black slaves. By the time he had roused the sleepy guard and closed the gates, the pretender's armed mass came up, and with foul abuse, imprecations, and with threats of instant death to all who opposed them, demanded admittance. Captain Paton told them, that the Resident had been directed by the British Government to place Nuseer-od Dowlah, the uncle of the late King, on the throne as the rightful heir;

that he was now in the palace, and all who opposed him would be treated as rebels; that the gates were all closed by order of the Resident, and all who attempted to force them would be put to death. All was in vain. They told him with fury that the Padshah Begum, and the son of the late King, and rightful heir to the throne, were among them, and must be instantly admitted. Captain Paton despatched a messenger to the Resident to say, that he could hold the gate no longer without troops: but before he could get a reply, the insurgents brought up an elephant to force in the gate with his head. The first failed in the attempt, and drew back with a frightful roar. A second, urged on by a furious driver, broke in the gate, one-half fell with a crash to the ground, and the elephant plunged in after it. Captain Paton was standing with his back against this half, and must have been killed; but Mukun, one of his chuprassies, seeing the gate giving way, caught him by the arm and dragged him behind the other half. The other three chuprassies ran off in a fright and hid themselves. Two of them were Surubdawun Sing and Juggurnath, two brothers, who will be mentioned elsewhere in this diary.*

The furious and confused mass rushed in through the half-opened gate, and beat Captain Paton to the ground with their bludgeons, the hilts of their swords, and the butt-ends of their muskets. Mukun, chuprassie, his only remaining attendant, was beaten down at the same time and severely bruised, but he soon got up, covered with blood, made his way out through the crowd, and ran to meet the five companies of the 35th Regiment, then not far distant, under Colonel Monteath. As soon as he heard from Mukun the state in which he had left his

* See Juggurnath chuprassie in Chapter V., Vol. II.

master, he sent on a party of thirty sipahees under Captain Cowley, with orders to make all possible haste to the rescue. They arrived in time to save his life from the fury of the assailants, but found him insensible from his wounds.

In a few minutes every court-yard within the palace walls was filled with the armed and disorderly mass. The Resident, Captain Shakespear, and their few attendants, tried to stop them by every impediment they could throw in their way, but in vain. The assailants rushed past or over them, brandishing their swords and firelocks, with loud shoutings and flaming torches, and soon filled all the apartments of the palace, save those occupied by the ladies and their female attendants, and the dead body of the late King. The Resident and his Assistant, and the Meer Moonshee, were soon separated from the new sovereign and his small party, who lay for some time concealed in the small room in which he had been left to repose, while they were confined to the northern verandah overlooking the river, and the long room leading into it. The armed and furious throng filled all the other rooms of the palace, the court-yard, eighty yards long, leading to the baraduree (or summer-house) and all the four great halls of that building, in one of which the throne stood.

The Resident felt that he was helpless in his present position, and unable to do anything whatever to prevent the temporary triumph of the insurgents, and the consequent tumult, pillage, and loss of life that must follow; and that it would be better to try any change than to remain in that helpless state. He thought that he might, if he could once reach the Begum, be able to persuade her of the impossibility of her ultimately succeeding in her attempt to keep the pretender on the throne; and if not, that it would be of advantage to get so much nearer to the place where the British troops must soon arrive, and be drawn up in a garden to the south of the baraduree, and to gain time for their arrival by a personal and open conference with the Begum, during which he thought her followers would not be likely to proceed to violence against his person, and those of his attendants. He therefore persuaded one of the rebel sentries placed over him to apprize the Begum that he wished to speak to her. She sent to him Mirza Allee, one of her Wakeels; and with him Captain Shakespear, and the Meer Moonshee, he forced his way through the dense crowd, and got safely into the baraduree.

They found all the four halls, small apartments, and verandahs, leading into them, filled with armed men in a state of great excitement, and in the act of placing the pretender, Moonna Jan, on the throne. The Begum sat in a covered palankeen at the foot of the throne; and as the Resident entered, the band struck up "*God save the King*," answered by a salute of blunderbusses within, and a double royal salute from the guns in the "*julloo-knana*," or northern court-yard of the palace through which the Begun had passed in. Other-guns, which had been collected in the confusion to salute somebody (though those who commanded and served them knew not whom), continued the salute through the streets without. A party of dancing-girls, belonging to the late King, or brought up by the Begum, began to dance and sing as loud as they could at the end of the long hall in front of the throne, at the same time that the crowd within and without shouted their congratulations at the top of their voices, and every man who had a sword, spear, musket, or matchlock, flourished it in the air amidst a thousand torches. A scene more strange and wild it would be difficult to conceive.

In the midst of all this the Resident and his Assistants remained cool under all kinds of foul abuse and threats from a multitude so excited, that they seemed more like demons than human beings, and resolved to force them to commit some act or make use of some expression that might seem to justify their murder. They fired muskets close to their ears, pointed others loaded and cocked close to their breasts and faces, flourished swords close to their noses, called them all kinds of opprobrious names, but all in vain. The Resident, in the midst of all this confusion, pointed out to the Begum the impossibility of her ultimately succeeding in her attempt to secure the throne for the pretender, since he was acting under the orders of his Government, who had declared the right to be another's; and if he and all his Assistants were killed, his Government would soon send others to carry out their orders. "I am," she said, "in my right place, and so is the young King, my grandson, and so are you. Why do you talk to me or to anybody else of leaving the throne and the baraduree?" But some of her furious followers, afraid that she might yield, seized him by his neckcloth, dragged him towards the throne, on which the boy sat, and commanded him to present his offerings of congratulation on the threat of instant death. They had, they said, placed him on the throne of his ancestors by order of the Begum, and would maintain him there. Had he or either of his Assistants lost their temper or presence of mind, and attempted to resent any of the affronts offered to them, they must have been all instantly put to death, and a general massacre of all their supposed adherents, and the pillage of the palace and city, would have followed.

The Begum's Wakeel, Mirza Allee, seeing the life of

the Resident and those of his Assistants and attendants in such imminent peril, since he so resolutely refused to give any sign whatever of recognition to the pretender, and aware of the consequences that would inevitably follow their murder, seized him by the arm, and in a loud voice shouted out that it was the Begum's order that he should conduct him out into the garden to the south. He pushed on with him through the crowd, followed by all his small party, and with great difficulty and danger they at last reached the garden, where Colonel Monteath had just brought in and drawn up his five companies in a line facing the baraduree. Finding the entrance to the north-west occupied by the Begum's party, Colonel Monteath marched along the street to the west of the palace, and entered the baraduree garden by the south-west gate. As the Resident went out, Colonel Roberts, who commanded a brigade in the Oude service, went in, and presented to the pretender his offering of gold mohurs, and then went off and hid himself, to wait the result of the contest. Captain Magness drew up his men and guns on the left of Colonel Monteath's, and was told to prepare for action. He told the Resident that he did not feel quite sure of his men in such a crisis, and the line of British sipahees was made to cover his rear, to secure them. The King and minister had commanded him to act precisely as directed by the Resident, and he himself knew this to be his only safe course, but the hearts of his men were with Moonna Jan and the Begum.

The Begum, as soon as the Resident left her, deeming all safe, went over to the female apartments, where her adopted son, the late king, lay dead; and after gazing for a minute upon his corpse, returned to the foot of the throne, on which the pretender had now been seated for more than three hours. It was manifest that nothing but force could now remove the boy and his supporters, but the Begum tried to gain more time in the hope of support from a popular insurrection from without, which might take off the British troops from the garden; and she sent evasive messages to the Resident by her wakeels, urging him to come once more to her, since it was impossible for her to make her way to him without danger of collision between the troops of the two States. He refused to put himself again in her power, and commanded her to come down with the boy to him and surrender; and promised that if she did so, and directed all her armed followers to quit the palace and city of Lucknow, all that had passed should be forgiven, and the large pension of fifteen thousand rupees a-month, promised by the late King, secured to her for life. All was in vain, and the Begum was gaining her object. Robberies of State property in the eastern and more retired parts of the palace-buildings had commenced. Gold, jewels, shawls, &c., to a large amount were being carried off. Much of such property lay about in places not guarded by Captain Paton in the morning, or known to the minister, or other respectable servants of the State, all holding out temptation to pillage. Acts of plunder and ill-treatment to unoffending and respectable persons in the city were every moment reported, and six or eight houses had been already pillaged, and attempts had been made on others by small parties, who were every moment increasing in numbers and ferocity.

Several parties of the King's troops had openly deserted their posts and joined the pretender's followers in the baraduree, and dense masses of armed men were crowding in upon the British troops, whose officer became anxious, and urged the Resident to action, lest they should no longer have room to use their arms. At one time these armed crowds got within two yards of the British front; and on Colonel Monteath's telling them to retire a few paces and leave him a clear front, they did so in a sullen and insolent manner, and one of them actually attempted to seize one of the sipahees by his whiskers, and an affray was with difficulty prevented.

Mostufa Khan, Kundaharee, who had command of a regiment of a thousand horse in the late King's service, was with many others commanded by the Begum to attend the young King on the throne; and he did so some time after Brigadier Johnstone reached the garden, in front of the baraduree, though he knew that Nuseer-od Dowlah had been declared the rightful heir to the throne, and was actually in the palace. He said that "he was the servant of the throne; that the young King was actually seated upon it, and that he would support him there, happen what might." He presented his offerings of gold to the young King, and was forthwith appointed to supersede all the other wakeels in the Begum's negotiations with the Resident. He merely repeated what the other wakeels had said, urging the Resident to go up to the Begum, since she could not come down to him. The Resident repeated to him what he had told the Begum herself, and taking out his watch, told him that unless his orders were obeyed in less than one-quarter of an hour, the guns should open upon the throne-room; that when once they opened, neither she nor her followers could expect favour, or even mercy; and unless he, Mostapha Khan, separated himself from her party, he should be hung as a traitor if taken alive.

Owing to the height of some houses and walls about the left part of the position of the British troops, the guns could not be conveniently brought to bear upon the south-western corner of the baraduree and throne-room, and two of the guns had to be taken round by a road one-third of a mile, to be placed in a better position. On seeing this the crowd shouted out, "The cravens are already running away!" and became more insolent and furious than ever.

The minister and Durbar Wakeel had been swept away by the crowd, who rushed into the palace, and separated from the Resident and his party, and as they passed through the balcony overlooking the river, the wakeel threw off his turban, and leaped over from a height of about twenty feet. The ground was soft, but he sprained both his ankles. He was taken up by some boatmen, who had put-to near the bank, and concealed in their boat till the affair was over. The new sovereign remained still unnoticed, and apparently unknown, having long led a secluded life; but his son, grandsons, and the rest of his attendants were at last discovered, very roughly treated by the insurgents, and would, it is said, have been put to death, had not Rajah Bukhtawur Sing and some others, who thought it safe to be on friendly terms with the ruffians, persuaded them that they would be useful hostages in case of a reverse. The minister had had all his clothes, save his trousers, torn from him, and his arms and legs pinioned preparatory to execution, and the princes had been treated with little more ceremony. All had given themselves up for lost.

The Begum remained firm to her purpose, her hopes from without increasing with the increasing noise, tumult, and reports of pillage in the city. The quarter of an hour had passed, and the Resident, turning to the Brigadier, told him, that the work was now in his hands, just an hour and twenty minutes after he had brought his troops into the garden. The guns from the British, and Captain Magness' parks opened at the same instant upon the throne-room and the other halls of the baraduree with grape; and after six or seven rounds, a party of the 35th Regiment, under Major Marshall, was ordered to storm the halls. With muskets loaded and bayonets fixed they rushed first through a narrow covered passage; then up a steep flight of steps, and then into the throne-room, firing upon the affrighted crowd as they advanced, and following them up with the bayonet as they rushed out over the two flights of steps on the north side, and through the court-yard which separates the baraduree from the palace. Other parties of sipahees ascended at the same time over ladders collected at the suggestion of Doctor Stevenson, and placed on the southern front of the baraduree; and the halls were soon cleared of the insurgents, who left from forty to fifty men killed and wounded on the floors of the four halls.* In this assault Mostufa Khan, Kundaharee, was killed. Moonna Jan was found concealed in a small recess under the throne, and the Begum in a small adjoining room, to which she had been carried as soon as the guns opened. They were taken into custody, and sent to the Residency, with Imam Buksh, a bihishtee, or water-carrier, a notorious villain, who had been her chief instigator in all this affair, and appointed Commander-in-Chief to the young King. Many who had been wounded got out of the halls, and some even reached their homes, but the killed and wounded are

* As they entered the hall at the end opposite the throne, they saw their own figures reflected in the large mirror, which stands behind the throne; and, taking them to be their enemy preparing to charge, they poured their first volley into the mirror, by which many lives were saved at the expense of the glass.

supposed to have amounted altogether to about one hundred and twenty. The Begum and the boy were accommodated in the Residency, and their *Commander-in-Chief* was made over to the King's Courts for trial. He is still in prison at Lucknow. No one was killed on our side, but three or four of our sipahees were wounded in the assault.

The Delhi princess, the chief consort of the deceased King, a modest, beautiful, and amiable young woman, who had been forced to join the Begum, in order to give some countenance to the daring enterprise, was, as soon as the guns opened, carried by her two female attendants in her litter to a small side-room, facing the palace at the east end of the throne-room. One of these females had her arm shattered by grape shot, but the other tied some clothes together, and let the princess and her wounded attendant down from a height of about twenty-four feet into a court-yard, whence they were conveyed to her palace by some of her attendants, and all three escaped. The sipahees occupied both of the flights of steps in the northern face of the baraduree. She was afraid to trust herself to them, and saw no other way of escape than that described.

It was nine o'clock before the palace could be cleared of the insurgents; and the Resident was very anxious that the new Sovereign should be crowned, as soon and as publicly as possible, in order to restore tranquillity to the city, which had become greatly disturbed from the number of loose and desperate characters that always abound in it, and are at all times ready to make the most of any tumult that may arise from whatever cause. The new Sovereign had become greatly agitated and alarmed at the danger to which he and his family had been so long exposed, and at the fearful scene which they witnessed at the close; and the Resident exerted himself to soothe and prepare him for the long and tedious ceremonies of the coronation, while the killed and wounded were being removed and the throne-room and the other halls of the baraduree cleaned out and properly arranged and furnished. When all was ready the Resident conducted him from the palace through the court-yard to the baraduree, accompanied by the brigadier and all the principal officers of the British force and the Court, seated him on the throne, placed the crown on his head, under a royal salute, repeated from every battery in the city, and proclaimed him King of Oude, in presence of all the aristocracy and principal persons of Lucknow, who had flocked to the place on hearing that the danger had passed away.

From the time that the Resident discovered that the King was dead, till the arrival of the five companies under Colonel Monteath, the whole of the British force in this vast city, containing a population of nearly a million persons, amounted to only two companies and a half of sipahees under native officers. One of the companies guarded the Resident's Treasury, one constituted the honorary guard of the Resident, and the half company guarded the gaol. A part of the honorary guard, with as many sipahees as could be safely spared from the Treasury and gaol, were taken by Captain Paton to the palace, and distributed as already mentioned. They all stood nobly to their posts during the long and trying scene, and no attempt was made to concentrate them for the purpose of arresting the tumultuous advance of the Begum's forces. Collectively they would have been too few for the purpose, and it was deemed unsafe to remove them from their respective charges at such a time. The Resident relied upon the minister's repeated assurances that he had taken all necessary precautions to prevent her approach; upon the two companies, called the Khas companies, under the command of Mujd-od Dowlah; and the squadron of one hundred and fifty horse, under Rajah Bukhtawur Sing, whom he had himself ordered to guard the passage by which they entered. Of all these men not one was employed for the purpose. They and their Commanders all stood aloof, and left the British soldiers to their fate.

The minister was a fool, under the tutelage of his deputy, Sobhan Allee Khan, a great knave, who disappeared as soon as he heard that the Begum was approaching with his son-in-law, Khadim Hoseyn. Mozuffer Allee Khan, a person in high office and confidence under the late King, did the same. The minister and the Durbar Wakeel were the only officers of the State of Oude who stood by the new King and the British Resident. The minister afterwards declared that a strong detachment of troops had been placed outside the gate through which the Begum ultimately forced her way, as well as at the other passages leading to the palace and baraduree; and Captain Shakespear, on his way to the new Sovereign, ascertained that guards had actually been posted outside all the other gates leading to the palace and baraduree. From this, the supineness and seeming apathy of many of the palace guards and servants, and the perversion of the orders sent by him before and during the tumult, the minister concluded that there must have been many about him interested in promoting the enterprise of the Begum; and that the approach to the gate through which she forced her way must have been purposely left unguarded. There is now little doubt that from the time that it became known, that the contest was between Moonna Jan and Nuseer-od Dowlah, a person but little known except as a prudent and parsimonious old man, a large portion not only of the civil and military establishments, but of the population of the city, felt anxious for the success of the Begum's enterprise; for both had, under the harsh treatment of the last two sovereigns, become objects of sympathy.

A good many of the members of the royal family, who were brought up from childhood with the deceased King, Nuseer-od Deen Hyder, and near his person to the last, declare that Moonna Jan was his son; but that the King was ashamed and afraid to acknowledge him after he had so frequently and so formally declared to the British Government that he was not his son, and that he had ceased to cohabit with the boy's mother for two years before his birth. But all such persons admit that Moonna Jan was a boy of ungovernable temper, and the worst possible dispositions; and that he must soon have forfeited the crown by his cruelty, bigotry, and injustice, had he been placed upon it by the British Government. I saw him in January 1838, at Chunar, and a more unpromising boy I have rarely seen.

The ministry dreaded being called to account for their malversations as much from the Begum, on account of their successful efforts to keep the King alienated from her and his son, as from Nuseer-od Dowlah, on account of his parsimony, prudence, and great experience in business during the reign of his able father, Saadut Allee Khan. But they would have a better chance of escape from the Begum and the boy than from the vigilant old man, who afterwards made them all disgorge their ill-gotten wealth; and, in consequence, they made no effort to obstruct her enterprise. The military and civil establishments were all in favour of the boy, who would probably be as regardless of their number and discipline as his father had been, while the old man would assuredly reduce the one, and endeavour, by rigorous measures, to improve the other. Hardly any one at Lucknow at present doubts that the minister and his associates caused the King to be poisoned, and employed Duljeet and the two sisters, Dhunneea and Dulwee, for the purpose, in expectation that the British Government would take upon itself the Oude administration, as the only possible means of improving it.

The respectable and peaceable portion of the city, though their sympathies were with the boy, had too much in property, and the honour of their families, at stake to aid in any movement in his favour, since it would involve a tumult, and for a time, at least, insure the supremacy of the mob. Their security and that of their families depended upon the success of the British troops; and they were all prepared to acquiesce in any cause which the British Government might adopt for the sake of order. They would rather that it should adopt that of the Begum and the boy than that of Nuseer-od Dowlah; but in either case were resolved to remain neuter, and let the representative of the British Government take his own course.

It is a fact not unworthy of remark, that more than three millions sterling, or three crores of rupees, in our Government securities, are held by persons who reside and spend the interest arising from them in the city of Lucknow; and that the fall in their value in exchange during the times that we have been engaged in our most serious wars has been less in Lucknow than in Calcutta, the capital of British India; so much greater assurance do the people feel of our resources being always equal to our exigencies. At such times the merchants of Lucknow commission their agents in Calcutta to purchase up Government securities at the rate to which they fall in Calcutta, for sale at Lucknow, where they seldom fall at all. About three crores and half of rupees, or three millions and half sterling, have been at different times contributed to our loans by the sovereigns of Oude as a provision for the different members of their respective families and dependents; and the interest is now paid to them and their descendants, at the rates which prevailed at the time of the several loans (four, five, and six per cent.) to the amount of fourteen lacs thirty-five thousand and four hundred and ten rupees a-year.

The Begum's haughty and violent temper, and inveterate disposition to meddle in public affairs, were the real cause of her continual disquietude and ultimate disgrace and ruin. The minister of the day dreaded the ascendancy of so imperious and furious a character, should she ever become reconciled to the King. During the whole reign of Ghazee-od Deen, her husband, from the 12th of July 1814, to the 20th of October 1827, her own frequent ebullitions, which often disfigured the King's robes and vests, and left even the hair on his head and chin unsafe, and Aga Meer's sagacious suggestions, satisfied him that his own personal safety and peace of mind, and the welfare of the State, depended upon his keeping as much as possible aloof from her. He was fond of his son, Nuseer-od Deen Hyder, but during his minority he always took the part of his adoptive mother, the Padshah Begum; and, in consequence, remained almost as much as she was alienated from the King, his father. His natural mother died soon after his birth; and people suspected that the Padshah Begum had her put to death that she might have no rival in his affections; and she had an entire ascendancy over him, acquired by every species of enervating indulgences; and he remained all his life utterly without character, ignorant of the rudiments of public affairs, and altogether incapable of taking any useful part in them.

She retained this ascendancy over him for some time after he became King, first from habit and affection, and latterly from the fears with which she continued to inspire him, that she could, by her disclosures, whenever she pleased, prevail upon the British Government to set him aside in favour of some other member of the royal family, as the Buhoo Begum of Fyzabad had set aside Wuzeer Allee. She made him dismiss his father's minister, Aga Meer, with disgrace, and confer the seals on Fuzl Allee, the nephew of her favourite waiting-woman, Fyzon Nissa; but when the shrewd and sagacious Hakeem Mehndee became minister three years after, he soon persuaded the young King, that all fears of his adoptive mother's disclosures or wishes were idle, and that nothing which she could do or say would induce the British Government to disturb his possession of the sovereignty of Oude. He is said to have been the first person who ventured to hint to him the murder of his natural mother by the Padshah Begum; and he was, or pretended to be, violently shocked and grieved. He then built a splendid tomb or cenotaph for her; and endowed it with the means for maintaining pious men to read the Koran in it, and attendants of all kinds to keep it in a condition suitable for the mother of a King. He shuddered, or pretended to shudder, at the mention of the name of the Padshah Begum, as the most atrocious of murderesses. The minister of the day always made it a point to bring the reigning favourite of the seraglio over to his views, by giving her a due share of the profits and patronage of his office; and it was for this reason, that the high-born chief consort, whose influence over the King could not be so purchased, was soon made to retire from the palace, and, ever after, to live separated from her husband.

The Padshah Begum had only one child, a daughter, who was united in marriage to Mehndee Allee Khan, by whom she had three children, Mohsen-od Dowlah, who was married to the daughter of Nuseer-od Dowlah, the new King; and two daughters who were married to Mirza Abool Kasim, and Mirza Aboo Torab. They lost their mother while yet children, and the Padshah Begum brought them up and became much attached to them. They had all from childhood been brought up with Nuseer-od Deen, and were all much attached to him and to each other. The ministers, fearing that this attachment might possibly lead to a reconciliation between the King and his adoptive mother, and to their ruin, left him and her no peace till, to save them, she forbade them her house, and sent the girls to their husbands, and the boy to his father-in-law, Nuseer-od Dowlah, whose succession to the throne of Oude has been here described. All objects of mutual interest and affection were in this manner carefully excluded from attendance on either, till they showed themselves to be entirely subservient to the minister of the day.*

* The mother always declared, and her two daughters and son all declare, Moonna Jan to have been the son of Nuseer-od Deen, and

Thus alienated from her son, all her affections were transferred to her grandson, Moonna Jan, and there is too much reason to believe, that in both cases she purposely did her best to prevent their ever becoming men of business, in order that she might have the guidance of public affairs in her own hands when they should be called to the throne.

The Resident accommodated the Begum, the boy, and her two female attendants in apartments at the Residency, and had a guard placed over them. The new King told him, " that the Begum was the most wicked and unscrupulous woman he had ever known, and that he could expect no peace at Lucknow while she remained." He promised to consult his Government as to her disposal, and on returning to the Residency he increased that guard to two companies of Native Infantry, and all remained quiet when he made his report to Government on the 9th. But towards the close of that day, the city became again agitated. Reports prevailed, that Government was to be consulted as to whether they preferred the rights of Moonna Jan to the throne or those of Nuseer-od Dowlah; that the Begum's adherents were ready at her call to fall upon the Resident and his party, and put them all to death, or to attack the apartments in which she was confined, rescue her and the boy from prison, and place him again on the throne. The Court favourites of the late King, and all the public military and civil establishments in the city, dreaded the rigid economy and strict supervision of the new King, who had conducted the duties of the ministry for some time, under his able and vigilant

exactly like him in person, voice, and temper. But he was indulged by the Padshah Begum in such habits of atrocious cruelties to other children, that he soon became detested by all around him but herself and the boy's natural mother, Afzul-mahal.

father, Saadut Allee Khan; and all that numerous class who benefit by the lavish expenditure of a thoughtless and profligate Court were equally anxious to have the Government in the hands of an extravagant woman and thoughtless boy, and ready to join and incur some risk in supporting their cause.

Under all these circumstances the Resident determined to send the Begum and her boy out of Oude as soon as possible. At midnight on the 11th, a detachment of three companies of Infantry, under Major Lane of the 2nd Regiment, marched from Cawnpore and arrived at Newulgunge, midway to Lucknow, a distance of twenty-two miles, in the morning of the 12th, with one troop of cavalry. Another troop proceeded to Onow, the first stage from Cawnpore, and a third to Rahmutgunge, the second stage, to relieve the first on their return. At each of these stages, relays of sixty palankeen-bearers and six torch-bearers were placed by the Post-Master at Cawnpore. As the bridge over the Ganges at Cawnpore had been washed away by the flood, a company of Native Infantry was placed on the Oude side of that river, to hold boats in readiness, and assist in escorting over the party when they came. About the same time, at midnight, the Begum, her boy, and two of her female attendants were placed in palankeens and sent off from the Residency under the escort of a regiment of Infantry, and a detail of artillery, attended by the Second Assistant, Captain Shakespear.

They marched without resting through one of the hottest days of the year, and the party reached Cawnpore in safety about half-past nine o'clock in the evening of the 12th, and were securely lodged in apartments prepared for them at the custom-house. So well had things been arranged between the Resident and Brigadier commanding the troops in Oude, and the Major-General commanding the Division at Cawnpore, that very few persons at Lucknow knew that the Begum and her party had left the Residency when she passed the Ganges at Cawnpore. The three companies under Major Lane, who had marched twenty-two miles in the morning, kept pace with the palankeens all the way back, making a march of forty-four miles, between midnight of the 11th, and half-past nine in the evening of the 12th, in so hot a day.

The Begum and Moonna Jan were sent off with their attendants to the fort of Chunar, where they were lodged as state prisoners. As it became safe, the restrictions to which they were at first subjected became by degrees relaxed, and they were permitted to enjoy all the freedom and comforts compatible with their safe keeping. Both died at Chunar, Moonna Jan some time before the Begum. He left three sons by two slave-girls at Chunar, and they still reside there, supported by a small stipend of three hundred rupees a-month from the Oude Government, under the protection of the commandant of the garrison, and the guardianship of Afzul mahal, the mother of the late Moonna Jan.

All these circumstances, as they occurred, were reported by the Resident to the Government of India, who took time to deliberate, and did not reply till the 19th of July 1837, when they signified their approval of all that the Resident had done, with the exception of the written declaration to which he had obtained the consent and signature of the new King. They did not think that it would be considered dignified or becoming the paramount power, to exact such a declaration, binding himself to absolute submission, from the sovereign of a country so much under their control, on ascending a throne to which he was called as of right; and were of opinion that his character as a prudent man of business, well trained to public affairs, during the time he acted as minister under his father, rendered such a declaration unnecessary. It was therefore annulled; and the Governor-General, Lord Auckland, addressed a letter to his Majesty expressing, in kind terms, his congratulations on his accession to the throne, and his hopes of a better administration of the Government of Oude under his auspicious guidance. This letter, despatched by express, the Resident received on the 25th of July.

The Resident concluded, on good grounds, that the Government deemed a new and more stringent treaty indispensable for the better government of the country, and that advantage should be taken of the occasion to prepare the new King for it. Government desired, that the negotiations for a new treaty should be based "upon reason and right, and not upon demand and submission." Had the declaration been allowed to stand good, there would have been *right* as well as *reason* in the treaty of 1837, which was soon after concluded.

The Resident intimated the receipt of these letters to the King, and on the 28th, he waited on his Majesty, to present the Governor-General's letter. He found him sitting up in his bed in a small apartment in the baradurree, in his dishabille, having spent a restless night from rheumatic pains; but he was cheerful and in good spirits, and requested the Resident to present his respectful compliments to the Governor-General, and grateful thanks for his consideration and congratulations. All his relations, the chief officers of the Government, and other persons of distinction about the Court, were assembled to hear the letters read, and make their offerings on this recognition of his authority by the paramount power. "The King assured the Resident, that the arrival of this recognition, and its public announcement, would greatly strengthen his hands in the exercise of public duties, for during the last few days bad reports had been industriously circulated by evil-disposed persons to the effect, that the delay in the recognition of his succession to the throne by the paramount power in India, had arisen from discussions between the members of the Government in Calcutta, as to the amount of money to be taken on the occasion from the new King, as the price of his sudden elevation; and that no letter was to be presented by the Resident until the money was paid, or security given for its punctual payment; that the Governor-General himself wanted *two crores* of rupees, but some members of the Government would be satisfied with *a crore and half* each, and others even with *one crore* each, provided that these sums were paid forthwith." In relating this story, which the Resident had heard from many others within the last few days, the King observed, "that he was too well acquainted with the character for honour and justice of the Honourable Company's Government, to give the slightest credit to such scandal, the more especially since no demand of the kind had been made on the accession of either of the last two Kings, who were known to be rich, while he was equally well known to be poor; but that nothing but the arrival of this despatch confirming him on the throne, could convince many, even well-disposed persons, of the utter groundlessness of such wicked rumours; that many poor but respectable persons, who had been weak enough to believe such rumours, would feel much relieved when they heard the salutes which were now being fired, for they had apprehended, that they might be severe sufferers by being compelled to contribute their own property, in order to enable him to make up the *peshkush*, or tribute, required by the British Government, since the late King had squandered the ten crores, which he found in the treasury on the death of his father."

It is certain, that a great portion of the population of Lucknow expected that some such demand would be made by the British Government from the new sovereign, since his right to the throne could be disputed, not only by Moonna Jan, the supposed son of the late King, but by the undoubted sons of Shums-od Dowlah, the elder brother of the present King, whose rights were barred only by that peculiar feature of the Mahommedan law, elsewhere adverted to in this Diary. Every day of delay, in promulgating the final orders of the Supreme Government, tended to add to this number; and by the time that these final orders came, by far the greater portion of the city were of the same opinion. The fears of the people tended to add to their numbers, and give strength to the opinion, for all knew, that there was but little left in the reserved treasury, that the expenses greatly exceeded the annual revenue, and that the troops and establishments were all greatly in arrear; and all believed that a general contribution would have to be levied to meet the demand when it came.*

* Nuseer-od Dowlah reigned under the title of Mahommed Allee Shah, from the 8th of July, 1837, to the 16th of May, 1842. Nuseer-od Deen Hyder, his predecessor, had reigned from the 20th of October, 1827, to the 7th of July, 1837. He, Nuseer-od Deen, found in the treasury, when he ascended the throne, ten crores of rupees, or ten millions sterling. He left in the treasury, when he died, only seventy lacs of rupees, including the fifty-three lacs left by the Koduseea Begum. Mahommed Allee Shah left in the treasury thirty-five lacs of rupees, one hundred and twenty-four thousand gold mohurs, and twenty-four

The assertion, on the part of the late King, that he had ceased to cohabit with Afzul mahal, the mother of Moonna Jan, for two years, or even for six months before his birth, is now known to have been utterly false, and known at the time to be so by his mother, the Padshah Begum, with whom they both lived. Afzul-mahal, though of humble birth and pretensions, maintained a fair reputation among those who knew her best in a profligate palace, and has continued to maintain the same up to the present day in adversity. In prison and up to the hour of her death, which took place some time after that of Moonna Jan himself, the old Begum declared that she had seen the boy born, and had never lost sight of him; and that the story of his not being the son of Nuseer-od Deen, was got up to prevent her ever becoming reconciled to the King through the means of his son; and her extraordinary affection for him never diminished while he lived. When she retired from the palace of Nuseer-od Deen to her new residence of Almas Bagh, she kept fast hold of the boy, and would never let him out of her sight till they entered the prison at Chunar, when they were obliged to occupy separate apartments. Up to his death she watched over him with the tenderest care; and always declared to the European officers placed over her, that the boy's father and mother always resided with her up to the time of his birth. The boy was remarkably like Nuseer-od Deen in form and features, as well as in temper and disposition.

---

lacs in our Government securities. Amjud Allee Shah reigned from the 16th of May, 1842, to the 13th of February, 1847; and left in the treasury ninety-two lacs of rupees, one hundred and twenty-four thousand gold mohurs, and the twenty-four lacs in our Government securities. His son, Wajid Allee Shah, has reigned from the 13th of February, 1847.

Afzul-mahal was a person of great good sense and prudence, and in all things trusted by the old Begum, who before her death executed a formal will, leaving to her the charge of Moonna Jan's three children, and all the establishments; and since the death of the old lady she has executed the trust conscientiously, and with great economy; and with much difficulty managed to maintain all in respectability upon the small stipend of three hundred rupees a-month, allowed for their support by the King of Oude. In this, she has been very much impeded and annoyed by the two slave-girls, the mothers of Moonna Jan's children, who have been always striving to get this stipend into their own hands, that they may share it with their paramours. At the death of the old lady most of her female companions and attendants refused to return to Lucknow, and remained at Chunar with Afzul-mahal and the children; and all have to be subsisted out of this small stipend. The slave-girls urge, that they might have had separate pensions, had they obeyed the orders to return to Lucknow on the death of the Begum, and that they ought not now to share in the stipend of the children. Five or six of the females were ladies of rank, and one of them, who died lately, was a widow of Saadut Allee Khan.

This pension may be discontinued when the boys become of age, or appropriated by them and their mothers for their own exclusive use, and the Government of Oude should be required to assign pensions for life to Afzul mahal, and the other females who are now supported from it.

The salary of the prime minister, during the five years that Roshun-od Dowlah held the office, was twenty-five thousand rupees a-month, or three lacs a-year, and over and above this, he had five per cent. upon the actual revenue, which made above six lacs a-year. His son, as Commander-in-Chief, drew five thousand rupees a-month, though he did no duty—his first wife drew five thousand rupees a-month, and his second wife drew three thousand rupees a-month, total eighty-eight thousand rupees a-month, or ten lacs and fifty-six thousand rupees a-year. These were the avowed allowances which the family received from the public treasury. The perquisites of office gave them some five lacs of rupees a-year more, making full fifteen lacs a-year.

Roshun-od Dowlah held office for only three months, under the new sovereign, Mahommed Allee Shah. He was then superseded by Hakeem Mahndee, thrown into prison, and made to pay twenty lacs to the treasury, and two lacs in gratuities to Court favourites. After paying these sums, he was permitted to go and reside at Cawnpore; but his houses in the city, valued at three lacs, were afterwards confiscated by the present King, on the ground of unpaid balances. He took into keeping Dulwee, the younger of the two sisters; but she was afterwards seduced away from him by one of his creatures, a consummate knave, Wasee Allee, whose wife she now is. Dhunneea, the eldest sister, is still residing at Lucknow. Roshun-od Dowlah's first wife took off with her more than three lacs of rupees in our Government securities; and his son, the Commander-in-Chief, took off eight lacs of rupees in the same securities. Roshun-od Dowlah carried off a large sum himself. She and his son afterwards left him, and now reside in comfort upon the interest of these securities at Futtehgur, while he lives at Cawnpore in poor circumstances.

Sobhan Allee, his deputy, was made to pay to the

treasury seven lacs of rupees, and in gratuities to court favourites five lacs more. Roshun-od Dowlah was one of the principal members of the old aristocracy of Lucknow, and connected remotely with the royal family; and he got off more easily in consequence, compared with his means, than his deputy, who had no such advantages, and was known to have been the minister's guide in all things, though he would never consent to hold any ostensible and responsible office.

Duljeet, a creature of Roshun-od Dowlah's, and prime favourite of the late King, carried off, while the King lay dead, money and jewels to the value of one lac of rupees, and concealed them in a vault at Constantia. His associates, not satisfied with what he gave them, betrayed him. The money and jewels were discovered and brought back, and he was made to pay another lac of rupees to the treasury as a fine. Dhunneea, the eldest of the two sisters, was made to disgorge two lacs of rupees. Many other favourites of the late King were fined in the same way.

The King had, in the case of Ghalib Jung, already described in this Diary, declared his resolution of looking more closely into his accounts in future, and punishing all transgressors in the same way; and Roshun-od Dowlah often expressed to the Resident his apprehensions that his turn to suffer must soon come. Sobhan Allee Khan had much stronger grounds to fear, since he had made himself utterly detested by the people generally, and had neither friends nor connexions in the royal family or aristocracy of Lucknow. Under the strong and general impression that the British Government was determined to interpose, and take upon itself the administration of the country, and that the King himself wished the independent sovereignty of Oude to terminate with his reign, they most earnestly desired his early death as their only chance of escape. The British Government would not, they knew, make them refund any of their ill-gotten wealth without full judicial proof of their peculations, and this proof they knew could never be obtained. Indeed they were satisfied that our Government, aware of the difficulty of finding such proof, and occupied in forming and working a new system, would not trouble themselves to seek for it; and that they should all be left to reside where they chose, and enjoy freely the fruits of their malversation.

The Resident had kept the instructions of the 15th of December, 1832, from the supreme Government, a profound secret, lest they might lead to intrigue and disturbance, and, above all, to the poisoning of many innocent persons who might be considered to have a claim of right to the throne; and all were surprised and confounded when it was announced that the paramount power had already decided in favour of Nuseer-od Dowlah, whose claims had never been thought of by the people, or apprehended by the ministers. The instant they heard this decision, they dreaded the scrutiny of the sagacious and parsimonious old man, and the enmity of the favourites by whom he had been surrounded in private life. These men, whom they had, in their pride and power, despised and insulted, would now have their revenge; and they wished for the success of the old woman and the boy, from whom they might have a better chance of escape, till they could get their wealth and their families out of the country.

I may here mention a similar repudiation of a supposed

eldest son by the late King. Mostafa Allee was brought up in the palace as his eldest son, and on all occasions treated as such. Mahommed Allee Shah, the late King's father, was always very fond of him, but shortly before his death he became angry with him for some outrages committed in the palace, and put him under restraint. The young man requested the late King, his supposed father, to mediate with his grandfather for his release. He refused to do so, and the young man drew his sword, and threatened to kill him. He was kept under more strict restraint till the grandfather died, and his father ascended the throne, on the 16th of May, 1842. The King then requested the Resident to assure the Governor-General that Mostafa Allee was not his son—that he was a year and a-half old when his mother entered the palace. The Resident reported accordingly on the 26th of that month. The Governor-General required the statement to be made under the King's own sign and seal, and it was transmitted on the 6th of June, 1842. The present King was then declared heir-apparent to the throne, and Mostafa Allee has ever since been in strict confinement under him. The general impression, however, is that he was the eldest son of the late King, and repudiated solely on account of his violent temper and turbulent conduct. That he was treated as such during the life of Mahommed Allee Shah, and that the late King dared not repudiate him while his father lived, is certain.

By the treaty of 1801 we bound ourselves to defend the territories of the sovereign of Oude from all foreign and domestic enemies; and to defray the cost of maintaining the troops required for this purpose, and paying some pensions at Furruckabad and Benares, the sovereign of Oude ceded to our Government the under-mentioned districts, then yielding the revenues specified opposite their respective names.*

Khyreegurh and Kunchunpore were re-ceded to the Oude sovereign in the treaty of the 11th of May, 1816, with the Turae lands, taken from Nepaul, between Khyreegurh and Goruckpore, in liquidation of the loan of one crore of rupees. In the same treaty, Handeea (*alias* Kewae) was ceded by Oude to the British Government, in lieu of Nawabgunge, which was made over to the Oude sovereign by the British Government. Handeea, or Kewae, now in the Allahabad district, yielded land revenue, for 1846-47, rupees one lac, fifty-two thousand, and nine hundred and five.

* *Districts ceded by Oude to the British Government by the treaty of* 1801.

Etawa, Korah, Kurra				55,48,577	11	9
Rehur and others				5,33,374	0	6
Furruckabad				4,50,001	0	0
Khyreegurh, and Kunchunpore				2,10,001	0	0
Azimgurh, Mounal, and Bunjun				6,95,624	7	6
Goruckpore	5,09,853	8	0			
Botwul	40,001	0	0	5,49,854	8	0
Allahabad and others				9,34,963	1	3
Bareilly, Moradabad, Bijnore, Budown, Pilibheet, and Shahjehanpore				43,13,457	11	3
Nawabgunge, Rehlee, &c.				1,19,242	12	0
Mohowl and others, with exception of Jaulluk Arwul				1,68,378	4	0
Total				1,35,23,474	8	3
Deduct						
Nawabgunge	1,19,242	12	0			
Khyreegurh	2,10,001	0	0	3,29,243	12	0
Total				1,31,94,230	12	3
Add						
Handeea or Kewae				1,52,905	0	0
Total				1,33,47,135	12	3

PRESENT REVENUES of the TERRITORIES we hold from OUDE under the treaty of 1801, according to the Revised Statistical Return of the Districts of the North-Western Provinces for 1846-47, prepared in 1848, A. D.

—	Land Revenue 1846-47.	Abkaree for 1846-47.	Stamp for 1846-47.	Total for 1846-47.
Rohilcund	64,44,341	2,47,854	2,04,576	68,96,771
Allahabad, including Handeea *alias* Kewae	21,29,551	1,41,409	61,802	23,32,762
Furruckabad	13,57,544	88,061	49,698	14,95,303
Mynpooree	12,33,901	24,822	20,484	12,79,207
Etawa	12,80,596	19,647	10,355	13,10,598
Goruckpore	20,80,296	2,10,045	96,549	23,86,890
Azimgurh, including Mahoul	14,89,887	81,257	53,925	16,25,069
Cawnpore	21,51,139	1,26,155	57,406	23,34,700
Futtehpore	14,25,431	60,370	21,063	15,06,864
Total	1,95,92,686	9,99,620	5,75,858	2,11,68,164

*** The lands are the same with the exception of Khyreegurh, Nawabgunge ceded since, and Handeea received ; but the names are altered.

The British Government retained the power to station the British troops in such parts of the Oude territories as might appear to it most expedient; and the Oude sovereign bound himself to dismiss all his troops, save four battalions of infantry, one battalion of Nujeebs and Mewaties, two thousand horsemen, and three hundred golundages, or artillerymen, with such numbers of armed peons as might be deemed necessary for the purpose of collecting the revenue, and a few horsemen and nujeebs to attend the persons of the amils. It is declared that the territories ceded, being in lieu of all former subsidies and of all expenses on account of the Honourable Company's defensive establishments with his Excellency the sovereign of Oude, no demand whatever shall be made upon his territory on account of expenses which the Honourable Company may incur by assembling forces to repel the attack, or menaced attack, of a foreign enemy; on account of the detachment attached to his person; on account of troops which may be occasionally furnished for suppressing rebellions or disorders in his territories; on account of any future charge of military stations; or on account of failures in the resources of the ceded districts, arising from unfavourable seasons, the calamities of war, or any other cause whatever.

The Honourable Company guarantees to him and to his heirs and successors, the possession of the territories which remain to him after the above cessions, together with the exercise of his and their authority within the said dominions; and the sovereign of Oude engages to establish, in his reserved dominions, such a system of administration, to be carried into effect by his own officers, as shall be conducive to the prosperity of his subjects, and calculated to secure the lives and property of the inhabitants; and to advise with, and act in conformity to the counsel of, the officers of the British Government.

In the time of Asuf-od Dowlah, who died on the 21st September, 1797, the military force of Oude amounted to eighty thousand men of all arms, and in the direct pay of Government. Saadut Allee Khan, his brother and successor, on the conclusion of the above treaty, and the transfer of half his territory, reduced the number to thirty thousand.

Relying entirely upon the efficiency of British troops to defend him against external and internal enemies, and to suppress rebellion and disorder, he laboured assiduously to reduce his expenditure within the income arising from the reserved half of his dominions. He resumed almost all the rent-free lands which had been granted with a lavish hand by his predecessor, and paid off and discharged all superfluous civil and military establishments; and, by his prudence and economy, he so reduced his expenditure within the income, that on his death on the 12th of July, 1814, he left fourteen millions sterling, or fourteen crores of rupees, in a treasury which he found empty when he entered upon the government in 1797. In this sum were included the confiscations of the estates of some favourites of his predecessors, Asuf-od Dowlah and Wuzeer Allee, who had grown rich upon bribery and frauds of all kinds. He never confiscated the estates of any good and faithful servants, who left lawful heirs to their property.

He had been freely aided by British troops, according to the stipulations of the treaty of 1801; but the British Government had been made sensible, on several occasions, of the difficulty of fulfilling its engagements with the sovereign with a due regard to the rights and interests of his subjects. Saadut Allee Khan was a man of great general ability, had mixed much in the society of British officers in different parts of India, had been well trained to habits of business, understood thoroughly the character, institutions, and requirements of his people, and, above all, was a sound judge of the relative merits and capacities of the men from whom he had to select his officers, and a vigilant supervisor of their actions. This discernment and discrimination of character, and vigilant supervision, served him through life; and the men who served him ably and honestly always felt confident in his protection and support. He had a thorough knowledge of the rights and duties of his officers and subjects, and a strong will to secure the one and enforce the other. To do so he knew that he must, with a strong hand, keep down the large landed aristocracy, who were then, as they are now, very prone to grasp at the possessions of their weaker neighbours, either by force or in collusion with local authorities. In attempting this with the aid of British troops, some acts of oppression were, no doubt, committed; and, as the sympathies of British officers were more with the landed aristocracy, while his were more with the humbler classes of landholders and cultivators who required to be protected from them, frequent misunderstandings arose, acts of just severity were made to appear to be acts of wanton oppression, and such as were really oppressive were exaggerated into unheard-of atrocities.

Our relations with the state of Oude, from the treaty of 1801 to the death of Saadut Allee, were conducted by able men; but they had a very difficult task to perform in conducting them to the satisfaction of both parties to that treaty; and when the Government devolved upon less able and well-disposed sovereigns, ministers, and public officers, our Government and its representative became less and less willing to comply with their requisitions for the aid of British troops in the collection of the revenue, and the suppression of rebellion and disorder. Our Government demanded, that the British Resident should be fully informed of the cause which led to the resistance complained of to legitimate authority; and be fully satisfied of the justice and necessity of such aid before he afforded it; and the sovereigns of Oude admitted the justice of this demand on the part of the paramount power. But the Resident could never hear fully and fairly both sides of the question, and the officers commanding the troops were seldom disposed to do so; and neither was competent to pass a sound judgment upon the justice and necessity of complying with the requisitions made for the aid of the British troops.

But when, under an imbecile and debauched sovereign, like Ghazee-od Deen, and an unscrupulous minister, creatures and favourites began to share so largely in the revenues of the country, this sort of scrutiny on the part of the Resident and officers commanding troops, employed in aid of the King's officers, became exceedingly distasteful; and the minister gradually increased the military force of Oude at his disposal, that he might do without it. During the last few years of Ghazee-od Deen's reign, the Oude forces of all arms amounted to about sixty thousand men. During the first few years of his successor's, Nuseer-od Deen's, reign, these forces were augmented by the ministers for the sake of the profit and patronage they gave them; and in the year 1837, the forces of all arms, paid from the treasury, amounted to more than sixty thousand men. A memorandum given to the British Resident by the minister on the 8th of April 1837, showed the men of all descriptions, belonging to the Oude army, to amount to sixty-seven thousand nine hundred and fifty-six. The artillery, cavalry, and infantry, composing what they call the regular army, amounted to twenty thousand, all badly paid, clothed, armed, accoutred, and disciplined; and for the most part placed under idle, incompetent, and corrupt commanders. The rest were nujeebs employed in the provinces under local officers of the revenue and police, and obliged to provide their own clothes, arms, accoutrements, and ammunition. They were altogether without discipline.

Government, on the 26th November, 1824, informs the Resident, "that our troops are to be actively and energetically employed in the Oude territory in cases of real internal commotion and disorder." And again on the 22nd of July, 1825, Government condemns the Resident for his disregard of the orders of the 26th of November, 1824, regarding the employment of British troops in Oude, and states, "that it is sincerely disposed to maintain the rights of the King of Oude to the fullest extent, as guaranteed to him by the treaty with his father, on the 20th of November, 1801; but observes, that upon the maturest consideration of articles 3rd, 5th, and 6th of that treaty, and of Lord Wellesley's memorandum in 1802, of the final results of discussions between him and Saadut Allee, whilst Government admits that, according to article the 3rd of the treaty, we were bound to defend his Majesty's present territories 'against all foreign and domestic enemies,' and that, in pursuance of the 4th article, the Company's troops are to be employed, without expense to his Majesty, not only 'to repel the attack, or menaced attack, of a foreign enemy,' but also for suppressing rebellion and disorder in his Majesty's territories; and that, in a strict adherence to the 6th article, the King of Oude is entitled to exercise complete sovereign authority within his own dominions, by a system of administration conducive to the prosperity of his subjects, to be carried into effect by his own officers, with the advice and counsel of the officers of the British Government (in conformity to which his Majesty is expressly engaged to act); yet the Governor-General in council considered it to be indispensable and inherent in the nature of our obligations, under the treaty referred to, that whenever the King of Oude requires the aid of British troops, to quell any disturbance, or to enforce any demand for revenue or otherwise, the British Government is clearly entitled, as well as morally obliged, to satisfy itself by whatever means it may deem necessary, that the aid of its troops is required in support of right and justice, and not to effectuate injustice and extortion.

"This principle, which has often been declared and acted upon during successive Governments, must still be firmly asserted, and resolutely adhered to; and the Resident must consider it to be a positive and indispensable obligation of his public duty, to refuse the aid of British troops until he shall have satisfied himself, on good and sufficient grounds (to be reported in each case as soon as practicable, and when the exigency of the case may admit of it, before the troops are actually employed), that they are not to be employed but in support of just and legitimate demands."

On the 13th of July, 1827, Government, in reply to the Resident's letter of the 30th May idem, expresses "its surprise that, under the circumstances therein stated, he should have suffered so long a period to elapse without adopting the most active and decided measures against a subject of Oude, whose conduct is that of a public robber and rebel against the authority of his Government; and whom the King has plainly stated that he is unable to reduce to subjection without the aid of British troops."

On the 20th of January, 1831, the Governor-General, Lord William Bentinck, held a conference with the King of Oude, and told his Majesty, in presence of his minister, that the state of things in Oude, and maladministration in all departments, were such as to warrant and require the authoritative interference of the British Government for their correction; that he declined to make himself a party to the nomination of the minister, or to have it understood that the measure was a joint resolution of the two governments, so that both should be responsible for its success in effecting reformation; that the act was his Majesty's own, and the responsibility must be his; that his Lordship hoped that a better system would be established by his minister's agency, but if he failed, and the same abuses and misrule continued, the King must be prepared to abide the consequences; that the Governor-General intended to make a strong representation to the authorities in England on the state of misrule prevailing, and to solicit their sanction to the adoption of specific measures, even to the length of assuming the direct administration of the country, if the evils were not corrected in the interim.

In the letter from Government dated the 25th of August, 1831, referring to this advice, the Resident is told that by treaty we are bound to give the aid of troops to quell internal resistance, as well as to keep off external enemies, but by the same treaty the Oude Government is bound to establish a good system of administration, and to conform to our advice in this respect; that, finding it impossible to procure the establishment of such an improved system, and seeing that our troops were liable to be made the instruments of violence, and vindictive and party proceedings, it was determined to withhold the aid of troops except after investigation into the cause which might lead to the application for them; that, by recent orders from the Court of Directors, the Government would be authorised in withholding them altogether, in the hope that the necessities of the Oude Government might compel a reform such as we might deem satisfactory; that matters had not, however, been brought to such an issue, for the Oude Government having been deprived of the services of British troops to execute its purposes, has entertained a body stated at sixty thousand men, cavalry, infantry, and artillery, whereof forty-five thousand are stationed in the interior for the special purpose of reducing refractory zumeendars without British aid. Government urges the necessity of reducing this number, and states that if British troops be employed to enforce submission, it seems impossible to avoid becoming parties to the terms of submission, and guarantees of their observance afterwards on both sides, in which case we should become mixed up in every detail of the administration; it is therefore required that each case shall be investigated and submitted for the specific orders of the Governor-General.

On the 15th of August, 1832, the Governor-General addressed a letter to his Majesty, the King of Oude, in the last sentence of which he says, "I do not use this strong language of remonstrance without manifest necessity. On former occasions the language of expostulation has been frequently used towards you with reference to the abuses of your Government, and as yet nothing serious has befallen you. I beseech you, however, not to suffer yourself to be deceived into a false security. I might adduce sufficient proof that such security would be fallacious, but I am unwilling to wound your Majesty's feelings, while the sincere friendship which I entertain for you prevents my withholding from you that advice which I deem essential to the preservation of your own dignity, and the prosperity of your kingdom."

The Resident is told that the allusion in the concluding sentence of his Lordship's letter refers to Mysore; that the King had probably heard of our actual assumption of the government of that country, and the Resident must avail himself of this topic to impress upon his mind the consequencos which a similar state of things may entail upon himself.

On the 11th of September, 1837, a subsidiary treaty was concluded with the new sovereign, Mahommed Allee Shah, on the ground that though a larger force was kept up by the King of Oude than was authorised by the treaty of 1801, still it was found inadequate to the duties that devolved upon it, and it was therefore expedient to relax the restrictions as to the amount of military force to be maintained by the King of Oude, on condition that an adequate portion of the increased forces should be placed under British discipline and control. It was stipulated accordingly that the King might employ such a military establishment as he might deem necessary for the government of his dominion; that it should consist of not less than two regiments of cavalry, five of infantry, and two companies of artillery; that the Government of Oude should fix the sum of sixteen lacs of rupees a-year for the expenses of the force, including their pay, arms, equipments, public buildings, &c.; that the expenditure on account of this force of all descriptions should never exceed sixteen lacs; that the organization of this force should not commence till eighteen months after the 1st of September, 1837; that the King should take into his service an efficient number of British officers for the due discipline and efficiency of this force; that this force should be fixed at such stations in Oude as might seem to both Governments, from time to time, to be best, and employed on all occasions on which its services might be deemed necessary by the King of Oude, with the concurrence of the Resident, but not in the ordinary collections of the revenue; that the King should exert himself, in concert with the Resident, to remedy the existing defects in his administration; and should he neglect to attend to the advice and counsel of the British Government, or its representative, and should gross and systematic oppression, anarchy, and misrule, at any time hereafter prevail within the Oude territories, such as seriously to endanger the public tranquillity, the British Government would have the right to appoint its own officers to the management of all portions of the Oude territory in which such misrule might have occurred for so long a period as it might deem necessary, the surplus receipts in such case, after defraying all charges, to be paid into the King's treasury, and a true and faithful account rendered to his Majesty of the receipts and expenditure of the territories so assumed; that should the Governor-General of India in Council be compelled to resort to the exercise of this authority, he would endeavour, as far as possible, to maintain (with such improvements as they might admit of) the native institutions and forms of administration within the assumed territories, so as to facilitate the restoration of those territories to the sovereign of Oude, when the proper period of such restoration should arrive.

This treaty was ratified by the Governor-General in Council on the 18th of September, 1837, but the Honourable the Court of Directors, with that anxious regard for strict justice which, after long and varied experience, I have always found to characterise their views and orders, disapproved of that part of the above treaty which imposed on the Oude state the expense of the auxiliary force; and on the 8th of July, 1839, the King was informed, amidst great rejoicings, that he was relieved from this burthen of sixteen lacs of rupees a-year, which the British Government took upon itself. Only part of this auxiliary force had been raised when these orders came, and only two regiments of infantry out of that part were retained, one stationed at Soltanpore, and the other at Seetapore.

Up to 1835, the British forces in Oude amounted to two companies of artillery, with fourteen guns, and six regiments of infantry. Early in that year (1835), four guns, with a proportion of artillerymen, and one regiment of Native Infantry, were withdrawn, leaving the British force in Oude one company and a-half of artillery, with ten guns, and five regiments of Native Infantry. In 1837, when two infantry regiments of the auxiliary force had been raised, four guns more, with a detail of artillery, and two regiments more of Native Infantry were withdrawn from the two stations of Soltanpore and Seetapore, leaving the force paid by the British Government one company of artillery, with six guns, stationed at Lucknow, three regiments of Native Infantry at Lucknow, one regiment of the Oude auxiliary force stationed at Soltanpore, and the other at Seetapore. There had been artillery and guns at Pertabgur, Soltanpore, Secrora and Seetapore, and a regiment of regular cavalry at Pertabgur. In 1815 this regiment of cavalry was withdrawn for the Nepaul war, and subsequently it was retained for the Mahratta war. It was sent back to Pertabgur in 1820, but finally withdrawn in 1821. The British Government now maintains no cavalry in any part of the King of Oude's dominions, and no artillery or guns at any place but Lucknow.*

In fairness there should be guns at Seetapore and Soltanpore, and a corps of regular or irregular cavalry at Lucknow, or some other more convenient station. The

* There is a small detachment of thirty sowars from an irregular corps attached to the Resident.

stations of Secrora and Pertabgur were done away with by general orders 28th January, 1835, when one regiment of Native Infantry was withdrawn altogether from Oude, and one added to the two theretofore stationed at Lucknow. In consequence of these arrangements, the British force in Oude is much less than it was when the treaty of the 11th of September, 1837, was made, and assuredly less than it should be with a due regard to our engagements and the Oude requirements. Our Government instead of taking upon itself the additional burthen of sixteen lacs of rupees a-year to render the Oude Government more efficient, has relieved itself of a good deal of that which it bore before the new treaty was entered into, and this is certainly not what the Court of Directors contemplated, or the Oude Government expected.

Our exigencies became great with the Affghan war, and have continued to be so from those wars which grew out of it with Gwalior, Scinde, and the Punjab; but they have all now passed away, and those of our humble ally should be no longer forgotten or disregarded. Though we seldom give him the use of troops in support of the authority of his local officers, still the prestige of having them at hand, in support of a just cause, is unquestionably of great advantage to him and to his people, and this advantage we cannot withhold from him with a due regard to the obligations of solemn treaties.

But in considering the rights which the sovereign of Oude has acquired by solemn treaties to our support, we must not forget those which the five millions of people subject to his rule have acquired by the same treaties to the protection of our Government; and it is a grave question, that must soon be solved, whether we can any longer support the present sovereign and system of government in Oude, without subjecting ourselves to the reproach of shamefully neglecting the duties we owe to these millions.

The present King ascended the throne on the death of his father, on the 13th of February, 1847. In a letter dated the 24th of July of that year, the Resident is told "that it will be his Majesty's duty to establish such an administration, to be carried out by his own officers, as shall insure the prosperity of the people; that any neglect of this essential principle will be an infringement of treaty; and that the Governor-General must, in the performance of his duty, require the King to fulfil his obligations to his subjects—that his Majesty must understand that, as a sovereign, he has duties to perform to, as well as claims to exact from, the people committed to his care."

In the month of November in that year, the Governor-General, Lord Hardinge, visited Lucknow; and in a conference held with the King, he caused a memorandum which he had drawn up for the occasion to be read and carefully explained to his Majesty. It stated, "that in all our engagements the utmost care had always been taken, not only to uphold the authority of native rulers, but also to secure the just rights of the people subject to their rule; that the same principle is maintained in the treaty of 1801 with Oude, in the sixth paragraph of which the engagement is entered into 'for the establishment of such a system of government as shall be conducive to the prosperity of the King's subjects, and calculated to secure to them their lives and properties;' that in the memorandum of 1802, signed by the Governor-General, the King engages to establish judicial tribunals for the free and pure administration of justice to all his subjects;

and that it is recorded in the sovereign's own hand in that document, 'let the Company's officers assist in enforcing obedience to these tribunals;' that it is, therefore, evident that in all these stipulations the same principle prevailed —namely, that while we engage to maintain the prince in the full exercise of his powers, we also provide for the protection of his people.

"That, in the more recent treaty of 1837, it is stated that the solemn and paramount obligation provided by treaty for the prosperity of his Majesty's subjects, and the security of the lives and property of the inhabitants, has been notoriously neglected by several successive rulers in Oude, thereby exposing the British Government to the reproach of having imperfectly fulfilled its obligations towards the Oude people; that his Lordship alludes to the treaty of 1837, as confirming the original treaty of 1801, and not only giving the British Government the *right* to interfere, but declaring it to be the intention of the Government to interfere, if necessary, for the purpose of securing good government in Oude; that the King can, therefore, have no doubt that the Governor-General is not only justified, but bound by his duty, to take care that the stipulations provided by treaty shall be fairly and substantially carried into effect; that if the Governor-General permits the continuation of any flagrant system of mismanagement which by treaty he is empowered to correct, he becomes the participator in abuses which it is his duty to redress; and in this case no ruler of Oude can expect the Governor-General to incur a responsibility so repugnant to the principles of the British Government, and so odious to the feelings of the British people.

"That, in the discussion of this important subject, advice and remonstrance have been frequently tried, and have failed; that the Governor-General hopes that the King will exercise a sounder judgment than those who have preceded him, and that he will not be compelled to exchange friendly advice for imperative and absolute interference; that when the Governor-General, Lord William Bentinck, had a conference with the former King, Nuseer-od Deen Hyder, on this subject, on the 20th of January, 1831, he deemed it right frankly to inform him that if the warning which he then gave was disregarded by his Majesty, it was his intention to submit to the home authorities his advice that the British Government should assume the direct management of the Oude dominions; that the Honourable the Court of Directors coincided in his Lordship's views; and, in order that no doubt may remain on the King's mind as to the sentiments of the home authorities on this point, he, Lord Hardinge, here inserts an extract from the despatch of that Court, for his information; that it is as follows:—'We have, after the most serious consideration, come to the determination of granting to you the discretionary power which you have requested from us for placing the Oude territories under the direct management of officers of the British Government; and you are hereby empowered, if no real and satisfactory improvement shall have taken place in the administration of that country, and if your Government shall still adhere to the opinion expressed in the minute of the Governor-General, to carry the proposed measure into effect, at such period and in such manner as shall appear to you most desirable;' that this resolution was communicated to the Resident and to the King, and advantage was taken of it to press upon his Majesty the necessity of an immediate reform of his administration; that the above extract will enable the

King to form a clear judgment of the position in which the sovereigns of Oude are placed by treaty; that the Governor-General is required, when gross and systematic abuses prevail, to apply such a remedy as the exigency of the case may appear to require—that he has no option in the performance of that duty.

"That by wisely taking timely measures for the reformation of abuses, as one of the first acts of his reign, his Majesty will, with honour to his own character, rescue his people from their present miserable condition; but if he procrastinates he will incur the risk of forcing the British Government to interfere, by assuming the government of Oude; that the former course would redound to his Majesty's credit and dignity, while the latter would give the British Government concern in the case of a prince whom, as our ally, we sincerely desire to honour and uphold; that for these reasons, and on account of the King's inexperience, the Governor-General is not disposed to act immediately on the power vested in him by the Honourable Court's despatch above quoted, still less is he disposed to hold him responsible for the misrule of his predecessors, nor does he expect that so inveterate a system of misgovernment can suddenly be eradicated; that the resolution, and the preliminary measures 'to effect this purpose,' can and ought at once to be adopted by the King; that if his Majesty cordially enters into the plan suggested by the Governor-General for the improvement of his administration, he may have the satisfaction, within the period specified of two years, of checking and eradicating the worst abuses, and, at the same time, of maintaining his own sovereignty and the native institutions of his kingdom unimpaired; but if he does not, if he takes a vacillating course, and fail by refusing to act on the Governor-General's advice, he is aware of the other alternative and of the consequences. It must, then, be manifest to the whole world that, whatever may happen, the King has received a friendly and timely warning."

On the 24th of December in that year, 1847, Government, in reply to the Resident's letter of the 30th November, states that it does not consider the King's reply in any respect satisfactory; that the Resident is to remind his Majesty that under paragraph the 23rd of the memorandum read out to him by the Governor-General's direction, the Resident has been required to submit periodical reports of the state of his dominions, and that his Majesty must be fully aware of the responsibility he incurs if he neglects, during the interval allowed him, to introduce the requisite reforms in his administration.

More than two years have elapsed since this caution was given, and the King has done nothing to improve his administration, abstained from no personal indulgence, given no attention whatever to public affairs. He had before that time tried to imitate his father, attend a little to public affairs, and see occasionally the members of the royal family and aristocracy, at least of the city, and heads of departments; but the effort was painful, and soon ceased altogether to be made. He had from boyhood mixed in no other society than that in which he now mixes exclusively, and he will never submit to the restraints of any other. The King has utterly disregarded alike the Governor-General's advice and admonitions, the duties and responsibilities of his high office, and the sufferings of the many millions subject to his rule. His time and attention are devoted entirely to the pursuit of personal gratifications; he associates with none but such as those who contribute to such gratifications—women, singers, and eunuchs; and he never, I believe, reads or hears read any petition from his suffering subjects, any report from his local officers civil or military, or presidents of his fiscal and judicial courts, or functionaries of any kind. He seems to take no interest whatever in public affairs, and to care nothing whatever about them.

The King had natural capacity equal to that of any of those who have preceded him in the sovereignty of Oude since the death of Saadut Allee in 1814, but he is the only one who has systematically declined to devote any of that capacity, or any of his time, to the conduct of public affairs; to see and occasionally commune with the heads of departments, the members of the royal family, and native gentlemen of the capital; to read or have read to him the reports of his local functionaries, and petitions or redress of wrongs from his suffering subjects.*

In the reports of the Resident on the state of affairs in Oude, and the replies of Government, much importance has been always attached to the change from the contract, or *ijara* system, to that of the *amanee*, or trust management system; and since the time of Lord Hardinge's visit

* This systematic disregard of his high duties and responsibilities still continues to be manifested by the King of Oude; and is observed, with feelings of indignation and abhorrence, by his well-disposed subjects of all classes and grades, who are thereby left to the mercy of men without any feeling of security in their tenure of office, any scruples of conscience, or feelings of humanity or of honour. So inveterate is the system of misgovernment—so deeply are all those, now employed in the administration, interested in maintaining its worst abuses—and so fruitless is it to expect the King to remove them, or employ better men, or to be ever able to inspire any men, whom he may appoint, with a disposition to serve him more honestly, and to respect the rights of others, or consider the reputation and permanent interests of their own master, that the impression has become strong and general, that our Government can no longer support the present Government of Oude, without seriously neglecting its duty towards the people.—1851, W. H. S.

many more districts have been put under the latter system; but this has not tended, in the smallest degree, to the benefit of the people of these districts. The same abuses prevail under the one system as under the other. The troops employed in the districts under the one are the same as those employed in the districts under the other, and they prey just as much upon the people. There is the same system of rack-rent in the one as in the other, and the same uncertainty in the rate of the Government demand. The manager under the *amanut* system demands the same secret gratuities and *nuzuranas* for himself and his patrons at Court from the landholders, as the contractor; and if they refuse to pay them they are besieged, attacked, and cut up, and their estates desolated in the same manner. The *amanut* manager knows that his tenure of office depends as much upon the amount which he pays to his sovereign, and to his patrons at Court, as that of the contractor, and he exacts and extorts as much as he can in the same manner. Unless he pays his patrons the same he knows that he shall soon be removed, or driven to resign by the want of means to enforce the payment of the revenues justly due.

The objections which are urged against the employment of British troops in support of the authority of revenue contractors, are equally applicable to their employment in support of that of amanee managers. Their employment is just as liable to abuse under the one as under the other. It is not a whit easier to ascertain whether a demand for balance of revenue from, or a charge of contumacy against, a landholder is just or unjust in the one than in the other. In neither is the demand set forth in public documents understood by either party to be the *real* demand. Both parties are equally interested in preventing a portion of the real demand from appearing in the public accounts; and the quarrel is almost always about the rate of this concealed portion—the collector trying to augment, and the landlord trying to reduce it.

In a letter to the Resident, dated the 29th of March, 1823, Government observes: "As some palliation of the mischief of our forces being constantly employed in what might be too often termed the cause of injustice and extortion, the Government in 1811 distinctly declared our right of previously investigating, and of arbitrating the demands which its troops might be called upon to support, as also its resolution to exercise that right on all future occasions. The execution of the important duty in question seems to be almost invariably delegated by the Resident to the officers commanding at the different stations, who, after receiving general powers to attend to the requisitions of the amils, become the sole judges of the individual cases, in which aid is to be afforded or withheld; and the discretion again unavoidably descends from them, in many instances, to the officers commanding parties detached from the main body. It is obvious that an inquiry of this description can afford but a partial check to, and a feeble security against, injustice and oppression where specific engagements rarely exist, and where the point at issue is frequently the demand for augmenting rates of revenue, founded on alleged assets sufficient to meet that increase.

"Neither is the aid thus afforded at all effectual for the purposes of the Government of Oude, whether present or future, as is clear from the annual repetition of the same scenes of resistance and compulsion. As fast as disorders are suppressed in one quarter they spring up in another. Forts that are this year dismantled are restored again the next; the compulsion exercised upon particular individuals in one season has no effect in producing more regularity on their parts, or on that of others in the ensuing season, until the same process has been again gone through; whilst the contempt and odium attaching to a system of collecting the revenues, by the habitual intervention of the troops of another State, infallibly tend to aggravate the evil, by destroying all remains of confidence in his Majesty, or respect for his authority."

The aid of British troops in the collection of the revenues of Oude has long ceased to be afforded; but when they have been afforded for the suppression of leaders of atrocious bands of robbers, who preyed upon the people, and seized upon the lands of their weaker neighbours, and they have been driven from their forts and strongholds, the privilege of building them up again, or re-occupying and garrisoning them with the same bands of robbers, to be employed in the same way, is purchased from the local authorities, or the patrons of these leaders at Court, during the same or the succeeding season. The same things continue to be done every season where no British troops are employed. Such privileges are purchased with as much facility as those for the supply of essence or spices in the palace; unless the Resident should interpose authoritatively to prevent it, which he very rarely does. Indeed it is seldom that a Resident knows or cares anything about the matter.

I may say generally, that in Oude the larger landholders do not pay more than one-third of their net rents to the Government, while some of them do not pay one-fifth or one-tenth. In the half of the territory made over to us in 1801, the great landholders who still retain their estates pay to our Government at least two-thirds of their net rents. In Oude these great landholders have, at present, about two hundred and fifty mud forts, mounting about five hundred guns, and containing on an average four hundred armed men, or a total of one hundred thousand, trained and maintained to fight against other, or against the Government authorities; and to pillage the peaceful and industrious around whenever so employed. In the half of the territory ceded to us in 1801, this class of armed retainers has disappeared altogether. Hence from the Oude half we have some fifty thousand native officers and sipahees in our native army, while from our half we have not perhaps five thousand.

One thing is clear, that we cannot restore to the Oude Government the territory we acquired from it by the treaty of 1801, and the people who occupy it; and that we cannot withdraw our support from that Government altogether without doing so. It is no less clear that all our efforts to make the Government of Oude, under the support which we are bound by that treaty to give it, fulfil the duties to its people to which it was pledged by that treaty, have failed during the fifty years that have elapsed since it was made.

The only alternative left, appears to be for the paramount power to take upon itself the administration, and give to the sovereign, the royal family, and its stipendiary dependents, all the surplus revenues in pensions, opening as much as possible all employments in the civil administration to the educated classes of Oude. The military and police establishments would consist almost exclusively of Oude men. Under such a system more of these classes would be employed than at present, for few of the officers employed in the administration are of these classes—the greater part of them are adventurers from all parts of India, without character or education. The number of such officers would be multiplied fourfold; and the means of paying them would be taken from the favourites and parasites of the Court who now do nothing but mischief.

Such a change would be popular among the members of the royal family itself, who now get their pensions after long intervals—often after two and even three years, and with shameful reductions in behalf of those favourites and parasites whom they detest and despise, but whom the minister, for his own personal purposes, is obliged to conciliate by such perquisites. It would be popular among the educated classes, as opening to them offices now filled by knaves and vagabonds from all parts of India. It would be no less so to the well-disposed portion of the agricultural classes, who would be sure of protection to life, property, and character, without the expensive trains of armed followers which they now keep up. But to secure this, we should require to provide them with a more simple system of civil judicature than that which we have at work in our old territories.

The change would be popular, with few exceptions, among all the mercantile and manufacturing classes. It would give vast employment to all the labouring classes throughout the country, in the construction of good roads, bridges, wells, tanks, temples, suraes, military and civil buildings, and other public works; but above all, in that of private dwellings, and other edifices for use and ornament, in which all men would be proud to lay out their wealth to perpetuate their names, when secured in the

P 2

possession by an honest and efficient Government; but more especially those who would be no longer able to employ their means in maintaining armed bands, to resist the local authorities and disturb the peace of the country. On the whole, I think that at least nine-tenths of the people of Oude would hail the change as a great blessing; always providing, that our system of administration should be rendered as simple as possible to meet the wants and wishes of a simple people.

Though the Resident has never been able to secure any substantial and permanent improvement in the administration, he often interposes successfully in individual cases, to relieve suffering, and secure redress for wrongs; and the people see that he interferes in no others. Their only regret is, that he does not interpose more often, and that his efforts, when he does, should be so often thwarted or disregarded. The British character is, in consequence, respected in the remotest village and jungle in Oude; and there is, I believe, no part of India where an European officer is received, among the people of all classes, with more kindness and courtesy than in Oude. There is, certainly, no city or town in any other native State in India where he is treated in the crowded streets with more respect. This must of course be accounted for in great measure from the greater part of the members of the royal family, and the relatives and dependents of the several persons who have held the highest offices of the State since 1814, either receiving their incomes from the British Government in treaty pensions, or in interest on our Government securities, or being guaranteed in those which they receive from the Oude Government by ours. A great many of the families of the middle classes depend entirely upon the interest which they receive from us on our Government securities. There is, indeed, hardly a respectable family in Lucknow that is not more or less dependent upon our Government for protection, and proud to have it considered that they are so. The works and institutions which would soon be created out of revenues, now absorbed by worthless Court favourites, would soon embellish the face of the country, improve the character, condition, and habits of the people, stimulate their industry in agriculture, manufactures, and commerce; and render our connection with the Oude Government honourable to our name in the estimation of all India.

CHAPTER V.

Baree-Biswa district—Force with the Nazim, Lal Bahader—Town of Peernuggur—Dacoitee by Lal and Dhokul Partuks—Gangs of robbers easily formed out of the loose characters which abound in Oude—The lands tilled in spite of all disorders—Delta between the Chouka and Ghagra rivers—Seed sown and produce yielded on land—Rent and stock—Nawab Allee, the holder of the Mahmoodabad estate—Mode of augmenting his estate—Insecurity of marriage processions—Belt of jungle, fourteen miles west from the Lucknow Cantonments—Gungabuksh Rawat—His attack on Dewa—The family inveterate robbers—Bhurs, once a civilized and ruling people in Oude—Extirpated systematically in the fourteenth century—Depredations of Parsees—Infanticide—How maintained—Want of influential middle class of merchants and manufacturers—Suttee—Troops with the Amil—Seizure of a marriage procession by Imambuksh, a gang leader—Perquisites and allowances of Passee watchmen over corn-fields—Their fidelity to trusts—Ahbun Sing, of Kyampoor, murders his father—Rajah Singjoo, of Soorujpoor—Seodeen, another leader of the same tribe—Principal gang leaders of the Dureeabad Rodowlee district—Jugurnath Chuprassie—Bhooree Khan—How these gangs escape punishment—Twenty-four belts of jungle preserved by landholders, always or occasionally, refractory in Oude—Cover eight hundred and eighty-six square miles of good land—How such atrocious characters find followers, and landholders of high degree to screen, shelter, and aid them.

February 14, 1850.—Peernuggur, ten miles south-east, over a plain of the same soil, but with more than the usual proportion of oosur. Trees and groves as usual, but not quite so fine or numerous. The Nazim of Khyrabad took leave of me on his boundary as we crossed it about midway, and entered the district of "Baree Biswa," which is held in farm by Lal Bahader,*

* This man was in prison at Lucknow as a defaulter, but made his escape in October, 1851, by drugging the sentry placed over him, and got safe into British territory.

a Hindoo, who there met us. This fiscal officer has under him the "Jafiree," and "Tagfore" Regiments of nujeebs, and eight pieces of cannon. The commandants of both corps are in attendance at Court, and one of them, Imdad Hoseyn, never leaves it. The other does condescend sometimes to come out to look at his regiment when *not on service*. The draft-bullocks for the guns have, the Nazim tells me, had a little grain within the last month, but still not more than a quarter of the amount for which the King is charged. Peernuggur is now a place of little note upon the banks of the little river Sae, which here flows under a bridge built by Asuf-od Dowlah some sixty years ago.

Gang-robberies are here as frequent as in Khyrabad, and the respectable inhabitants are going off in the same manner. One which took place in July last year is characteristic of the state of society in Oude, and may be mentioned here. Twelve sipahees of the 59th Regiment Native Infantry, then stationed at Bareilly, lodged here for the night, in a surae, on their way home on furlough. Dal Partuk, a Brahmin by caste, and a man of strength and resolution, resided here and cultivated a small patch of land. He had two pair of bullocks, which used to be continually trespassing upon other men's fields and gardens, and embroiling him with the people, till one night they disappeared. Dal Partuk called upon his neighbours, who had suffered from their trespasses, to restore them or pay the value, and threatened to rob, plunder, and burn down the town if they did not.

A great number of pausees reside in and around the town, and he knew that he could collect a gang of them for any enterprise of this sort at the shortest notice. The people were not disposed to pay the value of his lost bullocks, and they could not be found. While he was meditating his revenge, his relation, Dhokul Partuk, was by a trifling accident driven to take the field as a robber. An oil-vender, a female, from a neighbouring village, had presumed to come to Peernuggur, and offer oil for sale. The oil-venders of the town, dreading the consequences of such competition, went forthwith to the little garrison and prayed for *protection.* One of the sipahees went off to the silversmith to whom the oil-vender had sold twopence-worth of oil, and, finding the oil-vender still with him, proceeded at once to seize both, and take them off to the garrison as criminals. Dhokul Partuk, who lived close by, and had his sword by his side, went up and remonstrated with the sipahee, who, taking him to be another silversmith, struck him across the face with his stick. Dhokul drew his sword, and made a cut at the sipahee, which would have severed his head from his body had he not fallen backwards. As it was, he got a severe cut in the chest, and ran off to his companions. Dhokul went out of the town with his drawn sword, and no one dared to pursue him. At night he returned, took off his family to a distant village, became a leader of a band of pausee bowmen, and invited his kinsman, Dal Partuk, to follow his example.

Together, they made an attack at night upon the town, and burnt down one quarter of the houses. Dal Partuk offered to come to terms and live in the town again, if the people would pay the value of his lost bullocks, and give him a small income of five rupees a-month. This they refused to do, and the plunder and burning went on. At last they made this attack upon the party in the surae, which happened to be so full that several of the sipahees and others were cooking outside the walls. None of the travellers had arms to defend themselves, and those inside closed the doors as soon as they heard the alarm. The pausees, with their bows and arrows, killed two of the sipahees who were outside, and while the gang was trying to force open the doors of the surae, the people of the town, headed by a party of eight pausee bowmen of their own, attacked and drove them back. These bowmen followed the gang for some distance, and killed several of them with their arrows. The sipahees who escaped proceeded in all haste to the Resident, and the Frontier Police has since succeeded in arresting several of the gang; but the two leaders have hitherto been screened by Goorbuksh Sing and other great landholders in their interest. The eight pausees who exerted themselves so successfully in defence of the town and surae were expecting an attack from the pausees of a neighbouring village, and ready for action when the alarm was given.

These parties of pausee bowmen have each under their charge a certain number of villages, whose crops and other property they are pledged to defend for the payment of a certain sum, or a certain portion of land rent-free. In one of these, under the Peernuggur party, three bullocks had been stolen by the pausees of a neighbouring town. They were traced to them, and, as they would neither restore them nor pay their value, the Peernuggur party attacked them one night in their sleep, and killed the leader and four of his followers, to deter others of the tribe from trespassing on property under their charge. They expect, they told us, to be attacked in return some night, and are obliged to be always prepared, but have not the slightest apprehension of ever being called to account for such things by the officers of Government. Nor would Dal and Dhokul Partuk have any such apprehension, had not the Resident taken up the question of the murder of the Honourable Company's sipahees as an international one. After plundering and burning down a dozen villages, and murdering a score or two of people, they would have come back and reoccupied their houses in the town without any fear of being molested or *questioned* by Government officers. Nor would the people of the town object to their residing among them again, provided they pledged themselves to abstain in future from molesting them. Goorbuksh Sing, only a few days ago, offered the contractor, Hoseyn Allee, the sum of five thousand rupees if he would satisfy the Resident that Dal Partuk had nothing whatever to do with the Peernuggur dacoitee, and thereby induce him to discontinue the pursuit.*

The people of towns and villages, having no protection whatever from the Government, are obliged to keep up, at their own cost, this police of pausee bowmen, who are bound only to protect those who pay them. As their families increase beyond the means derived from this, their only legitimate employment, their members thieve in the neighbouring or distant villages, rob on the high-roads, or join the gangs of those who are robbers by profession, or take the trade in consequence of disputes and misunderstandings with Government authorities or their neighbours. In Oude—and indeed in all other parts of India, under a Government so weak and indifferent to the sufferings of its subjects—all men who consider arms to be their proper profession think themselves justified in using them to extort the means of subsistence from those who have property when they have

* Dhokul Partuk and Dal Partuk were at last secured. Dhokul died in the king's gaol, but Dal Partuk is still in prison under trial.

none, and can no longer find what they consider to be suitable employment. All Rajpoots are of this class, and the greater part of the landholders in Oude are Rajpoots. But a great part of the Mahommedan rural population are of the same class, and no small portion of the Brahmin inhabitants, like the two Partuks above named, consider arms to be their proper profession; and all find the ready means of forming gangs of robbers out of these pausee bowmen and the many loose characters to whom the disorders of the country give rise.

A great many of the officers and sipahees of the King's nujeeb and other regiments are every month discharged for mutiny, insubordination, abuse of authority, or neglect of duty, or merely to make room for men more subservient to Court favourites, or because they cannot or will not pay the demanded gratuity to a new and useless commandant appointed by Court favour. The plunder of villages has been the daily occupation of these men during the whole period of their service, and they become the worst of this class of loose characters, ready to join any band of freebooters. Such bands are always sure to find a patron among the landholders ready to receive and protect them, for a due share of their booty, against any force that the King's officers may send after them; and, if they prefer it as less costly, they can always find a manager of a district ready to do the same, on condition that they abstain from plundering within his jurisdiction. The greater part of the land is, however, cultivated, and well cultivated under all this confusion and consequent insecurity. Tillage is the one thing needful to all, and the persons from whom trespasses on the crops are most apprehended are the reckless and disorderly trains of Government officials.

February 16, 1850.—Biswa, eighteen miles east, over a plain of excellent soil, partly doomut, but chiefly mutteear, well studded with trees and groves, scantily cultivated for the half of the way, but fully and beautifully for the second half. The wheat beginning to change colour as it approaches maturity, and waving in the gentle morning breeze; intervening fields covered with mixed crops of peas, gram, ulsee, teora, surson, mustard, all in flower, and glittering like so many rich parterres; patches here and there of the dark-green *arahur* and yellow sugar-cane rising in bold relief; mango-groves, majestic single trees, and clusters of the graceful bamboo studding the whole surface, and closing the distant horizon in one seemingly-continued line of fence—the eye never tires of such a scene, but would like now and then to rest upon some architectural work of ornament or utility to aid the imagination in peopling it.

The road for the last six miles passes through the estate of Nawab Allee, a Mahommedan landholder, who is a strong man and a good manager and paymaster. His rent-roll is about four hundred thousand rupees a-year, and he pays Government about one hundred and fifty thousand. His hereditary possession was a small one, and his estate has grown to the present size in the usual way. He has lent money in mortgage and foreclosed; he has given security for revenue due to Government by other landholders, who have failed to pay, and had their estates made over to him; he has given security for the appearance, when called for, of others, and, on their failing to appear (perchance at his own instigation), had their lands made over to him by the Government authorities, on condition of making good the Government demand upon them; he has offered a higher rate of revenue for lands than present holders could make them yield, and, after getting possession, brought the demand down to a low rate in collusion with Government officers. Some three-fourths of the magnificent estate which he now holds he has obtained in these and other ways by fraud, violence, or collusion within the last few years. He is too powerful and wealthy to admit of any one's getting his lands out of his hands after they have once passed into them, no matter how.

The Chowka river flows from the forest towards the Ghagra, about ten miles to the east from Biswa, and I am told that the richest sheet of cultivation in Oude is within the delta formed by these two rivers.* At the apex of this delta stands the fort of Bhitolee, which I have often mentioned as belonging to Rajah Goorbuksh Sing, and being under siege by the contractor of the Khyrabad district when we passed the Ghagra in December. Biswa is a large town, well situated on a good soil and open plain, and its vicinity would be well suited for a cantonment or seat for civil establishments. Much of the cloth called sullum used to be made here for export to Europe, but the demand has ceased, and with it the manufacture.

February 17 *and* 18, 1850.—Detained at Biswa by rain.

February 19, 1850.—Yesterday evening came to Kaharpore, ten miles, over a plain of the same fine soil,

* This delta contains the following noble estates; 1, Dhorehra; 2, Eesanuggur; 3, Chehlary; 4, Rampore; 5, Bhitolee; 6, Mullahpore; 7, Seonta; 8, Nigaseen; and 9, Bhera Jugdeopore. The Turae forest forms the base of this delta, and the estates of Dhorehra, Eesanuggur, and Bhera Jugdeopore lie along its border. They have been much injured by the King's troops within the last three years. Bhitolee is at the apex.

mutteear of the best quality, running here and there into doomutteea and even bhoor. Cultivation good, and the plain covered with rich spring crops, except where the ground is being prepared to receive the autumn seed in June next. It is considered good husbandry to plough, cross-plough, and prepare the lands thus early. The spring crops are considered to be more promising than they have been at any other season for the last twenty years. The farmers and cultivators calculate upon an average return of ten and twelve fold, and say that, in other parts of Oude where the lands are richer, there will be one of fifteen or twenty of wheat, gram, &c. The pucka-beega, two thousand seven hundred and fifty-six square yards, requires one maund of seed of forty seers, of eighty rupees of the King's and Company's coinage the seer.* The country, as usual, studded with trees, single, and in clusters and groves, intermingled with bamboos, which are, however, for the most part, of the smaller or hill kind.

* The pucka-beega in Oude is about the same as that which prevails over our North-Western Provinces, two thousand seven hundred and fifty-six and a quarter square yards, or something more than one-half of our English statute acre, which is four thousand eight hundred and forty square yards. This pucka-beega takes of seed-wheat one maund, or eighty pounds; and yields on an average, under good tillage, eight returns of the seed, or eight maunds, or six hundred and forty pounds, which, at one rupee the maund, yields eight rupees, or sixteen shillings. The stock required in Oude in irrigated lands is about twenty rupees the pucka-beega. The rent on an average two rupees. In England an acre, on an average, requires two and three-quarter bushels of seed wheat, or one hundred and seventy-six pounds, or two maunds and sixteen seers, and yields twenty-four bushels, or one thousand five hundred and thirty-six pounds. This at forty shillings the quarter (512 lbs.) would yield six pounds sterling. The stock required in England is estimated at ten pounds sterling per acre, or ten times the annual rent. It is difficult to estimate the rate of rent on land in England, since the reputed owner is said to be "only the ninth and last recipient of rent."

On reaching camp, I met, for the first time, the great landholder, Nawab Allee, of Mahmoodabad. In appearance, he is a quiet gentlemanly man, of middle age and stature. He keeps his lands in the finest possible state of tillage, however objectionable the means by which he acquires them. His family have held the estates of Mahmoodabad and Belehree for many generations as zumeendars, or proprietors; but they have augmented them greatly, absorbing into them the estates of their weaker neighbours.*

Akram Allee held Mahmoodabad, and was succeeded in the possession by his son, Mosahib Allee, who died about forty years ago, leaving the estate to his widow, who held it for twenty-eight years up to A. D. 1838, when she died. She had, the year before, adopted her nephew, Nawab Allee, and he succeeded to the estate. The Belehree estate is held by his elder brother, Abud Allee, who is augmenting it in the same way, but not at the same rate. I may mention a few recent cases, as illustrative of the manner in which such things are done in Oude.

Mithun Sing, of an ancient Rajpoot family, held the estate of Semree, which had been held by his ancestors for many centuries. It consisted of twelve fine villages, paid to Government 4000 rupees a year, and yielded him a rent roll of 20,000. Nawab Allee coveted very much this estate, which bordered on his own. Three years

* Akram Allee and Muzhur Allee inherited the estate in two divisions. Akram Allee got Mahmoodabad, and had two sons, Surufraz Allee, who died without issue, before his father; and Mosahib Allee, who succeeded to the estate, but died without issue. Muzhur Allee got the estate of Belehree, and had two sons, Abud Allee, and Nawab Allee. Abud Allee succeeded to the estate of Belehree, and Nawab Allee to that of Mahmoodabad by adoption.

ago, he instigated the Nazim to demand an increase of 5000 rupees a-year from the estate; and at the same time invited Mithun Sing to his house, and persuaded him to resist the demand to the last. He took to the jungles, and in the contest between him and the Nazim all the crops of the season were destroyed, and all the cultivators driven from the lands. When the season of tillage returned in June, and Mithun Sing had been reduced to the last stage of poverty, Nawab Allee consented to become the mediator, got a lease from the Chuckladar for Mithun Sing at 4500 rupees a-year, and stood surety for the punctual payment of the demand. Poor Mithun Sing could pay nothing, and Nawab Allee got possession of the estate in liquidation of the balance due to him; and assigned to Mithun Sing five hundred pucka-beegas of land for his subsistence. He still resides on the estate, and supports his family by the tillage of these few beegas.

Amdhun Chowdheree held a share in the estate of Biswa, consisting of sixty-five villages; paying to Government 12,000 rupees a-year, and yielding a rent-roll of 65,000. His elder brother's widow resided on the estate, supported by Amdhun, who managed its affairs for the family. Nawab Allee got up a quarrel between her and her brother-in-law; and she assumed the right to authorize Nawab Allee to seize upon the whole estate. Amdhun appealed to his clan, but Nawab Allee, in collusion with the Nazim, was too strong for him, and got possession by taking a strong force, and driving out all who presumed to resist him. The estate had been held by the family for many centuries.

Mohun Sing held the estate of Mundhuna, which had been in his family for many generations. He was, by the usual process, five years ago, constrained to accept the security of Nawab Allee for the punctual payment of the revenue; and his estate was absorbed in the usual way, the year after. He is now, like a boa-constrictor, swallowing up Chowdheree Pertab Sing, who holds a large share in the hereditary estate of Biswa, which has been in the possession of the family for a great many generations. This share consisted of thirty-six villages, and paid a revenue to Government of fourteen thousand. Last year, Nawab Allee instigated the Nazim to demand ten thousand more. The Nazim, to prevent all disputes, assigned the twenty-four thousand to Mirza Hoseyn Beg, the commandant of a troop of cavalry, employed under him, in liquidation of their arrears of pay. The commandant gave him a receipt for the amount, which the Nazim sent to the treasury, and got credit for the amount in his accounts. But poor Pertab Sing could not pay, and was imprisoned by the cavalry, who kept possession of his person, and took upon them the collection of his rents. Nawab Allee came in and paid what was due; and gave security for the punctual payment of the revenue for the ensuing year. The estate was made over to him; and he put on score after score of *dustuk* bearers, who soon reduced Pertab Sing to utter beggary. Ten thousand rupees were due to Nawab Allee, and he had nothing left to sell; and under such circumstances no man else would lend him anything.

The dustuk bearers are servants of the creditor, who are sent to attend the debtor, extort from him their wages and subsistence, and see that he does not move, eat, or drink till he pays them. During this time the creditor saves all the wages of these attendants; and they commonly exact double wages from the debtor, so that he is soon reduced to terms. In this stage we found the poor Chowdheree on reaching Biswa. I had him released, and so admonished Nawab Allee, that he has some little chance of saving his estate.

Bisram Sing held the estate of Kooa Danda, which had been in the possession of his family of Ahbun Rajpoots for many centuries. It consisted of thirty-five villages, paid a revenue of six thousand rupees a-year, and yielded a rent-roll of eighteen thousand and five hundred. Nawab Allee coveted it as being on his border, and in good order. As soon as his friend, Allee Buksh, was appointed Nazim of the district, he prevailed upon him to report to the Durbar that Bisram Sing was a refractory subject, and plunderer; and to request permission to put him down by force of arms. This was in 1844, while Bisram Sing was living quietly on his estate. On receiving the order, which came as a matter of course, the Nazim united his force with that of Nawab Allee, and attacked the house of Bisram Sing, which had only twenty-two men to defend it against two thousand. Six of the twenty-two were killed, eight wounded, and eight only escaped; and Nawab Allee took possession of the estate.

Bisram Sing was at Lucknow at the time, trying to rebut the false charges of the Nazim; but his influence was unhappily too strong for him, and he got no redress. Soon after Nirput Sing, a sipahee in the 9th Regiment Native Infantry, presented a petition to the Resident, stating that he was the brother of Bisram Sing, and equally interested in the estate; and a special officer, Busharut Allee, was ordered by the Durbar to investigate and decide the case. He decided in favour of Nirput, the sipahee, and Bisram Sing. Another special officer was sent out to restore Bisram to possession. Nawab

Allee then pleaded the non-existence of any relationship between Nirput and Bisram; and a third special officer has been sent out to ascertain this fact.

Belehree, held by Abud Allee, consists of forty villages, pays a revenue of twelve thousand rupees a-year, and yields a rent-roll of forty thousand. Abud Allee holds also the estate of Pyntee, in the same district, consisting of eighty villages, paying a revenue of thirty-five thousand, and yielding a rent-roll of one hundred and forty thousand. It had been held by his relative, Kazim Allee, who was succeeded in the possession by Nizam Allee, the husband of his only daughter. Nizam Allee was in A. D. 1841 killed by a servant, who was cut down and killed in return by his attendants. Nizam Allee's widow held till 1843, when she made over the estate to Abud Allee, by whom she is supported.

Nawab Allee has always money at command to purchase influence at Court when required; and he has also a brave and well-armed force, with which to aid the governor of the district, when he makes it worth his while to do so, in crushing a refractory landholder. These are the sources of his power, and he is not at all scrupulous in the use of it—it is not the fashion to be so in Oude.

February 20th, 1850.—Came on sixteen miles to Futtehpore, in the estate of Nawab Allee, passing Mahmoodabad half way. Near that place we passed through a grove of mango and other trees called the "Lak Peree," or the grove of a hundred thousand trees, planted by his ancestors forty years ago. The soil is the same, the country level, studded with the same rich foliage, and covered with the same fine crops. As we were passing through his estate, and were to encamp in it again to-day, Nawab Allee attended me on horseback; and I endeavoured to impress upon him and the Nazim the necessity of respecting the rights of others, and more particularly those of the old Chowdheree Pertab Sing. "Why is it," I asked, "that this beautiful scene is not embellished by any architectural beauties? Sheikh Sadee, the poet, so deservedly beloved by you all, old and young, Hindoos and Mahommedans, says, 'The man who leaves behind him in any place, a bridge, a well, a church, or a caravansera, never dies.' Here not even a respectable dwelling-house is to be seen, much less a bridge, a church, or a caravansera." "Here, sir," said old Bukhtawur, "men must always be ready for a run to the jungles. Unless they are so, they can preserve nothing from the grasp of the contractors of the present day, who have no respect for property or person—for their own character, or for that of their sovereign. The moment that a man runs to save himself, family, and property, they rob and pull down his house, and those of all connected with him. When a man has nothing but mud walls, with invisible mud covers, they give him no anxiety; he knows that he can build them up again in a few days, or even a few hours, when he comes back from the jungles; and he cares little about what is done to them during his absence. Had he an expensive house of burnt brick and mortar, he could never feel quite free. He might be tempted to defend it, and lose some valuable lives; or he might be obliged to submit to unjust terms. Were he to lay out his money in expensive mosques, temples, and tombs, they would restrain him in the same way; and he is content to live without them, and have his loins always girded for fight or flight."

"True," said Nawab Allee, "very true; we can plant groves and make wells, but we cannot venture to erect costly buildings of any kind. You saw the Nazim of Khyrabad, only a few days ago, bringing all his troops down upon Rampore, because the landlord, Goman Sing, would not consent to the increase he demanded of ten thousand, upon seventeen thousand rupees a-year, which he had hitherto paid. Goman Sing took to the jungles; and in ten days his fine crops would all have been destroyed, and his houses levelled with the ground, had you not interposed, and admonished both. The one at last consented to take, and the other to pay an increase of five thousand. Only three years ago, Goman Sing's father was killed by the Nazim in a similar struggle; and landholders must always be prepared for them."

February 21*st*, 1850.—Bureearpore, ten miles south-east, over a plain of the same fine soil, well cultivated, and carpeted with the same fine crops and rich foliage. Midway we entered the district of Ramnuggur Dhumeree, held by Rajah Gorbuksh Sing under the security of Seoraj-od Deen, the person who attempted in vain to arrest the charge of the two regiments upon the Khyrabad Nazim by holding up the *sacred Koran* over his head. He met me on his boundary, and Nawab Allee and the Nazim of Baree Biswa took their leave. Nawab Allee's brother, Abud Allee, came to pay his respects to me yesterday evening. He is a respectable person in appearance, and a man of good sense. The landscape was, I think, on the whole richer than any other that I have seen in Oude; but I am told that it is still richer at a distance from the road, where the poppy is grown in abundance, and opium of the best quality made.*

* Opium sells in Oude at from three to eight rupees the seer, according to its quality. In our neighbouring districts it sells at fourteen rupees the seer, in the shops licensed by Government. Government, in our districts, get opium from the cultivators and manufacturers at

Still lamenting the want of all architectural ornament to the scene, and signs of manufacturing and commercial industry, to show that people had property, and were able to display and enjoy it, and gradations of rank, I asked whether people invested their wealth in the loans of our Government. "Sir," said Bukhtawur Sing, "the people who reside in the country know nothing about your Government paper; it is only the people of the capital that hold it or understand its value. The landholders and peasantry would never be able to keep it in safety, or understand when and how to draw the interest."

"Do they spend more in marriage and other ceremonies than the people of other parts of India, or do they make greater displays on such occasions?"

"Quite the reverse, sir," said Seoraj-od Deen; "they dare not make any display at all. Only the other day, Gunga Buksh, the refractory landholder of Kasimgunge, attacked a marriage-procession in the village of ——, carried off the bridegroom, and imprisoned him till he paid the large ransom demanded from him. In February last year Imam Buksh Behraleen, of Oseyree, having quarrelled with the Amil, attacked and carried off a whole marriage party to the jungles. They gave up all the property they had, and offered to sign bonds for more, to be paid by their friends for their ransom; but he told them that *money* would not do; that their families were people of influence, and must make the King's officers restore him to his estate upon his own terms, or he would keep them till they all died. They exerted themselves, and Imam Buksh got back his estate upon his own terms; but he still

---

three rupees and half the seer. The temptation to smuggle is great, but the risk is great also, for the police in our districts is vigilant in this matter.

continues to rob and plunder. These crimes are to them diversions from which there is no making them desist."

"There are a dozen gang leaders of this class at present in the belt of jungle which extends westward from our right up to within fourteen miles of the Lucknow cantonments; and the plunder of villages, murder of travellers, and carrying off of brides and bridegrooms from marriage processions, are things of every-day occurrence. There are also in these parts a number of pansee bowmen, who not only join in the enterprises of such gangs as in other districts, but form gangs of their own, under leaders of their own caste, to rob travellers and plunder villages.

"Gunga Buksh of Kasimgunge has his fort in this belt of jungle, and he and his friends and relations take good care that no man cuts any of it down, or cultivates the land. With the gangs which he and his relatives keep up in this jungle, he has driven out the greater part of the Syud proprietors of the surrounding villages, and taken possession of their lands. After driving out the King's troops from the town of Dewa, and exacting ransoms from many of the inhabitants, whom he seized and carried off in several attacks, he, in October last, brought down upon it all the ruffians he could collect, killed no less than twenty-nine persons—chiefly Syuds and land proprietors—and took possession of the town and estate. The chief proprietor, Bakur Allee, was killed among the rest; and Gunga Buksh burnt his body, and suspended his head to a post in his own village of Luseya. He dug down his house and those of all his relations who had been killed with him, and now holds quiet possession of his estate."

This was all true. The Resident, on the application of Haffiz-od Deen, a native judicial officer of Moradabad district—one of the family which had lost so many members in this atrocious attack—urged strongly on the Durbar the necessity of punishing Gunga Buksh and his gang. The Ghunghor Regiment of Infantry, with a squadron of cavalry, and six guns, was sent out in October 1849, for the purpose, under a native officer. On the force moving out, the friends of Gunga Buksh at Court caused the commandant to be sent for on some pretext or other; and he has been detained at the capital ever since. The force has, in consequence, remained idle, and Gunga Buksh has been left quietly to enjoy the fruits of his enterprise. The Amil having no troops to support his authority, or even to defend his person in such a position, has also remained at Court. No revenue has been collected, and the people are left altogether exposed to the depredations of these merciless robbers. The belt of jungle is nine miles long and four miles wide; and the west end of it is within only fourteen miles of the Lucknow cantonments, where we have three regiments of infantry, and a company of artillery.

February 22nd, 1850.—A brief history of the rise of this family may tend to illustrate the state of things in Oude. Khumma Rawut, of the pansee tribe, the great-grandfather of this Gunga Buksh, served Kazee Mahommed, the great-grandfather of this Bakur Allee, as a village watchman, for many years up to his death. He had some influence over his master, and making the most of this and of the clan feeling which subsisted among the pansees of the district, he was able to command the services of a formidable gang when the old Kazee died. He left a young family, and Khumma got possession of five or six villages out of the estate which the old Kazee left to his sons. The sons were too weak to resist the pansees, and when Khumma died he left them to his five sons:—1. Kundee Sing; 2. Bukhta Sing; 3. Alum Sing; 4. Lalsahae; 5. Misree Sing. As the family increased in numbers it has gone on adding to its possessions in the same manner, by attacking and plundering villages, murdering or driving off the old proprietors of the lands, and taking possession of them for themselves. Each branch of the family, as it separates from the parent stock, builds for itself a fort in one or other of the villages which belong to its share of the acquired lands. In this fort the head of each branch of the family resides with his armed followers, and sallies forth to plunder the country and acquire new possessions. In small enterprises each branch acts by itself; in larger ones two or more branches unite, and divide the lands and booty they acquire by amicable arrangement.

They seize all the respectable persons whom they find in the villages which they attack and plunder, keep them in prison, and inflict all manner of tortures upon them, till they have paid, or pledged themselves to pay, all that they have or can borrow from their friends, as their ransom. If they refuse to pay, or to pledge themselves to pay the sum demanded, they murder them. If they pay part, and pledge themselves to pay the rest within a certain time, they are released; and if they fail to fulfil their engagements, they and their families are murdered in a second attack. After the last attack above described upon Dewa, Gunga Buksh seized seven fine villages belonging to the family of Bakur Allee Khan, which they had held for many generations. He, Gunga Buksh, now holds no less than twenty-seven villages, all seized in the same manner, after the plunder and murder of their old proprietors. The whole of this family, descendants of

Khumma Rawut, hold no less than two hundred villages and hamlets, all taken in the same manner from the old proprietors, with the acquiescence or connivance of the local authorities, who were either too weak or too corrupt to punish them, and restore the villages to their proper owners.*

* Kundee Sing had two sons, 1. Cheytun Sing; 2. Ajeet Sing. Cheytun Sing had two sons, 1. Sophul Sing; 2. Thakurpurshad. Sophul Sing had two sons, 1. Keerut Sing; 2. Jote Sing. Ajeet Sing had two sons, 1. Bhugwunt Sing; 2. Rutun Sing. Thakur Purshad, Bhugwunt Sing, and Rutun Sing, reside in a fort which they have built in Bhetae, four miles from Dewa, in the north-west border of the belt of jungle. They hold forty villages, besides hamlets, which they have taken from the old proprietors of the Dewa and Korsee estates. Thakur Purshad has another fort, called Buldeogur, near that of Atursae, two coss south of Dewa; and Bhugwunt Sing has the small fort of Munmutpore, close to Bhetae. Bukta Sing had only one son, Bisram Sing, who had only one son, Gunga Buksh, who built the fort of Kasimgunge, on the north-eastern border of the same belt of jungle, two miles south of Dewa, and on the death of his father, he went to reside in it with his family and gang. He holds twenty-seven fine villages, with hamlets. Twenty of these he seized upon from six to twelve years ago; and the other seven he got after the attack upon Dewa, in October last. He has also a fort called Atursae, two coss south from Dewa; a mile west from Buldeogur. Alum Sing's descendants have remained peaceable cultivators of the soil in Dewa, and are, consequently, of too little note for a place in the genealogical table of the family.

Lalsahae had three sons, 1. Dheer Sing; 2. Bustee Sing; 3. Gokul Sing, all dead. Dheer Sing had two sons, Omed Sing and Jowahir Sing. Omed Sing had three sons, Dirgpaul Sing, Maheput Sing, and Gungadhur, who was murdered by Thakur Pershad, his cousin. Jowahir Sing had one son, Priteepaul Sing. Bustee Sing had two sons, Girwur Sing and Soulee Sing. Girwur Sing had two sons, Dhokul Sing and Shunker Sing. This branch of the family hold the forts of Ramgura and Paharpore, on the border of the jungle six miles south-west from Dewa, and twelve villages besides hamlets taken in the same manner from the old proprietors. Gokul Sing had two sons, Dulloo Sing and Soophul Sing. Dulloo Sing has one son. They reside with the families of Dheer Sing and Bustee Sing.

Misree Sing, the fifth son of Khumma, had three sons, 1. Bonead Sing; 2. Dureeao Sing; 3. name forgotten—all three are dead. Bonead Sing had two sons, 1. Anoop Sing; 2. Goorbuksh Sing. Dureeao Sing

To record all the atrocities committed by the different members of this family in the process of absorbing the estates of their neighbours, and the property of men of substance in the countries around, would be a tedious and unprofitable task; and I shall content myself with mentioning a few that are most prominent in the recollection of the people of thedistrict. About ten years ago, Gunga Buksh and his gang attacked the house of Lalla Shunker Lal, a respectable merchant of Dewa, plundered it, killed the tutor of his three sons, and carried them and their father off to his fort, where he tortured them till they paid him a ransom of nine thousand rupees. On their release they left Dewa, and have ever since resided in Lucknow. Two years after they attacked the village of Saleempore, two miles east from Dewa, killed Nyam Allee, the zumeendar, and seized upon his estate. About six years ago Munnoo, the son of Gunga Buksh, with a gang of near two thousand men, attacked the King's force in the town of Dewa, killed four sipahees, two artillery-men, and two troopers, and plundered the place. About six months ago this gang attacked the house of Ewuz Mahommed, in Dewa, plundered it, levelled it with the ground, and took off all the timbers to their fort of Kasimgunge. Soon after he made the attack in which he killed twenty-nine persons in Dewa, as above described.

Thakur Purshad, about fourteen years ago, attacked

---

had two sons, 1. Anokee Sing; 2. name forgotten. The third son of Misree Sing had three sons, 1. Mulung Sing; 2. Anunt Sing; 3. name forgotten—all three still live.

This branch of the family resides in Satarpore, one mile west from Kasimgunge, in this belt of jungle, and two miles from Dewa, in a fortified house built by them. They have got a small fort, called Pouree, near this place. They form part of Gunga Buksh's gang, and share with him in the booty acquired.

the village of Molookpore, two miles east from Dewa, plundered it, took possession of the land, seized and carried off the proprietor, Sheikh Khoda Buksh, and put him to death in his fort of Bhetae. Three years after he attacked the house of Gholam Mostafa, in Dewa, killed him, and seized upon all the lands he held. Three years ago he attacked the house of Janoo, a shopkeeper, plundered it, and confined and tortured him till he paid a ransom of two hundred and fifty rupees. Three months after he seized and carried off to his fort Roopun, another shopkeeper, and confined and tortured him till he paid a ransom of three hundred rupees. Last year he seized and took off Jhow Dhobee from Dewa, and extorted forty rupees from him. Six months ago he attacked a marriage-procession in Dewa, plundered it, took off the bridegroom, Omed Allee, and confined and tortured him till he paid eleven hundred and fifteen rupees. These men all levy black mail from the country around; and it is those only who cannot or will not pay it, or whose lands they intend to appropriate, that they attack. They created the jungle above described, of nine miles long by four wide, for their own evil purposes, and preserve it with so much vigilance, that no man dares to cut a stick, graze a bullock, or browse a camel in it without their special sanction; indeed, they are so much dreaded, that no man or woman beyond their own family or followers dares enter the jungle.

Omed Sing, fifteen years ago, invited to his house the four proprietors of the village of Owree, Gholam Kadir, Allee Buksh, Durvesh Allee, and Moiz-od Deen, residents of Dewa, and put them to death because they could not, by torture, be made to transfer their lands to him. He then seized their village, and built the fort of Rumgura Paharpore upon it. Omed Sing, Jowahir Sing, Dhokul Sing, and Soophul Sing all reside in this fort with the son of Dulloo Sing. This family of pansees, or, as they call themselves, Rawuts, form at present one of the most formidable gangs of robbers in Oude, and one of the most difficult to put down from their union and inveterate habit of plunder. They can always, at short notice and little cost, collect bands of hundreds of the same tribe and habit to join them in plunder and resistance to lawful authority.

On the 25th of February, 1838, Rajah Dursun Sing, then in charge of the district, wrote to the Durbar to say, "that Gunga Buksh of Dewa was the worst robber in the district, would pay no revenue, and instigated others to withhold theirs; that numerous complaints had been made against him to the Durbar by the people, and that he had been urged by Government to do his best to punish him; that he had long tried all he could to do so, but had not sufficient troops; that his evil deeds increased, however, so much, that he at last determined to run all risks, and on the 27th of that month, on Friday, he left Amaneegunge, and marched forty-eight miles without resting; and on Saturday, before daybreak, reached the fort of Kasimgunge, and invested it on all sides; that he found the fort large and strong, and surrounded with dense jungle; that he had only three guns with him, but, as the enemy were taken by surprise, he took all their outworks one after another; that the besieged got a crowd of their adherents to attack his force in the rear on Saturday night, that they might get off in the confusion, but his troops were ready to intercept them at all points; and, in attempting to cut his way through, Gunga Buksh was seized with all his followers, but the women and children were permitted to go their way; that a good many of the enemy had been killed, and he, Dursun Sing, had had one golundaz and five sipahees killed and ten persons wounded."

The King sent Dursun Sing a dress of honour with the title of Rajah on the 3rd of March, 1838, and ordered him to have the fort levelled with the ground. Dursun Sing, in reply, states that he had men employed in pulling down the fort; and, in reply to an order to send in a list of the property taken from the besieged, he states, on the 12th of March, 1838, that none whatever had been secured. Gunga Buksh soon bribed his way out of prison at Lucknow, returned to Kasimgunge, rebuilt his fort, and made it stronger than ever; and continued to plunder the country, and increase his landed possessions by the murder of the old proprietors. He became enlisted into the tribe of Rajpoots, and his sister was married to the Powar Rajah of *Etonda*, seven coss north from Lucknow. Jode Sing, the present Rajah of that place, is her son; and he is associated with Gunga Buksh in his depredations. *Sahuj Ram*, of Pokhura, of the Ametheea tribe of Rajpoots, in the Hydergurh purgunna, on the right bank of the Goomtee river, married a daughter of Gunga Buksh's, and has a strong fort, called Raunee, thirty miles east from Lucknow. He is said to have been present at the murder of the twenty-nine persons at Dewa in October last, and to have had with him four hundred armed men and two guns. He and all his followers are notorious and inveterate robbers, like Gunga Buksh himself. The descendants of Khumma, the village watchman, have already built ten forts upon the lands which they have seized, and there are no less than seventy of these forts or strongholds within a circuit of ninety miles round Bhetae and Khasimgunge, the centre being not more than eighteen miles from the Lucknow cantonments.

The Minister having informed the Resident that, without some aid from British troops, it was impossible for him to put down or punish these atrocious murderers and robbers, who had so many mud-forts well garrisoned by their gangs, he, on the 26th of March, 1850, ordered a wing of the 2nd Battalion of Oude Local Infantry under Captain Boileau to join the force, consisting of, 1. A wing of the 2nd Oude Local Infantry; 2. Captain Barlow's regiment, with two nine-pounders and one eight-inch howitzer; 3. Nawab Allee's auxiliaries, two thousand men and three small guns; 4. Sufshikum Khan, the Amil of the district, with one thousand men and five guns; 5. Seoraj-od Deen, the Amil of Ramnuggur, with one hundred and fifty men and two guns; 6. Ghalib Jung, with one thousand foot soldiers, forty camel jinjals (tumbooraks), seven guns, and one hundred troopers, in an attack upon Kasimgunge. The different parts of this force had been so disposed as to concentrate upon and invest the fort at daybreak on the morning of that day. The surprise was complete.

Shells were thrown into the fort from Captain Barlow's guns, but Captain Boileau did not consider the force sufficient to take the fort and secure the garrison, and wrote to request a reinforcement. The distance from Kasimgunge to the cantonments was twenty miles. A wing of the 10th Regiment Native Infantry, with two guns, was sent off under Captain Wilson; but the garrison had evacuated the fort and fled on the night of the 26th, and the wing was ordered to proceed direct to the fort of Bhetae, four miles nearer to the cantonments, which was to be invested by the same force on the morning of the 28th.

Captain Wilson had with him Lieutenant Elderton, as adjutant of the wing, and Ensigns Trenchard and Wish, with a native officer in charge of the two guns. They reached Bhetae at 7 A.M., were joined by the Bhetae force at 8 A.M., and the two forts of Bhetae and Munmutpore were forthwith invested. Munmutpore stood about three hundred yards to the west of Bhetae; and both forts were held by Thakur Purshad and Bhugwunt Sing, members of the same family of pansee robbers, and their gangs. Captain Wilson was the chief in command; and he, with his own and Captain Boileau's wing, took up his position on the north side of Bhetae, and placed Captain Barlow on the west side of Munmutpore. There was a deep dry ditch all round outside the outer wall, and a thick fence of bamboos inside. Between this fence and the citadel in both forts was a still deeper ditch. Between the fence of bamboos and the inner ditch was a small intricate passage, intersected by huts and trenches.

The wall of the citadel was about twenty feet high, and the upper part formed a parapet eight feet high, filled with loopholes for matchlocks. Between Bhetae and Munmutpore, midway, was a large bastion filled with matchlock-men, to keep open the communication and prevent an enemy from taking up any position between the two forts. The investing force was distributed all round, with orders to attack the nearest and weakest points as soon as Captain Wilson should commence his upon the main point, the northern face.

On the afternoon of the 29th, about half-past three, a small party of the garrison came out of the gate on the northern face, and appeared disposed to attack Captain

Wilson's two nine-pounders, and a third gun, which had all three been advanced on to within a short distance of the gate. During this time Captain Barlow was throwing shells into both forts from his position to the west of Munmutpore. The subahdar-major had command of the advanced party in charge of Captain Wilson's three guns. He charged and drove back into the fort the small party which threatened his guns, and Captain Wilson hastily assembled all his and Captain Boileau's force, and followed to support the subahdar-major. Finding his officers and men all excited and anxious to push on into the fort, Captain Wilson unfortunately yielded to the impulse, and entered the outer gate with one of his two nine-pounders, in the hope of taking the place by a *coup-de-main.*

The garrison all retired into the citadel as he entered, and kept up a distressing fire upon the assailants as they went along the narrow passage between the bamboo fence and the ditch in search of a way into the citadel. Several rounds were fired from the gun, in the hope of making a breach in the wall, but the balls penetrated and lodged midway in the wall, without bringing down any part of it; and musketry was altogether useless against a thick parapet with loopholes, so slender on the outside and so wide within. The huts, which might have sheltered officers and men, were set fire to by accident, and tended to increase the confusion. The entrance to the citadel was over a narrow mud causeway, which the garrison had not had time to remove; but it was hidden from the assailants by a projection which they could not attain, and the men began to fall fast before the fire from the loopholes of the parapet.

On hearing the firing on Captain Wilson's side, the officers commanding the troops on the other three sides, commenced their attack on the nearest and seemingly weakest points, as before directed.. Captain Barlow lost some men in an unsuccessful attempt to enter the fort of Munmutpore on the west side; but the auxiliary force of Nawab Allee effected an entrance on the east side of that fort. They were, however, arrested by the second ditch within, in the same manner as Captain Wilson's force had been, and a good many men were shot down, in the same manner, in attempting to get over it. The force under Sufshikum Khan, on the east side of Bhetae, effected an entrance, but was arrested by the second ditch in the same manner, and lost many men. The enemy in Bhetae had eleven men killed and nineteen wounded, a good many of them from the shells thrown in by Captain Barlow. The loss of the enemy in Munmutpore was never ascertained.

After Captain Wilson had been engaged within the wall about three-quarters of an hour, and the ammunition of the gun had become exhausted, Lieutenant Elderton, who had behaved with great gallantry during the whole scene, and was standing in advance with Captain Boileau, received a shot in the neck, and fell dead by his side. Having lost so many men and officers in fruitless efforts to penetrate into the citadel, and seeing no prospect of carrying the place by remaining longer under the fire from the parapet, Captains Wilson and Boileau drew off their parties; but the bullocks which drew the gun had been all killed or wounded, and they were obliged to leave it behind with the bodies of the killed. The men attempted to draw off the gun; but so many were shot down from above that it was deemed prudent to abandon it. About midnight both garrisons vacated the forts, and retired unmolested through the jungle to the eastward, where Ghalib Jung's troops had been posted. There is good ground to believe that he connived at their escape, and purposely held back from the attack as a traitor in connivance with some influential persons in the Durbar.

The 10th Native Infantry had one European officer, Lieutenant Elderton, ten sipahees, and one calashee, killed; five native officers and twenty-two privates, wounded.

The 2nd Oude Local Infantry, six sipahees, and one calashee, killed; and seven native officers and thirteen privates, wounded.

The artillery had one native officer and nine privates wounded.

This reverse arose from the commandant's yielding to the impetuosity of his officers and sipahees, and attempting to take by a rush a strong fort whose defences he had never examined and knew nothing whatever about, as he had never before seen any place of the kind, or had one described to him. He and all his men had courage in abundance, but they wanted prudence.

Gunga Buksh and his son, Runjeet Sing, were afterwards taken, convicted before the highest tribunal in Oude, of the murder of the twenty-seven persons in Dewa, in October, 1849, and executed on the 18th of September, 1850. Thakur Purshad and his cousin, Bhugwunt Sing, remained at large, and at the head of their gang of robbers continued to plunder the country, and levy black mail from landholders and village communities till the 1st of February, 1851, though pressed by a force of one thousand infantry, fifty troopers, and some ten guns. On the morning of that day, Captain Hearsey, commanding a detachment of the Oude Frontier Police, who had been ordered to co-operate with this force in putting down this gang, took advantage of a dense fog, fell upon them, and with the loss of one non-commissioned officer killed, and three non-commissioned officers and three sipahees wounded, killed one of the chief leaders, Bhugwunt Sing, and twenty-two of their followers, wounded many more, and took eight prisoners, among them the son of the leader Bhugwunt Sing. The other two leaders, Thakur Purshad and Keerut Sing, were bathing at the time in the river Goomtee, and escaped by swimming across.

Rajah Bukhtawur Sing declares, that the taking of daughters from families of this caste by Rajpoots is one of the punishments inflicted upon them for the murder of their own. They will not condescend to give daughters in marriage to such persons; and they take daughters from them merely to get their money, and assistance on emergency in resisting the Government, and murdering and plundering its subjects.

This part of Oude, comprising the districts of Dureeabad Rudowlee, Ramnuggur Dhumeree, Dewa Jahangeerabad, Jugdispoor, and Hydergur, has more mud forts than any other, though they abound in all parts; and the greater part of them are garrisoned in the same way by gangs of robbers. It is worth remarking, that the children in the villages hereabout play at fortification as a favourite amusement, each striving to excel the others in the ingenuity of his defences. They all seem to feel that they must some day have to take a part in defending such places against the King's troops; and their parents seem to encourage the feeling. The real mud forts are concealed from sight in beautiful clusters of bamboos or other evergreen jungle, so that the passer-by can see nothing of them. Some of them are exceedingly strong, against troops unprovided with mortars and shells. The garrison is easily shelled out by a small force, or starved out by a large one; but one should never attempt to breach them with round shot, or take them by an escalade or a rush.

It is still more worthy of remark, that these great landholders, who have recently acquired their possessions by the plunder and murder of their weaker neighbours, and who continue their system of pillage, in order to acquire the means to maintain their gangs, and add to these possessions, are those who are most favoured at Court, and most conciliated by the local rulers; because they are more able and more willing than others to pay for the favours of the one, and set at defiance the authority of the other. They often get their estates transferred from the jurisdiction of the local governors to that of the person in charge of the Hozoor Tuhseel at Lucknow. Almost all the estates of this family of Rawuts have been so transferred.

Local governors cannot help seeing or hearing of the atrocities they commit, and feeling some *sympathy* with the sufferers; or at least some apprehension, that they may lose revenue by their murder, and the absorption of their estate; but the officer in charge of the Hozoor Tuhseel sees or hears little of what they do, and cares nothing about the sufferers as long as their despoilers pay him liberally. If the local governor reports their atrocities to Government, this person represents it as arising solely from enmity; and describes the sufferers as lawless characters, whom it is meritorious to punish. If the Court attempts to punish or coerce such characters, he gives them information, and does all he can to frustrate the attempt. If they are taken and imprisoned, he soon gets them released; and if their forts and strongholds have been taken and pulled down, he sells them the privilege of rebuilding or repairing them. It is exceedingly difficult at all times, and often altogether impossible, to get one of these robber landholders punished, or effectually put down, so many and so formidable are the obstacles thrown in the way by the Court favourite, who has charge of the Hozoor Tuhseel, and their other friends at the capital. Those who suffer from their crimes have seldom any chance of redress. Having lost their all, they are no longer in a condition to pay for it; and without payment nothing can be got from the Court of Lucknow.

February 23, 1850.—Badoosura, ten miles south-east over a plain covered with rich crops and fine foliage; soil muteear generally, but in some parts doomut; tillage excellent. Passed over some more sites of Bhur towns. The Oude territory abounds with these sites, but nothing seems to be known of the history of the people to whom they belonged. They seem to have been systematically extirpated by the Mahommedan conquerors in the early part of the fourteenth century. All their towns seem to have been built of burnt brick, while none of the towns of the present day are so. There are numerous wells still in use, which were formed by them of the finest burnt brick and cement; and the people tell me that others of the same kind are frequently discovered in ploughing over fields. I have heard of no arms, coins, or utensils peculiar to them having been discovered, though copper sunuds, or deeds of grant from the Rajahs of Kunoje, to other people in Oude, six hundred years ago, have been found. The Bhurs must have formed town and village communities in this country at a very remote period, and have been a civilized people, though they have not left a name, date, or legend inscribed upon any monument. Brick ruins of forts, houses, and wells, are the only relics to be found of these people. Some few of the caste are still found in the humblest grade of society as cultivators, police officers, &c., in Oude and other districts north of the Ganges. Up to the end of the thirteenth century their sovereignty certainly extended over what are now called the Byswara and Banoda districts; and Sultanpore, under some other name, appears to have been their capital. It was taken and destroyed early in the fourteenth century by Allah-od Deen, Sultan of Delhi, or by one of his generals, and named Sultanpore. Chandour was another great town of these Bhurs. I am not aware of any temples having been found to indicate their creed.*

The landholders, who have become leaders of gang-robbers, are more numerous here than in any other part of Oude that I have seen, save Bangur: but they are not here, as there, so strongly federated. The Amil is so weak, that, in despair, he connives at their atrocities and usurpations as the only means of collecting the Government revenue, and filling his own pockets. The pausee bowmen are here much more formidable than they are even in Bangur. There they thieve, and join the gangs of the refractory landholders; but here they have powerful leaders of their own tribe, and form formidable independent gangs. They sometimes attack and plunder villages, and spare neither age nor sex. They have some small strongholds in which they assemble from different villages over pitchers of spirits, made from the fruit of the mhowa tree, and purchased for them by their leaders; and, having determined upon what villages to attack,

* The Bhur Goojurs must, I conclude, have been of the same race.

proceed at once to work before they get sober. Every town and village through which we pass has suffered more or less from their atrocities, and the people are in a continual state of dread.

In 1842, the pausees, who resided in the village of Chindwara, in the Dewa district, ran off to avoid being held responsible for the robbery of a merchant in the neighbourhood. They were pacified and brought back; but the landholder was sorely pressed by the Government collector to pay up his balance of revenue, and he, in turn, pressed the pausees to pay up the balances due by them for rents. They ran off again, but their families were retained by the landholder. The pausees gathered together all of their clan that they could muster from the surrounding villages, attacked the landholder's house, killed his mother, wife, four of his nephews, the wife of one of his nephews, two of the King's sipahees who attempted to defend them, and several of the landholder, Yakoob Husun's, servants, and plundered him of everything he had. The landlord himself happened to be absent on business, and was the only one of the family who escaped. In all twenty-nine persons were murdered by the pausees on that occasion. They were all permitted to come back and settle in the village, as if nothing had happened; the village was made over to another, and Yakoob Husun has ever since been supplicating in vain for redress at the King's gate.

About three miles from Badoosura, we passed from the Ramnuggur district into that of Dureeabad Rodowlee; but the above description is applicable to both, though in a somewhat less degree to Ramnuggur than to Dureeabad. It is equally applicable to the Dewa district, which we left on our right yesterday, midway between our road and Lucknow. There Gunga Buksh Chowdheree and his relatives have large gangs engaged in plundering towns, and seizing upon the lands of their weaker and more scrupulous neighbours. In the Dureeabad district, the leaders of gangs are chiefly of the Behraleea tribe of Rajpoots, so called after the district of Behralee, in which they reside.

I this morning asked Nowsing, a landholder of the Rykwar Rajpoot clan, who came to me, in sorrow, to demand redress for grievous wrongs, whether he did not think that all the evils they suffered arose from murdering their female infants. "No, sir, I do not." "But the greater part of the Rajpoot families do still murder them, do they not?" "Yes, sir, they still destroy them; and we believe that the father who preserves a daughter will never live to see her suitably married, or that the family into which she does marry will perish or be ruined." "Do you recollect any instances of this?" "Yes, sir, my uncle, Dureeao, preserved a daughter, but died before he could see her married; and my father was obliged to go to the cost of getting her married into a Chouhan family at Mynpooree, in the British territory. My grandfather, Nathoo, and his brother, Rughonath, preserved each a daughter, and married them into the same Chouhan families of Mynpooree. These families all became ruined, and their lands were sold by auction; and the three women returned upon us, one having two sons and a daughter, and another two sons. We maintained them for some years with difficulty, but this year, seeing the disorder that prevailed around us, they all went back to the families of their husbands. It is the general belief among us, sir, that those who preserve their daughters never prosper, and that the families into which we marry them are equally unfortunate."

"Then you think that it is a duty imposed upon you from above to destroy your infant daughters, and that the neglect and disregard of that duty bring misfortunes upon you?" "We think it must be so, sir, with regard to our own families or clan."

I am satisfied that these notions were honestly expressed, however strange they may appear to others. Habit has brutalized them, or rendered them worse than brutes in regard to their female offspring. They derive profit, or save expense and some mortification, by destroying them, and readily believe anything that can tend to excuse the atrocity to themselves or to others. The facility with which men and women persuade themselves of a religious sanction for what they wish to do, however cruel and iniquitous, is not, unhappily, peculiar to any class or to any creed. These Rajpoots know that the crime is detestable, not only to the few Christians they meet, but to all Mahommedans, and to every other class of Hindoos among whom they live and move. But the Rajpoots, among whom alone this crime prevails, are the dominant class in Oude; and they can disregard the feelings and opinions of the people around them with impunity. The greater part of the land is held by them, and in the greater part of the towns and villages their authority is paramount.

Industry is confined almost exclusively to agriculture. They have neither merchants nor manufacturers to form, or aid in forming, a respectable and influential middle class; and the public officers of the state they look upon as their natural and irreconcileable enemies. When the aristocracy of Europe buried their daughters alive in nunneries, the state of society was much the same as it now is in Oude. The King has prohibited both infanticide and suttee. The latter being essentially a public exhibition, the local authorities have continued, in great measure, to put down; but the former was certainly never more common than it is at present, for the Rajpoot landholders were never before more strong and numerous. That suttees were formerly very numerous in Oude is manifest from the numerous suttee tombs we see in the vicinity of every town and almost every village; but the Rajpoots never felt much interested in them; they were not necessary either to their pride or purse.*

February 24th, 1850.—Dureeabad, ten miles south-east, over a plain of good soil—doomut and mutteear—covered with the same rich crops and fine foliage. There is at present no other district in Oude abounding so much in gang robbery and other crime as this of Dureeabad Rodoulee, in which the Amil, Girdhara Sing, is notoriously conniving at these crimes from a consciousness of utter inability to contend with the landholders who commit them, or employ men to commit them. Yet he has at his disposal a force that ought to be sufficient to keep in order a district five times as large. He has the Jannissar battalion of nujeebs, under Seetla Buksh at present; the Zoolfukar Sufderee battalion of nujeebs, under Bhow-od Dowlah, who never leaves Court; and the Judeed, or new regiment, consisting of a thousand men. He has nine guns, and a squadron of horse. Of the guns, five are on the ground, utterly useless; four will bear firing a few rounds. For these four he has bullocks, but they are not yet in condition. Of the seer and half of corn, drawn for each bullock per diem, only half a seer is given. Of the

* Suttee, infanticide, suicide, the maiming of any one, or making any one an eunuch, were all prohibited by the King of Oude, on the 15th of May, 1833, as reported to Government by the Resident on the 6th November, 1834. These prohibitions were reported to the Resident, by the King, on the 14th of June, 1833.

corps, more than one-half of the men are at Lucknow, in attendance upon Court favourites; and of the half present not one-third are fit for the work of soldiers.

The Amil rode by my side, and I asked him about the case of the marriage-procession. "Sir," said he, "what you heard from Seoraj-od Deen is all true. Imam Buksh had a strong fort in his estate of Ouseyree, five miles to our right, where he had a formidable gang, that committed numerous dacoitees and highway robberies in the country around. I was ordered to attack him with all my force. He got intimation, and assembled his friends to the number of five thousand. I had not half the number. We fought till he lost seventy men, and I had thirty killed and fifteen wounded. He then fled to the jungles, and I levelled his fort with the ground. He continued, however, to plunder, and at last seized the bridegroom and all the marriage party, and took them to his bivouac in the jungles. The family was very respectable, and made application to me, and I was obliged to restore him to his estate, where he has lived ever since in peace. I attacked him in November 1848, and he took off the marriage party in February following." "But," said a poor hackery driver, who was running along by my side, and had yesterday presented me a petition, "you forgot to get back my two carts and bullocks which he still keeps, and uses for his own purpose, though I have been importuning you ever since." "And what did he do to you when he got you into the jungles?" "He tied up and flogged all who seemed respectable, and worth something—such as merchants and shopkeepers—and poked them with red-hot ramrods till they paid all they could get, and promised to use all the influence and wealth of their families to force the Amil to restore him to his estate on his own terms." "And were the parties married after their release?" "Yes, sir, we were released in April, after the Amil had been made to consent to his terms; and they were married in May; but I could not get back my two carts." "And on what terms did you restore this Imam Buksh to his estate?" "I granted him a lease, sir," said the Amil, "at the same rate of five thousand rupees a-year which he had paid before." *

Stopping to talk with the peasantry of a village who had come out to the roadside to pay their respects and see the procession, I asked them how, amidst such crimes and disorders, they could preserve their crops so well. "Sir," said they, "we find it very difficult and expensive to do so, and shall find it still more so when the crops are cut and stacked, or have been threshed and stored; then these gangs of robbers have it all their own way, and burn and plunder all over the country; we are obliged to spend all we have in maintaining watchmen for our fields." "But the pausee bowmen have an allowance for this duty, have they not?" "Yes, sir, they have all an allowance. Every cultivator, when he cuts his crop, leaves a certain portion standing for the pausee who has guarded it, and this we call his *Bisar*. Over and above this he has a portion of land from the proprietor or holder of the village, which he tills himself or gets tilled by others." "And they are strong and faithful watchmen, are they not?" "Yes, sir, they are; and though they

* This Imam Buksh, in April, 1850, went in disguise to the annual fair held at Bahraetch, in honour of the old saint. He was recognized by some of Captain Bunbury's soldiers, who attempted to seize him. He was armed with sword, spear, and shield, and defended himself as long as he could. Seeing no chance of escape, he plunged both sword and spear into his own belly, and died, though Captain Bunbury came up, had his wounds sewn up, and did all he could to save him.

will thieve and join gangs of robbers in any enterprise, they will never betray their trust. They consider it a *point of honour* not to trespass on fields or property under the guardianship of members of their own class with whom they are on good terms, or to suffer any persons whatever to trespass on what is under their own care. The money which we send to the treasuries is commonly intrusted to pausees, and their fidelity and courage may be relied upon. The gang robbers do little injury to our fields while the crops are green, for they take animals of hardly any kind with them in their enterprises; and having to move to and from their points of attack as quickly as possible, they could carry little of our crops with them; they are, too, afraid of the arrows of the pausee bowmen at night, if they venture to trespass upon our fields." "And are these pausee bowmen paid at the rate you mention all over the country?" "No, sir; they are in some parts paid in what is called the beega arhaeya, or two seers and half of grain from every beega. From a pucka beega they get pucka two and half seers; and from a kutcha beega, a kutcha two and half seers."* "Your crops, my friends, are finer than I have ever before seen them in Oude." "Yes, sir, they are very fine; but how we shall gather them God only knows, with such gangs of desperate robbers all around us. The alarm is sounded every night, and we have no rest. The Government authorities are too weak to protect us, or too indifferent to our sufferings; and we cannot afford to provide the means to protect ourselves."

As we went on, I asked the Amil what had become of Ahburun Sing, of Kyampore, the landholder who mur-

* The kutcha measure bears the same relation to the pucka in weight as in land measurement.

dered his father to get possession of his estate, as mentioned in the early part of this Diary. "Ahburun Sing, sir, is still in possession of his estate of Kyampore, and manages it exceedingly well." "I thought he had taken to the jungles with his gang, like the rest of his class after such a crime, in order to reduce you to terms?" "It was his father, sir, Aman Sing, that was doing this. He was the terror of the country; neither road nor village was safe from him. He murdered many people, and plundered and burnt down many villages; and all my efforts to put him down were vain. At last I came to an understanding with his eldest son, who remained at home in the management of the estate, and was on bad terms with his father. He had confidential persons always about his father for his own safety; and when he was one night off his guard, he went at the head of a small band of resolute men, and seized him. He kept him in prison for six months, and told me that while so much plunder was going on around, he did not feel secure of keeping his father a single night; that many of his old followers wanted him back as their leader, and would certainly rescue him if he was not disposed of; that he could not put him to death, lest he should be detested by his clan as a parricide; but if I would make a feigned attack on the fort, he would kill him, and make it appear that he had lost his life in the defence of it. I moved with all the force I had against the fort, discharged many guns against the walls, made a feigned attempt at escalade; and in the midst of the confusion *Aman Sing was killed.* As soon as this was done, I returned with my force; the son remained in possession of the estate, and all the surrounding country was delighted to hear that so atrocious a character had been got rid of."

This was all true, and the Amil did not seem to think that any one who listened to him could suppose that he had done anything dishonourable in all this: he seemed to think that all must feel as he did, seeing his utter inability to cope with these baronial robbers in any other way, and the evils they every day inflicted upon the people. This Aman Sing was the most formidable of these robbers in this district, and the high road from Lucknow to Fyzabad was for some time closed by his gang. Of those whom he robbed, he used to murder all who appeared likely to be able to get a hearing at Court or at the Residency.

The Behraleea Rajpoots, of the Soorujpore Behreyla purgunna, are now the most formidable and inveterate robbers and plunderers in the district. The Rajah of this estate, Singjoo, was for some years the most formidable robber in Oude. He had taken a dislike to the family of a sipahee of the Governor-General's body-guard; and, in an evil hour, he buried the sipahee's father, and some members of his family, alive. Strong remonstrances were made through the Resident, and Man Sing, the son of Dursan Sing, who has been already mentioned in this diary, had orders to seize him. In March, 1845, he made a march of forty miles at the head of five hundred active and brave men; and, on the night of the 20th of that month, reached the gate of the fort of Soorujpore, broke it open, entered, killed and wounded fifty of the Rajah's men, and lost five of his own.

The Rajah escaped and took shelter in the fort of Goura. After taking possession of the fort, eight guns, and some elephants, and releasing two hundred unhappy prisoners, Man Sing followed the Rajah to Goura, where he was joined by Captain Magness and his corps.

The gate of this fort was giving way before Man Sing's pickaxemen, when Singjoo surrendered. He was taken to Lucknow, and there died in gaol. The village, in which his father had been buried alive, Hukkamee, was given to the sipahee, and is still held by the family;* but they are a good deal worried in the possession by the widow of the old Rajah, who still lives at Soorujpore, and would be as formidable as her late husband was if she could.

Seodeen, another leader of the same tribe, had been seized in the same manner by Man Sing's father, Dursun Sino, in October, 1830; and soon after three of his nephews were seized, and all four died in gaol at Lucknow; but Chunda and Indul, the brothers of these three men, are still among the most formidable robbers of the district. Hardly a night passes without their plundering some village or other, though Chunda continues to hold his estate, which yields 2250 rupees a-year, under the security of Seetla Buksh, the commandant of the Jannissaree battalion, for the payment of four hundred and fifty rupees a-year. The other robbers of the Dureeabad Rodowlee district, most formidable, are—

1. Imambuksh, above described, as having seized the marriage party. In October last he attacked the town of Syud Mahomedpore, killed three of the Syud proprietors, and plundered it of all he could find. In the interval between his being driven out of his stronghold and re-

* In the interval, during which Singjoo held this village, he had added to its boundaries a good deal of land belonging to himself and others, under the impression that he was secure in the hereditary possession. The sipahee's family seized upon all these lands, while they paid Government only the old rate of revenue. The widow of Singjoo has been ever since trying to recover them, in the usual way, by night attacks, and a good many lives have been lost on both sides, but most on the side of the sipahee's family. December 4th, 1851.

stored, he attacked and plundered no less than twelve villages, in the same purgunna of Bussooree Mowae. In one of them, Myrmow, belonging to Ameer Chowdheree, he killed no less than twelve of the inhabitants. He still keeps up his gang, and plunders, though restored to his estate on his own terms.*

2. Junuck Sing, Behraleea, and his brother, Jeskurun, only twenty days ago, attacked, plundered, and burnt down the town of Meeangunge, through which we passed this morning, and carried off all the inhabitants from whom they thought they could extort any ransom. Only two days ago, they attacked and plundered the village of Bhojpore, belonging to Soorujbulee Canoongo, one of the most respectable men in the district; and cut off the hands of six persons, one of whom died from loss of blood. The next day they attacked and plundered Gorawa, a village belonging to the same person, and burnt it down. Two of the inhabitants were severely wounded, and many bullocks perished in the flames. Within the last year they have taken off more than two thousand head of cattle from the purgunna of Soorujpore Behreyla, in which these villages are situated. Their chief associates in the crimes they commit every day are Chunda and Indul, their clansmen above named.

3. Daood Khan, zumeendar of Sundona, in Mowae Bussooree. He has murdered several of his co-sharers in the estate, and taken their lands—frightened out others, and taken theirs, and at the head of his band of ruffians he robs on the highway, and plunders villages.

4. Benee Sing Kana, Rajpoot of Deeh, in the Mohlara purgunna. He is blind of one eye, and has a small but

* The death of this robber, Imam Buksh, has been already described in a note.

formidable gang. In November, 1850, the native collector of Mohlara, sent a detachment of one hundred men, accompanied by Seonath Sing, a co-sharer of Benee Sing, in the village of Deeh, and Oree Sing, a sipahee, in Captain Orr's Frontier Police, to attack his small gang in their stronghold at Atgowa, in the Rodowlee purgunna. They reached the place at the dawn of day, and forthwith commenced the attack. Benee Sing and his men made a stout defence. Rajah Man Sing came up, and great numbers of the armed peasantry joined in the attack. They took the place about nine o'clock; but Benee Sing, with fourteen of his stoutest men, defended his house as a citadel till morning, when the house was set fire to by the assailants. One of the fourteen was burnt and disabled, when Benee Sing and the remaining thirteen rushed out, sword in hand, to sell their lives as dearly as possible. Benee Sing and twelve of the thirteen were killed; and the thirteenth at last threw down his arms, and called for quarter. He got it, and was saved. Six of his men had before been killed in defending the place. Man Sing had three men wounded and one killed; three more of the assailants were killed, and seven wounded. The head of the "one-eyed robber" was sent in to the king, and was received with much joy.

5. Jeskurun Behraleea, zumeendar of Kiteya, in Soorujpore.

6. Rughbur Behraleea, of Kiteya, an associate of Imam Buksh and Chunda. Four months ago his gang seized two carts laden with valuable property belonging to Seodeen subahdar, of the Honourable Company's service. Through the interposition of the Resident they were restored fifteen days ago.

7. Jugurnath *Chuprassee*, a bhala soltan Rajpoot.

This is one of the most formidable of the leaders of banditti in this and the adjoining district of Jugdeespore. He and his elder brother, Surubdowun Sing, were chuprassees on the establishment of Captain Paton, when he was the First Assistant at Lucknow, and had charge of the Post-office, in addition to his other duties. A post-office runner was one night robbed on the road, and Jugurnath was sent out to inquire into the circumstances. The Amil of the district gave him a large bribe to misrepresent the case to his master; and as he refused to share this bribe with his fellow-servants, they made known his manifold transgressions to Captain Paton, who forthwith dismissed him. Surubdowun Sing was soon after dismissed for some other offence, and they both retired to their estate of Oskamow, in the Jugdeespore district.

This estate comprised fifteen villages. They obtained the leases of these villages by degrees, through the influence which their position at the Residency gave them. As soon as they got the lease of a village, they proceeded to turn out all the old proprietors and cultivators, in order the better to secure possession in perpetuity; and those among them of the military class, fought "to the death," to retain or recover possession of their rights. To defend what they had iniquitously acquired, Jugurnath and his brothers collected together bands of the most desperate ruffians in the country, and located them in the several villages, so as to be able to concentrate and support each other at a concerted signal. The ousted proprietors attacked only those who presumed to reside in or cultivate the lands of which they had been robbed; but Jugurnath and his brethren were less scrupulous; and as they could afford to pay such bands in no other way, they gave them free licence to plunder all the villages around, and all travellers on the highway. Their position and influence at the Residency enabled them to deter the local authorities from exposing their iniquities; and they went on till all the villages became waste, and converted into dens of robbers.

They were, in all, six brothers, and they found their new trade so profitable and exciting, that they all became leaders of banditti, by profession, long before the dismissal of the two brothers from the Residency, though no one, I believe, ventured to prefer charges against them to the Resident or the Durbar. Soon after their dismissal, however, Jugurnath one night attacked and murdered his eldest brother, Surubdowun Sing, in order to get the whole estate to himself, and put his widow and daughter into prison. His other four brothers became alarmed, separated from him, and set up each his separate gang. But Jugurnath contrived soon after, in a dark night, to shoot the third brother, Himmut, dead, with one ball through the chest. Purmode Sing, the youngest brother, was soon after shot dead by some villager, whose cattle he was driving off in a night attack. Bhugwunt Sing, the fourth, and Byjonath, still survive, and have gangs of their own, afraid to trust themselves with Jugurnath, who has built two forts, Oskamow and Futtehpore, in the Jugdeespore district, and a third in two small villages, which he has lately seized upon and made waste, in the Rodowlee district, in order that he may have a stronghold to fly to when pressed by the governors of other districts.

They pay no rent or revenue to Government for any of the villages they hold. The king's officers are afraid to demand any from them. They have plundered a great many villages, and are every month plundering others. They have murdered a great many persons of both sexes and all ages, and tortured more into paying ransoms in proportion to their supposed means. Jugurnath is still the terror of the surrounding country, and a reward of five hundred rupees has been offered for his apprehension.*

8. Moorut Sing, of *Kiteya*, which has eleven small villages depending upon it, all occupied by Rajpoot robbers. Nowgowa, in Mohlara, in Rodowlee, on the left bank of the Goomtee river, twenty miles below Lucknow, has, in the same manner, twelve villages depending upon it, all occupied by Rajpoots, who rob, or shelter robbers, when pursued from the east. On the opposite bank is the village of Kholee, in the Hydergurh purgunna, held by Surfraz Chowdheree, and occupied by Brahmans and Musulmans, who shelter robbers in the same way. When they are pressed in Nowgowa they take shelter in Kholee, and when pressed in Kholee they take shelter in Nowgowa. All the robbers above named find shelter in these villages when pursued, and share their plunder with the inhabitants.

9. Bhooree Khan. The great-grandfather of Bhooree Khan, Rostam Khan, was the leader of a large gang of Musulman freebooters. The estate of Deogon, containing thirty-seven villages, belonged to a family of Bys Rajpoots. Rostam Khan and his gang seized upon them all, and turned out the Rajpoot proprietors, and by force made three of them Musulmans, Kanhur, Bhooree, Geesee; and all their descendants are of the same creed.

Imam Buksh, the father of Bhoree Khan, built a fort

* See note to Chapter VI., Vol. II., on the capture of Maheput Sing. A reward of one thousand rupees has since been offered for Jugurnath's arrest. See in Chapter IV., Vol. II., an account of his desertion of his master, Captain Paton. He is still at large, and plundering. December 4th, 1851.

in Deogon, which the *family* still held. In 1829, Rajah Dursun Sing took the mortgage of the estate for twenty-eight thousand one hundred and ten rupees, to enable Imam Buksh to liquidate a balance of revenue due to Government. When the time of payment came, in 1832, Imam Buksh could pay nothing; and he transferred the estate to Dursun Sing, on a deed of sale or bynama. He continued to manage the estate for Dursun Sing in farm; but, falling in balance, he was put into confinement, where he remained till he died, three years after, in the year 1842. Bhooree Khan was then a boy, but he continued to receive the usual perquisites from the estate while Dursan Sing held it. In the year 1846, the governor of the district, Wajid Allee Khan, took the estate from Dursun Sing's family, and made it over to Bhooree Khan for a present of five thousand rupees. He ceased to pay the Government demand, collected a gang, and became a leader of banditti. He plundered all the people around, and all travellers on the road, seized and confined all who seemed likely to be able to pay ransom, and tortured and maimed them till they did pay; and those who could not or would not pay, he put to cruel deaths. The thirty-six villages on his estate became deserted by all save his followers, and those whom he could make subservient to his purposes, as robbers and murderers.

Ousan Opudeea resided at the village of Etapore, in the estate of Deogon, and possessed and cultivated lands in that and other villages around, for which he paid an annual rent of five hundred and ninety-nine rupees. In 1846, Bhooree Khan demanded from Ousan an increase of one hundred and fifty rupees, which he paid. The year after 1847, be demanded a further increase of the same amount, which he paid. He was then summoned to appear before Bhooree Khan, and was on his way when tol that he would be seized with all his family, and tortured. He, in consequence, took his family to the village of Patkhoree. Bhooree Khan followed with a gang of several hundred men, and two guns, attacked, plundered, and burnt down his house, and fifteen bullocks and buffaloes perished in the flames. One hundred and fifty head of cattle belonging to the village were taken off by the gang. Dwarka, one of Ousan's sons, was killed in defending the house; and the other two, Davey, aged sixteen, and Seochurun, aged seventeen, were seized, bound, and taken off to the jungle, with Ramdeen, Ousan's nephew, and many others of the respectable inhabitants of the village. After exacting a ransom from all the rest, he let them go; but retained the two sons of Ousan, and demanded twelve hundred rupees for their ransom. Ousan had lost all his property in the attack, and could raise no more than seven hundred rupees among his relatives and friends. This would not satisfy Bhooree Khan, who, after torturing and starving the boys for twelve months, and taking the seven hundred rupees, took them to the jungle of Gaemow, with fetters on their legs, and bamboo collars round their necks. He there had them tied to trees, and after firing at them as targets, for some time, with bows and arrows, he had them cut to pieces with swords, and then seized upon all the lands which their father held.

In 1848, Bhooree Khan attacked and plundered the house of Peer Khan, in Khanseepoor in Deogon, and bound and carried him off with his two brothers, Ameer Khan and Jehangeer Khan. He had them beaten with sticks, and caused small iron spikes to be driven up under their nails, and their eyelids to be sewn up with needle and thread, and their beards to be burned, till he extorted from them a ransom of eight hundred rupees.

While they were thus confined and being tortured, they saw four travellers brought in by the gang, and tortured and beaten to death, because they could not pay the ransom demanded from them.

Bhoree Khan, in this month of August 1848, attacked the house of Sirdar Khan, an invalid naek of the 36th Regiment of Bengal Native Infantry, and, after robbing it, burnt it to the ground, and bound and carried off to his fort in Deogon, Sirdar Khan himself and his three sons, Khoda Buksh, Allah Buksh, and Allee Buksh; the first fourteen years of age, the second eight, and the third seven years. He tortured all three, and demanded a ransom of nineteen hundred rupees. This sum was borrowed and paid by Jehangeer Khan, the brother of the naek, and the naek was released. Bhooree Khan would not, however, release either of the sons till he got five hundred rupees more; but Sirdar Khan was unable to procure this further sum, and, in April 1849, Bhooree Khan had two of the boys, Khoda Buksh and Alla Buksh, tied to trees and shot to death with arrows, for the amusement of his gang. They were then hacked with swords, and their bodies were thrown into a ditch, whence he would not permit their friends to remove them for burial. Sirdar Khan became for a time deranged on hearing of the sufferings of his sons, and wandered about the country. Bhooree Khan, with his gang, again attacked the village, and burned it all down, and drove off all the cattle, including all that Sirdar Khan possessed. He recovered, and changed his residence to the village of Deokalee. Bhooree Khan still retained the third son, Allee Buksh, alias Pulleen, and he is still in prison.*

* The Resident effected the release of the third son, Allee Buksh, in January, 1851, through the aid of Captain Orr, of the Frontier Police.

Sirdar Khan's ancestors were the Rajpoot proprietors of the estate of Deogon, and were forcibly converted to Mahommedanism by Bhooree Khan's ancestors when they seized upon the estate. Sirdar Khan cultivated eighteen beegahs of land in the village of Salteemow, in Deogon, for which he had long paid thirty-six rupees a-year rent. Bhooree Khan demanded sixty-five a-year before the attack, and this sum Sirdar Khan paid, but it had no effect in softening the robber leader.

In the year 1847, soon after he took possession of the estate, Bhooree Khan sent a gang under the command of his cousin, Mungul Khan, to attack the house of Dulla, the most opulent and respectable merchant of the district, who resided in the town of Mukdoompore. Dulla had two sons, Nychint and Pursun Sing. After plundering the house, the gang seized Dulla, his son Nychint, Golbay the son of Pursun Sing, and Ajoodheea the son of Nychint. Pursun Sing, the other son of the old merchant, had gone off to the Governor of the district, Rajah Incha Sing, to adjust his annual accounts. The females of the family got out through the back-door of the female apartments, and escaped to the village of Etwara, in the Jugdeespore district, where they had a residence. All the valuables had been buried in a pit in the house, some ten feet deep, and the females had no time to take them up.

The old man, his son Nychint, and his two sons, were sent off to Bhooree Khan, who, on learning that the valuables had not been found, came with fifty more armed men, accompanied by Baboo Mudar Buksh, the tallookdar of Silha in Jugdispore, his own agent Muheput, and a Brahmin prisoner named Cheyn, who knew Dulla, and the wealth he possessed. He brought with him the merchant's son Nychint, and commanded him to point out the place in which the valuables lay concealed. He would not do so, and Bhooree Khan then drove four tent-pins into the ground in the court-yard, placed Nychint on his face, and tied his hands and feet to these pegs. He then had him burnt into the bones with red-hot ramrods, but the young man still persisted in his refusal. He had then oil boiled in a large brass pot which they found in the house, and poured it over him till all the skin of his body came off. He became insensible for a time, and when he recovered his senses he pointed out the spot. Gold and silver ornaments and clothes of great value, and brass utensils belonging to the family, or held as pledges for money due to the old man, were taken up, with one hundred and fifty matchlocks and the same number of swords. They found also many pits, containing several thousand maunds of grain. The valuables, and as much of the grain as he could find carriage for, Bhooree Khan and his gang carried off, and the rest of the grain he gave to any one who would take it. The value of the whole plunder was estimated at one hundred and fifty thousand rupees.

Nychint was unbound, but died that night, and the body was made over to the Brahmin, Cheyn, who had now become a Mussulman. He took it to the jungle, where he had it burnt with the usual ceremonies. Bhooree Khan still detained Ajodheea, the son of Nychint, and Golbay, the son of Pursun Sing, and demanded a further ransom for them, but he released Dulla, who came home and died of grief and of the tortures inflicted upon him in less than a month after. Cheyn, Dabey Sookul, and Forsut, all Brahmins of

Mukdoompoor, were witnesses to the tortures inflicted upon Nychint, and to the plunder of the house. He kept Dulla's grandsons for a year more, with occasional tortures, but the surviving son, Pursun Sing, had nothing more to give, and no one would give or lend him anything. Golbay, his son, at last contrived to get a letter conveyed to him, stating that he was now less carefully guarded than he had been; that he and his cousin, Ajodheea, were sent to take their meals with a bearer, who lived in a hamlet on the border of the jungle, where they were guarded by only four pausee bowmen, and if his father could come with fifty armed men, and surprise them at a certain hour, he might rescue them. He assembled fifty men from surrounding villages, and at the appointed time, before daybreak, he surprised the guard, and rescued his son and nephew.

Gunga Purshad, son of Chob Sing, canoongo of Silha, in Deogon, left the place when Bhooree Khan took to plundering, and went off, in 1847, with his family to reside at Budulgur, a village held by Allee Buksh, a mile distant. A month after he had settled in that place, Bhooree Khan came with his gang, surrounded his house at night, plundered it, and seized and took off his brother, Bhowanee Purshad, two younger brothers, and his, Gunga Purshad's, daughter and son, with Gowree Lall and Gunesh Purshad, his relations, who had come on a visit to congratulate him on the prudence of his change of residence. Gunga Purshad was absent at the time on business. All the prisoners were taken to the jungles and tortured with red-hot iron ramrods, and put into heavy fetters. He demanded a ransom of nine hundred and fifty rupees for all. Gunga Purshad sold all he had except some cows and bullocks, and collected four hundred rupees, and his relations clubbed together and raised one hundred more. The five hundred were sent to Bhooree Khan, and he took them and released all but Bhowanee Purshad. His two younger brothers collected the cows and bullocks, and went with them to Mukdoompoor, in the hope of being allowed to till their lands; but Bhooree Khan and his gang came, seized and sold all the cows and bullocks they had saved, plundered them of everything, and took their lands from them. They all fled once more, and went to reside at Putgowa. At Mukdoompoor, Bhooree Khan had Bhowanee Purshad flogged so severely that he fell down insensible, and he then had red-hot iron spikes thrust into his eyes, and a few days after he died in confinement of his sufferings. The value of the property taken from the family, besides the five hundred rupees' ransom, was one thousand rupees. He, about the same time, seized and carried off from Mukdoompoor Gunga Sookul, a Brahmin, tortured him to death, and threw his body into the river.

About the same time, August 1847, he seized and carried off Cheyn, a Brahmin of Mukdoompoor, son of Bhowanee Buksh. He had come to him to pay the year's rent for the lands he held in that village. After paying his own rents and those of others who were afraid to put themselves into Bhooree Khan's power, and had sent by Cheyn all that was due, he demanded from him a ransom of four hundred rupees. He could give no more, and was put under a guard and tortured in the usual way. As he persisted in declaring his inability to pay more, a necklace of cow's bones was put round his neck, and one of the bones was thrust into his mouth, and the blood of a cow was thrown over him, from which he became for ever an outcast from his religion. He expected to be put to death, but a friend conveyed to him the sum of ten rupees, which he gave to the robbers employed to torture him, and they spared his life. His son had taken shelter in the village of Pallee, whence he sent a pausee bowman, named Bhowaneedeen, to inquire after *him*, and offered him ninety rupees if he would rescue his father. The pausee pledged himself to Bhooree Khan to pay the money punctually, and Cheyn was released. But Bhooree Khan had cut down all the crops upon the lands, and taken them away, and cut down also the five mango-trees which stood upon his land and had been planted by his ancestors. During his confinement, Cheyn saw Bhooree Khan torture and murder many men, and dishonour many respectable women, whom he had seized in the same way.

In the same month, August 1847, Bhooree Khan seized Sudhae, the son of Tubbur Khan, of Salteemow, in Deogon, and his (Sudhae's) two sons, Surufraz and Meerun Buksh, and took them to the jungle. Sadhae had paid him the eighty rupees rent due for the land he tilled, but Bhooree Khan demanded one hundred rupees more; and when he could not pay he made him over to the Jumogdar, to whom he had become pledged for the payment of a certain sum. The Jumogdar had him beaten till he saw that nothing could be beaten out of him, when he let him go to save the cost of keeping him. Bhooree Khan became very angry, and, with his gang, attacked and plundered the house of Sudhae's brother, Badul Khan, in Salteemow, with whom Sudhae lived. The two brothers and their families expected this attack, and escaped unhurt, and fled, but they lost all their property.

Bhooree Khan then ordered one of his followers,

Mirdae, to take Surufraz to a tank outside the village and cut off his nose. He took out at the same time Bukhtawur, a Brahmin, and cut off his nose first. Mirdae then ordered a Chumar, of Deogon, to cut off the nose of Surufraz, and standing over him with a sword, told him to cut it off deep into the bone. Surufraz prayed hard for mercy, first to Bhooree Khan and then to Mirdae; but his prayers were equally disregarded by both. The Chumar cut off his nose with a rude instrument into the bone, and with it all his upper lip. He was then let go; but he fell down, after going a little distance, from pain and the loss of blood, and was there found by his uncle, Badul Khan, who had gone in search of him. He was taken home, but died the same night. His brother, Meerun Buksh, was soon after released for a ransom of fifty rupees.

Golzar Khan, sipahee of the Dull Regiment, in the King of Oude's service, tilled some lands in the village of Mukdoompore, for which he paid rent to Bhooree Khan. In 1847 he first extorted from him double the rent agreed upon, then seized all the crops, and plundered his house, and lastly seized the sipahee's sister, and had her forcibly married to his servant and relative, Mungul Khan.

In 1846 Bhooree Khan attacked the house of Allah Buksh of Gaemow, in Deogon, plundered it, killed his brother, Meerun Buksh, cut off the hands of his relative, Peer Buksh, and wounded three other relatives who happened at the time to be on a visit with his family. The articles of property that were taken off by Bhooree Khan and his gang consisted of five horses and mares, fifteen matchlocks, four maunds of brass utensils, three hundred and twenty-five maunds of grain, five swords, four boxes of clothes, fifteen cows and bullocks, five hundred and forty rupees in money. The houses of all the rest of the village community were plundered in the same manner. They cut down all the mango and mhowa trees belonging to the family, as well as all those belonging to other people of the village.

In 1847 he attacked the house of Akber Khan, in the village of Kanderpore, in Deogon; and after plundering it, he bound and carried off his son, Rumzam, a lad of fifteen years of age; and the year after, 1848, he again attacked his house, and seized and took off his brother, Wuzeer Khan. He has them still in confinement under torture, because Akber Khan cannot get the sum demanded for their ransom; and all applications for their release to the Government authorities have been disregarded.*

In the month of August, 1848, Pransook, a Rajpoot, and Lullut Sing, his cousin, of Booboopore, in Rodowlee, went to purchase a supply of bhoosa for their cattle to Mukdoompore, in the Deogon estate, and were there seized by Aman Sing, an agent of Bhooree Khan, who pretended that they had given shelter to some of the cultivators who had fled from Deogon, and demanded their surrender. They protested that they had never seen any such cultivators, and knew nothing whatever about them. They were bound and taken off to Deogon to Bhooree Khan, who had them both put into the stocks. After having been in the stocks for five days, they were again taken to Bhooree Khan, who ordered them to produce the cultivators, or pay a ransom of one hundred and five rupees. They were then taken back to prison, and con-

* The Resident could not effect the release of these two persons, the son and brother of Akber Khan, till January, 1851.

fined for eighteen days more; and having no food supplied them, they were obliged to sell all the clothes they wore to procure a scanty supply.

To frighten them, Bhooree Khan one day ordered his followers to make outcasts in their presence of two respectable men whom he had in prison, Deena Sing, a Chowan Rajpoot of Jooreeum, and a Brahmin of Poorwa, a small hamlet near Deogon, while he sat on the roof of his house to look on. One of his Musulman followers forced open Deena Sing's mouth, and spit into it; and the others tied the bones of a neelgae round the neck of the Brahmin, by which both of them were deprived of their caste. They then told Pransook and Lullut Sing that they would be served in the same manner unless they paid the ransom demanded. They became alarmed, and sent to their friends to request them earnestly to borrow all they could, and send it for their ransom. Their cousin, Sheobuksh Sing Jemadar, an invalid pensioner from the 2nd Regiment of Bengal Native Infantry, collected one hundred and eighteen rupees, and sent them. Bhooree Khan took one hundred and five for himself, and his servants took thirteen, and they were released; but they were made to swear on the tomb of the saint Shah Sonder that they would not complain of the treatment they had received, and had their swords and shields taken from them. They had been confined twenty-seven days.

In 1846 Davey Sookul, a Brahmin, cultivated land in Mukdoompore, for which he paid an annual rent of seventy-one rupees. In consequence of murders and robberies perpetrated by Bhooree Khan and his gang, he went off with his family to reside at Budulgur, under the protection of Rajah Allee Buksh, a mile distant. He had witnessed the murder of Bhowanee Purshad and the torture of many other persons. One morning his brother, Gunga Purshad, returned to Mukdoompore to gather some mangoes from trees there planted by their ancestors. He was there seized by Bhooree Khan and his gang, who were lying in wait for him. They demanded a ransom of three hundred rupees, which Davey Sookul could not raise. He kept Gunga Purshad in prison for four months, and had him tortured every day. Finding that the money was not forthcoming, Bhooree Khan had a firebrand thrust into one of his eyes, and then had him flogged with bunches of sticks till he died. Khoda Buksh, of Kurteepore, one of the followers of Bhooree Khan, went and reported this to his brother and widow, who wept over the tale of his sufferings. His brother, Boodhoo Sookul, a sipahee of the 45th Regiment, presented a petition to the Resident, describing these atrocities, and praying redress, but none was afforded.

Bukhtawur, son of Kaushee, a Brahmin, tilled lands in Deogon, for which he paid an annual rent of sixty-eight rupees. In 1847 Bhooree Khan demanded double that sum; and when he could not pay, he seized and sold all the stock on the land, and seized and took off to the jungles Bukhtawur and his two brothers, Heeralall and Jankee, and seized upon all their lands, and all the property they had to the value of five hundred rupees. He kept them in prison for six months, and then had Bukhtawur's nose cut off by a Chumar, because he could not pay him the ransom demanded. The nose of Surufraz was cut off at the same time, as above described, and he died in consequence. Bukhtawur's two brothers made their escape three months afterwards.

In 1848 he attacked the house of Choupae Tewaree, a

Brahmin of Ottergow, and after plundering it he took off the son of Choupae, then thirteen years of age, and his, the son's, wife, and his young son and his wife, and tortured all, till Choupae borrowed and begged all he could, and paid the ransom demanded.

Purotee Aheer tilled sixteen beegahs of land in Deogon, for which he paid an annual rent of thirty-two rupees a-year. As soon as Bhooree Khan got the estate from Maun Sing, in November, 1846, he demanded double the sum, and exacted it. He, in 1848, demanded two hundred and fifty, seized Purotee, sold all his cows and bullocks, sixteen in number, and other property, and then released him. Purotee then sent off secretly all his family to Duheepore, two miles distant; but Bhooree Khan sent off his servants, Bundheen and Bugolal pausees, to trace them. They seized his two daughters, one fourteen and the other ten years of age, and his son Nihal's wife, and his son, then only four years of age. Bhooree Khan ravished the two girls, and then released them, with Nahal's wife and her little son. Purotee saw the noses of Bukhtawar and Surufraz cut off while he was in confinement, and saw Bhooree Khan put them on a plate, which he placed in a recess in the wall. It was in March, 1848, when he went to pray that his daughters might be released after they had been ravished. The family went to reside in the village of Mohlee, in Khundara, but have all been turned out of their caste in consequence of the dishonour of his daughters.

In the same year he attacked the house of Foorsut Aheer of Dehpal ka Poorwa, made him prisoner, and tortured him till he paid eight hundred rupees. After this he made his escape; but Bhooree Khan seized and sold all his bullocks, cows, and buffaloes, and stores of grain

In 1845 Bhoore Khan and his gang attacked the house of Buldee Sing, subahdar in the Honourable Company's service, in the village of Ghurwae, and, after plundering him of all the property they could find, they seized him and his wife, and took them to the jungles, where they tortured them till they gave all they could borrow or beg to the amount of many thousand rupees.

About the same time he seized and carried off Eesuree Purshad, a Brahmin, who had fled from Palpore, in Deogon, and gone for shelter to the Bazaar of Ottergow; and after cutting off his nose, he put him on an ass with a young pig tied to his neck, and paraded him through the bazaar, with a drummer before him, to render him an outcast.

In the same year, 1848, he seized Rampurshad Tewaree, and his son Runghoor, cultivators of Deogon, and demanded from them four times the rent due for the land they tilled; and when they could not pay, he sold all their cattle, grain, and other property, and had iron spikes driven up under their nails. Unable to extort money by this means, he caused Sotun Bhurbhoonja, or grain-parcher, to —— in his father's face, and then released him.

In 1848 he demanded from Junga Salor, a cultivator of Bhudalmow, in Deogon, double rent for the land he tilled; and when he could not pay, seized and took off his wife, and cohabited with her four or five days, and then made some of the followers do the same before he released her.

In the same year, 1848, he and his gang attacked the village of Byrampore, in the Kisnee purgunna, and seized Omrow Sing, a Bys Rajpoot, and Boodhea, a Goojur, and all the respectable inhabitants they could get hold of, with their families. After torturing the rest for eight days, and extorting from them all they could pay, he let them go; but detained Omrow Sing, and had him flogged every day till he reduced him to a dying state, when he let him go. He was taken off to his home; but he died as soon as he entered the house and saw his family. The wife of Boodheea, the Goojur, he confined and violated. Bukhtawur deposes that he saw all this while he was in confinement.

He, in 1848, seized and carried off to his stronghold Kaseeram, a Brahmin, of Deogon, and cut off his nose, and tortured him with hot irons till he got from him all that he and his relations could be made to pay, and then let him go.

In the same year and month he attacked and plundered the village of Puttec, in the Jugdeespore purgunna, carried off all the shopkeepers of the place, and tortured them till they paid him altogether three thousand rupees.

In the same year he attacked the village of Koteea, in the Rodowlee district, carried off one of the shopkeepers, and drove iron pins up under his nails till he paid a ransom of one hundred and fifty rupees. He drove off and sold all the cattle of the village.

In the same year he attacked and plundered the village of Budulgur, in the Jugdeespore purgunna, in the same way.

In the same year he attacked and plundered the village of Khorasa, in Rodowlee, carried off Sopae, the Putwaree, with his mother and wife, and tortured them till they paid a ransom of two hundred rupees. He murdered about the same time the son of Buksh Khan, the holder of the village of Gaepore, and two members of the family of Poorae, a carpenter of Almasgunge, in Deogon.

After plundering the house of Sungum Doobee, a respectable Brahmin of Mukdoompore, he seized him and his nephew, took them off to his fort, and, because they could not pay the ransom he demanded, he caused melting lead to be poured into their ears and noses till they died. About the same time he, with his own hands, for some slight offence, cut the throat of his table-attendant, Khyratee, of Kunhurpore.

About the same time he seized two travellers; and, because they could not pay the ransom demanded, he suspended one of them to a tree in the village of Sathnee, on the bank of the Goomtee river, and the other to a tree in the village of Mukdoompore. He had their arms first broken with bludgeons, and then their feet cut off, and at last they were beaten over the head till they died.

[Bhooree Khan, in March, 1850, went with a gang of three hundred men to assist Gunga Buksh and his family in the defence of Kasimgunge and Bhetae; but he was too late. On his way back, in the beginning of April, he left his gang in a grove, six miles from Lucknow, and entered the city alone in a disguise to visit a celebrated dancing-girl of his acquaintance, named Bunnee. He had been with her two days, and on the 15th of April he went to see the magnificent tomb of Mahommed Allee Shah, of which he had heard much. While sauntering about this place he was recognised by three or four persons belonging to another dancing-girl of his acquaintance, named the Chhotee Gohur, or "Little Gem," whom he had formerly visited. They seized him. As soon as Bunnee heard of this she sent ten or twelve of her own men, and rescued him from the followers of the "Little Gem." They took him to Bunnee, who made a virtue of necessity, and went off with him forthwith to the Minister, who rewarded her with a pair of shawls, and made suitable presents to her followers.

It is said that he was pointed out to the followers of the "Chhotee Gohur" by Peer Khan, of Khanseepore, in Deogon, whom Bhooree Khan had some time before plundered and tortured for a ransom, as already stated. Bhooree Khan was sentenced to transportation beyond seas for life, and sent off in October, 1851.]

After reading such narratives, an Englishman will naturally ask what are the means by which such atrocious gangs are enabled to escape the hands of justice. He will recollect the history of the MIDDLE AGES, and think of strong baronial castles, rugged hills, deep ravines, and endless black forests. They have no such things in Oude.* The whole country is a level plain, intersected by rivers, which, with one exception, flow near the surface, and have either no ravines at all, or very small ones. The little river Goomtee winds exceedingly, and cuts into the soil in some places to the depth of fifty feet. In such places there are deep ravines; and the landholders along the border improve these natural difficulties by planting and preserving trees and underwood in which to hide themselves and their followers when in arms against their Government. Any man who cuts a stick in these jungles, or takes his camels or cattle into them to browse or graze without the previous sanction of the landholder, does so at the peril of his life. But landholders in the open plains and on the banks of rivers, without any ravines at all, have the same jungles.

In the midst of this jungle, the landholders have gene-

* The Terae forest, which borders Oude to the north, is too unhealthy to be occupied by any but those who have been born and bred in it. The gangs I am treating of are composed of men born and bred in the plains, and they cannot live in the Terae forest.

rally one or more mud forts surrounded by a ditch and a dense fence of living bamboos, through which cannon-shot cannot penetrate, and man can enter only by narrow and intricate pathways. They are always too green to be set fire to; and being within range of the matchlocks from the parapet, they cannot be cut down by a besieging force. Out of such places the garrison can be easily driven by shells thrown over such fences, but an Oude force has seldom either the means or the skill for such purposes. When driven out by shells or any other means, the garrison retires at night, with little risk, through the bamboo fence and surrounding jungle and brushwood, by paths known only to themselves. They are never provided with the means of subsistence for a long siege; and when the Oude forces sent against them are not prepared with the means to shell them out, they sit down quietly, and starve or weary them out. This is commonly a very long process, for the force is seldom large enough to surround the place at a safe distance from the walls and bamboo fence, so as to prevent all access to provision of all kinds, which the garrison is sure to get from their friends and allies in the neighbourhood, the garrison generally having the sympathy of all the large landholders around, and the besieging force being generally considered the common and irreconcilable enemy of all.

As soon as the garrison escapes, it goes systematically and diligently to work in plundering indiscriminately all the village communities over the most fertile parts of the surrounding country, which do not belong to baronial proprietors like themselves till it has made the Government authorities agree to its terms, or reduced the country to a waste. The leaders of the gang may sometimes condescend to quicken the process by appropriating a portion of their plunder to bribing some influential person at Court, who gets an injunction issued to the local authorities to make some arrangement for terminating the pillage and consequent loss of revenue, or he will be superseded or forfeit his contract. The rebel then returns with his followers, repairs all the mischief done to his fort, improves its defences, and stipulates for a remission of his revenue for a year or more, on account of the injury sustained by his crops or granaries. The unlucky Amil, whose zeal and energy have caused the necessity for this reduction, is probably thrown into gaol till "he pays the uttermost farthing," or bribes influential persons at Court to get him released on the ground of his poverty.

I may here mention the jungles in Oude which have been created and are still preserved by landholders, almost solely for the above purposes. They are all upon the finest soil, and in the finest climate; and the lands they occupy might almost all be immediately brought into tillage, and studded by numerous happy village communities.

I may, however, before I begin to describe them, mention the fact that many influential persons at Court, as well as the landholders themselves, are opposed to such a salutary measure. If brought under tillage and occupied by happy village communities, all the revenue would or might flow in legitimate channels into the King's treasury; whereas in their present state they manage to fill their own purses by gratuities from the refractory landholders who occupy them, or from the local authorities, who require permission from Court to coerce them into obedience. Of these gratuities such a salutary measure would deprive them; and it is, in consequence, exceedingly difficult to get a jungle cut down, however near it may be to the city where wood is so dear, and has to be brought from jungles five or ten times the distance.

In the Sultanpore District.

1st.—The Jungle of Paperghat, about one hundred miles south-east from Lucknow, on the bank of the Goomtee river, ten miles long, and three wide, or thirty square miles.

In this jungle Dirgpaul Sing, tallookdar of Nanneemow, has a fort; and Rostum Sing, tallookdar of Dera, has another.

2nd.—The Dostpore Jungle, one hundred and twenty miles south-east from Lucknow, on the bank of the Mujhoee river, twelve miles long, and three broad, or thirty-six square miles.

3rd.—The Khapra Debee Jungle, one hundred miles south-east from Lucknow, on the plain, about ten miles long, and six miles broad, or sixty square miles.

4th.—The Jugdeespore Jungle, on the bank of the Goomtee river, fifty miles south-east from Lucknow, sixteen miles long, and three miles broad, forty-eight square miles.

Allee Buksh Khan, tallookdar, has the fort of Tanda in this jungle, on the bank of the Kandoo rivulet, which flows through it into the Goomtee. The fort of Bechoogur in this jungle is held by another tallookdar.

5th.—Gurh Ameytee, seventy miles from Lucknow, south-east, on the bank of the Sae river, nine miles long and three broad, or twenty seven square miles.

Rajah Madhoe Sing has a fort in this jungle, and is one of the very worst, but most plausible men in Oude.

6th.—Daoodpoor Jungle, seventy miles south-east from Lucknow, on the plain, four miles long and three broad, or twelve square miles.

The Beebee or Lady Sagura has her fort and residence in this jungle.

7th.—Duleeppore Jungle, one hundred and ten miles east from Lucknow, on the bank of the Sae river, ten miles long, and three miles wide, thirty square miles.

Seetla Buksh, who is always in rebellion, has a fort in this jungle.

8th.—The Matona Jungle, fifty miles south-east from Lucknow, on the bank of the Goomtee river, twelve miles long and three wide—square miles, thirty-six.

Allee Buksh Khan, a notoriously refractory tallookdar, has a fort in this jungle.

In the Uldeemow District.

9th.—Mugurdhee Jungle, one hundred and forty miles east from Lucknow, on the bank of Ghogra river, eight miles long and three broad—square miles, twenty-four.

10th.—Putona Jungle, one hundred and twenty miles east from Lucknow, on the bank of the Tonus river, eight miles long and four miles broad—square miles, thirty-two.

11th.—Mudungur Jungle, one hundred and twenty miles east from Lucknow, on the bank of the Tonus river, six miles long, and three miles broad—square miles, eighteen.

Amreys Sing and Odreys Sing, sons of Surubdowun Sing (who was killed by the King's troops thirty years ago), hold the fort of Mudungur in this jungle.

12th.—Bundeepore Jungle, east from Lucknow one hundred and forty miles, on the plain, seven miles long and one broad—seven square miles.

13th.—Chunderdeeh, south-east from Lucknow one hundred and ten miles, on the bank of the Goomtee river, seven miles long, and three miles wide—square miles, twenty-one.

In the Dureeabad District.

14*th.*—Soorujpore Behreyla Jungle, east from Lucknow forty miles, on the bank of the Kuleeanee river, sixteen miles long, and four miles broad—square miles, sixty-four.

Chundee Sing has a fort in this jungle, and the family have been robbers for several generations. The widow of the late notorious robber, Rajah Singjoo, the head of the family, has a still stronger one.

15*th.*—Guneshpore Jungle, sixty miles south-east from Lucknow, on the bank of the Goomtee river, six miles long and two broad—twelve square miles.

Maheput Sing, an atrocious robber, holds his fort of Bhowaneegur in this jungle.

In the Dewa Jehangeerabad District.

16*th.*—The Kasimgunge and Bhetae Jungle, eighteen miles north-east from Lucknow, sixteen miles long, and four miles wide—square miles, sixty-four, on the bank of the little river Reyt.

Gunga Buksh holds the forts of Kasimgunge and Atursae in this jungle; Thakur Purshad those of Bhetae and Buldeogur; and Bhugwunt Sing that of Munmutpore. Other members of the same family hold those of Ramgura Paharpore. The whole family are hereditary and inveterate robbers.

In the Bangur District.

17*th.*—Tundeeawun Jungle, on the plain, west from Lucknow, seventy-two miles, twelve miles long and six broad—square miles, seventy-two.

In the Salone District.

18*th.*—The Naen Jungle, eighty miles south from Lucknow, on the bank of the Sae river, sixteen miles long and three wide—square miles, forty-eight.

Jugurnath Buksh, the tallookdar, holds the fort of Jankeebund, in this jungle; and others are held in the same jungle by members of his family.

19*th.*—The Kutaree Jungle, on the bank of the Kandoo river, south-east from Lucknow sixty miles, eight miles long and three broad—square miles, twenty-four.

Surnam Sing, the tallookdar, has a fort in this jungle.

In the Byswara District.

20*th.*—The Sunkurpore Jungle, south of Lucknow seventy miles, on the plain, ten miles long and three wide—square miles, thirty.

Benee Madhoe, the tallookdar, has three forts in this jungle.

In the Hydergur District.

21*st.*—The Kolee Jungle, fifty miles south-east from Lucknow, on the bank of the Goomtee river, three miles long and one and a half wide—square miles, four and a half.

The rebels and robbers in this jungle trust to the natural defences of the ravines and jungles.

22*nd.*—Kurseea Kuraea Jungle, south-east from Lucknow fifty miles, on the bank of the Goomtee river, three miles long and one wide—square miles, three.

The landholders trust in the same way to natural defences.

In the Khyrabad and Mahomdee Districts.

23*rd.*—Gokurnath Jungle, north-west from Lucknow

one hundred miles, extending out from the Terae forest, and running south-east in a belt thirty miles long and five wide—square miles, one hundred and fifty.

Husun Rajah, the tallookdar of Julalpore, has a fort in this jungle. Sheobuksh Sing, the tallookdar of Lahurpore, holds here the fort of Katesura; and Omrow Sing, the tallookdar of Oel, holds two forts in this jungle.

In the Baree and Muchreyta Districts.

24th.—The Suraen Jungle, north-west from Lucknow thirty-four miles, along the banks of the Suraen river, twelve miles long and three miles wide—square miles, thirty-six.

In this jungle Jowahir Sing holds the fort of Basae Deeh; Khorrum Sing, that of Seogur; Thakur Rutun Sing, that of Jyrampore. They are all landholders of the Baree district, and their forts are on the *north* bank of the Saraen river. Juswunt Sing holds the fort of Dhorhara; Dul Sing, that of Gundhoreea; Rutun Sing holds two forts, Alogee and Pupnamow.—They are all landholders of the Muchreyta district, and their four forts are on the *south* bank of the Saraen river.

This gives twenty-four belts of jungle beyond the Terae forest, and in the fine climate of Oude, covering a space of eight hundred and eighty-six square miles, at a rough computation.* In these jungles the landholders find shooting, fishing, and security for themselves and families, grazing ground for their horses and cattle, and

* The surface of the Oude territory, including the Terae forest, is supposed to contain twenty-three thousand seven hundred and thirty-nine square miles. The Terae forest includes, perhaps, from four to five thousand miles; but within that space there is a great deal of land well tilled and peopled.

fuel and grass for their followers; and they can hardly understand how landholders of the same rank, in other countries, can contrive to live happily without them. The man who, by violence, fraud, and collusion, absorbs the estates of his weaker neighbours, and creates a large one for himself, in any part of Oude, however richly cultivated and thickly peopled, provides himself with one or two mud forts, and turns the country around them into a jungle, which he considers to be indispensable as well to his comfort as to his security.

The atrocities described in the above narrative were committed by Bhooree Khan, in the process of converting his estate of Dewa into a jungle, and building strongholds for his gang as it increased and became more and more formidable. Having converted Deogon into a jungle, and built his strongholds, he would, by the usual process of violence, fraud, and collusion with local authorities, have absorbed the small surrounding estates of his weaker neighbours, and formed a very large one for himself. The same process, no doubt, went on in England successively under the Saxons, Danes, and Normans; and in every country in Europe, under successive invaders and conquerors, or as long as the baronial proprietors of the soil were too strong to be coerced by their Sovereign as they are in Oude.

An Englishman may further ask how it is that a wretch guilty of such cruelties to men who never wronged him, to innocent and unoffending females and children, can find, in a society where slavery is unknown, men to assist him in inflicting them, and landholders of high rank and large possessions to screen and shelter him when pursued by his Government. He must, for the solution of this question, also go back to the MIDDLE AGES, in England

and the other nations of Europe, when the baronial proprietors of the soil, too strong for their sovereigns, committed the same cruelties, found the same willing instruments in their retainers, and members of the same class of landed proprietors, to screen, shelter, and encourage them in their iniquities.

They acquiesce in the atrocities committed by one who is in armed resistance to the Government to-day, and aid him in his enterprises openly or secretly, because they know that they may be in the same condition, and require the same aid from him to-morrow—that the more sturdy the resistence made by one, the less likely will the Government officers be to rouse the resistance of others. They do not sympathise with those who suffer from his depredations, or aid the Government officers in protecting them, because they know that they could not support the means required to enable them to contend successfully with their Sovereign, and reduce him to terms, without plundering and occasionally murdering the innocent of all ages and both sexes, and that they may have to raise the same means in a similar contest to-morrow. They are satisfied, therefore, if they can save their own tenants from pillage and slaughter. They find, moreover, that the sufferings of others enable them to get cultivators and useful tenants of all kinds upon their own estates, on more easy terms, and to induce the smaller allodial or khalsa proprietors around, to yield up their lands to them, and become their tenants with less difficulty. It was in the same manner that the great feudal barons aggrandised themselves in England, and all the other countries of Europe, in the MIDDLE AGES.

In Oude all these great landholders look upon the Sovereign and his officers—except when they happen to be in collusion with them for the purpose of robbing or coercing others—as their natural enemies, and will never trust themselves in their power without undoubted pledges of personal security. The great feudal tenants of the Crown in England, and the other nations of Europe, did the same, except when they were in collusion with them for the purpose of robbing others of their rights; or fought under their banners for the purpose of robbing or destroying the subjects and servants of some other Sovereign whom he chose to call his enemy.

Only one of these sources of union between the Sovereign and his great landholders is in operation in Oude. Some of them are every year in collusion with the governors of districts for the purpose of coercing and robbing others; but the Sovereign can never unite them under his banners for the purpose of invading and plundering any other country, and thereby securing for himself and them present *glory*, wealth, and high-sounding titles, and the admiration and applause of future generations. The strong arm of the British Government is interposed between them and all surrounding countries; and there is no safety-valve for their unquiet spirits in foreign conquests. They can no longer do as Ram did two thousand seven hundred years ago—lead an army from Ajodheea to Ceylone. They must either give up fighting, or fight among themselves, as they appear to have been doing ever since Ram's time; and there are at present no signs of a disposition to send out another "Sakya Guntama" from Lucknow, or Kapila vastee to preach peace and good-will to "all the nations of the earth." They would much rather send out fifty thousand more brave soldiers to fight "all the nations of the east," under the banners of the Honourable East India Company.

An English statesman may further ask how it is that so much disorder can prevail in a small territory like Oude without the gangs, to which it must give rise, passing over the border to depredate upon the bordering districts of its neighbours. The conterminous districts on three sides belong to the British Government, and that on the fourth or north belongs to Nepaul. The leaders of these gangs know, that if the British Government chose to interpose and aid the Oude Government with its troops, it could crush them in a few days; and that it would do so if they ventured to rob and murder within its territory. They know, also, that it would do the same if they ventured to cross the northern border, and rob and murder within the Nepaul territory. They therefore confine their depredations to the Oude territory, seeing that, as long as they do so, the British Government remains quiet.

CHAPTER VI.

Adventures of Maheput Sing, of Bhowaneepoor—Advantages of a good road from Lucknow to Fyzabad—Excellent condition of the artillery bullocks with the Frontier Police—Get all that Government allows for them—Bred in the Tarae—Dacoits of Soorujpoor Bareyla—The Amil connives at all their depredations, and thrives in consequence—The Amil of the adjoining districts does not, and ruined in consequence—His weakness—Seetaram, a capitalist—His account of a singular *Suttee*—Bukhtawar Sing's notions of *Suttee*, and of the reason why Rajpoot widows seldom become *Suttees*—Why local authorities carry about prisoners with them—Condition of prisoners—No taxes on mango-trees—Cow-dung cheaper than wood for fuel—Shrine of "Shaikh Salar" at Sutrik—Bridge over the small river Rete—Recollection of the ascent of a balloon at Lucknow—End of the pilgrimage.

Poorae Chowdheree, of Kuchohee, held a share in the lands of the village of Bhanpoor in Radowlee. He mortgaged it in 1830, to a co-sharer, who transferred the mortgage to *Meherban Sing*, of Guneshpoor. Poorae disliked the arrangement, and made all the cultivators desert the village of Bhanpoor, and leave the lands waste. Meherban attacked the village of Kuchohee in consequence, killed Porae, and seized upon all the lands of Bhanpoor for himself. Rajah Ram, one of the ousted co-sharers in these lands, attacked and killed Meherban in 1832, and seizéd upon all the lands of Bhanpoor.

After the death of his first wife, Meherban had attacked the house of Bhowanee Sing, Rajpoot, of Teur, carried off his daughter, who had been affianced to another, and forcibly made her his wife. By her he had one daughter and one son, named *Maheput Sing*, who now inherited from his father a fifteenth part of one of the six and half shares into which the lands of Guneshpoor were divided. He, by degrees, murdered, or drove out of the village, all his co-sharers, save Gunbha Sing and Chungha Sing, joint proprietors of a small part of one of the shares, known by the name of the Kunnee Puttee. From the year 1843, Maheput Sing became a robber by profession, and the leader of a formidable gang; and in three years, by a long series of successful enterprises, he acquired the means of converting his residence, on the border of the town of Guneshpoor, into a strong fort, among the deep ravines of the Goomtee river. This fort he called *Bhowaneegur*, after Bhowanee, the patroness of the trade of murder and robbery, which he had adopted.

I shall now mention, more circumstantially, a few of the many atrocities committed by him and his gang, during the last few years of his career, as illustrative of the state of society in Oude. Bulbhudder Sing, a subadar of the 45th Regiment of Bengal Native Infantry, resided at Rampoor Sobeha, in the Dureeabad district. By degrees he purchased thirteen-sixteenths of the lands of these two small villages, which adjoin each other, out of the savings from his pay, and those of his nephew, Mugun Sing, havildar of the 43rd Regiment Bengal Native Infantry. On his being transferred to the invalid establishment, the subadar resided with his family in Rampoor, and in May, 1846, his nephew, Mugun Sing, came home on furlough to visit him. Gujraj, an associate of Maheput Sing's, held the other three-sixteenths of the lands of these two villages; and by the murder of the subadar and all his family, he thought he should be able to secure for himself the possession of the whole estate in perpetuity. The family consisted of the subadar and his wife,—Mugun

Sing, the son of his deceased brother, Man Sing, and his wife; and his son Bijonath and his wife,—Dwarka Sing, son of Ojagur Sing, another deceased brother of the subadar,—Mahta Deen, the son of Chundun Sing, another deceased brother of the subadar, and his wife and young son, Surubjeet Sing, seven years of age,—Kulotee Sing, son of Gobrae, another deceased brother of the subadar, —Bag Sing, a relative,—Bechun Sing, a servant,—Seo Deen, the gardener,—Jeeawun Sing, the barber, and the widow of Salwunt Sing, another son of Mugun Sing, havildar.

When the family were all assembled, Maheput Sing, with Gujraj and other associates, and a gang of one hundred and fifty armed followers, proceeded to the village at midnight, and carefully reconnoitred the premises. It was, after consultation, determined to defer the attack till daybreak, as the subadar and his nephews were known to be brave and well-armed men, who kept watch till towards morning, and would make a desperate resistance, unless taken by surprise. They remained concealed within the enclosure of Gujraj's house, till just before daylight, when they quietly surrounded the subadar's house. As day dawned the subadar got up, opened the door and walked out, as usual, to breathe the fresh air, thinking all safe. He was immediately shot down, and on Mugun Sing's rushing out to assist his uncle, he received a shot in the eye, and fell dead on his body. The robbers then rushed in, cut down Jeeawun, the barber, while attempting to shut the door, and wounded Kulotee Sing,* Bag Sing, and others of the party. Finding that they could no longer stand against the numbers, rushing in at the doors

* Kulotee Sing was murdered, a few days afterwards, by Maheput and Gujraj, as he was superintending the cultivation of his lands.

and windows, the defenders climbed from the inside to the flat roof of the house, over the apartments of the men, fired down upon the robbers, who were still inside, and shot one of them. The robbers, finding they could not otherwise dislodge them, set fire to that part of the house, and the men were obliged to leap off to save themselves. In doing this, Bag Sing hurt his spine, and Seo Deen sprained his ankle, and both lay where they fell, pretending to be dead, till night. The others all went off in search of succour.

The robbers found the boy, Surubjeet, lying sick on his bed, attended by his mother. They seized him and dashed his head against the ground; and when he still showed signs of life, Gujraj cut him to pieces with his sword. They then seized and stripped the females naked, and sprinkled boiling oil over their bodies, till they pointed out all the property concealed in the house. Seventeen hundred rupees were found buried in the floor; and the rest of the property in clothes, gold and silver ornaments, and brass utensils, amounted to about ten thousand rupees.

About noon, while the robbers were still in the house, the Amil of Mohlara came with a large force and one gun, and surrounded them; but stood at a safe distance, whence he kept up for some time a fire from his gun and his matchlocks, which had no effect whatever. The robbers fired in return from the house, merely to show that they were not to be frightened from their booty in that way. This went on till after dark in the evening, when the robbers all retired to the jungles with their booty, unmolested by the Amil.

Byjonath, who had brought the Amil to the spot, urged him on as much as he could to save the property and females, and avenge the death of those who had fallen, and he killed one man and seized another, the son of one of the leaders; but he was obliged to give him up to the Amil as an hostage, for the recovery of the property, and a witness to the robbery. The Amil kept him for six months, and then let him go on the largest ransom he could get for him from his father. The circumstances were all represented, through the Resident, to the Durbar, and redress prayed for, but none was ever obtained.*

In May 1846, Maheput attacked the house of Seobuksh, a gardener, and after plundering it, he seized and carried off to the jungle the gardener's brother, Puroutee, and tortured him to death with hot irons, because he could not raise the sum demanded for his ransom.

In August 1847, Maheput Sing and his gang attacked the house of Meherban Tewaree, subadar of the Gwalior Contingent, in the village of Hareehurpoor, in the district of Rodowlee. It was about ten at night, and the whole family were asleep. The subadar lay on his cot below, near the door; his brother, Angud Tewaree, slept on the upper story. Some placed ladders and entered the upper story through a window; Maheput, with others, broke open the door, near which the subadar slept below. The brother got a sword-cut in the hand, and called out from the upper story as loud as he could for help; but their neighbours were all too much alarmed to come to their aid. Maheput seized and bound the subadar with his own waistband, and commanded his brother to come down, saying, that he need not call for help, as the villagers all knew him too well to molest him; and if he did not come

* When the Resident visited this place, in his tour, in January, 1850, Dwarka Sing and other members of the family described all the circumstances of this attack, and they were taken down; and have been confirmed since by a judicial investigation.

down instantly he would set fire to the house. Seeing no chance of help, he came down, and was bound with his own waistband in the same manner. When the subadar remonstrated against this treatment, Maheput struck him over the face. They then plundered the house of all the property it contained, to the value of six hundred and fifty rupees; and took the subadar and his brother to the jungles; and, in the morning, demanded a ransom of one thousand rupees. At last they came down to four hundred rupees and the horse, which the subadar kept for his own riding. The subadar consented, and his brother was released to get the money and horse. He borrowed the money and sent it with the horse through Bhowanee Deen Tewaree, landholder of Ladeeka Poorwa, and the subadar was released. He presented three petitions, through the Resident, and orders were sent from the Durbar to the local authorities, Hurdut Sing and Monna Lal, but they were both in league with the robbers, and tried to get the subadar made away with, to save further trouble, and he sought security with his regiment.*

In January 1847, Maheput and his gang attacked the village of Bahapoor, in the Rodowlee district; and after plundering all the houses, seized and carried off among others Seetul, the spirit-dealer, and the two sons of Reehta, the widow of Bhosoo, one twenty-two years of age, and the other eighteen. They tortured them with red-hot irons, and tied bamboos round their necks every day for fifteen days. Maheput then shot the eldest son, and cut his body to pieces with his sword. The younger son, at night, made his escape while they were asleep, and

* Meherban Tewaree, subadar, was present, as a witness at the subsequent trial of Maheput and Gujraj, who were sentenced to transportation beyond seas for life.

returned to tell the tale of his brother's murder to his mother. Seetul, the Kalwar, got his uncle to lend him twenty-eight rupees, for which he was released.[1]

In April 1847, Maheput Sing and his gang attacked the house of Ramoutar, Brahmin, of the Brahmin village of Guneshpoor, in Rodowlee; plundered it of property valued at one hundred rupees, and then bound Ramoutar, his father and two sons, and took them off to the jungles; and there tortured them all for seven days. He then had the two boys, one nine years old and the other five, suspended to a tree and flogged; and Ramoutar himself tied to a thorny tree and beaten till the blood flowed down and drenched his waistband, because he could pay nothing, and would not sign a bond to pay two thousand rupees. His sufferings and the sight of those of his two sons made him at last sign one for one thousand rupees. He was flogged again till his friends brought four hundred out of the thousand, and Cheyt Sing, Thakoor, a respectable landholder of Koleea, in Rodowlee, consented to give security for the payment of two hundred and forty-two rupees more. Ramoutar and his family were then released, after they had been confined and tortured for thirty-six days, and they went off and resided at Bookcheyna in Khundasa. A year after his house was there attacked by Maheput Sing and his gang, and plundered of all it contained; and his brother Seetul, and his youngest son were seized and taken off to his fort at Bhowaneegur, and there tortured and starved for six months. Ramoutar then borrowed one hundred and sixty rupees, and obtained the release of his brother Seetul, and a year after he was able to raise forty-seven rupees more, with which he ransomed his son.

In May 1847, Maheput Sing attacked the house of

Seolal Tewaree of Torsompoor, in Rodowlee, at midnight; and after plundering it and stripping his mother and wife, and the wife of his brother, Jurbundun Sing, of all the clothes and ornaments they had, he bound and carried off to the jungle the two brothers, Seolal and Jurbundun. They were flogged, and had hot irons applied to their bodies every day for twenty days, and had only a little flour to eat and water to drink, once in three days. After twenty days they contrived to make their escape one dark and stormy night, and got home; but three days after he again attacked their house and burnt it to the ground, with all they possessed. He, at the same time, burnt down the house of their uncle, in the same village, and that of one of their ploughmen; and two cows and one bullock were burnt to death in the flames.

In July 1847, Maheput Sing and his gang attacked the house of Chubbee Lal, Brahmin, in the village of Bunnee, in the Rodowlee district, and after plundering it of property to the value of five hundred rupees, he bound and took the old Brahmin off to the jungles, and demanded from him a ransom of eight thousand rupees. This sum the old man could not pay, and he was flogged with thorns, and had red-hot irons applied to his body every day. Maheput then sent a letter to the old man's son, Dwarka, desiring him to send the eight thousand rupees if he wished his father to live. The house having been plundered, the family had nothing left, and could persuade no one to lend them. On receiving a reply to this effect, Maheput had the old man's body plastered all over with moist gunpowder, and made him stand in the sun till it was dry. He then set fire to the powder, and the poor man was burnt all over. He then cut off both his hands at the wrists, and his nose, and sent them to his family;

and in this condition he afterwards sent the poor man to his home upon a cot. The son met his father at the door, but the old man died as soon as his son had embraced him.

Maheput carried off Pem, the son of Teeka, at the same time, and tortured him till his family paid the ransom demanded. He was witness to the tortures of the old Brahmin.

In August 1847, Maheput and his gang attacked the house of Bichook, a Brahmin, in the village of Torsompoor, in Rodowlee, at midnight, while he was sleeping, and bound and carried him off to the jungle. The next day, when he was about to have him tortured for a ransom, one of his followers interceded for him, and he was released. But a month after, Maheput and his gang again attacked his house, and after plundering it of all it contained, they burnt it to the ground. Bichook had run off on hearing their approach, and he escaped to Syudpoor.

In November, 1846, Maheput Sing attacked the house of Sook Allee, in Guneshpoor, at midnight, with a gang of one hundred men; and, after plundering it of all the property it contained, to the amount of four hundred rupees, he burnt it to the ground, and bound and carried off Sook Allee to the house of his friend, Byjonath Bilwar, a landholder in the village of Kholee, eight miles distant. He there demanded a ransom of five hundred rupees; and on his declaring that he neither had nor could borrow such a sum, he had him tortured with hot irons, and flogged in the usual way. He kept him for two months at Kholee, and then took him to Tukra, in the Soorajpoor purgunnah, where he kept him for another month, torturing, and giving him half a meal every other day. At the end of three months, Akber Sing and Bhowanee

Deen, Rajpoot landholders of Odermow, contrived to borrow two hundred rupees for Sook Allee, and he was released on the payment of this sum. The marks of the hot irons, applied to his body by Maheput Sing, with his own hands, are still visible, and will remain so as long as he lives.*

About the same time—the latter end of 1846—Maheput Sing sent to Sheik Sobratee, of the same place, a message through a pausee, named Bhowanee Deen, demanding twenty-five rupees. This sum was sent; but six weeks had not elapsed ,before Sheik Sobratee received another demand for the same amount, through the same person. He had no money, but promised to send the sum in ten days. At midnight, on the fourth day after this, Maheput and his gang attacked his house, and plundered it of all they could find, female ornaments, and clothes, and brass utensils. Sobratee was that night sleeping at the house of his friend Peree, the wood-dealer, in the same town. Maheput tried to make his mother and wife point out where he was, by torturing them, but they either would not or could not do so. After some search, however, they discovered him, and bound and took him off, with handcuffs, and an iron collar round his neck, to the Kurseea jungle, in the Hydergur pergunnah. His son, a boy, had escaped. After torturing him in the usual way for eight days, they sent a message to his mother by Maheput's servant, Salar, to say, that unless she sent a ransom of five hundred rupees, her son's nose and hands should be cut off and sent to her as those of *Chubbee Lal*, Brahmin, of Bunnee, had been. She prevailed upon Baroonath Gotum to lend the money; and Maheput sent Sobratee to him, accompanied by one of his armed

* I saw these marks on the sufferer.

retainers, with orders to make him over to the Gotum, if he pledged himself in due form to pay. He did so, and Sobratee was made over to him, and the next day sent home to his wife and mother. Some months after, however, when he had completed his fort of Bhowneegur, Maheput sent to demand two hundred rupees more from Sobratee, and when he found he could not pay, he had his house pulled down, and took away all the materials to his fort. What he did not require he caused to be burnt. He got from Sobratee, in ransom and plunder, more than three thousand rupees; and he has been ever since reduced to great poverty and distress.

In November 1847, Maheput Sing and his gang seized and carried off Khosal, a confectioner, of Talgon, in Rodowlee, who had gone to his sister at Buhapoor, near Guneshpoor, to attend a marriage—took him to the jungle, and tortured and starved him in the usual way for five weeks. He had him burnt with red-hot irons, flogged and ducked in a tank every day, and demanded a ransom of two hundred rupees. At last, his brother, Davey Deen, borrowed thirty-three rupees from Rambuksh, a merchant of Odermow, and offered to pay it for his ransom. Maheput sent Khosal, with his agent, Bhowanee Deen, to Rambuksh, and he released him on getting the money. He still bears on his body the marks of the stripes and burnings.*

In December 1847, Maheput and his gang attacked the house of Motee Lal Misser, a Brahmin, in the village of ——, and after robbing it of all that it contained, he seized and carried off his nephew, Ram Deen, a boy of seven years of age, and tortured him for a month in the jungle. He then cut off his left ear and the forefinger

* These marks I have seen.

of his right hand, and sent them to the uncle in a letter, stating, that if he did not send him one thousand rupees, he would send the boy's head in the same manner. The boy's father had died, and his uncle, with great difficulty, prevailed upon his friends and neighbours to lend him two hundred and twenty rupees, which he sent to Maheput, and his nephew was released. The boy declares to me that Maheput cut off his ear and finger with his own hands.*

In June 1848, Forsut Pandee, of Resalpandee-ka-Poorwa, in Rodowlee, accompanied Girwar Sing, a Rajpoot of Bowra, in Rodowlee, to Guneshpoor, on some business. They were smoking and talking together at the house of Mungul Sing, Thakoor, a large landholder of that place, when five of Maheput's armed men came up, and told Forsut Pandee to attend them to their master. Girwar Sing remonstrated and declared that his honour had been pledged for Forsut Pandee's personal safety. Mungul Sing, Thakoor, however, told him, that he must offer no opposition, as they seized all travellers who came that way, and it was dangerous to oppose them. He was taken to Maheput Sing, in his fort at Bhowaneegur, situated half a mile from Guneshpoor. Maheput told him that he had heard of his having a good flint gun, and a shawl in his house, and that he must have them. Forsut Pandee swore on the Ganges that he had no such things. He then had him tied up to a tree and flogged him with his own hands with thorny bushes, the scars of which are still visible. He then demanded a ransom of three hundred rupees, and had him flogged and tortured every day for a month, while he gave him to eat only half a pound of flour every two or

* This boy was present, as a witness, at the trial of Maheput.

three days. The prisoner's brother, Bhoree Pandee, sold all the clothes and ornaments of his family, utensils, and furniture, and their hereditary mango and mhowa grove, and raised two hundred and six rupees, which he sent to Maheput, through Baldan Sing, a landholder of Bharatpoor, two miles from Guneshpoor. On the receipt of this Forsut Pandee was released.

In October 1848, Maheput Sing sent ten of his gang to seize a cultivator, by name Khosal, who was engaged in cultivating his land in a hamlet, one mile south of the town of Syudpoor. They seized and bound him and took him off to their leader, Maheput, who had him tortured for a month in the usual way. He had him tied up to a ladder and flogged. He had red-hot irons applied to different parts of his body—he put dry combustibles on the open palms of his hands and set fire to them, so that he has lost the use of his fingers for life. For the whole month he gave him only ten pounds of flour to eat; but his friends contrived to convey a little more to him occasionally, which he ate by stealth. He was reduced, by hunger and torture, to the last stage, when his family, by the sale of all they had in the world, and the compassion of their friends, raised the sum of one hundred and twenty-six rupees, which they sent to Maheput, by Thakoor Persaud, a landholder of the village of Somba, and obtained his release. The tortures have rendered him a cripple, and the family are reduced to a state of great wretchedness.*

The village of Guneshpoor yielded a revenue to Government of twenty-one thousand rupees a-year, and was divided into six and half shares each, held by a different

* This man was a witness at the trial of Maheput, and I saw the signs of his sufferings.

person. One belonged to Omrow Sing, Rajpoot, the father of Hunmunt Sing, a corporal in the 44th Regiment Bengal Native Infantry, and descended to Omrow Sing's eldest son, Davey Sing. One share was held, jointly, by Maheput Sing and Chotee Sing, when, in October 1848, Maheput assembled a gang of about two hundred men, and attacked the house of Davey Sing, while his brother Hunmunt Sing was at home on recruiting service. There were in the house the corporal and his three brothers, and all mounted, with their friends, to the top of the house, with their swords and spears, but without fire-arms. The robbers, unable to ascend from the outside, broke open the doors, but the brothers descended and defended the passage so resolutely, that the gang was obliged to retire and watch for a better opportunity.

Three months after, in January 1849, Maheput attacked the house again, with a gang of five hundred men and good scaling-ladders. Some ascended to the top on the ladders, while others broke open the doors and forced their way in. The brothers and the other male members of the family defended themselves resolutely. One of the brothers, Esuree Sing, his uncle, Runjeet Sing, sipahee of the 11th Regiment Bengal Native Infantry, his cousin, Beetul Sing, sipahee of the 8th Regiment Bombay Native Infantry, were all killed, and hacked to pieces by Maheput and his gang. No person came to the assistance of the family, and the robbers retired with their booty, consisting of five hundred and ten rupees in money, four muskets, and four swords, and twelve hundred maunds of corn, and all the clothes, ornaments, and utensils that could be found. They burnt down the house, and dispossessed the family of their share in the estate, and plundered all the cultivators. Davey Sing, the eldest brother, went to reside at Bhanpoor, in the neighbourhood. While he was engaged in cutting a field of pulse, in the morning, about seven o'clock, in the month of March following, Maheput Sing, with a gang of two hundred men, attacked his house, killed his two brothers, Gordut and Hurdut Sing, and their servant, Omed, and shot down his nephew, Gorbuksh Sing. Ramsahae, the nephew of Maheput Sing, ran up to despatch him with his sword, but Gorbuksh rose, cut him down, and killed him with his sword before he himself expired.

The corporal, Hunmunt Sing, of the 44th Native Infantry, described all these things in several petitions to the Resident, and prayed redress, but no redress was ever obtained. Saligram and other relatives of the corporal had been plundered and wounded by Maheput Sing and his gang, and he describes many other atrocities committed by the same gang. His petition of the 27th September 1849, was sent to the King by the Resident, who was told, that the Amil of the district of Dureeabad, Girdhara Lal, had been ordered to seize Maheput Sing and his gang. This Amil was always in league with them.

In December 1847, Maheput Sing and his gang attacked the house of a female, named Arganee, the widow of Sheik Rozae, in the village of Pertab Pahae. It was midnight, and she was sleeping with her two grandchildren, the sons of her son, who was a sipahee in the 66th Regiment of Bengal Native Infantry. They bound her hands: and leaving her young grandchildren alone, took her off to the jungle eight miles distant. There Maheput demanded from her the seven hundred rupees which she was said to have accumulated; and when she pleaded poverty, and said that the sipahee's pay was their only means of subsistence, he had her stripped naked and flogged in the usual way. For a month he had her stripped and flogged in the same manner every day. She then signed a bond to pay one hundred rupees on a certain day, and was released. She sold all she had, and borrowed all she could, and on the fourth day sent him fifty, and the other fifty on the fifteenth day; but he afterwards had the poor widow's house pulled down and all the wood-work carried to his fort of Bhowaneegur.

In April 1849, Maheput Sing and his gang attacked the house of Seodeen Misser, sipahee of the 63rd Regiment Bengal Native Infantry; and after plundering it, seized and carried off to the jungle his brother and that brother's two sons—one seven years of age and the other five—and his sister. He sold the two boys as slaves for two hundred rupees to a person named Davey Sookul, of Guneshpoor; and tortured the brother and sister till the sipahee and his friends sold all they had in the world for their ransom, when he released them.

In the month of May 1849, Maheput Sing and his gang at midnight attacked the house of Eseree Sing, a Rajpoot of the Chouhan tribe, in the village of Salpoor, in Dureeabad; and after stripping his mother and all the other females of the family of their clothes and ornaments, plundering the house of all it contained, rupees, twenty-five in money, two handsome matchlocks, two swords, two spears, and two shields, and brass utensils, weighing one hundred and sixty pounds, he bound Eseree Sing himself, and took him off with his sister, four years of age, and his daughter, only three, to a jungle, four miles distant. He there released Eseree Sing himself, but took on the girls, and made over his daughter to Akber, one of his followers, and his sister to Bechoo, another of his gang, to be united to them in marriage. It was at their instigation, and for that purpose chiefly, that he made the attack.*

In August 1849, Maheput and his gang attacked the houses of Seetul, Gorbuksh, and Sook Lal, Brahmins, of Guneshpoor; and after plundering them, he carried off Gorbuksh and his son, Ram Deen, and Bhowanee, the son of Seetul, and Sook Lal, and murdered them. He carried off and tortured, in a shocking manner, Benee, of the same place, till he paid a ransom; and Ongud, son of Khunmun, an invalid Khalasie, of the 26th Regiment Native Infantry.

In September 1849, Maheput attacked and plundered the house of Ongud Sing, sipahee of the 24th Regiment Bengal Native Infantry, and confined the sipahee for some time. His petition was sent to the King on the 11th November 1849.

On the 15th of December 1849, Monowur Khan, havildar of the 62nd Regiment Bengal Native Infantry, complained that Maheput Sing had seized him as he was walking on the high road, and extorted eleven rupees from him. His petition was sent to the King, with a request, that all local authorities might be urged to aid in his arrest; and orders were again sent to the Frontier Police.

On the 24th December 1849, Madho Sing, sipahee of the 11th Regiment Bengal Native Infantry, complained that Maheput Sing had attacked and plundered his house twice, burnt it down, and cut down all the trees which the family had planted for generations, and turned them all out of the village—that in the second attack he had murdered his daughter, a girl of only nine years of age. His petition was sent to the King, who, on the 13th of

* Akber and Bechoo are now in prison, with Maheput, at Lucknow.

February 1850, replied that he had proclaimed Maheput as a robber and murderer, and offered a reward of three thousand rupees for his arrest.

On the 16th of March 1850, Goverdhun complained, that Maheput had attacked and plundered his house, and carried off his father to the jungles, and extorted from him a ransom of one hundred and ten rupees. His petition was sent to the King, who, on the 27th March, replied, that he had given frequent and urgent orders for the arrest of Maheput Sing.

Gunga Deen, a trooper of the Governor-General's body-guard, complained to the Resident, on the 9th of August 1844, that Maheput Sing had attacked and killed with his own hand his agent, Thakoor Sing, while he was taking seven hundred and seventy-four rupees to the revenue-collector. On the 11th of September 1849, he again complained to the Resident, that Maheput Sing had plundered Bhurteemow and other villages, in Dureeabad, of property to the value of six thousand seven hundred and fifty-nine rupees, and murdered five men, besides Thakoor Sing, his servant, and had committed numerous robberies in other villages during the year 1848. Among them one in Bhurteemow, in which he killed Ramjeet and four other men—that he had soon after committed a robbery in which no less than twenty-two persons were killed and wounded, and property to the value of two thousand rupees was carried off. The King was frequently pressed most earnestly to arrest this atrocious robber; and on the 9th of December 1849, the Frontier Police was, at the King's request, directed to do all in their power to seize him.

In July 1847, Maheput Sing and his gang attacked the house of Mungul Sookul, a corporal of the 24th Regiment of Bengal Native Infantry, at midnight, robbed it of property to the value of five hundred rupees, and so rent the ears of his little son, by the violence with which he tore the gold rings from them, that the boy was not likely to live. The commanding officer of the regiment sent the corporal's petition for redress, through the Resident, to the Durbar; and orders were sent to the local authorities to afford it, but they were unable or unwilling to do anything.

Gunga Aheer, of Buroulee, in the district of Rodowlee, had been for three years a sipahee in the 48th Regiment of Bengal Native Infantry, under the name of Mata Deen. Continued sickness rendered him unfit for duty, and he obtained his discharge, and came home to his family. In March 1850, having been long without employment, and reduced, with his family, to great distress, he went to his relation, Ramdhun, of the Intelligence Department, in the service of the King of Oude, and then on duty at Dureeabad, with the Amil. A reward of three thousand rupees having been offered by the King for the arrest of Maheput Sing, the Amil ordered Ramdhun to try his best to trace him out, and he took Gunga Aheer with him to assist, on a promise of securing for him good service if they succeeded. They went to a jungle, about two miles from Guneshpoor, and near the foot of Bhowaneegur. While they were resting at a temple in the jungle, sacred to Davey, Maheput came up, with twenty followers, to offer sacrifice; and as soon as they recognized the Harkara, Ramdhun, they seized both, and took them off in the evening to a jungle, four miles distant. In the hope of frightening Maheput, the Harkara pretended to be in the service of the Resident at Lucknow; but as the reward for his arrest had been offered on the requisition of the Resident, on the application of injured sipahees of the British army, this did not avail him. Their hands were tied behind their backs, and as soon as it became dark, they took Ramdhun off to a distance of twenty paces from where Maheput Sing sat, and made him stand in a circle of men with drawn swords. One man advanced, and at one cut with his sword, severed his right arm from his body, and it fell to the ground. Another cut into the side, under the stump, while a third cut him across the left side of the neck with a back cut, he all the time calling out for mercy, but in vain. On receiving the cut across the neck he fell dead, and the body was flung into the river Goomtee. Maheput sat looking on without saying a word.

They then amused themselves for some time by flogging Gunga Aheer with thorn bushes, while he in agony cried for mercy. The next day, by Maheput's orders, they laid him upon a bed of thorns and beat him again, while he screamed from pain, and they laughed at his cries. One of the followers told Maheput, that they had been cautioned by the outlaw, Jugurnath, the chuprassie, not to murder Ramdhun and his companion, or the English would some day avenge them; but he laughed and said that spies must be punished, to deter others from pursuing them. One of his followers then sat on Gunga's chest while another held his arms, and a third his legs, while a fourth cut off his nose, and one of his hands at the wrist, and the fingers of the other hand. He became senseless, and Maheput and his followers all left him in this state. In the evening a servant of Seochurn Chowdheree, of Bhowaneepoor, on his way to the jungle, saw him and reported his condition to his master, who sent people and had him taken to him on a litter. He had his wounds dressed by a village surgeon, and the next day sent him home to his wife and mother. The landlord of the village reported the case to Captain Orr, of the Frontier Police, at Fyzabad, who had Gunga taken off to the hospital at Lucknow, where he remained under the care of the Residency surgeon till he recovered. This poor man had to support his mother, wife, and daughter by his labour. His mother came in with him, and attended him in hospital, while his wife and child remained at their village.

While in hospital recovering, Maheput Sing was brought before him, by the Frontier Police, to be recognized. As soon as he saw him all the terrible scene of Ramdhun's murder and his own torture came so vividly before him, that he trembled from head to foot, like a man in an ague fit, and was for some time unable to speak. At last, when he saw the fetters on Maheput's legs, and the handcuffs on his wrists, and armed Government servants around him, he recovered his senses; and by degrees, recorded what he had witnessed and suffered at his hands.

On the 25th March 1850, Rajah Maun Sing, under orders from the Durbar, with all the force he could muster, invested the fort of Bhowaneegur, while the force under Captains Weston, Thomas, Bunbury, and Magness, attacked the three forts belonging to Rajah Prethee Put, of Paska. Maheput Sing left the fort on the 27th, with eleven followers, to collect reinforcements and harass the besiegers, and the garrison was commanded by his nephew.

On the 28th, Maun Sing had three men killed and several wounded, from the fire of the garrison, and wrote for reinforcements to Captain Weston, who was at

Dureeabad, twelve miles distant. As soon as he got the letter, he mounted his horse, and leaving the force to follow, rode with his Assistant, Captain Orr, to the place, which is half a mile from Guneshpoor south, and two hundred yards from the left bank of the Goomtee river north. They were attended by a few sowars, under Seo Sing, and they reached the place before daybreak, on the 29th; and as soon as day appeared, proceeded with Captain Magness, who had galloped on in advance of his regiment to reconnoitre the fort, and were fired upon by the garrison wherever they were seen. Maun Sing's people had retired after the loss of a few men, to the distance of a mile, and lay scattered over the jungle.

The Infantry came up before sunset, and the guns before it grew dark, and all were placed in position, and a fire opened upon the fort till it grew too dark to point the guns. The garrison soon after attempted to escape by the west side, and were fired upon by the parties posted on that quarter. Captain Weston, hearing the fire, collected all the men he could, and getting with difficulty into the fort, found it empty. In the attempt to cut their way through, the garrison had two men killed and fifteen wounded and taken, and five managed to escape, under cover of the night, into the thick jungle. Bikhai, one of the most atrocious of Maheput's followers, was killed; but he killed two of the besiegers, and wounded two more before he fell. Akber Sing, the most atrocious of all the gang, had his arm taken off by a cannon-shot, and was seized. Maheput's nephew, the commandant of the garrison, was taken, with one of Maheput's secretaries and advisers.

Of Maun Sing's party, four were killed and thirteen wounded, and Captain Magness had one havildar severely wounded. The fort was levelled, and the jungle around cut down. The force then proceeded and took possession of the forts of Futtehpoor, Oskamow, Sorrea, Dyeepoor, and Etonja, all belonging to Jugurnath Chuprassie, another leader of banditti of that district. They were only a few miles distant from Bhowaneegur, and were deserted by his gangs on their seeing a British force and hearing the guns open upon Bhowaneegur. Two hundred head of stolen cattle were found in the forts of Jugurnath, and restored to their proper owners. Parties were sent in pursuit of Maheput Sing, and two of his followers were secured; but he himself escaped for the time. The forts were all destroyed. Captain Orr, the Assistant Superintendent, in charge of the Frontier Police at Fyzabad, had been long in pursuit of Maheput Sing, and his parties, knowing all his haunts and associates, gave him no rest. His subadar, Seetul Sing, became acquainted with Prethee Paul, tallookdar of Ramnuggur, who had been deprived of his estate for defalcation, and become associated with Maheput Sing. The subadar persuaded this landholder that it would be to his advantage to aid in the arrest of so atrocious a robber and murderer; and when Maheput next came to him to seek some repose from his pursuers, and consult about future plans, he sent intimation to Seetul Sing, whose detachment of sipahees was at no great distance. On receiving the intimation, the subadar marched forthwith, and reached the place at the dawn of day, on the morning of the 1st of July 1850. Maheput Sing had just left the house to perform his ablutions, but on seeing them, he suspected their designs and re-entered the house. The subadar's party saw him, immediately surrounded the house, and demanded his surrender. Maheput Sing begged Prethee Paul to join him in defending the house or cutting their way through; but

Prethee Paul told him that he had ruined himself by his atrocities, and must now submit to his fate, since he could not involve himself and all his family in ruin merely to assist him. Prethee Paul then took him by the arm, brought him out, and made him over to Seetul Sing, who had threatened to set fire to the house forthwith unless he did so. He was then secured and taken off, well guarded, and in all possible haste, to Captain Orr, lest his gang might collect and attempt a rescue. Captain Orr sent him off, under a strong guard and well fettered, to Lucknow, to Captain Weston, the Superintendent of the Frontier Police.

Prethee Paul, the tallookdar, for the good service, got back his estate from the Oude sovereign, and an addition of five hundred rupees a-year to his nankar or personal allowance. Gunga Aheer is now a pensioner on the Residency fund, and his family has been provided for. Maheput Sing and his associate Gujraj were sentenced to transportation beyond seas, and sent off in October 1851.

It is remarked by the people, that few of these baronial robbers ever die natural deaths—that they either kill each other, or are killed sooner or later by the servants of Government. More atrocious crimes than those which they every month commit it is difficult to conceive. In the Bangor district, through which we passed last month, this class of landholders are certainly as strong and as much disposed to withhold the just dues of Government, and to resist its officers and troops, as they are here, but they do not plunder and burn down each other's villages, and murder and rob each other's tenants so often as they do here. The coalition has introduced among them a kind of *balance of power*, which makes them respect each other's rights, and the rights of each other's tenants, for the chiefs are dependent upon the attachment and fidelity of their respective tenants. The above list contains only a part of the leaders of gangs, by which the districts of Dureeabad, Rodowlee, Sidhore, Pertabgunge, Dewa, and Jehangeerabad, are infested. We have seen no manufacture of any exportable commodity in Oude, nor have we seen traffic on any road in Oude, save that leading from Cawnpore to Lucknow.

In consequence of some bad seasons, a good deal of the grain required at the Capital, and in the districts to the north-east, comes from Cawnpore over this road. Were the road from Fyzabad to Lucknow good and safe, a good deal of land produce would, in ordinary seasons, come over it from the Goruckpoor district, and those intervening between Lucknow and Fyzabad. It would, however, be useless to make the road till the gangs which infest it are put down. A good and secure road from Lucknow through Sultanpoor to Benares, would be of still greater advantage.

Febuary 25, 1850.—Halted at Dureeabad. I here saw the draft-bullocks attached to the guns, with Captain Orr's companies of Frontier Police. They are of the best kind, and in excellent condition. They have the same allowance of a seer and half of grain a-day, which is drawn for every bullock attached to his Majesty's artillery. The difference is that they get all that is paid for in their name, while the others get one-third; and really got none when on detached duty till lately. On Fridays, Captain Orr's bullocks get only half; and this is, I believe, the rule with all the others that get any at all. His bullocks are bred in the Nanpara, Nigasun, Dhorehra, and other districts in the Oude Tarae, and are of an excellent quality for work. They cost from 40 to

75 rupees a-pair. In these districts of the Tarae forest, the cows are allowed to go almost wild in large grass preserves, where they are defended from tigers; and the calves are taken from them, when a year old, to be taken care of at home, till sold for the dairy or for work. Captain Orr's bullocks have no grazing-ground, nor are they sent out at all to graze—they get nothing but bhoosa (chaff) and corn. Of bhoosa they get as much as they can eat, when on detached duty, as they take it from the peasantry without payment; but when at Lucknow, they are limited to a very small quantity, as Government has to pay for it. On the 15th of May, 1833, the King prohibited any one from taking bhoosa without paying for it, either for private or public cattle; and directed that bhoosa, for all the Artillery bullocks, should be purchased at the harvests, and charged for in the public accounts; but the order was disregarded like that against the murder of female children.

February 26, 1850.—Sidhore, sixteen miles, W. S. W. The country, a plain, covered as usual with spring crops and fine foliage; but intersected midway by the little river Kuleeanee, which causes undulations on each side. The soil chiefly doomut and light, but fertile. It abounds more in white ants than such light soil generally does. We passed through the estate of Soorujpoor Behreylee, in which so many of the baronial robbers above described reside, and through many villages beyond it, which they had lately robbed and burnt down, as far as such villages can be burnt. The mud-walls and coverings are as good as bomb-proofs against the fire, to which they are always exposed from these robbers. Only twenty days ago, Chundee Behraleea and his party attacked the village of Siswae, through which we passed a few miles from this—

plundered it, and killed three persons, and six others perished in the flames. They served several others in the neighbourhood in the same manner; and have, within the same time, attacked and plundered the town of Sidhore itself several times.

The boundary which separates the Dureeabad from the Sidhore district we passed some four miles back; and the greater part of the villages lately attacked are situated in the latter, which is under a separate Amil, Aga Ahmud, who is, in consequence, unable to collect his revenue. The Amil of Dureeabad, Girdhara Sing,* on the contrary, acquiesces in all the atrocities committed by these robbers, and is, in consequence, able to collect his revenue, and secure the favour of the Court. Some of the villages of the estate, held by the widow of Singjoo, late Rajah of Soorujpoor, are under the jurisdiction of the Sidhore Amil; and, as she would pay no revenue, the Amil took a force a few days ago to her twelve villages of Sonowlee, within the Dureeabad district, and seized and carried off some three hundred of her tenants, men, women, and children, as hostages for the payment of the balance due, and confined them pell-mell, in a fort. The clamour of the rest of the population as I passed was terrible, all declaring that they had paid their rents to the *Ranee*, and that she alone ought to be held responsible. She, however, resided at Soorujpoor, within the jurisdiction, and under the protection of the Amil of Dureeabad.

The Behraleea gangs have lately plundered the five villages of Sadutpoor, Luloopoor, Bilkhundee, and Subahpoor, belonging to Soorujbulee, the head Canoongo,

* Girdhara Sing's patron is Chundee Sahaee, the minister's deputy, whose influence is paramount at present.

or Chowdheree of Dureeabad, who had never offended them. Both the Amils were with me for the latter part of the road; and the dispute between them ran very high. It was clear, however, that Girdhara Sing was strong in his league with the robbers, and conscious of being able to maintain his ground at Court; and Aga Ahmud was weak in his efforts to put them down, and conscious of his being unable much longer to pay what was required, and keep his post. He has with him two Companies of Nujeebs and two of Telingas, and eight guns. The guns are useless and without ammunition, or stores of any kind; and the Nujeebs and Telingas cannot be depended upon. The best pay master has certainly the best chance. It is humiliating and distressing to see a whole people suffering such wrongs as are every day inflicted upon the village communities and town's people of Dureeabad, Rodowlee, Sidhore, and Dewa, by these merciless freebooters; and impossible not to feel indignant at a Government that regards them with so much indifference.*

A respectable young agricultural capitalist from Biswa, Seetaram, rode along by my side this morning, and I asked him, "over whom these suttee tombs, near Biswa, and other towns were for the most part raised.—"Sir," said he, "they are chiefly over the widows of Brahmins, bankers, merchants, Hindoo public officers, tradesmen, and shopkeepers." "Are there many such tombs in

* Poor Aga Ahmud was put into gaol, for defalcation, at the end of the season; but Girdhara Sing was received with great favour by the Court. His government of the district, for the next season, was confirmed, and the usual dress of honour was conferred upon him, but the Resident deemed it to be his duty to interpose and insist upon his not being sent out. The government of the district was, in consequence, taken from him, and made over to Rajah Maun Sing.

Oude, over the widows of Rajpoot landholders?"—"I have not seen any, sir, and have rarely heard of the widow of a Rajpoot landholder burning herself." "No, sir," said Bukhtawar Sing, "how should such women be worthy to become suttees? They dare not become suttees, sir, with the murder of so many innocent children on their heads. Sir, we Brahmins and other respectable Hindoos feel honoured in having daughters; and never feel secure of a happy life hereafter till we see them respectably married. This, sir, is a duty the Deity demands from us, and the neglect of which we do not believe he can ever excuse. When the bridegroom comes, sir, to fetch our daughter, the priest reads over the marriage-service, and the parents of the girl wash her feet and those of her bridegroom; and, as they sit together after the ceremonies, put into her arms a tray of gold and silver jewels, and rich clothes, such as their condition in life enables them to provide; and then invoke the blessing of God upon their union; and then, and not till then, do they feel that they have done their duty to their child. What can men and women, who murder their daughters as soon as they are born, ever hope for in this life or in a future state? What can widows, conscious of such crimes, expect from ascending the funeral pile, with the bodies of their deceased husbands who have caused them to commit such crimes?" "And you think that there really is merit in such sacrifices on the part of widows, who have done their duties in this life?" —"Assuredly I do, sir; if there were none, why should God render them so insensible to the pain of burning? I have seen many widows burn themselves in my time, and watched them from the time they first declared their intention to their death; and they all seemed to me to feel nothing whatever from the flames: nothing, sir, but support from above could sustain them through such trials. Depend upon it, sir, that no widow of a Rajpoot murderer of his own offspring would ever be so supported; they knew very well that they would not be so; and, therefore, very wisely never ventured to expose themselves to the trial: faithful wives and good mothers only could so venture. The Rajpoots, sir, and their wives were pleased at the prohibition, because others could no longer do what they dared not do!" "What do you think, Seetarum?"—"I think, sir, that this crime of infanticide had its origin solely in family pride, which will make people do almost anything. These proud Rajpoots did not like to put it into any man's power to call them *salahs* or *sussoors*,* (brothers-in-law or fathers-in-law).

"I remember an instance of a woman burning herself at Lasoora, six miles from Biswa, when I was fifteen years of age, and I am now twenty-five. She certainly seemed to suffer no pain. One forenoon she told her husband that in a former birth she had promised him that when he should be born a *maha brahman* at Biswa, she would unite herself in marriage to him, and live with him as his wife for twelve years; that these twelve years had now expired, and that she had that night received intimation from Heaven that her real husband, *Rajah Kirpah Shunker*, of Muthura, had died without having been married in this birth; that she was in reality his wife, and had already burnt herself five times with his body, and would now mix her ashes with his for the sixth time, and he must forthwith send her to the village of

* These are terms too often made use of as abuse all over India. To call a man sussoor or salah, in abuse, is to say to him, I have dishonoured your daughter or your sister!

Lasoora, where she would become a suttee. The husband was astounded, for they had always lived together on the best possible terms, and out of the four children they had had two still survived. He and all their relations did all they could to dissuade her, but she disregarded them, and ran off to the Sewala (temple) in Biswa, which was built by my father. Thence she sent a Brahmin, by name Gokurn, to call me and my elder brother, Morlee Munohur, then seventeen years of age. We went, and she told us that she had been our mother in a former birth, and wished to see us once more before she died; she blessed us, and prayed that we might have each five sons, and then told us to arrange for her funeral pile at Lasoora, as all her former five suttees had been performed at that place.

"We thought she was delirious, and no one supposed that she would really burn herself. She, however, left the temple and proceeded towards Lasoora on foot, followed by a party of women and children, and by her husband, who continued to implore her to return home with him. He had a litter with him to take her, but she would not listen to him or to any one else. We reached Lasoora about an hour and a half before sunset, and she ordered the people to collect a large pile of wood for her, and told them that she would light it with a flame from her own mouth. They seemed to regard her as an inspired person, and did so. She mounted the pile, and it soon took fire, how I know not! Many people said they saw the flame come from her mouth, and all seemed to believe that it did so. The flames ascended, for it was in the month of March, and the wood was dry, and she seemed to be quite happy as she sat in the midst of them, and was burnt to death. Her husband told us, that she had lost one son some years before, and another only four days before she burnt herself, and that she had been much afflicted at his death. Whether there really had been such a person as Rajah Kirpah Shunker, no one ever thought it necessary to inquire. Her suttee tomb still stands at Lasoora among many others. Our mother was alive, though our father had been dead many years, and she used to say that the poor woman must have become deranged at the death of her child. The people all believed that she told the truth, and the husband was obliged to yield, though he seemed much afflicted. Her two sons still live, and reside at Biswa." *

I asked the Amil, "How he fed, clothed, and lodged his prisoners?" He said, "We always take them with us in our marches, secured in stocks or fetters. We cannot leave them behind, because we have no gaols or other places to keep them in, and require all our troops to move with us. As to food and clothing, they are obliged to provide themselves, or get their families or friends to provide them, for Government will not let us charge anything for their subsistence and clothing in the accounts."

"I understand that you and all other public servants who have charge of prisoners not only make them provide themselves with food and clothing, but make them pay for lamp-oil, whether they have a lamp burning at night or not?"—"When they require a lamp they must of course pay for it, sir; prisoners are always a source of much anxiety to us, for if we send them to Lucknow,

* Moorlee Monowur, a very respectable agricultural capitalist, tells me, that all that his younger brother, Seetaram, told me, about this suttee, is strictly true, and can be proved by a reference to the poor woman's husband and sons, who still survive, and to the people of Biswa and Lasoora.

they are almost sure to be let out soon, on occasions of thanksgiving, or on payment of gratuities, and enabled to punish all who have assisted us in the arrest; and with hosts of robbers around us, we are always in danger of an attempt to rescue them, which may cost us many lives."

"If the gaol darogahs at Lucknow had not the power to sell his prisoners, sir," said Bukhtawar Sing, "how should he be able to pay so much as he does for his place? He is obliged to pay five hundred rupees or more for his place, and is not sure of holding it a month after he has bought it, so many are the candidates for a place so profitable!" "But he gets a share of the subsistence money, paid for the prisoners from the Treasury, does he not?"—"Yes, sir; of the four pice a-day paid for them by the King, he takes two, and sends them to beg through the city for what more they require." "If they get more than what he thinks they require from the public or their friends, he takes the surplus from them, I am told?" —"It is very true, sir, I believe. Fellows, sir, who have no substantial friends, and cannot and will not beg, soon sink under this scanty supply of food."

February 27, 1850.—Sutrick, sixteen miles west, over a plain of muteear soil, tolerably well cultivated, and very well studded with trees of the finest kinds, single, in clusters and in groves. The mango-trees are in blossom, and promise well. The trees are said to bear only one season out of three, but some bear in one season, and others in another, so that the market is always supplied, though in some seasons more abundantly than in others. A cloudy sky and easterly wind, while the trees are in blossom, are said to be very injurious. A large landholder told me that they never took a tax upon any of the trees, not even the mhowa-trees, but the owner could not, except upon particular occasions, dispose of one to be cut down, without the permission of the zumeendar upon whose lands it stood. He might cut down one without his permission for building or repairing his house, or for fuel, on any occasion of marriage in his family, but not otherwise. A good many fine trees were, he said, destroyed by the local officers of Government. Having no tents, they collected the roofs of houses from a neighbouring village in hot or bad weather, cut away the branches to make rafters, and left the trunks as pillars to support the roofs, and under this treatment they soon died. He told me that cow-dung was cheaper for fuel than wood in this district, and consequently more commonly used in cooking; but that they gathered cow-dung for fuel only during four months in the year, November, December, January, and February; all that fell during the other eight months was religiously left, or stored for manure. In the pits in which they stored it, they often threw some of the inferior green crops of autumn, such as kodo and kotkee; but the manure most esteemed among them was *pigs' dung*—this, he said, was commonly stored and sold by those who kept pigs. The best muteear and doomut soils, which prevail in this district, are rented at two rupees a kutcha beegah, without reference to the crop which the cultivator might take from them; and they yielded, under good tillage, from ten to fifteen returns of the seed in wheat, barley, gram, &c. There are two and half or three kutcha beegahs in a pucka beegah; and a pucka beegah is from 2750 to 2760 square yards.

Sutrick is celebrated for the shrine of Shouk Salar, alias *Borda Baba*, the father of Syud Salar, whose shrine is at Bahraetch. This person, it is said, was the husband of the sister of Mahmood, of Ghuznee. He is supposed to have died a natural death at this place, while leading the armies of his sovereign against the Hindoos. His son had royal blood in his veins, and his shrine is held to be the most sacred of the two. A large fair is held here in March, on the same days that this fair takes place at Bahraetch. All our Hindoo camp followers paid as much reverence to the shrine as they passed as the Mahommedans. It is a place without trade or manufactures; but a good many respectable Mahommedan families reside in it, and have built several small but neat mosques of burnt bricks. There is little thoroughfare in the wretched road that passes through it.

The Hindoos worship any sign of manifested might or power, though exerted against themselves, as they consider all might and power to be conferred by the Deity for some useful purpose, however much that purpose may be concealed from us. "These invaders, however merciless and destructive to the Hindoo race, say they must have been sent on their mission by God for some great and useful purpose, or they could not possibly have succeeded as they did: had their proceedings not been sanctioned by Him, he could at any moment have destroyed them all, or have interposed to arrest their progress." These, however, are the speculations of only the thinking portion. At the bottom of the respect shown to such Mahommedan shrines, by the mass of Hindoos, there is always a strong ground-work of *hope* or *fear*: the soul or spirit of the savage old man, who had been so well supported on earth, must still, they think, have some influence at the Court of Heaven to secure them good or work them evil, and they invoke or propitiate him accordingly. They would do the same to the tomb of Alexander,

Jungez Khan, Tymour, or Nadir Shah, without any perplexing inquiries as to their creed or liturgy.

February 28, 1850.—Chinahut, eleven miles west, over a plain intersected by several small streams, the largest of which is the Rete, near Sutrick. There is a good deal of kunkur-lime in the ground over which we have passed today; but the tillage is good where the land is at all level, and the crops are fine. The plain is cut up here and there by some ravines, but they are small and shallow, and render but a small portion of the surface unfit for tillage. The banks of the small streams are, for the most part, cultivated up to the water's edge.

We passed the Rete over a nice bridge, built by Rajah Bukhtawar Sing twenty-five years ago, at a cost of twenty-five thousand rupees, out of his own purse. He told me that one morning, in the rains, he came to the bank of this river, on his way to Lucknow from Jeytpoor, a town which we passed yesterday, and found it so swollen that he was obliged to purchase some large earthen jars, and form a raft upon them to take over himself and followers. While preparing his raft, which took a whole day, he heard that from five to ten persons were drowned, in attempting to cross this little river, every year, and that people were often detained upon the bank for four or five days together. He resolved to save people from all this evil; and as soon as he got home set about building this bridge, and got it ready before the next rains. It is a substantial work, with three good arches. About two miles on this side of the bridge he pointed out to me the single tree, near a mango-grove, where some eighteen or twenty years ago he overtook a large balloon, which the King, Nuseer-od Deen Hyder, had got made in the Dilkosha Park at Lucknow. It was made, he tells me, by a tall and slender young English gentleman, who visited Lucknow, with his uncle, for the special purpose of constructing and ascending in this machine. "When it was all ready, sir, the young man got into a small boat that was suspended under it, taking with him a gun and some artificial fish. We asked him what he intended to do with a gun in the clouds; and he told us, that in the sky he was in danger of meeting large birds that might hurt the balloon, and the gun was necessary to frighten them off. As the balloon began to ascend the old gentleman's eyes filled with tears, and I asked him why. He told me, that this young man's father had fallen into the sea, and been drowned; and he was always afraid, when the son went up, that he might never see him alive again.

"The King was sitting at the window in the upper story of the Dilkosha house, with some English gentlemen, when the balloon passed up close by, and the gentleman took off his hat and bowed gracefully as he passed, at which the King seemed much pleased. I commanded a regiment of Dragoons, and the King told me to take a party of my boldest and best-mounted men and follow the balloon. I selected seventeen, and we were all ready in our saddles. The balloon went straight up, and we lost sight of the man and the boat in which he sat. The machine, though it was sixty feet long, including boat and all, and twelve feet wide, seemed at last to be no larger than a small water-jug. Below we had no wind, but we soon saw the balloon driven by an upper current to the eastward, along the Fyzabad road. We followed as fast as the horses could carry us, crossed the Goomtee river over the old stone bridge, and passed many travellers on the road staring at the extraordinary machine, for they had heard nothing about it, and we had no time to tell them. When we had gone about seventeen miles, the balloon began to descend. It was in the month of March, and the weather was hot, and I had lost three horses before it came to the ground. The young man then began to let go his fish, and they came fluttering down, while the oil-cloths about the balloon made a noise like the growling of a wild beast. Seeing the enormous machine going at this rate, followed by us at full speed, the people along the road, who are always numerous in the morning, became so panic-struck that a great many fell down senseless upon their faces, and some of them could not be got to rise for some hours afterwards.

"We were not far from it when it approached the ground, and swept along on the border of this grove, on our left. Fortunately for the young man, it did not strike any trees. He was dressed all in black, and a very tall, handsome young man he was. As soon as he found himself near enough to the ground, he jumped out, holding one rope in his hand, and tried to stop the balloon, calling out to the people on the road, as loud as he could, *puckaro, puckaro!*—seize, seize! We were then within two hundred yards of it, and at full speed; and, instead of helping the young man, the people on the road, thinking the order was to seize them, fell down flat on their faces, unable to look upon the balloon, or utter a word. They all thought that it was some terrible demon from above come to seize and devour them. When we had headed it a little, we all sprang from our saddles, joined the young man at the ropes, and lashed them round anything we could find, as we were being dragged along. The young man took out his penknife, and gave the balloon a gash in the side, to let out the *smoke* that inflated it, and it collapsed and stopped. The first thing, sir, that the young man did was to call for fire, take a cigar from his waistcoat pocket, and begin to smoke, while we went to the assistance of the panic-struck travellers, many of whom were still lying senseless on the ground. We got water, and threw it in their faces; and when they were able to sit up, we mounted the young man upon one of our horses, and took him back slowly to Lucknow. He told me that it was so very cold above, that it gave him a severe headache, and that he found a cigar a good thing to remove it. The King was very glad when we brought him back, and he gave him several thousand rupees over and above the cost of making the balloon, and providing him and his uncle during their stay. They soon after left Lucknow for Lahore, and what became of them I know not."

Passing a Mahommedan village, I asked some of the landholders, who walked along by the side of my elephant, to talk of their grievances, whether they ever used *pigs' dung* for manure. They seemed very much surprised and shocked, and asked how I could suppose that Mahommedans could use such a thing. "Come," said Bukhtawar Sing, "do not attempt to deceive the Resident. He has been all over India, and knows very well that Mahommedans do not keep or eat pigs; but he knows, also, that there is no good cultivator in Oude who does not use the dung of pigs for manure; and you know that there is no other manure, save pigeons' dung, that is so good." "We often purchase *manure* from those who prepare it," said the landholders, "and do not ask questions about what it may be composed of; but the greater part of the manure we use is the cow-dung which falls in the season of the rains, and is stored exclusively for that purpose. In the dry months, sir, the dung of cows, bullocks, buffaloes, &c., is gathered, formed into cakes, and stacked for fuel; but in the rains it is all thrown into pits and stored for manure."

Chinahut is the point from which we set out on the 2nd of December, and here I was met by the prime minister, Nawab Allee Nakee Khan, and the chancellor of the exchequer, Maharajah Balkrishun, to whom I explained my views as to the measures which ought to be adopted to save the peaceful and industrious portion of his Majesty's subjects from the evils which now so grievously oppress them.

Here closes my pilgrimage of three months in Oude; and I can safely say that I have learnt more of the state of the country, and the condition and requirements of the people, than I could possibly have learnt in a long life passed exclusively at the capital of Lucknow. Any general remarks that I may have to make on what I have seen and heard during the pilgrimage I must defer to a future period.

At four in the afternoon, I left Chinahut, and returned to Lucknow. At the old race-stand, about three miles from the Residency, I was met by the heir-apparent, and drove with him, in his carriage, to the Furra Buksh Palace, where we alighted for a few minutes, to go through the usual tedious ceremonies of an Oriental Court. On the way we were met by Mr. Hamilton, the chaplain, and his lady, Dr. and Mrs. Bell, and Captain Bird, the First Assistant, and his brother and guest. After the ceremony, I took leave of the Prince, and reached the Residency at six o'clock. My wife and children had left me at Peernuggur, to return, for medical advice, to the Residency, where I had the happiness to find them well, and glad to see me. Having broken my left thigh bone, near the hip joint, in a fall from my horse, in April, 1849, I was unable to mount a horse during the tour, and went in a tonjohn the first half of the stage, and on an elephant the last half, that I might see as much as possible of the country over which we were passing. The pace of a good elephant is about that of a good walker, and I had generally some of the landholders and cultivators riding or walking by my side to talk with.

END OF THE TOUR.

PRIVATE CORRESPONDENCE

RELATING TO THE ANNEXATION OF THE KINGDOM OF OUDE TO BRITISH INDIA.

Camp, Nawabgunge, 5th December, 1849.

MY DEAR BIRD,

I HAD heard from Mahomed Khan what you mention regarding the imposition practised on the King by the singers; but from his having conferred a khilaut on the knaves, they supposed that he had, as usual, pardoned all. If you have grounds to believe that the King is prepared to punish them, or to acquiesce in their punishment, pray ask an audience and ascertain his Majesty's wishes. When we last went, I was in hopes that he would tell me that he wished to be relieved of their presence, and did all I could to encourage him to do so. If the King wishes to have them removed, encourage him to give immediate orders to the minister to confine them; and offer any assistance that may be required to take them across the Ganges, or put them into safe custody. When it is done, it must be done promptly.

As to the Taj Mahal, I went on an order by Richmond, "that the King should put a Mahaldarnee upon her if he wished." I was told that such was Richmond's order, and I give mine in consequence. I will refer to the Dufter for his order. But you must at once insist upon all sipahees being withdrawn from her house. This order was given by me and should be enforced by you. I said that the Mahaldarnee might remain, but it must be alone, without sipahees, &c.

On emergency, act of course on your own discretion. I only wish that the King may be induced to consent to the removal of all the singers, and meddling eunuchs also.

Yours sincerely,
(Signed) W. H. SLEEMAN.

To Captain Bird,
First Assistant.

Sadik Allee should be secured, and punished with the rest.

(Signed) W. H. SLEEMAN.

Camp, Bahraetch, 10th December, 1849.

MY DEAR BIRD,

THE conduct of the singers which exasperated the King had no reference to public matters with which he was pledged not to permit them to interfere; and my only request was, that you should offer your aid in removing them should his Majesty indicate any wish for it. The King said he would himself punish them for their conduct by banishment across the Ganges, and he must be left to do so: it was not from any demand made by us, but from resentment for a personal affront, or an affront to his understanding. We cannot call upon the King to do what he said he would do under such circumstances, but must leave it to himself. The removal of two out of a dozen fellows of this description will be of no use—their places will soon be filled by others. Any attempt on your part to supply their places by better men will only tend to indispose the King towards them; and it is no part of our duty to dictate to his Majesty with whom he shall associate in his private hours.

I have had abundant proof that, to reduce the influence of the present favourites, has no tendency to throw the power into better hands—no authority of any kind taken from them has, by the minister, been confided to better men; the creatures of one are not a whit better than the creatures of the other. If his Majesty were to rouse himself, and apply his own mind to business, we might hope for some good, and I see little chance of this.

You are not to order that the King fulfil his promise, because, as I have said, it was no pledge made on the requisition of our Government on the Resident. If he does not fulfil it, it is only one proof more added to a hundred of his exceeding weakness. There are at least a dozen worse men now influencing all that the King and minister do than Kotab Alee and Gholam Ruza. The last order given regarding Taj Mahal by me was, that she should admit a Mahaldarnee from the King, but that no sipahees should be forced upon her. I wrote to the King to this effect, and my order must be enforced. I am told by the moonshee, that when the King expressed a wish to have such guardians upon many, Richmond replied that he might have one upon Taj Mahal, who had given such proof of profligacy. It was not a judicial decision, to be referred to as a guide under all circumstances, but a mere arrangement which might any day require to be altered. Taj Mahal is so profligate and insolent a woman, that if she refuses to obey my order, and receive the King's Mahaldarnee, I shall withdraw the Residents.

After what the Governor-General had told the King in November, 1847, regarding what our Government would feel itself bound to do, unless his Majesty conducted the duties of a sovereign better than he had hitherto done; and after the experience we have since had of his entire neglect of those duties, you should not, I think, have said what you mention having said to him, that our Government had no wish to deprive him of one iota of the power he had. It was a declaration not called for by the circumstances, or necessary on the occasion, and should have been avoided, as it is calculated to impair the impression of his responsibility for the exercise of his power. No sovereign ever showed a greater disregard for the duties and responsibilities of his high office than he has done hitherto, and as our Government holds itself answerable to the people of Oude for a better administration, he should not be encouraged in the notion that he may always show the same disregard with impunity—that is, continue to retain every iota of his power whether he exercised it properly or not. No man, I believe, ever felt more anxious for the welfare of the King, his family, and country, than I do; but unless he exercises his fearful power better, I should be glad, for the sake of all, to see the whole, or part of it, in better hands.

The minister has his Motroussil with me, and I have daily communications of what is done or proposed to be done, and you may be sure that I lose no occasion of admonition. I did not mention anything you said regarding your interview with the King in your letter to Mahomed Khan; but in a few hours after your letter came he got the whole from the minister, and reported it to me. He wants us to undertake the work of turning out the King's favourites, that he may get all the power they lose, without offending his master by any appearance of moving in the matter.

We go hence to-morrow; hope to be at Gonda on the 14th, and Fyzabad on the 18th. I have requested the post-master to send all our letters to Fyzabad by the regular dawk from Thursday next, the 13th. From Fyzabad I will arrange for their coming to my camp.

Yours sincerely,

(Signed) W. H. SLEEMAN.

To Captain Bird,
&c. &c.

Camp, Ghunghole, 12th December, 1849.

MY DEAR BIRD,

I GOT your letter of the 9th instant last night, at our last ground. In what you have done, you have not, I think, acted discreetly. You asked me whether, in any case of emergency, you should act on your discretion, and I told you in reply that you might do so; but surely, whether the King should have a dozen singers or only ten could not be considered one of such pressing emergency as not to admit of your waiting for instructions from me, or, at least, for a reply to your letter. The King has told you truly, that the matter in which the offenders had transgressed had reference to his house, and not to his Government or ours. This is a distinction which you appear to have lost sight of from the first. If I demand reparation from another for wrong or insults suffered from his servants, and he promises to punish them by dismissal from his service, but afterwards relents and detains them, I consider it due to myself and my character to insist upon the fulfilment of his promise; but if I voluntarily visit any friend who has at last become sensible of the impositions of his servants which had long been manifest to all his neighbours, with a view to encourage him in his laudable resolution to dismiss them from his service, and to offer my aid in effecting the object should he require it, and he promises me not to swerve from it, but afterwards relents and retains the impostors, I pity his weakness, but I do not consider it due to myself, or to my character, to insist upon his fulfilling his promise. By considering two cases so very distinct, the same, you have placed yourself in a disagreeable situation, for I cannot support you; that is, I can neither demand that the requisitions made by you be complied with, nor can I tell the King that I approve of them. Had you waited for my reply, which was sent off from Bahraetch on the 10th, you would have saved yourself all this annoyance and mortification. It has arisen from an overweening confidence in your personal influence over his Majesty; the fact is, I believe that no European gentleman ever has had or ever will have any personal influence over him, and I very much doubt whether any real native gentleman will ever have any. He never has felt any pleasure in their society, and I fear never will. He has hitherto felt easy only in the society of such persons as those with whom he now exclusively associates, and to hope that he will ever feel easy with persons of a better class is vain. I am perfectly satisfied, in spite of the oath he has taken in the name of his God, and on the head of his minister, that he made to you the promise you mention; and I am no less satisfied that the minister wished for the removal of the singers, provided it should be effected through us without his appearing to his master to move in the matter, and that he wished their removal solely with a view to acquire for himself the authority they had possessed. You should not have any more audiences with the King without previous reference to me; nothing is likely to occur to require it.

Yours sincerely,
(Signed) W. H. SLEEMAN.

To Captain Bird,
&c. &c.

Camp, Fyzabad, 18th December, 1849.

MY DEAR BIRD,

I SEND you the letter which you wish to refer to. As you quote my first letter, pray let me see it. I kept no copy, but have a distinct recollection of what I intended to say in it regarding this affair of the singers. It shall be sent back to you. The term "indiscreet" had reference only to your second visit, and demand from the King of the fulfilment of his promise. I had no fault whatever to find with your first visit. The term "private" must have had reference, not to the promise or to the person to whom it was made, but to the offence with which the singers stood charged. It was an affront offered to the King's understanding that he took affront at, and whether he had made a promise to resent it as such to me or to you could make no difference. If he did not fulfil it, we should pity this further instance of his weakness, but could have no right to insist upon his doing so. Even had the offence been an interference in public affairs, and breach of the King's engagements, I should not have demanded their banishment without a reference to the Governor-General, because the delay of waiting for instructions involved no danger or serious inconvenience; that is, I should not have demanded it when the King was so strongly opposed to it. I must distinctly deny that you demanded the King's fulfilment of his promise in conformity to any instructions received from me, or in accordance with my views of what was right or expedient in this matter. Your second visit and demand were neither in conformity to the one nor in accordance with the other. You must have put a construction upon what I wrote which it cannot fairly bear. By "requisitions" I mean your requirements that the two men should be banished by the King, according to his promise. No notice has been made to me of your visit by the Court, and I have therefore had no occasion to say anything whatever about it in my communications to the Court, nor shall I have any I suppose. In your letter of the 4th instant, you say, with regard to the Taj Mahal's case, "Not knowing whether you do or do not wish me to act in any sudden emergency during your absence, I suppose, therefore, that had you had any such wish you would have instructed me on the subject." In reply, I requested that you would so act on your own discretion in any such sudden case of emergency.

Yours sincerely,
(Signed) W. H. SLEEMAN.

To Captain Bird,
&c. &c.

Camp, Mahomdee, 2nd February, 1850.

MY DEAR SIR ERSKINE,

HAD it not been too late for you to join my camp conveniently, I should have asked you to run out and see a little of the country and people of Oude, after you had seen so much of those of the Honourable Company's dominions. A few years of tolerable government would make it the finest country in India, for there is no part of India with so many advantages from nature. I have seen no soil finer; the whole plain of which it is composed is capable of tillage; it is everywhere intersected by rivers, flowing from the snowy chain of the Himmalaya, which keep the moisture near the surface at all times, without cutting up any of the land on their borders into deep ravines; it is studded with the finest groves and single trees, as much as the lover of the picturesque could wish; it has the boldest and most industrious peasantry in India, and a landed aristocracy too strong for the weak and wretched Government; it is, for the most part, well cultivated; yet with all this, one feels, in travelling over it, as if he was moving among a people suffering under incurable physical diseases, from the atrocious crimes every day perpetrated with impunity, and the numbers of suffering and innocent people who approach him, in the hope of redress, and are sent away in despair.

I think your conclusion regarding the source of the signs you saw of beneficial interference in the north-west provinces a fair one. A Lieutenant-Governor is able to see all parts of the country under his charge every year, or nearly all; and while he is sufficiently "monarch of all he surveys" to feel an interest in, and to provide for the general good, he has a sufficient knowledge of the internal management of particular districts to control the proceedings of the local officers. He is also well seconded in a very efficient Board of Revenue. But I must not indulge in these matters any further, till I have the pleasure of meeting you where we can talk freely about them.

I trust that all at Lucknow will be conducted to your satisfaction and that of Mrs. Erskine. I have this morning received a note from Mr. Erskine, who left you, it appears, before the little heir-apparent returned your visit. I expect to complete my tour and return to Lucknow on the 20th, when I shall have seen all that I required to see, to understand the working of the existing system, and the probable effects of any suggested changes.

With kind regards to Mrs. Erskine,

Believe me,

Yours very sincerely,

(Signed) W. H. SLEEMAN.

To Sir Erskine Perry.

P.S.—I must not omit to thank you for the expression of your favourable opinion of the "Rambles." There is one thing of which I can assure you, that the conversations mentioned in it are genuine, and give the real thoughts and opinions of the people on the subjects they embrace.

W. H. S.

Lucknow, 26th April, 1850.

MY DEAR ELLIOT,

I DID not send Weston's letters with the other papers, because they were not written in an official form.

He was the senior officer with the force, and had authority from the Durbar to call upon all local, civil, and military authorities to co-operate in the work; but he did not take upon himself the command, or write in official form. He inspired all with harmony and energy, and brought the whole strength of the little force to bear upon the right points at the right time.

The head of Prethee Put of Paska was cut off by Captain Magness's sipahees after his death, to be sent to the King as a trophy, but Captain Weston would not let it come in. The body was offered to his family and friends for interment, but none of the family or tribe (Kolhun's Rajpoots) would have anything to do with the funeral ceremonies of a man who had murdered his eldest brother and the head of his tribe. The body was, with the head, put into a sheet, taken to the river Ghagra, and committed to the stream, to flow to the Ganges, as the best interment for a Hindoo. These sipahees knew nothing of the man's history; but the people who saw the affair from the Dhundee Fort mentioned that the body was thrown into the river at the precise place where he had thrown in that of his eldest brother, after murdering him in the boat with his own hands, as stated in the extract from my Diary; and all believe that this retribution arises from an interposition from above. The eldest son of the murdered brother will, I hope, be put into possession of the estate.

The Governor-General may like to peruse these letters, and I send them. They give, perhaps, a fuller and better account of what was done, and the manner in which it was done, than more studied compositions, in an official form, would have given.

Yours sincerely,

(Signed) W. H. Sleeman.

To Sir H. M. Elliot, K.C.B.

Lucknow, 8th July, 1850.

MY DEAR SIR JAMES,

I FEEL that my Indian career, which has now lasted forty years, must be drawing to a close, and I am anxious for the settlement in life of my only son, now between seventeen and eighteen years of age. Having no personal claims upon any member of the Home Government of India, I solicit the insertion of his name on his Grace the Duke of Wellington's list of candidates for a commission in the Dragoons; and he is now preparing for his examination under the care of Mr. Yeatman, at Westow Hill, Norwood, Surrey, near London. But he is ambitious to obtain an appointment to Bengal, where his father has served so long, and may, possibly, have friends and recollections that might be useful to him in the early part of his career. It falls to the lot of few to have the opportunities that I have had to carry out the benevolent views of Government in measures of great and general benefit to the people, and to secure their gratitude and affection to their rulers. All the measures which I have been employed to carry out have tended to display the benevolent solicitude of the Government of India for the welfare of the people committed to its charge; the object of all has been the greater security of life and property throughout the country, the greater confidence of the people in the wisdom and efficiency of our rule, and their greater feeling of interest in this stability. These measures, as far as they have been confided to my care, have all succeeded; but, as I have stated (p. 79) in a printed report, a copy of which will be sent to you, they have neither flattered the vain-glory of any particular nation, nor enlisted on their side the self-love of any influential class or powerful individual, and they have, in consequence, been attended with little *éclat*. They have, however, tended to secure to the Government the gratitude and affection of the people of

India, and are measures of which that Government may justly feel proud. The stability of our Government in India must depend less upon our military victories than upon the confidence and affection with which our civil and political administration may inspire the great mass of the people. The general belief is, that our object is their substantial good, and that we are instruments in the hands of Divine Providence to effect that object. In our military glory they can feel no sympathy, and in our territorial acquisitions little interest; but they can and do appreciate every measure which tends to improve the security of life, property, and industry through the land—to restore the bond of good feeling between the Government and governed, where it has for a time been severed or impaired by accident—to provide the people with works tending to improve their comfort and convenience—to mitigate sufferings from calamities of season, and to encourage all to exert themselves honestly in their proper sphere. In carrying out the views of Government in such measures, and such only, has my life in India been spent; and for doing so to the best of my humble ability I have, I believe, done much to make its rule revered throughout India. It is by such measures that the respect and confidence of the great mass of the people have been secured, so as to enable Europeans, male and female, to pass from one end of the country to the other with the assurance, not only that they will suffer no personal injury, but no mark of disrespect. Should anything occur to deprive us of this confidence and respect among the great mass of the people, the recollection of our victories, and assurance of our superior military organization will avail us but little; and it is as one who has zealously and successfully aided Government in securing them, that I now venture to address you, in the hope that you will—if you can do so consistently with your public duties and pledges to others—open to my son the same career of usefulness by conferring upon him a nomination to the civil service of India. He is now five months above seventeen years of age; and by the time he is eighteen, he will, I hope, under Mr. Yeatman's judicious care, be able to pass his examination for Haileybury, should he, through your means, obtain this the utmost object of his ambition. Over and above the desire to follow his father's footsteps in India, he is anxious to avoid the necessity of encroaching so much upon the small means I have to provide for his four sisters, by entering so expensive a branch of the public service as the Dragoons. I know the great nature of the favour I ask from you. It is the first favour that I have ever asked from any member of the Home Government of India; and I solicit it from you solely on the ground of service rendered to the Government and people of India. I am told that I must address my application to an individual; and I address it to you, under the impression that you are the member with whom such ground is likely to meet with most consideration;—not that I think any member of the Honourable Court would disregard it; for I believe, after long and varied experience in public affairs, and much thought and reading, that no body intrusted with the Government of a distant possession ever performed their duties with more earnest solicitude for its welfare than the Court of Directors of the Honourable East India Company; but because your public career has inspired me with more confidence than that of any other member of the Court as now constituted. If you cannot grant me the favour I ask, you will, I know, pardon the liberty I have taken in asking it.

And believe me, with great respect,

Yours faithfully,

(Signed) W. H. SLEEMAN.

To Sir James Weir Hogg, Bart.

Lucknow, 20th September, 1850.

MY DEAR SIR CHARLES,

THE papers give us reason to hope that it is your intention to visit Lucknow on your way down from the hills, and if you can make it convenient to come, I shall be rejoiced to have the opportunity of showing you all that is worth seeing, and be able to afford all who come with you, ladies and gentlemen, accommodation.

The only road to Lucknow for carriages is from Cawnpore, and if you come that way, I will have carriages sent for you. If you come by any other road, I will have elephants sent to whatever place you may mention, and tents if required. It has been usual, when the Commander-in-chief visits Lucknow, for Government to intimate the intention to the King through the Resident in Oude, that preparation may be made for his reception in due form.

I mention this that you may make known your wish or intention to the Governor-General, in time for me to prepare the King and his Court.

From Cawnpore to this is only a drive of six hours, the distance being fifty miles, and the road good. All officers, &c., will be glad to have an opportunity of paying their respects to their distinguished Chief.

Believe me,

Yours very faithfully,

(Signed) W. H. SLEEMAN.

To his Excellency
Sir Charles Napier, G.C.B.,
&c. &c. &c.

Lucknow, 7th November, 1850.

MY DEAR ALLAN,

In the "Englishman" of the 28th, and the "Hurkaru" of the 29th, there are some strictures on Oude affairs. The editors of both papers are, I believe, sturdy, honest men; but their correspondents are not acquainted with the merits of the particular case referred to, or with Oude affairs generally. I vouch for the truth of everything stated in the enclosed paper, and shall feel obliged if you will give it to the one most likely, in your opinion, to make a fair use of it. There can be no harm in putting an editor in possession of the real truth in a question involving not only individual but national honour; for he must be anxious to make his paper the vehicle of truth on all such questions.

I do not like to address either of the editors, because Government expect all their servants will abstain from doing so in their own vindication, and will leave their honour in their keeping. I have done so since 1843, and should now do so were I alone concerned in this affair. You may mention my name as authority for what is stated, but pray let it be mentioned confidentially. Government has been informed of the truth, and it is well that the public should be so.

Yours sincerely,
(Signed) W. H. SLEEMAN.

To J. Allan, Esq.

Lucknow, 17th November, 1850.

MY DEAR SIR JAMES,

I THANK you for your very kind letter of the 7th ultimo: my son is preparing for his examination, and expects his commission in some regiment of cavalry very soon. He has not only become reconciled to it, but would, I believe, now prefer remaining at home as a cavalry officer to coming to India in any capacity. As I have only one son, and he has four sisters to look after, I should be unwilling to have him sent out to India as a cadet, were he anxious to be so. A good regiment is an excellent school for a young man, but no school could be worse than a bad regiment; and among so many, there must always be some bad. I have seen some of the sons of my old friends utterly ruined in character and constitution by being posted to such regiments when too young to think for themselves. I feel, however, as grateful to you for your very kind offer as I should be, were I to avail myself of it.

If I return to England, I shall take advantage of the earliest opportunity to pay my respects and become personally acquainted with you; but I have no intention to leave India as long as I feel that I can perform efficiently the duties intrusted to me.

I had a few days ago, in referring to Government an important question that must some day come before you, occasion to mention an important and interesting fact. During the last collision with the Seiks, I found that the Government securities kept up their value here, while in Calcutta they fell a good deal; and the merchants here employed agents in Calcutta to purchase largely for sale here. Paper to the value of more than three millions sterling, or three crores of rupees, is held by people residing in the city of Lucknow, and the people had never the slightest doubt that we should be ultimately triumphant. The question was whether heirs and executors of persons domiciled here and leaving property in Government securities, should apply to Her Majesty's Supreme Court in Calcutta, for probates to wills and letters of administration, or whether an act should be passed to render the decision of the highest Court at Lucknow, countersigned by the Resident, as valid as the certificate of a judge in our own provinces, as far as such property in Government securities might be concerned. A provision of this sort had been omitted in Act 20 of 1841, which was considered applicable to all British India, of which the kingdom of Oude was held to form a part.

We have now a fair prospect of long peace, during which I hope our finances will improve. The lavish life-pensions granted after wars in Central and Southern India will be lapsing with the death of the present incumbents, many of whom are becoming old and infirm, and our means of transit and irrigation will increase with the new works which are being formed, and we shall always have it in our power to augment our revenue from indirect taxation, as wealth and industry increase.

Believe me, my dear Sir James,
Very faithfully and obligedly yours,
(Signed) W. H. SLEEMAN.

To Sir James Weir Hogg, Bart.

Lucknow, 2nd March, 1851.

MY LORD,

THE mail of the 24th January has just come in, and I find my only son Henry Arthur gazetted for the 16th Dragoons. He told me by the last mail that he was to be so if he passed his examination on the 10th of that month, which he hoped to do; but I deferred writing to thank you for your kind exertions in his behalf till his name should appear in the "Gazette." I pray your Lordship to accept my most grateful acknowledgments for this act of kindness, added as it has been to the many others which I have received at your hands. It is not the less valuable that it is the only favour I have received from England since I left it more than forty years ago, though, I believe, few have done more to benefit the people of its eastern dominions, and to secure for it their esteem and affection.

I trust that my son will never do anything to make your Lordship regret the favour conferred upon me and him on this occasion. He is, I believe, in disposition, manners, and education a little gentleman; and in time he will, I hope, become a good officer.

If I might take the liberty, I would pray your Lordship to offer, in such terms as may appear to you suitable, my grateful acknowledgments for the consideration I have received, to his Grace the Duke of Wellington, and to Lord Fitzroy Somerset. My London Agents, Messrs. Denay, Clark, and Co., of Austin Friars, have been instructed to pay for my son's commission and outfit, and to provide him with the funds indispensably necessary in addition to his pay.

We shall now look with much interest to the Parliamentary discussions on Indian affairs, for we must expect some important changes on the renewal of the Charter. Whatever these changes may be for the home or local Government, I trust the benefit of the people of India will be considered the main point, and not the triumph of a party. The statesman who shall link India more closely with New Zealand will be a benefactor to both England and India, and that colony also. It might, with advantage to itself, take those children of Indian officers who cannot find employment of any kind in India, and ought not to be thrown back upon the mother-country. With this view, it might be useful to transfer our orphan institutions to that island, to direct that way our invalid and pensioned officers, who, while subsisting upon their pensions or stipends, would be able to establish their children in a climate suitable to the preservation of their race, which that of India certainly is not.

India is at present tranquil, and likely to remain so. We have no native chiefs, or combination of native chiefs, to create uneasiness; and if we continue to satisfy the great body of the people that we are anxious, to the best of our ability, to promote their happiness and welfare, and are the most impartial arbitrators that they could have, we shall have nothing to fear. The moment that this mass is impressed with the belief that we wish to govern India only for ourselves, or as the French govern Algiers, from that moment we must lose our vantage ground and decline. We may war against the native chiefs of India, but we cannot war against the people—we need not fear what may be called political dangers, but we must guard carefully against those of a social character which would unite against us the members of all classes and all creeds.

But I must no longer indulge in speculations of this sort, in which you can now feel little interest amidst the important changes which are now taking place in the institutions and relations of European nations. With grateful recollections of kindness received, and great respect,

I remain,

Your Lordship's obedient servant,

(Signed) W. H. SLEEMAN.

To the Right Hon.
the Earl of Ellenborough.

P.S.—Since writing the above, I have received your Lordship's letter of the 18th of January, and have been much gratified with the favourable opinion you entertain of the commandant and officers. It is the best assurance I could have of my boy being safe. Nothing could be more auspicious than the opening of the lad's career, and I trust he will profit by the advantage.

Lucknow, 18th March, 1851.

MY DEAR SIR ERSKINE,

I HAVE read over with much interest the two small works you have done me the favour to send me, the one on Buddhism, and the other on Law Reform; but I have not ventured upon the Seventh Report of the Board of Education yet, because I have had a good deal to do and think about; and a good deal of it is in small print, very trying for my eyes, which are none of the strongest. I shall, however, soon read it.

I concur in all your views about the necessity of throwing overboard the whole system of special pleading, and have been amused with Sir J. P. Grant's horror of your proposed innovations. It is not less than that which he expressed at the little Macaulay Code, intended to blow up the whole pyramid raised by "the wisdom of our ancestors," in which so many illustrious characters lie entombed. He was, indeed, as you say, a great *laudator temporis acti;*" but the number of those like him at all times in England and its distant possessions is fearful. One likes to look to America in this as in all things tending to advancement; but there the "damned spot" stares us in the face, blights our hopes, and crushes our sympathies—hideous slavery—hideous alike in the recollection of the past, the contemplation of the present, and the anticipation of the future. I wish two things—1. That you would write a work on the subject less "sketchy and perfunctory," as you call it, so that any one not versed in English law and procedure might be able to understand it and appreciate it thoroughly. 2nd. That you would, when relieved from your present office, come out as our law member of council, to press your views on our Government with effect. With these law reforms, as with railroads, there were less impediments in India than in England; but there is one thing that I would observe. In our own Indian Courts our judges would—for a time at least—want the aid of honest *masters* to condense and report upon cases under trial. Such men would be made in time; and in considering such things, we must recollect that almost the only persons in India who can send agents into all parts of it, with a perfect assurance of honest dealing, are the native merchants and bankers. But I won't dwell on this subject. I can't find amongst the numerous Buddhists here, one who knows anything about "Kapila vasta," which you place near to Lucknow. I should like to visit the birth-place of a man who did so much for mankind as Sakeen Gantama.

He would hardly have done as I have, placed my only son in the 16th Lancers. However, I may console myself, for he may be in it a long time without doing much mischief, for I do hope that the people of the nations of modern Europe are too strong and too wise to let their sovereigns and ministers play such fantastic tricks as they were "wont to play," when George the 3rd, and Edward the 3rd, and Henry the 5th were kings. Property, good sense, and good business have greatly increased and spread, and are every day producing good fruits.

Believe me,
Yours very trusting,
(Signed) W. H. SLEEMAN.

To Sir Erskine Perry,
&c. &c.

Lucknow, 31st March, 1851.

MY DEAR SIR,

I GRIEVE to say that I can do nothing whatever for the son of my late friend Colonel Ouseley, and have been obliged to write to him to that effect, as to many other sons of old and valued friends whom I should be glad to aid if I could.

Tens of thousands of the most happy families I have seen in India owe all they have to the able and judicious management of the late Colonel Ouseley when in the civil charge of the districts of Houshengabad and Baitool, in the Saugor territories; and no man's memory is more dear to the people of those districts than his now is. The family of a man who had done so much to make his government beloved and respected over so large a field should never want if I could prevent it; but I have no situations whatever in my gift, nor have I any influence over any persons who have such situations to bestow.

Believe me,

Yours truly,

(Signed) W. H. SLEEMAN..

To Captain Harrington.

Lucknow, 24th November, 1851.

MY LORD,

LUCKNOW affairs are now in a state to require the assumption of the entire management of the country; and the principal question for your Lordship's consideration is, whether this shall be done by a new treaty or by simple proclamation. Treaties not only justify but enjoin the measure; our pledges to the people demand it; and all India are, I believe, satisfied of its justice, provided we leave the revenues for the maintenance of the royal family in suitable dignity, and for the benefit of the people.

We may disencumber our Government of the pay of two regiments of Oude Local Infantry, and incorporate them with the Oude force to be raised, and of that of the officers of the residency, altogether about two lacs and a-half of rupees; and when things are settled down a little, the brigade now here—of three infantry regiments and a company of artillery, costing some four lacs more —may be dispensed with, perhaps.

If I may be permitted to give an opinion as to the best

mode of the two, I should say proclamation, as the more dignified.

I have prepared all the information I believe your Lordship will require, and am ready to wait upon you with it when and where it may seem most convenient.

The treasury is exhausted, and fifty lacs are required to pay the stipendiaries of the royal family and establishments; and assuredly all the members of that family, save the King's own household, are wishing for some great measure to place them under the guarantee of the British Government. The people all now wish for it, at least all the well-disposed, for there is not a man of integrity or humanity left in any office. The King's understanding has become altogether emasculated; and though he would not willingly do harm to any one, he is unable to protect any one. He would now, I believe, willingly get rid of his minister; and, having exhausted the treasury, the minister would not much dislike to get rid of him. I shall do my best to prevent his being released from the responsibility of his misdoings till I meet your Lordship. I should like, if possible, to meet your Lordship where there is likely to be the least crowd of expectants and parade to take up your time and distract your attention. If at Cawnpore, I hope you will permit me to have my camp on the Oude side of the river, with a tent in your camp for business during the day. With your Lordship's commands to attend, it will be desirable to have an order to make over my treasury to the First Assistant, to prevent delay. Should you desire any memoranda to be sent, they shall be forwarded as soon as ordered. If any further public report upon the state of Oude affairs appears to be required, I must pray your Lordship to let me know as soon as convenient. I shall not propose any native gentlemen for the higher offices; but it will be necessary to have a great many in the subordinate ones, to show that your Lordship wishes to open employment in all branches of the new administration to educated native gentlemen.

I remain,
Your Lordship's obedient servant,
(Signed) W. H. SLEEMAN.

To the Most Noble
The Marquis of Dalhousie,
Governor-General,
&c. &c. &c.

Lucknow, 18th March, 1852.

MY LORD,

I WAS favoured with your Lordship's letter of the 24th ultimo in due course, and did not reply immediately as I had stated, or was about to state, in a public form, all that seemed to be required about Captain Bird and Dr. Bell. Dr. Bell had apologised for indiscretions in conversation, but denied ever having authorised Mr. Brandon to make use of his name; and pretended utter ignorance of the intrigues which he was carrying on at the time that he was doing his utmost to convey wrong impressions to the Durbar. I feel grateful for the support your Lordship has given me. I cared nothing about the intrigues of these very silly men while under the impression that it was your intention to interpose effectually for the benefit of the people of Oude, because the new arrangements would have rendered them harmless; but when I found that you could not do so at present, it became necessary, for my own dignity and that of the Government, to do my best to put a stop to them. Most assuredly Captain Bird had been trying hard to persuade the King and his minister that our Government could not interfere, and that all the threats of the Governor-General would continue to be what they had hitherto been, and might be disregarded.

I find that your Lordship has departed slightly from your original plan in regard to Burmah, by sending a detachment to make a demonstration upon Rangoon and Martaban. There is no calculating upon the result of such a demonstration in dealing with a Government so imbecile, and so ignorant of our resources. The places are too far from the capital, and the war party may succeed in persuading the King that in this demonstration we put forth all our strength. I can appreciate your motive—the wish to avoid, if possible, a war of annexation, which a war upon any scale must be. We should have to make use of a vast number of suffering people, whom we could not abandon to the mercy of the old Government.

In the last war our great difficulties were the want of quick transit for troops and stores by sea, the want of carriage cattle, and sickness. These three impediments will not now beset us. Our own districts on the coast will supply land-carriage, steam-vessels will carry our troops and stores, and subsequent experience will enable us to avoid sources of endemial diseases. I have no map of the country; but some letters in the papers about the Busseya river interested me much. Our strong point is steam; and the discovery of a river which would enable us to use it in getting in strength to the rear or flank would be of immense advantage. There must be healthy districts; indeed Burmah generally must be a healthy country, or the population would not be so strong and intelligent as they are known to be. In religious feeling they are less opposed to us than any other people not Buddhists. Indeed, from the people we should have nothing to fear; and the army must be insignificant in numbers as well as equipments. I am very glad to find that so able and well-trained a statesman as Fox Maule has been put at the head of the Board of Control; and trust that your Lordship will remain at our head till this Burmah affair is thoroughly settled.

The little affair of the Moplars, on the Malabar coast, may grow into a very big one unless skilfully managed. A brother of the Conollys is the magistrate, I believe. We can learn nothing of the cause of the strong feeling of discontent that prevails among this fanatical people. No such strong feeling can exist in India without some "canker-worm" to embitter the lives and unite the sympathies of large classes against their rulers or local governors, and make them think that they cannot shake it off without rebelling and becoming martyrs. I must pray your Lordship to excuse this long rambling letter, and

Believe me, with great respect,
Your obedient servant,
(Signed) W. H. SLEEMAN.

To the Most Noble
The Marquis of Dalhousie,
Governor-General,
Calcutta.

Lucknow, 4th April, 1852.

MY DEAR SIR JAMES,

YOUR present of the cadetship for her son made the poor widow's heart glad, and I doubt not that she has written to express her grateful feelings. The young man will, I hope, prove himself deserving of the favour you have conferred upon him so gracefully. The Court has called for a copy of my Diary of the tour I made through Oude soon after I took charge of my office; and I have sent off two copies, one for Government and the other for the Court. I purchased a small press and type for the purpose of printing it in my own house, that no one but myself and the compositor might see it. I will send home two copies for yourself and the chairman as soon as they can be bound in Calcutta. The Diary contains a faithful picture of Oude, its Government, and people, I believe. I have printed only a few copies, and they will not be distributed till I learn that the Court consider them unobjectionable. In spirit they will be found so. I intend, if I can find time, to give the history of the reigning family in a third volume. My general views on Oude affairs have been given in my letters to Government, which will, I conclude, be before the Court. A ruler so utterly regardless of his high duties and responsibilities, and of the sufferings of the people under his rule, as the present King, I have never seen; nor have I ever seen ministers so incompetent and so unworthy as those whom he employs in the conduct of his affairs. We have threatened so often to interpose for the benefit of the poor people, without doing anything, that they have lost all hope, and the profligate and unprincipled Government have lost all fear. The untoward war with Burmah prevents our present Governor-General from doing what he and I believe the Honourable Court both wish. We certainly ought not any longer to incur the odium of supporting such a Government in its iniquities, pledged as we are by treaties to protect the people from them. I do not apprehend any serious change in the constitution of the Court of Directors in the new charter. No ministers would hazard such a change in the present state of Europe. The Court is India's only safeguard. No foreign possession was ever so governed for itself as India has been, and this all foreigners with whom I have conversed, admit. The Governor-General of the Netherlands India was with me lately on his way home. He is a first-rate statesman, and he declared to me that he was impressed and delighted to see a country so governed, and apparently so sensible of the benefits conferred upon it by our paternal rule. He will tell you the same thing if you ever meet him. His name is Rochasson. The people appreciate the value of the Court of Directors, and no act, as far as it is known to them, has tended more to strengthen their confidence in it than that which has brought retribution on the great sinner in Scinde, Allee Murad. No punishment was ever more just or merited. Scinde, however, is too remote for the people in general to feel much interest in its affairs or families. Our weak points in the last Burmese war were :—1. The want of transport for troops and stores; 2. The want of carriage by land, for arms and stores; 3. Sickness. All these things have been remedied, and the war, when begun in earnest, can last but a short time. We know more of the country and shall avoid the sources of endemial disease; our steam provides for the rapid transport of troops and stores; and draft-cattle will be supplied from our own districts on the coast. Where our Government has no representative as Resident or Consul, all Europeans should be told that they remain entirely on their own responsibility. Unless this is done, the Governments must be eternally in collision. If war be carried on in earnest, it must be one of annexation: we must make use of persons whom we cannot abandon to the mercy of the Burmese Government. We have nothing to fear from the people: they have no religious feeling against us, being all Buddhists; and they have seen too much of the benefits conferred by us on the territories taken during the last war to have any dread of our dominion. Lord Dalhousie has, I believe, been most anxious to avoid a war—it has been forced upon him.

Believe me,

Yours very faithfully,

(Signed) W. H. SLEEMAN.

To Sir James W. Hogg,
Deputy Chairman,
India House.

Lucknow, 6th April, 1842.

MY DEAR MR. HALLIDAY,

WE are all wrong here in the Martinière institution, and you have now an admirable opportunity of setting all right and doing an infinite deal of good with little trouble. I know how little you have of time and attention to devote to such things, and conclude that Mr. Devereux cannot have much more, and you may feel assured that I shall do all in my power to assist you. We are here attempting to give the education of gentlemen to beggar-boys, who must always depend upon their daily work for their daily bread. The senior boys are in despair, for they find that they have learnt hardly anything to fit them for the only employments open to them, and this tends to discourage the younger ones. The Roorkee Civil Engineering School seems to have been eminently successful, and a fine field is open to all who are taught in it. We shall no doubt have a similar field open in Oude when Government interposes in behalf of the suffering people, and we might prepare for it by converting the Martinière into a similar school or college. The committee has just expressed to you a hope that Mr. Crank, the officiating principal, may be able to pass an examination in the native languages. This hope can never be realised; and if he does I shall have to record my opinion that he is otherwise unfitted. The power of nominating a principal rests entirely with the trustees; and if you concur in my views you might at once prepare for the change by getting a man from England or elsewhere, such as Mr. Maclagan, the late superintendent of the Roorkee school, fitted to teach civil engineering in all its branches. You have the command of funds to provide him with assistants of all kinds; and we have accommodations and funds to raise more, and provide machinery, books, &c. The thing might be set going at once, after you send a competent man to superintend it; and the work will be honourable to our Government and ourselves, and of vast benefit to the boys brought up at the Martinière, and to their parents and families. If you think favourably of the proposed change, and will direct the committee to take it into consideration, I will do my best to make it respond cordially to your call; or if you direct the measure to be adopted at once, I will see that it is worked out as it should be. Mr. Crank has a good knowledge of mathematics and mechanics, and will make a good second under a good first; but he would be quite unfit for a first. Mr. Maclagan intended going home, *viâ* Bombay, as soon as relieved by Captain Oldfield, and has embarked by this time. He might be written to, to send out a competent person and the required machinery. Constantia is admirably adapted for such an establishment; the river Goomtee flows close under it; the grounds are ample, open, and level, and the climate fine. It would interest the whole of the Oude aristocracy, and induce them to send their sons there for instruction. It would be gratifying to the Judges of the Supreme Court to know that the funds available were devoted to a purpose so highly useful; and you would carry home with you the agreeable recollection of having engrafted so useful a branch upon the almost useless old trunk of the Martinière.

Yours very truly,
(Signed) W. H. Sleeman.

To F. J. Halliday, Esq.
Secretary to Government,
Calcutta.

Mr. Maclagan is a Lieutenant of Engineers, and lives in Edinburgh.

Lucknow, 10th April, 1852.

My Lord,

In September 1848, I took the liberty to mention to your Lordship my fears that the system of annexing and absorbing native States—so popular with our Indian service, and so much advocated by a certain class of writers in public journals—might some day render us too visibly dependent upon our native army; that they might see it, and that accidents might occur to unite them, or too great a portion of them, in some desperate act. My only anxiety about Burmah arises from the same fears. Our native army has been too much *petted* of late; and they are liable to get into their heads the notion that we want them more than they want us. Had the 38th been at first ordered to march to Aracan, they would, in all probability, have begged their European officers to pray Government to permit them to go by water.

We committed a great mistake in not long ago making all new levies general service corps; and we have committed one not less grave in restricting the admissions into our corps to high-caste men: and encouraging the promotion of high-caste men to the prejudice of men equally deserving but of lower caste. The Brahmins in regiments have too much influence, and they are at the bottom of all the mischief that occurs. The Rajpoots are too numerous, because they are under the influence of the Brahmins, and feel too strong from their numbers.

We require stronger and braver men than the Madras Presidency can afford, with all their readiness for general service. The time may not be distant when England will have to call upon India for troops to serve in Egypt; and the troops from Madras, or even from Bombay, will not do against Europeans. Men from Northern or Western India will be required, and, in order to be prepared, it would be well to have all new corps—should new corps be required—composed of men from the Punjaub or the Himmalayah chain, and ready for any service. Into such corps none but Seiks, Juts, Goojurs, Gwalas, Mussulmans, and Hillmen should be enlisted. Too much importance is attached to height, merely that corps may look well on parade. Much more work can be got out of moderate-sized than tall men in India. The tall men in regiments always fail first in actual service—they are fit only for display at reviews and on parades: always supposing that the moderate-sized men are taken from Western and Northern India, where alone they have the strength and courage required.

No recruit should henceforward be taken except on condition of general service; and by-and-by the option may be given to all sipahees, of a certain standing or period of service, to put their names down for general service, or retire. This could not, of course, be done at present. No commanding officer can say, at present, what his regiment will do if called upon to aid the Government in any way not *specified in their bond.* They have too commonly favourites, who persuade them, for their own selfish purposes, that their regiments will do anything to meet their wishes, at the very time that these regiments are watching for an occasion to disgrace these favourites by refusal. I have known many occasions of this. None but general service corps or volunteers should be sent to Burmah from Bengal during this campaign, or we shall hazard a disaster. There are, I believe, several that your Lordship has not yet called upon. They should be at hand as soon as possible, and their present places supplied by others. In the mean time, corps of Punjaubies and Hillmen should be raised for general service. Not only can no commanding officer say what his corps will do under circumstances in which their religion or prejudices may afford a pretext for disobedience, but no officers can say how far their regiments sympathise with the recusant or discontented corps, and are prepared to join them.

In case it should ever be proposed to make all corps general service corps, in the way I mention, a donation would, of course, be offered to all who declined of a month's pay for every year of past service, or of something of that kind. A maximum might be fixed of four, five, or six months. It would not cost much, for but few would go. I must pray your Lordship to excuse the liberty I take in obtruding my notions on this subject, but it really is one of vital importance in the present state of affairs in India, as well as in Europe.

With great respect, I remain, &c.,
(Signed) W. H. SLEEMAN.

To the Most Noble
The Marquis of Dalhousie, K.T.
Governor-General of India,
Calcutta.

Memorandum.

In the year 1832 or 1833 the want of bamboos of large size, for yokes for artillery bullocks, was much felt at Saugor and the stations of that division; and the commissariat officer was authorised to form a bamboo grove, to be watered by the commissariat cattle, in order to supply the deficiency for the future. Forty beegas, or about twenty acres of land, were assigned for the purpose, and Government went to the expense of forming twelve pucka-wells, as the bamboos were planted upon the black cotton-soil of Central India, in which kutcha-wells do not stand. The first outlay was, therefore, greater than usual, being three thousand rupees. The establishment kept up consisted of one gardener, at five rupees a month, and two assistants at three rupees each. The bamboos were watered by the artillery bullocks and commissariat servants.

In a few years the bamboos became independent of irrigation, and no outlay has since been incurred upon them. The bamboos are now between forty and fifty feet high, and between four and five inches in diameter. They are used by the commissariat and ordnance departments at Saugor, but are not, I believe, required for yokes for the artillery bullocks.

There is a grove of sesum trees near the Lucknow cantonments formed in the same way, but with little or no outlay in irrigation. The trees were planted, and all the cost incurred has been in the people employed to protect them from trespass. In a dryer climate they might require irrigation for a few years. Groves of saul, *alias* sukhoo trees, might be formed in the same manner in the vicinity of all stations where there are artillery bullocks; and the bullocks themselves would benefit by being employed in the irrigation. The establishments kept up for the bullocks would be able to do all the work required.

The complement of bullocks for a battery of 6 guns, 6 waggons, and 2 store carts, is 106. The number yoked to each gun and waggon is 61, and to each cart 4, leaving a surplus of 26 for accidents. There would, therefore, be always a sufficient number of bullocks available for the irrigation of such groves where such a battery is kept up. These bullocks are taken care of by 4 sirdars and 59 drivers; and an European sergeant of artillery is appointed as bullock-sergeant to each battery, to superintend the feeding, cleaning, &c. &c. The officer on duty sees the bullocks occasionally, and the commanding officer sometimes. Such groves might be left to the care of the commandant of artillery at small stations, and to the commissariat officer at large ones.

At every large station there might be a grove of sesum,

one of sakhoo, and one of bamboos, each covering a hundred acres; and at all stations with a battery, three groves of the same kind, covering each twenty acres or more. For the convenience of carriage by water, such groves might be formed chiefly in the vicinity of rivers, or in that of the places where the timber is most likely to be required; but no battery should be without such groves. The men and bullocks would both benefit by the employment such groves would give them. The men, to interest them, might each have a small garden within the grove which he assists in watering.

Such groves would tend to improve the salubrity of the stations where they are formed, and become agreeable and healthful promenades for officers and soldiers. In most stations, kutcha-wells, formed at a cost of from 20 to 50 rupees, would suffice for watering such groves. They might be lined, like those of the peasantry, by twisted cables of straw and twigs; and the men who attend the bullocks might be usefully employed in weaving them, as all should learn to make fascines and gabions. Willows should be planted near all the wells, to supply twigs for making the cables for lining the wells, and the manure of the artillery draft-bullocks should be appropriated to the groves.

[Submitted to the Governor-General through the Private Secretary, in March, 1852, with reference to a conversation which I had with his Lordship in his camp.]

Lucknow, 23rd August, 1852.

My Lord,

Permit me to offer my congratulations, not only on the success which has hitherto attended your Lordship's arrangements in Burmah, but on the very favourable impression which that success has made upon the Sovereign and people of England. It has enabled you to show that the war is not with the people of Burmah, but with a haughty, insolent, and incompetent Government, with whom that people has no longer any sympathy; and that, should circumstances render the annexation of any portion of its territory necessary, the people of that portion would consider the measure a blessing, and be well pleased to live in harmony under the efficient protection of the new rule.

They are not in any way opposed to us from either religious or political feelings, for they seem to consider Christianity as a branch only of their own great system of Buddhism, which includes almost half of the human race; and they are evidently weary of the political institutions under which they now live, and which have ceased to afford them protection of any kind. In the annexation of Pegu—should it be forced upon your Lordship—there would be nothing revolting to the feelings of its people or to those of the people of England; on the contrary, both would be satisfied, after the disposition the people of Pegu have manifested towards us, that the measure was alike necessary to their security and to the honour and interest of our Government.

Nor do I think that there would be any ground to apprehend that the resources of the territory taken would not, after a time, be sufficient to defray the costs of the establishments required to retain and govern it. Among the people of Pegu we should find men able and willing to serve us faithfully and efficiently in both our civil and military establishments, and the drain for the maintenance of foreigners would not be large. I have heard the mental and physical powers of the men of Pegu spoken of in the highest terms by persons who have spent the greater part of their lives among them; and a country which produces such men cannot be generally insalubrious. This early demonstration has enabled your Lordship to ascertain and expose the determination of the Government of Ava not to grant the redress justly demanded for wrongs suffered, so as to enlist on our side the sympathy of all civilized nations, and at the same time to discover the real weakness of the enemy and the facilities offered to us, in their fine rivers, for the use of our strong arm—the steam navy. Not a single "untoward event" has yet occurred to dispirit our troops, or give confidence to the enemy, or to prejudice the people of Burmah against us: and there certainly is nothing in this war to make us apprehend "that our political difficulties will begin when our military successes are complete." It is not displeasing to perceive the strong tendency to an early onward move, while your Lordship has so prudent a leader in General Godwin to restrain it within due bounds.

I remain, &c.,
(Signed) W. H. SLEEMAN.

To the Most Noble
The Marquis of Dalhousie, K.T.
Governor-General of India,
Calcutta.

Lucknow, September, 1852.

MY LORD,

THE longer the present King reigns, the more unfit he becomes to reign, and the more the administration and the country deteriorate. The State must have become bankrupt long ere this, but the King, and the knaves by whom he is governed, have discontinued paying the stipends of all the members of the royal family, save those of his own father's family, for the last three years; and many of them are reduced to extreme distress, and without the hope of ever getting their stipends again unless our Government interferes. The females of the palaces of former sovereigns ventured to clamour for their subsistence, and they were, without shame or mercy, driven into the streets to starve, beg, or earn their bread by their labour. This deters all from complaining, and they are in a state of utter dismay. No part of the people of Oude are more anxious for the interposition of our Government than the members of the royal family; for there is really no portion more helpless and oppressed: none of them can ever approach the King, who is surrounded exclusively by eunuchs, fiddlers, and poetasters worse than either; and the minister and his creatures, who are worse than all. They appropriate at least one-half of the revenues of the country to themselves, and employ nothing but knaves of the very worst kind in all the branches of the administration. The King is a crazy imbecile, who is led about by these people like a child, and made to do whatever they wish him to do, and to give whatever orders may best suit their private interests. At present, the most powerful of the favourites are Decanut od Doula and Husseen od Doula, two eunuchs; Anees od Doula and Mosahib od Doula, two fiddlers; two poetasters, and the minister and his creatures. The minister could not stand a moment without the eunuchs, fiddlers, and poets, and he is obliged to acquiesce in all the orders given by the King for their benefit. The fiddlers have control over the administration of civil justice; the eunuchs over that of criminal justice, public buildings, &c. The minister has the land revenue; and all are making enormous fortunes. The present King ought not certainly to reign: he has wilfully forfeited all right to do so; but to set him aside in favour of his eldest, or indeed any other son, would give no security whatever for any permanent good government. A well-selected regency would, no doubt, be a vast improvement upon the present system; but no people would invest their capital in useful works, manufactures, and trades, with the prospect o. being handed over a few years hence to a prince brought up precisely in the same manner the present King was, and as all his sons will be. What the people want, and most earnestly pray for is, that our Government should take upon itself the responsibility of governing them well and permanently. All classes, save the knaves, who now surround and govern the King, earnestly pray for this—the educated classes, because they would then have a chance of respectable employment, which none of them now have; the middle classes, because they find no protection or encouragement, and no hope that their children will be permitted to inherit the property they may leave, not invested in our Government securities; and the humbler classes, because they are now abandoned to the merciless rapacity of the starving troops, and other public establishments, and of the landholders, driven or invited into rebellion by the present state of misrule. There is not, I believe, another Government in India so entirely opposed to the best interests and most earnest wishes of the people as that of Oude now is; at least I have never seen or read of one. People of all classes have become utterly weary of it. The people have the finest feelings towards our Government and character. I know no part of India, save the valley of the Nurbuddah, where the feeling towards us is better. All, from the highest to the lowest, would, at this time, hail the advent of our administration with joy; and the rest of India, to whom Oude misrule is well known, would acquiesce in the conviction, that it had become imperative for the protection of the people. With steamers to Fyzabad, and a railroad from that place to Cawnpore, through Lucknow, the Nepaul people would be for ever quieted, with half of the force we now keep up to look after them; and the N. W. Provinces become more closely united to Bengal, to the vast advantage of both. I mentioned that we should require a considerable loan to begin with; but I think that an issue of paper money, receivable in Oude in revenue, and payable to public establishments in Oude, might safely be made to cover all the outlay required to pay off odd establishments and commence the new work. Little money goes out of Oude, and the increased circulating medium, required for the new public works and new establishments, would soon absorb all the paper issued. It might be issued at little or no cost by the financial department of the new administration. Though everybody knows that the King has become crazy and imbecile, it would be difficult to get judicial proof that he is so, where the life and property of every one are at his mercy and that of the knaves who now govern him. His every-day doings sufficiently manifest it. There is not the slightest ground for hope that he will ever be any other than what he now is, or that his children will be better. There are too many interested in depriving them of all capacity for a part in public affairs that they may retain the reins in their own hands when the children come of age to admit of their ever becoming better than their father is. I have not lately made the reports which Lord Hardinge directed the Resident to make periodically, but shall be prepared to resume them whenever your Lordship may direct. I suspended them on account of hostilities with Burmah. I have printed eighteen copies of the establishments, as they are and were last year, and as I proposed for the new system. I shall not let any one have a copy till your Lordship permits it, and they are all at your disposal if required. This, and the "Substantive Code," are the only papers connected with Oude, except the Diary that I have had printed, or shall have printed, unless ordered by you.

I remain, with great respect,
Your Lordship's obedient servant,
(Signed) W. H. SLEEMAN.

P.S.—I believe that it is your Lordship's wish that the whole of the revenues of Oude should be expended for the benefit of the royal family and people of Oude, and that the British Government should disclaim any wish to derive any pecuniary advantages from assuming to itself the administration.

(Signed) W. H. SLEEMAN.

To the Most Noble
The Marquis of Dalhousie, K.T.
Governor-General,
&c. &c. &c.

Lucknow, 21st September, 1852.

MY DEAR SIR,

I WILL reply to the queries contained in your letter of the 16th instant to the best of my recollection. I was in Calcutta in January, 1838, when the late Dyce Sombre was there, and about to embark for England. I had seen a good deal of him at Sirdhanah, in March 1836, soon after the Begum Sumroo's death, and he afterwards spent a short time with me at Mussoorie, and consulted me a good deal on the subject of a dispute with his father.

Colonel James Skinner and Dr. Drener were, I believe, executors to his will. Colonel Skinner was at Delhi, and Dr. Drener had either gone home or was going, I forget which, and Dyce Sombre asked me to consent to become one of his trustees, for the conduct of his affairs in this country. I consented, and I think the circumstance was inserted in a codicil or memorandum added to his will or deed; but my recollection on this point is not distinct.

I had, however, nothing to do with the conduct of his affairs in this country until the death of Colonel James Skinner, which took place in December, 1841, when Mr. Reghilini, the overseer or agent at Sirdhanah, got my sanction to the outlay for establishments, &c. At this time I corresponded with Dyce Sombre, and continued to do so until his affairs were thrown into Chancery. I then sought a lawyer's opinion as to my proper course, and refused to give Mr. Reghilini any further orders. The opinion was, "that my only safe course was to do nothing whatever in the conduct of his affairs;" and I never afterwards did anything. I never heard of any Colonel Sheerman, and his name may have been inserted by mistake for mine; but I was then (1838) only a major, and was not promoted until 1843. I never heard of any desire on the part of Dyce Sombre, or the Begum Sumroo, to found a college other than as an appendage to the Sirdhanah church, nor of his having given the residue of his property for the purpose; at least, I have no recollection of having heard of such desire. I always hoped, and expected, until I heard of his marriage, that he would return and reside at Sirdhanah.

Dyce Sombre always spoke to me of Mrs. Troup and Mrs. Soloroli as his sisters: he regarded them alike as such, and so did the Begum Sumroo. I always understood them to be the children of the same mother; but the question was never mooted before me, and I have always heard that Mrs. Troup was very like Dyce Sombre in appearance, and that Mrs. Soloroli was not so.

Mr. Reghilini, who is, I believe, still at Sirdhanah, may know whether a Colonel Sheerman was appointed executor or not. Dr. Drener must know. The notes which passed between me and Dyce Sombre, after he left India, were on the ordinary topics of the day, and were destroyed as soon as read. I have none of them to refer to, nor would they furnish any confirmation on the matter in question if I had.

Believe me, yours, very truly,
(Signed) W. H. SLEEMAN.

Charles Prinsep, Esq.,
Barrister-at-Law,
Calcutta.

To Messrs. Molloy, Mackintosh, and Poe, Calcutta.

DEAR SIRS,

IN reply to your letter of the 16th instant, I enclose the copy of a letter addressed by me on the 21st ultimo to Mr. Charles Prinsep, in reply to similar queries. To what I stated in that letter I can add but little.

Dyce Sombre always spoke to me of Mrs. Soloroli and Mrs. Troup as his sisters, and of the former as the eldest of the two; and Mrs. Troup spoke of Mrs. Soloroli as her eldest sister. They were always treated by the Begum Sumroo as his sisters; and when Dyce Sombre went to England I think he left the same provision for both in addition to what they had received from the Begum.

I was introduced to Mrs. Troup by her husband as an old friend on my way back from Mussoorie in November, 1837, but I did not see Mrs. Soloroli, though she and her husband were at the same place, Sirdhanah, at that time. They both lived under the curtain, secluded from the sight of men, after the Hindoostanee fashion, as long as they remained in India, I think; and I was introduced to Mrs. Troup as a friend of the family, whom all might require to consult. Her husband only was present during the interview. Dyce Sombre had left the place for Calcutta. I never heard a doubt expressed of their being sisters by the same mother and father till the new will came under discussion at the end of last year.

I may refer you to pages 378 and 396 of the second volume of a work by me, entitled "Rambles and Recollections," in which you will find it mentioned that the grandmother of Dyce Sombre died insane at Sirdhanah in 1838. She must have been insane for more than forty years up to her death. Her son Zuffer Yab Khan was a man of weak intellect, and he was the father of Dyce Sombre's mother, of whom I know nothing whatever.

Dyce Sombre showed no symptoms of derangement of mind while I knew him; but he inherited from his grandmother a predisposition to insanity, which I apprehended might become developed by any very strong feelings of excitement; and I urged him to return and settle at Sirdhanah, when he had seen all he wished to see in Europe.

He saw a good deal of English society in India, and understood well the freedom which English wives enjoy in general society; but I doubted whether he could ever thoroughly shake off his early predilections for keeping them secluded. It would, I thought, be always to him a source of deep humiliation to see his wife mix with other men in the manner in which English married ladies are accustomed to do. Since his affairs were put into Chancery I have always felt persuaded that this must have been the principal "exciting cause" acting upon the predisposition derived from his grandmother, which led to it. I have never had the slightest doubt that he suffered under an aberration of mind upon this point, though he never mentioned the subject in any of his short letters to me from England, nor did he in any of them show signs of such aberration.

Believe me, yours, faithfully,
(Signed) W. H. Sleeman.

26th October, 1852.

Lucknow, 28th October, 1852.

MY DEAR SIR JAMES,

YOUR letter of the 6th ultimo reached me by the last mail, and I trust we shall see your hopes of an early renewal of the Charter with few alterations realised. I entirely concur with you in opinion that the power of recall is indispensable to the due authority of the Court; and was much surprised to find Maddock opposed to it. Many thinking men at home have been of opinion that the Ministers would secure for the Queen the nomination of a certain number to the Direction, on the ground that many of the best men from India are deterred from becoming candidates by the time and pledges required in the canvass. The late elections, however, seem to have come in time to increase the jealousy of ministerial influence, and prevent such a measure.

Hostilities with Burmah have prevented my making public periodical reports to Government about Oude affairs since I submitted my Diary. I took the liberty to send, through my London agents, a copy to yourself and the Deputy Chairman. Things have not improved since it was written. The King is as regardless of his high duties and responsibilities as ever: he is, indeed, an imbecile in the hands of a few fiddlers, eunuchs, and poetasters, and the minister, who is no better than they are, and obliged to provide for all these men out of the revenues and patronage of the country, and sundry women about the Court, also, to secure their influence in his favour.

The King contrives to get the stipends of those immediately about him, and of his mother, brothers, and sisters, paid out of the revenues; but is indifferent about those of his more distant relatives, and hardly any of them have had any stipends for the last two and even three years. Those who happen not to have a little

Company's paper given to them by former Sovereigns, or pensions guaranteed by our Government and paid out of our Treasury, are starving, and pray for the day when our Government may interpose in the administration. The expenditure is much above the income, and the reserved treasury is exhausted; but the King has his jewels and some personal property in Government notes, derived from his father and grandmothers. He thinks himself the best of kings and the best of poets, and nothing will induce him willingly to alter his course or make room for a better ruler or better system.

If our Government interpose, it must not be by negotiation and treaty, but authoritatively on the ground of existing treaties and obligations to the people of Oude. The treaty of 1837 gives our Government ample authority to take the whole administration on ourselves, in order to secure what we have often pledged ourselves to secure to the people; but if we do this we must, in order to stand well with the rest of India, honestly and distinctly disclaim all interested motives, and appropriate the whole of the revenues for the benefit of the people and royal family of Oude. If we do this, all India will think us right, for the sufferings of the people of Oude, under the present system, have been long notorious throughout India; and so have our repeated pledges to relieve the people from these sufferings, unless the system should be altered. Fifty years of sad experience have shown to us and to all India, that this system is incapable of improvement under the present dynasty; and that the only alternative is for the paramount power to take the administration upon itself.

Under the treaty of 1801, we took one-half of the territory of Oude, and that half yields to us above two crores of rupees; though, when taken, it was estimated at one hundred and thirty-three lacs. The half retained by the Oude Sovereign was estimated at the same; but it now yields to the Sovereign only one crore. The rest is absorbed by the knaves employed in the administration and their patrons at Court. All that is now so absorbed would come to the Treasury under us, and be employed in the maintenance of efficient establishments, and the construction of useful public works; and we should have ample means for providing for all the members of the royal family of Oude.

We should derive substantial benefit from the measure, without in any degree violating our declaration of disinterestedness. We now maintain five regiments of Infantry, and a company of Artillery, at a cost of from five to six lacs a-year. We maintain the Residency and all its establishments at a cost of more than one lac of rupees a-year. All these would become fairly chargeable to the Oude revenues under the new administration; and we might dispense with half the military forces now kept up at Cawnpore and Dinapore on the Ganges, as the military force in Oude would relieve us from all apprehension as to Nepaul.

Oude would be covered with a network of fine macadamised roads, over which the produce of Oude and our own districts would pass freely to the benefit of the people of both; and we should soon have the river Ghagra, from near Patna on the Ganges, to Fyzabad in Oude, navigable for steamers: with a railroad from Fyzabad, through Lucknow to Cawnpore, to the great benefit of the North-West Provinces and those of Bengal.

Were we to take advantage of the occasion to *annex* or *confiscate* Oude, or any part of it, our good name in India would inevitably suffer; and that good name is more valuable to us than a dozen of Oudes. We are now looked up to throughout India as the only impartial arbitrators that the people generally have ever had, or can ever hope to have without us; and from the time we cease to be so looked up to, we must begin to sink. We suffered from our conduct in Scinde; but that was a country distant and little known, and linked to the rest of India by few ties of sympathy. Our conduct towards it was preceded by wars and convulsions around, and in its annexation there was nothing manifestly deliberate. It will be otherwise with Oude. Here the giant's strength is manifest, and we cannot "use it like a giant" without suffering in the estimation of all India. Annexation or confiscation are not compatible with our relations with this little dependent state. We must show ourselves to be high-minded, and above taking advantage of its prostrate weakness, by appropriating its revenues exclusively to the benefit of the people and royal family of Oude. We should soon make it the finest garden in India, with the people happy, prosperous, and attached to our rule and character.

We have at least forty thousand men from Oude in the armies of the three Residencies, all now, rightly or wrongly, cursing the oppressive Government under which their families live at their homes. These families would come under our rule and spread our good name as widely as they now spread the bad one of their present ruler. Soldiers with a higher sense of military honour, and duty to *their salt*, do not exist, I believe, in any country. To have them bound to us by closer ties than they are at present, would of itself be an important benefit.

I can add little to what I have said in the latter end of the fourth chapter of my Diary (from p. 187, vol. ii.), on the subject of our relations with the Government of Oude; and of our rights and duties arising out of those relations. The diaries political, which I send every week or fortnight to the Government of India, are formed out of the reports made every day to the Durbar, by their local or departmental authorities. The Residency News-writer has the privilege of hearing these reports read as they come in; and though the reports of many important events are concealed from him, they may generally be relied upon as far as they go. The picture they give of affairs is bad enough, though not so bad as they deserve.

There are so many worthless and profligate people about the Court, interested in smothering any signs of common sense and good feeling on the part of the heir-apparent to the throne, in order to maintain their ascendancy over him as he grows up, that he has not the slightest chance of becoming fit to take any part in the conduct of public affairs when he comes of age. The present King has three or four sons, all very young, but it is utterly impossible for any one of them to become a man of business; and it would be folly to expect any one of them to make a better Sovereign than their father. He is now only twenty-eight or twenty-nine years of age; but his understanding has become quite emasculated by over-indulgencies of all kinds. He may live long, but his habits have become too inveterate to admit of his ever becoming better than he now is or fit to be intrusted with the government of a country.

I shall recommend that all establishments, military, civil, and fiscal, be kept entirely separate from those of our own Government, that there may be no mistake as to the disinterestedness of our intentions towards Oude. The military establishments being like Scindiah's contingent, in the Gwalior state, or the Hydrabad contingent in the Nizam's. I estimate the present expenditure at, civil and fiscal establishments, and stipendiaries, 38 lacs. Military and police, 55. King's household, 30. Total, 123 lacs. Establishments required for an efficient administration—civil and fiscal—at 22 lacs. Military, 26 lacs. Families and dependents of former Sovereigns, 12 lacs. Household of the Sovereign, his sons, brothers, and sisters, 15 lacs. Total, 75 lacs.

This would leave an abundant store for public works, military stores, contingent charges, pension establishments for the civil and military officers employed under us, &c. To pay off all the present heavy arrears of stipends, salaries, to provide arms, ammunition, and stores, and to commence upon all the public works, our Government would have either to give or guarantee a loan; or to sanction the issue of a certain amount of paper money, to circulate exclusively in Oude, by making it receivable in the Oude Treasuries in taxes.

The revenues would be at once greatly increased, by our taking for the treasury all that is now intercepted and appropriated by public officers and Court favourites for their own private purposes, by our making the great landholders pay a due portion of their assets to the state, and by our securing the safe transit of raw produce and manufactured goods to their proper markets.

By adopting a simple system of administration, to meet the wishes of a simple people, we should secure the good-will of all classes of society in Oude; and no class would be more pleased with the change than the members of the royal family themselves, who depend upon their stipends for their subsistence, and despair of ever again receiving them under the present Sovereign and system.

I hope a happy termination of the present war with Burmah will soon leave Lord Dalhousie free to devote his attention to Oude affairs. As far as I am consulted, I shall advocate, as strongly as may be compatible with my position, the measures above described, because I think they will be found best calculated to benefit the people of Oude, to meet the wishes of the home Government, and to sustain his Lordship's own reputation, and that of the nation which he represents throughout our Eastern empire.

You are aware of some of the difficulties that I have had to contend with, in carrying out important measures beneficial to the people, and honourable to the Government of India; but in no situation in life have I ever had to struggle with so many as here, in pursuing an honest and steady course of policy, calculated to secure the respect of all classes for the Government which I represent. Such a scene of intrigue, corruption, depravity, neglect of duty, and abuse of authority, I have never before been placed in, and hope never again to undergo; and I have had to contend with bitter hostility where I had the best right to expect support. I have never yet failed in the performance of any duty that Government has intrusted to me, and, under Providence, I hope that I shall ultimately succeed in the performance of that which I have committed to me here.

Lucknow is an overgrown city, surrounding an overgrown Court, which has, for the last half century, exhausted all the resources of this fine country; and so alienated the feelings of the great body of the people that they, and the Sovereign, and his officers, look upon each other as irreconcileable enemies. Between the city, the pampered Court and its functionaries, and the people of the country beyond, there is not the slightest feeling of sympathy; and if our troops were withdrawn from the vicinity of Lucknow, the landholders and sturdy peasantry of the country would, in a few days, rush in and plunder and destroy it as a source of nothing but intolerable evil to them.

Though I have written a long letter, I may have omitted many things which you wished me to notice. In that case I must rely upon your letting me know; and in the mean time, I shall continue to write whenever I have anything to communicate that is likely to interest you.

Believe me, dear Sir James,
Yours very faithfully,
W. H. SLEEMAN.

To Sir James Weir Hogg, Bart.
&c. &c. &c.

P.S. By treaty, we are bound to keep up a certain force near the capital for the protection of the Sovereign; and we should be obliged, till things were quite settled under the new system, to retain the brigade we now have of our regular troops in the cantonments, which are three miles from the city.

W. H. SLEEMAN.

Lucknow, 20th November, 1852.

MY DEAR SIR JAMES,

To be prepared for accidents, I deem it right to send a duplicate of the letter which I sent to you by the last mail, addressed to the care of my London agents, Messrs. Denny and Clark, Austin Friars. I have nothing new or interesting to communicate from Oude. The Burmese war seems likely to divert the Governor-General's attention from Oude and Hydrabad affairs for some time to come; and the death of the Duke of Wellington, and probable changes in the ministry at home, may prevent him from venturing upon any important change in the Oude administration when that war closes.

The war is an "untoward event," arising from a very small cause; and it should prevent our ever guaranteeing British subjects in countries where we have no accredited agents to conduct our relations with the Government. All such subjects, and all the subjects of our

European and American allies, should in future be made to understand that they enter such countries entirely upon their own responsibility. Without some such precaution we must always be liable to be involved in war with bordering countries by adventurers of one kind or another; and as war is almost always followed by annexation or confiscation, our Indian empire, like that of the Romans, must soon sink from its own weight. The people will think that we are perpetually seeking pretexts for war in order to get new territories, and the general or universal impression will be dangerous.

When the public press of England abuse those who have to conduct the present war for delay, they do not sufficiently consider our ignorance of the state of the rivers and of the military resources of the country in which it was to be carried on when we entered upon it. We did not know that the rivers were navigable, nor did we know how they were defended; nor did we know what forces Burmah could muster, nor how they were distributed. It was not intended to commence the war till after the rains, when it would be safe to move troops over the country; for it was not reasonable to suppose that the Government of the country could be so haughty and insolent without military force to support its pretensions, and we have often had sad experience of the danger of underrating the power of an enemy. The object of the earlier movement was merely to secure some points of support, at which to concentrate our forces as they came up, and not to advance at once on the capital or into the country at a season when no troops could move by land.

Our strong arm was, no doubt, the steam flotilla; but it would have been madness in us, with our ignorance of the rivers and resources of the country, to have calculated upon conquering Ava by steamers alone. With what we now know, people may safely say that General Godwin has failed to make all the use he might of the flotilla, as Lord Gough failed to make all the use he might of his "strong arm," the artillery, in the battles of the Punjaub; but Lord Gough was not ignorant of the country in which he had to operate, nor of the resources of the country he had to contend with. According to previous calculations, the war ought not to have begun till this month. The earlier movement has, however, been of great advantage —it has taught us what the rivers and resources of the country are; and, what is of still more importance, what the people and their feelings towards their Government and ours are. It is manifest that they fully appreciate the value of the protection which the people, under our rule, enjoy; and that they have neither religious nor political feelings of hostility towards us; and that the people of Pegu, at least, would hail the establishment of our rule as a blessing.

You were so kind as to express a wish to see my son. He is now with his regiment, the 16th Lancers, in Ireland, and has lately obtained his Lieutenancy. He will be twenty years of age in January. I will make known to him your kind wish, and doubt not that he will pay his respects when he visits London.

Believe me, my dear Sir James,

Yours very faithfully,

W. H. Sleeman.

To Sir James Weir Hogg, Bart.,
&c. &c. &c.

P.S.—In page 217, line 4, vol. i., of my Diary, the printer has put "months" for weeks. Pray do me the favour to have this corrected.—W. H. S.

My Lord,

Your Lordship's wishes in regard to the papers on Oude affairs shall be strictly attended to. They are locked up in my box, and no one shall see them. I had no wish to print any but those I mentioned in my last letter, and they are locked up with the others, which I have not looked at since I left your Lordship's camp; the Diary, excepted.

Things in Oude are just as they were; and the King's ambition seems to be limited to the reputation of being the best drum-beater, dancer, and poet of the day. He is utterly unfit to reign; but he is himself persuaded that no man can be more fit than he is for anything, and he will never willingly consent to make over the reins of Government to any one. It would be impossible to *persuade* him to abdicate even in favour of his own son, much less to resign his sovereignty in perpetuity. If our Government interpose, it must be by the exercise of a right derived from the existing relations between the two Governments, or from our position as the paramount power in India.

Of this your Lordship will have to consider and decide when your mind is relieved from Burmese affairs, which appear to be drawing very *quietly* to a close. I shall not write publicly about Oude affairs generally till I have your Lordship's commands to do so. The Diary will continue to be transmitted regularly; but the Periodical General Report will be suspended.

Mr. Bushe remained a few days at Lucknow. He has since seen Agra, Bhurtpoor, and other places, and is now on his way back to Calcutta, well pleased with his tour.

With great respect,

Your Lordship's obedient Servant,

W. H. SLEEMAN.

To the Most Noble
The Marquis of Dalhousie, K.T.,
Governor-General of India.

Lucknow, 2nd January, 1853.

MY DEAR SIR JAMES,

I enclose two sets of Tables of Errata for the Diary, and must pray you to do me the favour to have one set put into the two volumes of the copy you have, and the other sent to the Deputy-Chairman for insertion in his copy. I did not take the liberty to send a copy to the President of the Board of Control, but if you think I should do so, I will.

The King of Oude is becoming more and more imbecile and crazy, and his servants continue more and more to abuse their power and neglect their duty. The King every day manifests his utter unfitness to reign, in some new shape. He, on several occasions during the Mohurrum ceremonies which took place lately, went along the streets beating a drum tied round his neck, to the great scandal of his family and the amusement of his people. The members of his family have not been paid their stipends for from two to three years, and many of them have been reduced to the necessity of selling their clothes to purchase food. All classes, save the knaves who surround him, and profit by his folly, are become disgusted with and tired of him.

I do not interfere, except to protect our pledges and guarantees; and to conduct the current duties of the Residency in such a manner as to secure the respect of all classes for the Government which I represent. While the present King reigns, or has anything whatever to do with the Government, no interference could produce any substantial and permanent reform. The minister is a weak man and a great knave; but he has an influence over his master, obtained by being entirely subservient to his vices and follies, to the sacrifice of his own honour; and by praising all that he does, however degrading to him as a man and a sovereign.

Though the King pays no attention whatever to public affairs or to business of any kind, and aims at nothing but the reputation of being the best dancer, best versifier, and best drummer in his dominions, it would be impossible to persuade him that any man was ever more fit to reign than he is. Nothing would ever induce him willingly to abdicate even in favour of his own son, much less to make him willingly abdicate in perpetuity in favour of our Government, or make over the conduct of the administration to our Government. If, therefore, our Government does interfere, it must be in the exercise of a right arising out of the existing relations between the two States, or out of our position as the paramount power in India. These relations, under the Treaty of 1837, give our Government the *right* to take upon itself the administration, under present circumstances; and, indeed, imposes upon our Government the *duty* of taking it: but, as I have already stated, neither these relations nor our position, as the paramount power, gives us any right to *annex* or to *confiscate* the territory of Oude. We may have a right to take territory from the Nizam of Hyderabad in payment for the money he owes us; but Oude owes us no money, and we have no right to take territory from her. We have only the right to interpose to secure for the suffering people that better Government which their Sovereign pledged himself to secure for them, but has failed to secure.

The Burmese war still prevents the Governor-General from devoting his attention to Oude and Hyderabad. In the last war we did not march our armies to the capital because we were not prepared to supply a new Government for the one which we should thereby destroy; and insurrection and civil war must have followed. Our conduct in that was wise and benevolent. When we moved our armies to Rangoon this time, we upset one Government without providing the people with another.

The Governor-General could not provide for the Civil Government, because he could not know that the Government of Ava would force us to keep possession of any portion of its dominions; and taking upon ourselves the civil administration would compromise the people, should he have to give them up again to their old rulers. The consequence has been great suffering to a people who hailed us as deliverers. The folly of supposing that any country can be taken by steamers on their rivers alone has now become sufficiently manifest. The Governor-General has, however, adopted the best possible measures for securing ultimate good government to Pegu. It would have been more easily effected had they been taken earlier, but this circumstance prevented.

There is a school in India, happily not yet much patronised by the Home Government nor by the Governor-General, but always struggling with more or less success for ascendancy. It is characterised by impatience at the existence of any native State, and its strong and often insane advocacy of their absorption—by honest means, if possible—but still, their absorption. There is no pretext, however weak, that is not sufficient, in their estimation, for the purpose; and no war, however cruel, that is not justifiable, if it has only this object in view. If you know George Clerk or Mr. Robertson, both formerly Governors of our North-West Provinces, they will describe to you the school I mean. They, I believe, with me, strongly deprecate the doctrines of this school as more injurious to India and to our interest in it, than those of any other school that has ever existed in India. Mr. George Campbell is one of the disciples of this school.—See the 4th chapter of his "Modern India." The "Friend of India" is another, and all those whom that paper lauds most are also disciples of the same school. The Court of Directors will have to watch these doctrines carefully;

and I wish you would speak to George Clerk and Mr. Robertson about them. They are both men of large views and sound judgment.

Believe me, my dear Sir James,

Yours sincerely,

(Signed) W. H. SLEEMAN.

To Sir James Weir Hogg,
&c. &c. &c.

Lucknow, 12th January, 1853.

MY DEAR SIR JAMES,

I WROTE to you on the 23rd October, 20th November, and the 2nd of this month; I mention this lest any of my letters miscarry; of the first letter I sent a duplicate on the 2nd, but I shall not send duplicates of the last two, or of this. I now write chiefly to call your attention to a rabid article in the "Friend of India," of the 6th of this month, written by Mr. Marshman, when about to proceed to England, to become, it is said, one of the writers in the London "Times." Of course, he will be engaged to write the Indian articles; and you will find him advocating the doctrines of the school mentioned in my last letter of the 2nd of this month. I consider their doctrines to be prejudicial to the stability of our rule in India, and to the welfare of the people, which depends on it. The Court of Directors is our only safeguard against these Machiavellian doctrines; and it may be rendered too powerless to stem them by the new arrangements for the Government of India. The objects which they propose for attainment—religion, commerce, &c.—are plausible; and the false logic by which they attempt to justify the means required to attain them, however base, unjust, and cruel, is no less so. I was asked by Dr. Duff, the editor of the "Calcutta Review," before he went home, to write some articles for that journal, to expose the fallacies, and to counteract the influences of the doctrines of this school; but I have for many years ceased to contribute to the periodical papers, and have felt bound by my position not to write for them. Few old officers of experience, with my feelings and opinions on this subject, now remain in India; and the influence of this school is too great over the rising generation, whose hopes and aspirations they tend so much to encourage. Mr. Elphinstone, Mr. Robertson, and George Clerk will be able to explain their danger to you. India must look to the Court of Directors alone for safety against them, and they will require the exertion of all its wisdom and strength.

Mr. Robertson will be able to tell you that, when I was sent to Bundelcund, in 1842, the feelings of the people of that province were so strongly against us, under the operation of the doctrines of this school, that no European officer could venture, with safety, beyond the boundary of a cantonment of British troops; and their servants were obliged to disguise themselves in order to pass from one cantonment to another. In a brief period, I created a feeling entirely different, and made the character of British officers respected and beloved. In the Gwalior territories the same result was obtained by the same means. However impulsive on other occasions, Lord Ellenborough behaved magnanimously after his victories over the Gwalior troops; but in sparing the State, he acted, I believe, against the feelings of his Council, amongst whom the doctrines of the absorbing, annexing, and confiscating schools prevailed; and the "Friend of India" condemned him, though the invasion was never justified, except on the ground of expediency. Had I, on these occasions, adopted the doctrines of the absorbing school, I might have become one of the most popular and influential men in India; but I should, at the same time, have rendered our rule and character odious to the people of India, and so far have injured our permanent interest in the country. I mention all this merely to show that my opposition to the doctrines of this school is not new, nor in theory only, but of long standing and practice, as far as my influence has extended. I deem them to be dangerous to our rule in India, and prejudicial to the best interests of the country. The people see that these annexations and confiscations go on, and that rewards and honorary distinctions are given for them, and for the victories which lead to them, and for little else; and they are too apt to infer that they are systematic, and encouraged, and prescribed from home. The native States I consider to be breakwaters, and when they are all swept away, we shall be left to the mercy of our native army, which may not always be sufficiently under our control. Such a feeling as that which pervaded Bundelcund and Gwalior in 1842 and 1843, must, sooner or later, pervade all India, if these doctrines are carried out to their full extent; and our rule could not, probably, exist under it. With regard to Oude, I can only say that the King pursues the same course, and every day shows that he is unfit to reign. He has not the slightest regard for the duties or responsibilities of his high position; and the people, and even the members of his own family, feel humiliated at his misconduct, and grow weary of his reign. The greater part of these members have not received their stipends for from two to three years, and they despair of ever receiving them as long as he reigns. He is neither tyrannical nor cruel, but altogether incapable of devoting any of his time or attention to business of any kind, but spends the whole of his time with women, eunuchs, fiddlers, and other parasites. Should he be set aside, as he deserves to be, three courses are open: 1. To appoint a regency during the minority of the heir-apparent, who is now about eleven years of age, to govern with the advice of the Resident; 2. To manage the country by European agency during the regency, or in perpetuity, leaving the surplus revenue to the royal family; 3. To confiscate and annex the country, and pension the royal family. The first plan was prescribed by Lord Hardinge, in case of accident to the King; the second is what was done at Nagpore, with so much advantage, by Sir Richard Jenkins in 1817; the third is what the absorbing school would advocate, but I should most deprecate. It would be most profitable for us, in a pecuniary point of view, but most injurious, I think, in a political one. It would tend to accelerate the crisis which the doctrines of that school must, sooner or later, bring upon us. Which course the Governor-General may prefer I know not.

Believe me,
My dear Sir James,
Yours very faithfully,
(Signed) W. H. SLEEMAN.

To Sir James Weir Hogg, Bart.,
&c. &c. &c.

Lucknow, 12th January, 1853.

MY DEAR SIR,

I SHALL send you by this mail a copy of my Diary under cover, addressed, as you suggest, to Mr. Secretary Melvill. It is coarsely bound, as I could find no good binder here. I printed eighteen copies, and have sent one to Government, in Calcutta, for itself, and one for the Court of Directors; one to the Governor-General, and one each to the Chairman and Deputy-Chairman. I have also sent one to a brother, and one to each of my five children. All to whom I have sent it of my family have been enjoined to consider it as private and confidential, and they will do so. Government may publish any portion of it they please. A memorandum of errata has been added to the copy to be sent to you.

Over and above what you justly observe as to the cultivation and population not being much diminished, and the State not having incurred any public debt, I may mention the fact noticed, I believe, somewhere in the Diary, that the landed aristocracy of the half of Oude, reserved in 1801, has been better preserved than that of the half made over to us. Had they not combined generally against the Government, they would all have been crushed ere this, as ours have been. This makes me mention a school of too much influence in India, of whose doctrines I have a great abhorrence. They are best expounded by the so-called "Friend of India," in the last number of which (6th January, 1851) there is a rabid article on the subject worthy of your perusal, and that of all men interested in the welfare of India and the stability of our rule over it. It is in the true Machiavellian spirit, which justifies, or would persuade the world to justify, every means, however base, dishonest, and cruel, required to attain any object which they have persuaded themselves to be desirable for ourselves. This school is impatient at the existence of any native principality in India, however related to or dependent upon us. Mr. George Campbell is a disciple of this school, almost as rabid as the "Friend of India," as you will see in the fourth chapter of his book on "Modern India." If Mr. Marshman is to write the Indian articles for the "Times," as reports give out, you will see these doctrines advocated in that influential journal. The Court of Directors is the only safeguard of India, and of our stability in it, against those doctrines which, in my opinion, tend strongly to the injury of both; and its power may be rendered too powerless to shun them.

Believe me,
My dear Sir,
Yours sincerely,
(Signed) W. H. SLEEMAN.

To Colonel Sykes,
Director Hon. East India Company,
London.

P.S.—I have felt much interested in the geology of Central and Southern India; and if you have seen any satisfactory account of the origin of the stratum which caps the basaltic plateau, shall feel obliged if you will point it out to me.

Lucknow, 24th April, 1853.

MY DEAR SIR,

BY the last mail I received from a friend in London two articles, whose merits had been much canvassed at the clubs, one from the London "Times," of the 9th February, and the other from the "Daily News," a Manchester paper. The "Times" article must have been written by Mr. J. Marshman, or one of the most rabid members of the school of which he is the great organ, and whose chief characteristic is impatience at the existence of any native territorial chief or great landholder in India. The other article is a reply to it, and generally supposed to have been written by Sir George Clerk. I feel quite sure that it was written either by him or by Mr. T. C. Robertson, who preceded him in the government of our North-West Provinces. The article from the "Times" has been noticed in most of the Indian papers—the "Friend of India," April 7th, 1853, and the "Englishman," 15th April. But I have not seen that in the "Daily News" noticed in any Indian papers, though admirably written. I intended to send it to you, but have mislaid it. I think you can advocate the cause it adopts more consistently, more powerfully, and more wisely than any other editor now in India. I hope you will do so; for I consider the doctrines of the "Times" disgraceful to our morality, and dangerous to the stability of our rule. As I consider the welfare of the people of India to depend upon the stability of our rule, I am very anxious to see the fallacies of the atrocious doctrines which endanger it ably exposed. In no publication are these fallacies more obvious or more numerous than in Mr. George Campbell's "Modern India," chapter fourth, with, perhaps, the exception of the "Friend of India." With the "Friend," the theory of confiscation and annexation has become a disease, and he cannot praise or even tolerate any public officer or statesman who is not known to be a convert to the doctrines of this school.

I forget the date of the "Daily News" in which Sir George Clerk's article appeared, but it was immediately after the article appeared in the London "Times" of the 9th February. I hope you will give the article a prominent place in your paper, for it really deserves to be printed in letters of gold. Though I feel that the character of our nation, and our safety in India, are compromised by the open avowal of such atrocious doctrines in our leading journals, still the orders against officers in political employ writing in the papers are so strict, that I dare not attempt to expose the fallacies on which they are based, or express the indignation which they excite in me, in any public paper. To my superiors, and in the discharge of my public duties, I shall never cease to express my abhorrence of such doctrines, for I look upon them as worse than any that Machiavelli ever wrote.

Believe me,

Yours very sincerely,

(Signed) W. H. SLEEMAN.

To G. Buist, Esq.

P. S.—Of course, this note will be considered as confidential.

(Signed) W. H. S.

Lucknow, 24th April, 1853.

DEAR SIR,

AN article in your paper of the 15th instant, on the subject of the international law of India, has interested and pleased me much. It has reference to an article in the London "Times" of the 9th February last; and I write to invite your attention to an article which appeared in the "Daily News," a Manchester paper, in reply to it, written by Sir G. Clerk, lately Governor of Bombay. Both these articles have been much discussed at the London clubs, and the morality of the "Daily News" article has been very favourably contrasted with that of the article in the "Times."

The article in the "Times" is supposed to have been penned by Mr. J. Marshman himself, or by one of the most rabid members of the school whose Machiavellian doctrine he advocates.

These doctrines are considered by some of our wisest statesmen to be as dangerous to the stability of our rule in India as they are disgraceful to our morality; and as these statesmen consider the well-being of the people of India to depend upon that stability, they are always glad to see their fallacies exposed and their iniquities indignantly denounced by the most able and steady of our public journalists. I hope you will be able to find the able article in the "Daily News" to which I refer, and consent to give it a prominent place in the "Englishman." It was sent to me by a friend in London, but I have, unfortunately, mislaid it. This note will, of course, be considered as confidential.

Yours sincerely,
W. H. SLEEMAN.

To W. C. Harry, Esq.

Lucknow, 5th June, 1853.

MY LORD,

I HAVE read with great interest in the English journals your Lordship's able Minute on the Burmese war, and am glad that it has been published, as it cannot fail to disabuse the public mind at home, and bring about a reaction in the feeling of the people excited by some very unfair articles in the London "Times." I attributed these articles to the Napiers, who, however talented, are almost always wrong-headed.

I am persuaded that the new Sovereign will acquiesce in your possession of Pegu, and that he would not have ceded it by treaty under any circumstances. The old Sovereign might have done it, though at great risk; but the new Sovereign could not dare to do it.

Our own history affords us instances enough of powerful ministers anxious, for the public good, to get rid of conquered, but expensive and useless possessions, but deterred from proposing the measure by the dread of popular odium, which ambitious and factious rivals are always ready to excite.

There is one argument against the advance which I do not think that your Lordship has urged with the force of the rest. While the new Sovereign remains undisturbed in the rest of his dominions he will maintain his authority over them, and do his best to prevent our new frontier from being disturbed, knowing that we can advance to his capital and punish him if he does not. But, were he to be driven from his capital, all the rest of his dominions would soon fall into a state of anarchy, and our frontiers would soon be disturbed by leaders of disorderly bands, anxious to carve out principalities for themselves, and having no other means than plunder to maintain their followers. For the acts of such men we could hold no one responsible, after we had driven their Sovereign from his capital to the hills and jungles; and half a century might elapse before order could be restored. In the mean time, wealth would be growing up within our border to invite their aggression, while they would become poorer and poorer from disorders, and more and more anxious to seize upon it.

With regard to an advance upon Amarapoora, it will not be difficult after the rains, if circumstances render it necessary. The Madras cattle are much better for hard work and all climates than those of Bengal, and sufficient could be collected for the occasion by sea. Your Lordship's reasons for not trusting to steamers alone are unanswerable, and it seems impossible for a land and river force to act jointly. In this, we almost realize the contest between the winds and the moschettoes before the court of the genii in the Arabian tale: when the winds appeared, the moschettoes could not, and when they appeared, the winds could not. For the prestige of our own name in the rest of India, to advance to the capital and then give the rest of the country to the Sovereign might, perhaps, be the best; but for the security of our new acquisition, and that of the people of the rest of Burmah, it would certainly be better to stay where we are. The benefits of our rule might, by degrees, be imparted to that of the rest of Burmah. The Government would be obliged to treat their people better than they have done in order to keep them.

Here everything still is what I have described it to be so often; that is, as bad as it can be. The King is the same, and the officers and favourites whom he employs are the same. I shall not write public reports on the state of affairs till I learn that your Lordship wishes it, which will be, I conclude, when you have carried out your arrangements in Burmah.

The terrible war of races in China, to which I have been looking forward for some years, seems to be coming slowly on. I wrote to Sir H. M. Elliot about it some two or three years ago, and recommended him to write a better life than we have of Jungez Khan, in order to show what the Tartars now really are. When he led his swarms of them over China, Central Asia, and a great part of Europe, they worshipped the god of war; they now worship the god of peace: but there are millions of Lamas in Tartary who would change their crosiers for the sword at the call of a kindred genius, and are now impatient to do so, and prophesying his advent, just at the time that the rebels threaten the capital of China and the extinction of the Tartar dynasty. That dynasty will throw itself upon Tartary, and a new one will be raised by the successful leader.

Your Lordship's faithful and obedient servant,

(Signed) W. H. Sleeman.

To the Most Noble
The Marquis of Dalhousie, K.T.,
Governor-General.

Lucknow, 24th June, 1853.

Dear Sir,

Your letter of the 20th instant perplexes me a good deal. I have no place in my own office to offer you, and I never recommended any one for employment to the King. You cannot, according to rules laid down for our guidance, act as an advocate in any case before the Resident or his assistants. All landholders in Oude, except the few whose estates are included in what is called the Hozoor Tuhseel, transact their business through the Amils, Chuckladars, and Nazims of districts, and have nothing to do directly with the Durbar at Lucknow. Having nothing to do with their affairs, I cannot have anything to say with the employment by them of wakeels, or advocates. They, the landholders, generally employ native wakeels, who are willing to bear a good deal of ill-treatment on the part of Durbar officials for the sake of very small salaries. Your situation as a wakeel on their part would be ill remunerated and exceedingly humiliating.

If the son of Ghalib Jung has offered to introduce you to the minister, and to assist in getting employment for you at Lucknow, he must, I think, do so in the hope of being able to make use of you in some intrigue; for those only who can aid in such intrigues are fostered and paid at Lucknow. Honest men can get nothing, and find no employment about the Court. If you secure employment about the Court, I cannot hold any communication with you. I should compromise myself by doing so. In your situation, I would rather be a section writer in Calcutta, or at Agra, than hold any employment in the Oude Durbar that you can get by honest means. One of the tasks imposed on you would be, I conclude, to praise bad persons and things, and abuse good, in the newspapers. This, of course, you would not do, and you would be punished accordingly. I strongly advise you to have nothing to do with Oude at present.

Yours very truly,
(Signed) W. H. Sleeman.

To G. Norton, Esq.,
Azimgurh.

Lucknow, 11th August, 1853.

MY DEAR SIR,

YOUR brother, the late Lieut.-Colonel Ouseley, was a valued friend of mine. Before his appointment as Governor-General's Agent of the south-eastern frontier districts, he had for many years held the civil charge of different districts in the Sangor and Nerbudda territories. I had for many years the civil charge of districts bordering on those under his charge, and abundant opportunity of seeing how much he had made himself beloved, and the character of his Government respected, by the manner in which he conducted the duties confided to him.

When I became Commissioner over those territories in 1844, I passed through the districts which had so long been under his charge, and I can honestly say that I have never known a man who had made himself more beloved and revered by the people. Thousands of happy families were proud to acknowledge that they owed all their happiness to the careful and liberal revision of the settlement of the land-revenue made by him, in which he had provided for the interests of the higher and middle classes connected with the land, while he secured the rights of the humblest.

I visited at the same time the districts of those territories which bordered upon his then charge of the south-east frontier, and communed with many people from that quarter. They all spoke of him as beloved and respected by all classes as much in his then charge as he had been in his old one. In a country where it is the duty of every Englishman to make the character of his Government and his nation respected and beloved, one cannot but feel proud to hear a countryman and fellow-labourer spoken of by tens of thousands of respectable, contented, and happy people as your brother was and still is. I know no part of India where the people of all classes and all grades are so attached to our character and our Government as that of the Saugor and Nerbudda territories, and I believe that no man did more to establish that fine feeling than your brother.

Your brother's temper was warm, and he was not always happy in putting his thoughts and feelings to paper. Hence arose occasional misunderstandings with his official superiors. But while those superiors were men who could understand and appreciate his noble nature, such occasional misunderstandings never led to serious consequences. In the bitterness of his anguish, after his removal from the south-east frontier, he wrote to me; and it was most painful to me to feel that I was not in a position, or in circumstances, to advocate his cause, and describe the value of such a man as the representative of the Government and the national character among a wild and half-civilized people like those over whom he had been placed. I think it was on the representation of the late Mr. Launcelot Wilkinson, one of the most able and estimable members of the India Civil Service, that he was sent to the south-east frontier. He had seen his value in the Saugor and Nerbudda districts while he was political agent at Bhopaul, which bordered on the districts under your brother's charge.

It has been to me a source of much regret that I have not had it in my power to aid his son in getting employment in India.

Believe me,

Yours very truly,

(Signed) W. H. Sleeman.

To Major Ouseley,
&c. &c.

Lucknow, 14th September, 1853.

DEAR SIR,

THE King of Oude will certainly not assist you to get up a newspaper at Lucknow; and you will certainly be disappointed if you come in expectation of such assistance from him. If you can get into his service in any other capacity, I am not aware of any objections to it; but as I have already told you and many others, I cannot recommend any one for employment under him. The humiliations to which honest and respectable Christians have to submit in his service, from the jealousies of influential persons about the Durbar, are such as few can or ought to submit to; and I certainly would not advise any one to enter such a service. Under whatever pledge or whatever influence they might enter it, their tenure of office and their pay would be altogether precarious, and the Resident would be unable to assist them in retaining the one or recovering the other.

Yours faithfully,

(Signed) W. H. SLEEMAN.

To G. Norton, Esq.

P.S.—The King of Oude and his family are in no danger from the British Government, on whose good faith they repose. I only wish that his honest and industrious subjects were as safe from the officers whom he employs in all branches of the administration, and from whom they are nowhere safe I fear.

(Signed) W. H. SLEEMAN.

Lucknow, 27th September, 1853.

MY DEAR JAMES,

UNDER the circumstances you mention, I see but one course open to you; and that is, to recommend to the Government of Bombay to do as Lord William Bentinck did in the Bengal Presidency under similar circumstances, appoint a special Commissioner for the trial of offenders under Acts XX. of 1836, and XXIV. of 1843; or for the revision of trials under these Acts, conducted by Sessions' Judges.

The first would be the best if feasible; but the second would do, since the Sessions' Judges seem now to be disposed to give their aid to Government in putting down the evil, and the Sudder Judges do not. Formerly, I believe, the Sudder Judges were so disposed, and the Sessions Judges not. In my reply to the Government of Bombay, you will see reference made to Lord William's appointment of Mr. Stockwell as special Commissioner. He was at the time Commissioner of the Allahabad division, and the work was imposed upon him in addition to his other duties.

If the Bombay Government does not think it has authority to appoint such a special Commission, they may apply to the Legislative Council to pass an Act authorising the Government of every Presidency to appoint such a Commission when circumstances may render it necessary.

This will be better and safer than to frame and enforce new rules of evidence for the guidance of existing Judicial Courts. The one would be for a special emergency, and temporary; and Government would not be very averse to it; but the other they certainly would not venture upon, particularly at this time. A great fuss would be made about it here and at home; and lawyers are too influential in both places.

You can show that there is no alternative—that this system of crime must be left to prosper in the Bombay Presidency, where alone it now prevails, or such a Commission must be appointed; and as the Acts and the machinery for giving effect to them have succeeded in putting it down in all the rest, it would be hard to leave the people of Bombay exposed to all the evils arising from the want of such a special Commission. Such Commissions have been adopted to relieve the people from the hardships of the resumption laws, which affected but a small portion of the community; and you hope it would not be considered unreasonable in you to propose one for the relief of the whole community; for the life and property of no family will be safe an hour, if these classes of offenders by hereditary profession are assured that they may carry on their trade with impunity, as they must be if your agency be withdrawn, and all the prisoners be released.

If you make a forcible representation to the Bombay Government in this strong case, they will adopt the measure if they have the power, or ask the power from the supreme Government; and I think the supreme Government will give it. I would say a special Commission for the trial of commitments under XXX. of 1836, and XXIV. of 1843, or a special Commission for the revision of trials under these Acts, as may seem best to Government; but you can say that you think the first would answer the purpose best in the Bombay Presidency. You may offer to run down to Bombay and submit your views to the Government in Council if required. They would not think it necessary, but would be pleased with the offer. Where men are committed on the general charge, it has always been thought necessary to show that the gang committed a murder or a robbery, though it is not so to show what part the prisoners took in them. If your assistant has not done this, he has failed in a material point. He should be very cautious in dealing with whole classes. The fault of our Bombay assistants has always been a disposition to make offenders of whole classes, when only some of the members are so.

You must make your best of the present case—show the necessity of the remedy clearly, and urge it respectfully without pretending to find fault with the Judges; merely say that their interpretation of the laws of evidence laid down for their guidance, however conscientious, forms an insurmountable obstacle to the conviction of offenders by hereditary profession, whose system has been founded upon the experience of their ancestors in the most successful modes of defeating these laws, and the technicalities of ordinary Judicial Courts. This is, I think, all that I can say on the subject at present.

The Moncktons leave us this evening, and Amelie intends to set out for the hills on the 6th proximo.

Yours affectionately,
(Signed) W. H. SLEEMAN.

To Captain J. Sleeman.

Lucknow, 28th September, 1853.

MY DEAR JAMES,

ON further consideration, I think that you should say nothing about the second proposal of a special Commissioner to revise the trials of offenders tried by Sessions Judges. You should suggest the first proposal for a special Commissioner to try all prisoners committed for trial under Acts XXX. of 1836, and XXIV. of 1843, and perhaps also XI. of 1841. See my Printed Report, page 357.

You may mention that such Commissioner should be required to submit his sentences for the consideration and final orders of Government, as all political officers did till March, 1835; or merely for the information of Government, as political officers did after that time.

On the 23rd of March, 1835, the Secretary to the Government of India forwarded to the Resident of Lucknow, for his guidance, the copy of a letter addressed on that date to the Agent of the Governor-General in the Saugor and Nerbudda territories, requesting that he would carry into execution his sentences on Thugs, and not make any reference to Government for confirmation, but merely submit to Government abstract statements of sentences; but desiring that the sanction of the King of Oude should be required before any capital sentence was carried into effect. No capital sentence was from that time passed. As all prisoners will be tried on the general charge, no capital sentence will ever be passed by the special Commissioner, and the Bombay Government may be disposed to give him the same orders. But the Governor in Council at Bombay will be the best judge of that.

Lord Falkland may possibly be deterred by apprehensions that late events may have altered the tone of feeling at home towards him; but I am persuaded that he would be glad to carry this measure into effect. I will send you a copy of the Government letter to the Resident here; and you may get from the agent's office a copy of that sent on the same date to him, though you may not readily find that office under the new arrangements. You will, I think, have a strong case, and I wish you success in it.

Yours affectionately,
(Signed) W. H. SLEEMAN.

To Captain Jas. Sleeman.

Lucknow, 4th November, 1853.

MY DEAR MALCOLM,

I SHOULD recommend for the Baee a money stipend for life of five thousand rupees a-month, with the understanding that if she adopted a child she would have to provide for him out of her savings from this stipend, and out of her private property. All the Rajah's private property, save what he may will away to others, will of course be left to her, to be disposed of as she may think fit. But this stipend should be independent of those to be continued to the stipendiaries of the Rajah. There are several who have nothing else to depend on but the stipends which they now receive from the Rajah; and it must be borne in mind that they have no longer Bajee Rao, Benaek Rao, the Jhansi and Saugor chief, to go to. This will be the last of the Brahmin dynasties founded in that part of the world by the Peshwas. Our Government should therefore be liberal in taking possession of the estate as an escheat.

The Mahratta language in accounts should at once be done away with; but out of the revenues of the estate, Government should found a good school for English and Hindoo, and Persian; and, above all, for a very good hospital and dispensary, under well educated and tried surgeons, native and European, capable of throwing out branches.

All the public officers of the Rajah should have stipends or employment, or both, in proportion to their period of service and respectability. If they take employment the stipends should be deducted from their salaries while in office, as in our own service.

In the case of the Baee Regent at Saugor, we continued a small part of her pension to her adopted son,—one thousand rupees a-month,—to enable him to provide for her non-pensioned dependents. We took the management long before her death, and left her only a private lady, with a large pension of, I think, eight thousand rupees a-month; besides pensions—too large—to the family of her manager, Benaek Rao: this will be unnecessary at Jhansi. All the large hereditary landholders of the Jhansi estate should have liberal settlements at fixed rates. They are all from the landed aristocracy of Bundelcund, and should be treated with consideration.

The first settlement of the land revenue should be very moderate. The lands will lose the most valuable market for their produce in the breaking up of the Court and establishment of the Rajah at the capital, and yield less money, &c., than before. This must be borne in mind.

You may freely use these my views as you think best on the Jhansi question.

As to the management, I should make as little change as possible, till the final orders arrive from the Court of Directors, that you may have nothing to undo of what you have done. I would leave the management to Ellis, under your supervision, and interfere only on references in special cases, except, of course, on emergency. I know not what the system is to be, or what system the Governor-General has recommended, except that there is to be one head, as in Rajpootana; and that all correspondence with Government is to go through that head. In this state of the matter I know not what to suggest or say.

Yours sincerely,

(Signed) W. H. SLEEMAN.

To Major Malcolm,
&c. &c.

Lucknow, 11th November, 1853.

MY LORD,

I FEEL grateful for your Lordship's letter of the 27th ult., but cannot say that I have any hope of discovering the instruments employed, or the employer, in the late affair. The whole power of the Government is in the hands of men who are deeply interested in concealing the truth, and making it appear that no attempt was really made. The minister has, by his intrigues, put himself so much in the power of the knave whom I suspect, that he dares not do anything to offend him. The man could at once ruin him by his exposures if he chose, and he would do so if he found it necessary for his own security. The man is biding his time, as he has often done with former ministers; and the time would have come ere this had not the King, to save himself, married one of the minister's pretty daughters.

The King's chief consort was the niece of the minister, and her son is the heir-apparent; so that it was her interest, and that of her uncle, the minister, to get rid of the King as soon as possible. She is a profligate woman, and the King's mother is supposed to have given him a hint of his danger. He took a liking to one of the daughters, and married her, in order to make it the minister's interest to keep him alive as long as possible. He now contrives to make the King believe that neither his life nor reign can be in any danger as long as he is in his present position.

The night after this affair took place, a sipahee of the 35th Native Infantry, standing sentry at one end of the house, fell asleep while he was leaning with his right wrist on the muzzle of his musket. The musket went off; the ball passed through his wrist, grazed a large beam above him, struck against a stone in the roof of the portico, and fell down flattened by the side of the sentry, as he lay insensible and bleeding on the ground below. The wrist was sahttered, and several of the arteries cut through. He bled profusely, and when taken up he talked incoherently, declaring that some man had fired at him from behind the railing, twenty paces off. I have seen similar cases of incoherency, arising from a similar cause. As soon as day appeared the ball was found, and its marks on the beam and stone above showed the real state of the case. His right knee was probably leaning on the lock of the musket when he fell asleep. I have made no public or official report of this circumstance to Government.

I have now before me a curious instance of the difficulty of getting at the truth when it is the interest of the minister and others about this Court to prevent it. A wanton attack was made in April last by about one hundred armed men, led by one of the King's collectors, on a native British subject coming from Cawnpore to visit a brother in Oude. The man himself received a wound, from which he some days afterwards died at Cawnpore; two of his attendants were killed, and twenty thousand rupees were taken from him. I have investigated the case myself, with the aid of my assistant, Captain Hayes, and with the attendance of an assessor on the part of the King. The case is a very clear one, but they have produced about thirty witnesses to swear that no man of the poor merchant's party was hurt; and that, instead of being attacked, he invaded the Oude territory with more than one hundred armed followers, and wantonly attacked the King's party of only fifteen unoffending men, while engaged in the discharge of their duty in collecting the revenue. I have translated the depositions with the prospect of having ultimately to submit the case to Government, unless the King consents to punish the offenders and afford redress. The assessor, an old man, bewildered by the conflicting testimony, and anxious to escape from all responsibility, slept soundly through the greater part of the inquiry, which has been a very tedious one.

I remain, your Lordship's
Most obedient and humble servant,
(Signed) W. H. SLEEMAN.

To the Most Noble
the Governor-General of India.

Lucknow, 28th December, 1853.

MY DEAR MR. COLVIN,

I WAS glad to see your handwriting again, and to find that time had made so little alteration in it.

Oude affairs are, as you suppose, much as they used to be, save that the King is now persuaded by his minister and favourite that, had his predecessors had men and women about them so wise as they are, they never would have acted as if they believed that the Government of India ever really intended to carry into effect the penalty of misgovernment, so often threatened. Our Government has cried "wolf" so often that no one now listens to it. The King is an utter imbecile, from over-indulgences of all kinds; and the knaves whom he employs in his administration contrive to persuade him that the preservation of his life and throne depends entirely upon their vigilance and his doing nothing. Had I come here when the treasury was full, and Naseer-od Doon Hyder was anxious to spend his money in the manner best calculated to do good and please our Government, I might have covered Oude with useful public works; and much do I regret that I came here to throw away some of the best years of my life among such a set of knaves and fools as I have to deal with.

I think you will do much good in your present charge in the subject to which you refer. In the matter of discourtesy to the native gentry, I can only say that Robert Martin Bird insulted them whenever he had the opportunity of doing so; and that Mr. Thomason was too apt to imitate him in this as in other things. Of course their example was followed by too many of their followers and admirers; but, like you, I have been delighted to see a great many of the elder members of the civil service, in spite of these bad examples, treat the native gentry with all possible courtesy, and show them that they had their sympathy as long as they deserved it by their conduct.

It has always struck me that Mr. Thomason, in his system, did all he could to discourage the growth of a middle and upper class upon the land—the only kind of property on which a good upper and middle class could be sustained in the present state of society in India. His village republics and the Ryutwar system of Sir Thomas Munro had precisely the same tendency to subdivide minutely property in land, and reduce all landholders to the common level of impoverishment. The only difference was that the impoverished tenants in the North-Western Provinces were supposed to manage their own affairs, while those at Madras had them managed by a very mischievous class of native public officers. He (Mr. Thomason) would have forced his village republics upon any new country or jungle that came under his charge, and thereby rendered improvement impossible. I would have introduced into all such new countries a system of paternal government in imitation of our Government of India itself, which would have rendered improvement certain, and the growth of a middle and higher class no less so. He would have put the whole under our judicial courts, and thereby have created a middle class of pettifogging attorneys to swallow up all the surplus produce of the land. I would have kept the whole of the land in the hands of our fiscal courts, by making it all leasehold property, and maintaining the law of primogeniture in all estates of villages. Mr. Thomason, I am told, systematically set aside all the landed aristocracy of the country as a set of *middlemen*, superfluous and mischievous.

The only part of our India in which I have seen a middle and higher class maintained upon the land is the moderately-settled districts of the Saugor and Nerbudda territories; and there is no part of India where our Government and character are so much beloved and respected. You have sent Mr. Read to that part; and if he be bigoted to Mr. Thomason's system, he will upset all this, and, in my opinion, lay the foundation of much evil. We found a system of paternal government in every village, and maintained and improved it. They were all little principalities; and by the printed rules of the Sudder Board of Revenue, which are very good, all the sub-tenants were effectually secured in their rights.

In making a tour through Oude in the end of 1849 and beginning of 1850 I had a good deal of talk with the people. Many of them had sojourned in our territories in seasons of disturbance. The general impression was that they would be glad to see the country taken under British management, provided we could dispense with our tedious procedure in civil cases. They all had a very unfavourable impression of our civil courts, and of the cost and delay of the procedure. Mills and Harrington, to whom the duty, which was to have devolved on you, has been confided, may do much good, and I hope will, for there really is nothing in our system which calls so much for remedy. I am persuaded that, if it were to be put to the vote among the people of Oude, ninety-nine in a hundred would rather remain as they are, without any feeling of security in life or property, than have our system introduced in its present complicated state; but that ninety-nine in a hundred would rather have our Government than live as they do, if a more simple system, which they could understand, were promised at the same time.

In 1801, when the Oude territory was divided, and half taken by us and half left to Oude, the landed aristocracy of each were about equal. Now hardly a family of this class remains in our half, while in Oude it remains unimpaired. Everybody in Oude believes those families to have been systematically crushed. If by-and-by we can get the people to take an interest in our railroads, and outlays upon other great public works, it will tend to create the middle class upon which I set so much value, and to give that feeling of interest in the stability of our rule which we so much require. We shall then have objects of common interest to talk and think about, and become more united with them in feeling.

Maddock is in Ceylon, but intends to return by the steamer which is to leave Calcutta on the 5th proximo. His speculations there have been failures. Had he looked after his estates there instead of joining the effete party of the Derbyites he might have done well. He has made great mistakes, and he now suffers for them. His support of Lord Torrington was his first.

Believe me,

Yours very sincerely,

(Signed) W. H. SLEEMAN.

To Mr. Colvin.

MY DEAR LOW, Lucknow, 5th March, 1854.

I HAVE to-day written to Government a letter, which you will of course see, on the subject of a proposal made to me by Mr. B. Government will, I have no doubt, consider the reason assigned by me for refusing to permit him to send an European agent to Lucknow, ostensibly to collect debts, sufficient; but whether it will consent to adopt my suggestion, and empower the Resident to assure the King that it will not again consent to permit Mr. B. to return and reside at Lucknow, after he has been twice expelled for his misdeeds, I know not. One thing is certain, that his residence at Cawnpore, under the assurance from the minister that he shall come back and be made wealthy if he can aid in getting rid of the Resident, is very mischievous.

B., Wasee Allee, and the Minister, succeeded in persuading the King that Shurfod Dowla, and all the most respectable members of the Lucknow aristocracy, had signed a memorial to the Government of India, praying that it would set aside the present King as an incompetent fool, and put Mostafa Alee on the throne in his place. All this was reported by me to Government on the 2nd of March, 1853.

The seals were all forged or filched here at Lucknow, but the papers were written in Calcutta, under the agency, I believe, of Synd Jan, Sir H. E.'s moonshee, from Bilgram, where his family have long enjoyed an estate rent-free, for the aid he has given to the minister in his intrigues. I have never been able to remove this delusion from the mind of the imbecile King; and it is the "*raw*" on which these knaves have been ever since acting; for it enables the minister to persuade him that his vigilance alone preserves his life and crown.

The minister is aware that I know all this, and may some day be able to show the King how he has been deluded and befooled by him; and he would give all he is worth to get rid of me in any way. He would give any sums to B. and his other agents to bribe editors to write against me; but the only editors who have yielded have been those of the "Mofussilite," before Mr. C. took the management. Mr. B. complains at Cawnpore, that he gave Mr. L. a large sum to do his dirty work at home; but that he did nothing for it. This is not unlikely. That the minister and Wasee Alee got up the attempt at the Residency, either to make away with me, or to alarm me into going away, I am persuaded; but to get judicial proof of it I shall not attempt. It would be vain here, where the minister has all the revenues of the State to work with.

All the native gentlemen whose seals were forged to this document, look to me for protection; and they have been ever since in a state of great alarm. It was to keep up this alarm that they tried to turn Shurfod Dowla out of Oude. I had rarely seen him before that time; and I have only seen him once since he went to the cantonments; and then only for five minutes during my walk in the garden, to talk about Mulki Jahan's affairs. They punish any one who ventures to approach the King; and they would ruin any one who ventured to approach the Resident if they could, lest he might open the eyes of the King to the iniquities they commit. The troops are starved, and almost all the old members of the royal family, who had no Government paper or guarantees, have been already starved or driven out. Oude has never before been afflicted by a Sovereign so utterly imbecile and regardless of his duties and the sufferings of his people; nor has there ever been a minister so utterly regardless of his own reputation and that of his master. He bribes with money, power, and patronage, every one who has access to the King, to sound his praise in prose or verse; and the King is persuaded that his life and throne depend upon his abstaining altogether from interfering in the conduct of affairs.

When I was in the Governor-General's camp at Futtehgur, M. H., the son of S. A. K., came there armed, I knew, with four lacs of rupees. He was an old acquaintance of E.'s, and he (E.) told me that he had asked for an interview, and asked me whether he ought to consent to see him. I told him that, if he did see him, he must make up his mind to the man's persuading the King that he had given him the greater part of the money, though the man himself kept all that he did not give to his moonshee. He refused to see the man; but he has ever since been with Mr. L. at Allahabad, intriguing with his people to chouse men out of their ancient possessions; or with the Oude people, to keep up the *raw* they have established on the King's mind. The King, by over-indulgence, has reduced his intellect below the standard of that of a boy of five years of age. It is painful to talk to a man with a mind so utterly emasculated.

Our Government would be fully authorized at any time to enforce the penalty prescribed in your treaty of 1837, and it incurs great odium and obloquy for not enforcing it. But Lord D. has, no doubt, solid reasons for not taking such responsibility upon himself at this time. I do all I can to save the people, and the people are sensible of what I do, and grateful for it; for the Resident is the only person they can look up to with any hope. If Government can comply with my wish to have the King assured that it will not permit Mr. B. to return and reside at Lucknow again, it will be of great use to me and to the people, for the hopes held out to him are like a premium offered for my head, or for my ruin; and one never feels very comfortable under such offers, at any time or in any country. The reckless lies which this man gets adventurers at Cawnpore to write for him, and careless or corrupt editors to publish, are apt to stagger those who do not know the vile character of the individual, or the true nature of the facts referred to.

I am glad you saw W. He is a man of high character and first-rate ability, and has abundance of sagacity and energy. I miss him very much. He will be a credit to his regiment if engaged on active service.

Yours sincerely,

(Signed) W. H. SLEEMAN.

To Colonel Low, C.B.

P.S.—I shall say nothing in this of your domestic bereavement, though I have felt much for you.

W. H. S.

In my public letter, I have referred to that of the Marquess of W. to L., when he was Resident. Do refer to it. Page 388, Vol. I., "Despatches."

Lucknow, 1st June, 1854.

MY DEAR LOW,

IN my letter of the 10th of November, 1853, I solicited permission to retain Weston with me for reasons stated therein. In reply, I was told, in Mr. Dalrymple's letter of the 2nd of December, "that the Governor-"General in Council had every wish to consult my views, "but, for the present at least, his Lordship in Council "thinks that Lieutenant Weston must in fairness be "required to join his regiment, like other officers."

I am so very anxious to have his services again in the office he filled, that I have to-day ventured, in a public letter to the Foreign Secretary, to request that he will submit my wishes to the Governor-General in Council, should they deem the state of affairs in Burmah at present to be such as to admit of his being withdrawn from his regiment. I have said, in my public letter, that should any exigency arise he could, of course, quickly join his regiment on service again.

If you can give me any assistance in obtaining his services, I shall feel very much indebted to you, for I have that confidence in his abilities and high-mindedness which I cannot feel in those of his *locum tenens;* and I am very anxious to keep things in good train here till the end of the cold weather, when I must go on leave to recruit. I am really in a very difficult position here, not with regard to the King, for he has, I believe, entire confidence in me; but he has become so entangled with his minister, that he is afraid of him; and the minister would give all he has (and he has all the revenues of the country) to get me out of the way.

I carried the Government orders regarding Shurfod Dowla into effect, and he is now, with his family, quiet and safe. The King behaved very well, and resisted all the attempts of the minister to persuade him to remonstrate. I am to-day to submit Shurfod Dowla's letter of grateful thanks to Government. I hope Government will not write to him in reply, as this might mortify and vex the King, since he is not written to by the Governor-General.

I think I told you of the *raw* the minister, Wasee Alee and Co., had established on the King's mind—the belief that a party of the members of the royal family and native gentlemen at Lucknow had been trying to persuade Government to set him aside, and put his reputed brother, Mostafa Alee, on the throne. Whenever they want to make the King angry with any one, they tell him that he is a leader in this cabal. But the King is, by degrees, growing out of this folly. There never was on the throne, I believe, a man more inoffensive at heart than he is; and he is quite sensible of my anxious desire to advise him rightly, and see justice done in all cases. But I am a sad stumbling-block to the minister and the other bad and incompetent officers employed in the administration.

If you wish it, I will be more circumstantial about Weston's *locum tenens*, Lieut. B., of the 1st Cavalry. For his own repute, and that of the Government, I think the less he has to do with the political department the better. He would be better in a military staff appointment than a political one.

Yours sincerely,

(Signed) W. H. SLEEMAN.

To the Hon. Colonel Low, C.B.

Lucknow, 11th September, 1854.

MY LORD,

THE post which this morning brought me your Lordship's letter of the 6th instant brought me also one from Bombay, which I enclose for your Lordship's perusal. Should you think it worth while, Colonel Outram will be able to sift the matter to which it refers. I have long been aware of the intrigue, and have taken care to let the King know that I am so; but as I knew, at the same time, that the object was merely to get money out of him, and to strengthen his confidence in his minister, which had begun to give way, I did not think it necessary to trouble your Lordship with any reference on the subject. I knew that letters had been forged as from the King of Persia to the King of Oude, proposing to divide Hindoostan between them, and I thought it to be my duty to tell him so, in order to warn him; but, as he denied ever having received such letters, I told him that I should take the word of a King, and say no more about it. He is certainly not of sound mind, and things must, ere long, come to a crisis. His mind may have been of an average kind when he was young, but it has long become emasculated by over-indulgence; and the minister and his minions can make him believe or do what they please. They know that it cannot last long, and they have agents in Bombay and Calcutta to assist them in fleecing the King of money on all manner of false pretences.

The minister, a consummate knave, and one of the most incompetent men of business that I have ever known, has all the revenues and patronage of the country to distribute among those who have access to the King exclusively—they are poets, fiddlers, eunuchs, and profligate women; and every one of them holds, directly or indirectly, some court or other, fiscal, criminal, or civil, through which to fleece the people. Anything so detestable as the Government I have nowhere witnessed, and a man less competent to govern them than the King I have never known.

Had your Lordship left the choice of a successor to me, I should have pointed out Colonel Outram; and I feel very much rejoiced that he has been selected for the office, and I hope he will come as soon as possible. There are many honest men at Lucknow, and a finer peasantry no country can boast. But no honest man can obtain or retain office under Government with the present minister and heads of departments.

But where the whole revenues of a fine country are available to suborn witnesses to prove the King to be a *Solomon*, no Resident would be able to find judicial proof of his being a fool; but that he is so I have had abundance of, to me, satisfactory evidence ever since I have been here. It must soon, however, become clear, without the Resident's efforts to make it so. Where the Government of India is so solemnly pledged to see justice done to the people of a country, it cannot fairly permit them to be reigned over much longer by so incompetent a Sovereign. Proofs enough of bad government and neglected duties were given in my Diary; and a picture more true was, I believe, never drawn of any country. The duty of remedying the evils, and carrying out your Lordship's views in Oude, whatever they may be, must now devolve on another.

No one of my present assistants knows anything whatever about Oude, its Government, or its people; and Colonel Outram will, therefore, labour under great disadvantages. I hope, therefore, that your Lordship will pardon the liberty I take in suggesting that he be allowed the aid of Captain Weston. He went over the whole of Oude with me, and knows almost all who have made themselves prominent for good or for evil within the last five years. I know that, as soon as I go, some of the most atrocious villains whom I have kept out of office will try to purchase their way back; and there is no man too bad for the minister, provided he pays for his restoration.—The murderer of the banker, mentioned in my Diary, vol. i., p. 131, and the murderer of thousands, mentioned in the same volume. Captain Weston is high-minded, sagacious, energetic, hard-working, conciliatory, and, to Colonel Outram, his services in the new charge would be invaluable.

I have the honour to remain,
Your Lordship's faithful and obedient servant,
(Signed) W. H. SLEEMAN.

To the Most Noble
The Marquis of Dalhousie, K.T.
Governor-General.

THE END.